ADOLESCENCE AND WORK:

Influences of Social Structure, Labor Markets, and Culture

Edited by

David Stern
Dorothy Eichorn
University of California, Berkeley

Routledge
Taylor & Francis Group

NEW YORK AND LONDON

First published by
Lawrence Erlbaum Associates, Inc., Publishers
365 Broadway
Hillsdale, New Jersey 07642

Transferred to Digital Printing 2009 by Routledge
270 Madison Ave, New York NY 10016
27 Church Road, Hove, East Sussex, BN3 2FA

Library of Congress Cataloging-in-Publication Data

Adolescence and work : influences of social structure, labor markets,
   and culture / edited by David Stern, Dorothy Eichorn.
      p. cm.
   Includes bibliographies and indexes.
   ISBN 0-89859-964-4
      1. Vocational education—United States. 2. Career education-
   -United States. 3. Teenagers—Employment—United States.
   4. Educational anthropology–United States. I. Stern, David, 1945–
   II. Eichorn, Dorothy H.
   LC1045.A63 1989
   373.2'46'0973—dc19   88-39070
                                                                              CIP

Publisher's Note
The publisher has gone to great lengths to ensure the quality of this reprint
but points out that some imperfections in the original may be apparent.

Contents

PART III: WORK EXPERIENCE AND ADOLESCENT VOCATIONAL DEVELOPMENT

PART IV: SOCIAL CHANGE AND VOCATIONAL DEVELOPMENT

INTRODUCTION

1 Overview

David Stern
Dorothy Eichorn
University of California, Berkeley

Career counselors are concerned with helping people, especially young people, to make wise decisions about the kind of work they will prepare to do. Vocational psychologists provide the theories and tests that career counselors use. This volume illustrates connections between the concerns of vocational psychology and the adjoining disciplines of sociology, cultural anthropology, and labor economics. The intent is to suggest how vocational psychology and career counseling might recognize more explicitly the ever-changing social influences and institutional constraints that affect individuals as they begin, or contemplate beginning, their adult work. By incorporating insights from other social sciences, vocational psychology may reach an understanding of individual development that is more generalizable across cultures and historical epochs. The perspective of other disciplines also may help vocational psychologists and career counselors envision how social institutions themselves could be altered to facilitate more effectively the vocational development of young people.

ADOLESCENT VOCATIONAL DEVELOPMENT IN HISTORICAL CONTEXT

Historically, the emergence of the career counseling profession and the science of vocational psychology are, in large part, responses to the creation of "adolescence" in the 20th century. Economist Norton Grubb's chapter in this volume describes the origin of our current concept of adolescence, and relates the "social construction of adolescence" to fundamental changes in economic and social structure. The most important of these changes was that, as a result of industrialization, families lost control over economic production (see also President's

3

Science Advisory Committee, 1973; Coleman & Husen, 1985). In preindustrial America, families typically owned the agricultural or craft enterprises in which children worked alongside adults. Career choice was not an issue for most children because they would grow up doing the same kind of work their parents did. Industrialization, which removed work to enterprises not owned by employees, left parents without any direct way to teach their children how to make a living.

Children of the 20th century in industrialized societies therefore face the developmental task of preparing themselves for adult work without being able to rely on direct instruction by parents or other adults to whom parents delegate specific authority (as in traditional apprenticeship arrangements where parents could "bind out" children to another household for a period of time). In preindustrial times, only children who were very privileged, very poor, or unusual in some other way had to face this problem. Now, however, most children cannot rely on their parents to teach them, in any detail, what work to do when they grow up.

Adolescence is the time of life when this question becomes salient. Indeed, getting ready to do some kind of adult work is said to be the main problem for contemporary adolescents. Erik Erikson (1963), whose writings on adolescent identity formation have had a strong influence on clinical and developmental psychology, observed that "In most instances . . . it is the inability to settle on an occupational identity which disturbs individual young people" (p. 262). Because adolescence has emerged historically as the period in industrial societies when individuals must make the transition from childhood dependence to economically independent adulthood, the search for occupational identity can be considered the defining characteristic of contemporary adolescence.

SCHOOLS AND VOCATIONAL DEVELOPMENT

Erikson (1968) described adolescence as a *"psychosocial moratorium* during which the young adult through free role experimentation may find a niche in some section of his society, a niche which is firmly defined and yet seems to be uniquely made for him" (p. 156). As Grubb's chapter here describes, the notion of a moratorium has been institutionalized in the expectation that adolescents will attend school at least until age 17 or 18. The spread of mass secondary schooling in the United States, concomitant with enforcement of laws restricting child labor and setting minimum wages, all occurred in the early decades of this century, with the recognition of "adolescence" as a new and distinctive phase of life. As a result of these historical developments, high schools and, increasingly, colleges have been given major responsibility for helping young people navigate through the moratorium period and find their occupational "niche."

However, schools are beset by two major dilemmas. One stems from the fact that not all jobs are equally desirable. Some occupations offer more pay, higher prestige, and better working conditions than others. Since access to attractive occupations depends in large part on successful school completion, the schools are in the position of gatekeepers. This is awkward for the schools because they are agencies of society as a whole—taxpayers support them and all children are required by law to attend—and the egalitarian, or at least meritocratic, ideals of American society commit the schools to helping all students achieve their "maximum potential." To suggest that one child has the potential to be, say, an engineer while another only a minimally skilled laborer is inconsistent with American values—especially if perceived potential is correlated with race, sex, or social class. Schools, therefore, are highly sensitive to charges that they are channeling students into different "tracks" on the basis of characteristics other than ability.

Sociologists have been very attentive to this issue. Their "status attainment models" are designed to measure the extent to which educational attainment and subsequent occupational status depend not only on ability but also on other characteristics, especially social class, which children derive from their family of origin. Alan Wilson's chapter in this volume builds on previous status attainment models, using the same data set on which some of the classic research has been based. Like previous studies, Wilson's analysis here confirms the significant and substantial influence of social class (measured by parents' occupational status, income, and education) on success in school and subsequent access to high-status jobs. Wilson also modified the conventional status attainment model in a way that produced a surprising result, with interesting implications for vocational psychology. The modification has to do with high school students' stated aspirations for their future educational attainment and occupational status. In both the conventional model and Wilson's modified version, these stated aspirations are treated as possible influences on subsequent behavior. In the conventional model, a student's aspirations depend on the influences of friends, teachers, and parents, and on the student's academic performance. In Wilson's model, aspirations depend on these same things, but they also may act, in a reciprocal way, as *influences* on peers, teachers, parents, and the student's own performance in school. This change enables Wilson's model to account for a larger fraction of the variance in adult educational attainment and occupational status.

However, in Wilson's model virtually all the variance in aspirations themselves appears to be unexplained. That is, high school students' aspirations are a significant explanatory variable, but they cannot themselves be explained by Wilson's model. This finding suggests it would be useful to combine vocational psychologists' understanding of how interests and aspirations develop with the sociologists' model of status attainment. This kind of synthesis is also recommended by Fitzgerald (1986) in her critique of sociological and economic research on education and work.

Three other chapters in this volume also consider vocational development in the context of schooling. Sociologist Donald Hansen and psychologist Vicky Johnson analyze the task behavior of children in elementary school and suggest how certain behavioral patterns may carry over into adolescence and paid work. They find that children often respond to teachers' assignments in ways that enable them to fend off teachers' demands, but without actually engaging in the assigned task. Hansen and Johnson make a basic distinction between "dissembling" and "evading." Dissembling is what students do when they want to accomplish the task but feel unable. Evading is the students' response when they feel able to do the assignment but are not interested. If teachers do not respond appropriately, they may reinforce and aggravate these patterns, leading to apathy or eventual rebellion. This is part of the process by which schools, sometimes quite inadvertently, may cause some children to be labeled as failures at an early age. Even if the result is not so dramatic, later vocational development must build on these early experiences with school work. More research would be useful here.

Anthropologist John Ogbu illuminates the difficulties schools face in trying to promote the vocational development of black students in particular. Because blacks in this country have been treated as what Ogbu calls a "caste-like minority," young blacks may doubt that they can obtain desirable jobs even if they do well in school. Ogbu's respondents also feel that school is sometimes particularly demeaning to black people. The dilemma of schools—how to maintain American meritocratic values in the face of social stratification—is most acute in the case of blacks. For those who succeed in school and graduate from college, there is some evidence that existing theories of vocational psychology are applicable (Walsh, Bingham, & Sheffey, 1986). However, for young blacks who are caught up in what Ogbu calls the "oppositional identity" of the black culture, some modification of conventional theory seems warranted. This echoes the recommendation of Harmon and Farmer (1983), who want generally to extend the theoretical and empirical basis of vocational psychology beyond the "relatively privileged groups" (p. 70) who have been the main focus of study to date. (See also Smith, 1983).

The influence of schooling on vocational development is also evident in the chapter by vocational psychologist John Crites, explaining the construction of his Career Maturity Inventory. This work was done at a time when vocational psychology was going through a major transitional phase: from being exclusively concerned with the differential psychology of occupations, to studying also the developmental psychology of careers (Super, 1983). Crites used his instrument to profile the development of career decision-making maturity in boys and girls from grades 7 through 12. He found, serendipitously, a pronounced "dip" in measured maturity immediately following the transition from junior to senior high school. This result demonstrates the difficulty of constructing normative age profiles independent of the institutional context. Vocational development clearly does not occur in a vacuum.

To summarize: a complete theory of adolescent vocational development must incorporate some understanding of schools. This should include an understanding of how vocational development is affected by schools' internal operations, as suggested in the Hansen-Johnson and Crites chapters. A complete theory also must take into account how schools relate to the wider society. The relationship of schooling to occupational status or income has been the focus of much research by social scientists interested in vocational development. Vocational psychologists have emphasized that status or prestige or income is not the only dimension that is useful for describing occupations (Osipow, 1979), and have conceived other dimensions based on the intrinsic nature of the work itself (e.g., Holland, 1973). However, the task of integrating the vocational psychologists' multi-dimensional view of occupations with the social scientists' one-dimensional view remains largely undone. It is important to move ahead with this task of integration, since adolescents' vocational development is strongly affected by schools, which are preoccupied with the status dimension as they try to cope with the dilemma of upholding meritocratic principles in a stratified society.

WORK EXPERIENCE AND ADOLESCENT VOCATIONAL DEVELOPMENT

A second major dilemma of schools in industrialized societies is that they have been given increased responsibility to prepare young people for employment, yet schools themselves do not engage students in productive work for other people. Academic and vocational subjects are part of the school curriculum, but actual employment—production of goods or provision of services for people other than oneself—is not. Students are expected somehow to learn how to do this sort of work, without being given any actual practice.

Evidence of this dilemma is manifest in widespread dissatisfaction expressed by high school students. Throughout western Europe, Japan, and North America, students complain that classes are irrelevant to the work they will do after graduation, even though they recognize the necessity of finishing secondary school in order to get a decent job (Centre for Educational Research and Innovation, 1983; Coleman & Husen, 1985). In a 1977 survey, high school principals in the United States cited "student apathy" as a serious problem more often than they cited lack of resources, bureaucratic regulation, or any other issue (Abramowitz, Tenenbaum, Deal, & Stackhouse, 1978, p. 86). Likewise, high school teachers report "lack of student interest" as the biggest problem for them (Goodlad, 1984, p. 72). The Goodlad study also asked high school students what was the "one best thing" about their school. The top choice was "my friends," by 34% of the students. Only 7% chose "classes I'm taking," and 3% said "teachers"—while 8% chose "nothing"! (p. 77). A survey by the National Association of Secondary School Principals (1984) found the same thing: Friends and sports ranked much higher for students than did teachers, classes, or learning. The fact that high school students in the U.S. typically report spending as much time watching television during one *weekday* as they spend on homework in a whole *week* (Jones et al., 1983) likewise reflects little preoccupation with school work.

In the United States, growing numbers of high school students have been getting paid jobs when they can, during summers or after school. Table 9-4 in economist Paul Osterman's chapter shows how the number grew from 1964 to 1979 (see also Greenberger & Steinberg, 1986). Like housewives in recent decades, adolescents are trying to escape from their economically dependent role. Recent surveys in the U.S. have found that 50% to 60% of high school students are holding paid jobs at any given time, and 80% or 90% of the seniors have held at least one paid job at some time during their high school years (Lewin-Epstein, 1981; Lewis, Gardner, & Seitz, 1983).

Students often find their jobs a welcome relief from school. For example, a high school junior quoted in the Boyer (1983) report said her classes were:

> pretty boring, but then I suppose that's the way school classes are supposed to be . . . This year I've been working at McDonalds so I can buy some new clothes and a stereo set. The work isn't all that hard or exciting, but still it makes me feel on my own and that I'm an adult person, that I'm doing something useful. In school, you never feel that way. Not ever. (p. 202)

This is not an unusual reaction. In 1980, the High School and Beyond survey estimated that, nationwide, 51.5% of the seniors who had ever worked for pay considered their present or most recent job "more enjoyable than school" (Jones et al., 1983, p. 8–19).

Yet, by a substantially larger majority, 85% of the same seniors said their jobs were *not* "more important" than school. Students see high school as important for hard-headed, instrumental reasons. They know they need a diploma to go to college, to get a good job, or generally to compete in the world. As the proportion of the U.S. labor force with high school diplomas or more has grown from less than half in 1959 to more than three quarters in 1982, high school dropouts have been at an increasing disadvantage in finding paid work. If they do find jobs, dropouts now earn much less, compared to other workers, than they did only thirty years ago (Grant & Snyder, 1983, p. 191). Therefore, while many students are indifferent to school work and impatient with the student role, they stay in high school because they would rather be bored than sorry.

Since high schools give students little or no actual practice in producing goods or services for other people, those who intend to enter the labor force full time after graduation can learn directly about working only through experience in the part-time and summer jobs they find on their own. Psychologist Emmy Werner's chapter in this volume describes how the native Hawaiians on Kauai, who are less likely to go to college than are the ethnic Japanese or Filipino living on the island, are much more likely to have had paid jobs during high school. They are also more likely to say they are working because they want the experience, not only to make money. For teenagers who are not bound for college, vocational preparation requires work experience outside of high school, and they are more likely than college-bound youth to see their high school jobs as similar to the work they will do as adults (this is also evident in national surveys of U.S. high school students; see Bachman, Johnston, & O'Malley, 1984).

Work experience for adolescents is not always an unalloyed blessing, however (see Greenberger & Steinberg, 1986). The chapter by economists Stern and Nakata examines qualitative characteristics of jobs held by a nationally representative sample of high school seniors in the U.S. Compared to adults, teenagers are more likely to perform physical labor or low-skilled service jobs. However, there is variation among high school students' jobs in quality and quantity of social contacts, opportunities for using and developing valuable skills, and potential intrinsic interest of the work itself. Stern and Nakata find that, among high school graduates who do not attend college, success in the labor market after high school is more likely among individuals whose jobs during high school gave them more opportunity to use and develop skills. In addition to the specific content of the skills required on a particular job, teenagers in the more skill-demanding and skill-enhancing jobs are also developing or demonstrating a general capacity for learning on the job (cf. Kohn & Schooler, 1978). This is said to be an increasingly important requirement for workers in an increasingly fast-changing economy.

Paul Osterman's chapter also focuses on the labor market experience of young people who do not go to college. Even after they leave high school, the adolescent moratorium continues for these young people, as they frequently move from one short-term job to another in haphazard fashion. The existence of an exploratory period in the labor market has been known to vocational psychologists since the work of Donald Super and his colleagues in the 1950s. However, Osterman raises doubts about whether the moratorium period can be construed as intentional information-gathering leading to deliberate career choice. Instead, he points out, information about available jobs most often comes randomly from outside sources, rather than being systematically sought out by the young job-seekers themselves. Furthermore, the young workers in Osterman's study usually accepted the first job offered. Osterman concludes that individual choice plays only a small part in determining the kind of work these non-college youth eventually do. The limited role of individual choice in the youth labor market is underscored by Osterman's analysis of involuntary unemployment among young blacks. Osterman's argument is a direct challenge to the choice-centered theories of vocational psychology.

To summarize: Vocational development of adolescents occurs not only through schooling, but also through experience in the labor market itself. Given the paucity of actual work experience in schools, paid jobs during adolescence are especially important for individuals who do not expect to attend college. Instead of continuing their adolescent moratorium in college, non-college youth extend the moratorium through a series of short-term jobs in the secondary labor market, before settling into real, long-term jobs. There is some evidence that differences in quality among teenagers' early jobs do affect their subsequent labor market success.

SOCIAL CHANGE AND VOCATIONAL DEVELOPMENT

We have seen that the concept of adolescence, and the major social institutions that govern it, took their current form during the present century. Both the concept and the institutions are continuing to evolve in response to external forces and internal dilemmas. Adolescent vocational development, therefore, must be understood in its historical context.

The influence of historical circumstances is explicit in the chapter by Ravenna Helson, Teresa Elliott, and Janet Leigh, and also in the chapter by John Connor and George DeVos. The Helson, Elliott, and Leigh chapter analyzes the process of vocational identity formation in a sample of college-educated women during the 1960s and 1970s, when social norms governing women's work roles were changing dramatically. Theories of female vocational development written when these women were in college became outmoded by the time the women reached mid-career. Similarly, Connor and DeVos present data indicating changes over time in levels of achievement motivation among Japanese and American youth, and they offer an historical-cultural explanation. In addition to the substantive findings they present, these two chapters serve to remind us that vocational development for any individual takes place in a particular culture within a particular historical epoch, and that the spirit of the times may have a powerful influence. As Erikson (1968) wrote about the general process of identity formation: It is located *"in the core of the individual* and yet also *in the core of his communal culture,"* and therefore "establishes, in fact, the identity of those two identities" (p. 22).

Since social change affects the conditions and meaning of individual vocational development, it is important to consider which aspects of vocational psychology are most dependent on historical context, and which aspects may be relatively less dependent. It seems likely to us that the differential psychology of occupations would be relatively time-bound, because the nature and content of different occupations changes over time. In contrast, the development of general work-related skills and competence may be less dependent on changing social and economic patterns. Whatever the occupational mix, communication and problem-solving remain basic elements of vocational competence. The final chapter in this volume, by psychologists Dorothy Eichorn and Sheri Mainquist, pulls together the psychological literature on these general dimensions of competence. It thus provides a framework for a vocational psychology that may be more enduring in the face of social change.

CONCLUSION

The various chapters in this volume invite career counselors and vocational psychologists to explore the boundaries between their own discipline and related fields of social science. Some chapters present new research findings, others review existing literature, and some do both. All attest to the importance of adolescent vocational development for the reproduction and evolution of society. It is our hope that this volume will be a useful stimulus and guide to further research, policy and practice related to adolescence and work.

REFERENCES

Abramowitz, S., Tenenbaum, E., Deal, T. E., & Stackhouse, E. A. (1978). *High school '77: A survey of public school principals*. Washington, DC: The National Institute of Education, U.S. Department of Health, Education, and Welfare.

Bachman, J. G., Johnston, L. D., & O'Malley, P. M. (1984). *Monitoring the future: Questionnaire responses from the nation's high school seniors, 1982*. Ann Arbor, MI: Survey Research Center, University of Michigan.

Boyer, E. L. (1983). *High school: A report on secondary education in America*. New York: Harper & Row.

Centre for Educational Research and Innovation. (1983). *Education and work, the views of the young*. Paris: Organisation for Economic Cooperation and Development.

Coleman, J. S., & Husen, T. (1985). *Becoming adult in a changing society*. Paris: Centre for Educational Research and Innovation.

Erikson, E. H. (1963). *Childhood and society* (2nd ed.). New York: Norton.

Erikson, E. H. (1968). *Identity: Youth and crisis*. New York: Norton.

Fitzgerald, L. F. (1986). On the essential relations between education and work. *Journal of Vocational Behavior, 28*, 254–284.

Goodlad, J. I. (1984). *A place called school: Prospects for the future*. New York: McGraw-Hill.

Grant, W. J., & Snyder, T. D. (1983). *Digest of education statistics 1983-1984*. Washington, DC: National Center for Education Statistics.

Greenberger, E., & Steinberg, L. (1986). *When teenagers work*. New York: Basic Books.

Harmon, L. W., & Farmer, H. S. (1983). Current theoretical issues in vocational psychology. In W. B. Walsh & S. H. Osipow (Eds.), *Handbook of vocational psychology: Vol. I: Foundations*. Hillsdale, NJ: Lawrence Erlbaum Associates.

Holland, J. L. (1973). *Making vocational choices: A theory of career choices*. Englewood Cliffs, N.J.: Prentice-Hall.

Jones, C., Sebring, P., Crawford, I., Spencer, B., & Butz, M. (1983, April). *High school and beyond 1980 sophomore cohort first follow-up (1982) data file users manual*. Chicago: National Opinion Research Center, report to the National Center for Education Statistics, (contract OE-300-78-0208).

Kohn, M., & Schooler, C. (1978). The reciprocal effects of the substantive complexity of work and intellectual flexibility: A longitudinal assessment: *American Journal of Sociology, 84,* 24–52. 52.

Lewin-Epstein, N. (1981). *Youth employment during high school.* Washington, DC: National Center for Education Statistics.

Lewis, M. V., Gardner, J. S., & Seitz, P. (1983). *High school work experience and its effects.* Columbus, OH: National Center for Research in Vocational Education, Ohio State University.

National Association of Secondary School Principals. (1984). *The mood of American youth.* Reston, VA: National Association of Secondary School Principals.

Osipow, S. H. (1979). Career choices: Learning about interests and intervening in their development. In A. M. Michell, G. B. Jones, & J. D. Krumboltz (Eds.), *Social learning and career decision making.* Cranston, RI: Carroll Press.

President's Science Advisory Committee. (1973). *Youth: Transition to adulthood.* Washington, DC: U. S. Government Printing Office.

Smith, E. J. (1983). Issues in racial minorities' career behavior. In W. B. Walsh & S. H. Osipow (Eds.), *Handbook of vocational psychology: Volume I: Foundations.* Hillsdale, NJ: Lawrence Erlbaum Associates.

Super, D. E. (1983). The history and development of vocational psychology: A personal perspective. In W. B. Walsh & S. H. Osipow (Eds.), *Handbook of vocational psychology: Volume I: Foundations.* Hillsdale, NJ: Lawrence Erlbaum Associates.

Walsh, W. B., Bingham, R. P., & Sheffey, M. A. (1986). Holland's theory and college educated working black men and women. *Journal of Vocational Behavior, 29,* 194–200.

2 Preparing Youth for Work: The Dilemmas of Education and Training Programs

W. Norton Grubb
University of California, Berkeley

American youth always seem to be in a terrible state. At the turn of the century educators worried about excessive school drop-outs, unprepared for labor markets. Others emphasized the increasing numbers of immigrant and black youth poorly socialized for adult life, and the growth in juvenile delinquency. The current dilemmas are similar: Youth unemployment has been a serious issue for at least 20 years, illiteracy has become a new problem, teenage pregnancy and sexuality seem out of hand, and juvenile crime has become more prevalent and more violent. Even for middle-class youth, the turmoil of adolescence seems to be a constant feature of the teenage years.

The persistence of such problems suggests that our youth policy—such as it is—has not worked very well. Every generation has addressed some version of the "youth problem," by elaborating and revising the major social institutions of youth. In fact, both our conception of adolescence and a basic policy towards youth were shaped around the turn of the century (the subject of the first section of this paper). Ever since, the dominant strategy to prepare young people for work life has been the elaboration and extension of training institutions—first the schools, and more recently manpower programs and other out-of-school programs of training and guidance (the subject of the second and third sections).

But an uncertainty about the training strategy has emerged since the 1960s. With the expansion of work among teenagers and the development of formal work experience programs, the issue of whether training or work itself is the best preparation for work has become more prominent. This in turn generates another problem: While education has been largely a public function, subject in theory to democratic control, work tends to take place in private firms, and many aspects of the labor market (including the youth labor market) are not subject to public

13

control. This creates the dilemma of whether, and how, government policy should intervene to change the offerings of the youth labor market.

In fact, our youth programs most explicitly concerned about work—including vocational education, career education, guidance and counseling, manpower programs outside the schools, and various forms of work experience—have always been in the position of responding to forces they cannot control. These forces include socialization within families, which tend to vary with class, race, and gender; the cultural influences on youth from diverse sources, including the media; and the labor market itself. Squeezed among other powerful institutions, schools and other youth institutions have been relatively powerless to make the changes asked of them. The result is a set of programs that often seem ineffective and a sense that there has been no real progress against the enduring problems of youth.

THE SOCIAL CONSTRUCTION OF ADOLESCENCE

Adolescence obviously falls between childhood and adulthood, but the need to make the transition from dependence to independence does not explain why youth should be such a troubled period. Nor is it useful to claim that adolescent rebelliousness is an eternal part of human development: Such an idea blurs the specific problems that American youth face with those of youth from preindustrial cultures, or ancient Greece, or other times and places so remote that they are linked with our own only through the medium of "human nature." Instead, the stage of youth has been a social construction, since the tasks and choices that youth face are shaped by social and economic institutions (Grubb & Lazerson, 1982b).

In colonial America, the category of youth was ill-defined. The transition from childhood to adulthood, signified by marriage and ownership of the family farm or established occupational status, was gradual and could last until the late 20s or early 30s. Momentous decisions were almost nonexistent, and the stresses of transition were unremarkable. During the first half of the 19th century, youth as a stage of life became more clearly demarcated, as young people (especially boys) engaged in periods of semidependence, moving in and out of their homes, school, and work. A growing advice literature codified a new consciousness of youth as a critical stage. As Joel Hawes, a 19th-century writer of advice to youth, described the period in *Lectures Addressed to The Young Men of Hartford and New Haven,* published in 1828, it was "the forming, fixing period . . . It is during this season more than any other, that the character assumes its permanent shape and color. . . ." He regarded youth as a period in which young people were "exceedingly liable to be seduced into the wrong paths—into those fascinating but fatal ways, which lead to degradation and wretchedness." Yet the experiences of young people were too varied, with too much mixing of age groups in families, schools, and work settings, for youth to be considered a special stage.

During the last half of the century, teenagers began to live at home for longer periods, losing much of their independence. They stayed in school longer and were less likely to enter the labor market. By the first decades of the 20th century, the retention of young people in age-graded schools and their progression from school into work and then into marriage had become more regular. Schooling became the dominant way of preparing for adult occupations. As child labor declined, as teenagers withdrew from or were pushed out of the labor market, and as years at school lengthened, teenagers found themselves in age-segregated settings: junior high school, high school, and (for middle-class youth) college; the juvenile court for those in trouble; and youth groups like the Boy Scouts. By the 1920s, the activities of the teenage years had become ordered in a defined progression and were therefore more predictable.

The greater uniformity of teenage experiences was important in defining youth, but the expansion of choices facing them generated the real *Sturm und Drang* of adolescence. During much of the 19th century, occupational and marital decisions were less troubling: Boys tended to follow their father's occupations, girls became homemakers, and parents played a major role in the choice of a spouse. Several developments—the expansion of occupations, the decline of small-scale farming and independent craftwork, the decrease in self-employment and the increase in wage labor—made occupational choice a more conscious decision, especially for boys but increasingly in the early 20th century for girls, too. The concept of romantic love which spread in the late 18th and early 19th centuries supported the choice of a spouse as an individual's own decision, rather than a selection dictated by parents, business alliances, or community concerns. More generally, society had changed from one in which children succeeded their parents to one in which children were expected to become individuals different from their parents, a change that generated the conditions of both choice and anxiety.

By the Progressive Era, youth had come to be a period of critical decisions about an occupational identity (including schooling decisions) and about a sexual identity, including the choice of a spouse. As youth became more free to make their own decisions, a range of now-familiar problems emerged, all involving the dangers of making the *wrong* choices: problems of delinquency; fears about teenage sexuality; concern for the ''wasted years syndrome,'' the period between leaving school and assuming ''adult'' employment that was blamed for the shiftlessness of youth. These problems were of concern not only because they were intrinsically troubling, but also because their long-range consequences were potentially serious.

The most forceful statement of the new stage came from G. Stanley Hall, whose *Adolescence, Its Psychology and Its Relation to Physiology, Anthropology, Sex, Crime, Religion, and Education* (1904) set the terms for all subsequent discussion of young people. "Adolescence," Hall wrote, "is a new birth," a time of promise and pain, achievement and failure, and of turmoil. In adolescence "the higher and more complete human traits are now born", but the perils of adolescence were severe:

> Momentum of heredity often seems insufficient to enable the child to achieve this great revolution and come to complete maturity, so that every step of the upward way is strewn with wreckage of body, mind, and morals. There is not only arrest, but perversion at every stage, and hoodlumism, juvenile crime, and secret vice. . .

Six years later, Jane Addams echoed Hall:

> We may either smother the divine fire of youth or we may feed it. We may either stand stupidly staring as it sinks into a murky fire of crime and flares into the intermittent blaze of folly or we may tend it into a lambent flame with power to make clean and bright our dingy city streets.

In describing youth as a period of plasticity, these extravagant commentaries reflected both the centrality of decisions open to teenagers and the adult fears that "perversion and arrest" might result. Conceptions of adolescence have changed somewhat since then—adolescence begins earlier and ends later than it did at the turn of the century—but the central conception remains that of a period when crucial decisions are made, when there is a logical progression through schooling to adult life, and when evil influences can lure youth from the path of normal development.

The ideal of a uniform progression through school to adult work, protected from the dangers of "hoodlumism, juvenile crime, and secret vice," was itself a middle-class conception, shaped by the ideal of professional jobs arrayed in an orderly career, with schooling a necessary prerequisite (Kett, 1982). Contrary to this ideal, most semiskilled or working-class jobs, at the turn of the century as now, did not promise much in the way of advancement, were not arrayed in logical steps, and did not require schooling to learn job-related skills. The typical patterns of working class boys at the turn of the century—of working in dead-end jobs for a few years before settling into a more permanent and adult position—therefore violated the conception of how youth should behave.

As a result, the social construction of youth has always revealed sharp class divisions. The wasted years and juvenile crime of lower-class and immigrant youth were treated by harsh discipline and the juvenile court, while sexual excesses and a lack of discipline associated with middle-class youth were more gently corrected with advice literature, in voluntary organizations like the Boy Scouts, or in school programs. The class-based distinctions have continued to the present: The gangs of the 1950s, juvenile crime of the 1970s and 1980s, teenage pregnancy and youth unemployment are predominantly lower-class issues; the political and cultural rebellions of the 1960s, the sexual excesses of youth (excluding pregnancy), and the identity crises of college students are middle-class problems. Adolescence as a time before entering the work force and choosing a mate starts earlier for working class youth and ends earlier, as they leave school, begin work, or get married at earlier ages; adolescence for middle-class youth extends later, primarily because of extended school and college attendance.

In even more obvious ways, the social construction of youth has been divided by gender as well as by class. The crises of adolescence for girls have always been related more to sexual identity and marriage, when the dominant problems for males have been those of occupational decisions. Sexual activities are considered a problem for girls, not for the boys who impregnate them. In the juvenile system, unacceptable behavior for girls—for which they are adjudicated status offenders—is likely to be linked to charges of promiscuity, whereas sex-related charges are almost nonexistent for boys (save in the extreme case of rape). The social programs to cope with the problems of youth are similarly sex-typed— pregnancy prevention programs for girls, employment and training programs for boys. The policies are not entirely irrational, although as in the case of class distinctions the differences are more than descriptive: Boys participate in teenage sex and conception as much as girls do, unemployment rates are as high for girls as they are for boys, and labor market participation rates for men and women have narrowed considerably. The distinctions between "male" and "female" problems among youth reflect sex-stereotyped conceptions of how boys and girls should prepare for their adult futures and what activities will dominate their adult lives.

The assumed plasticity of youth has often led to exaggerated reactions from adults, fearing that the smallest influences can lead young people astray. At the turn of the century, various efforts emerged to segregate and protect young people from bad influences—most obviously in the juvenile institutions located away from the cities, but more pervasively in the idea that teenagers belonged in schools, rather than at work or in the streets where they might be corrupted; often the desire to protect young people became more controlling than paternalistic, especially when lower-class youth were involved. Thus youthful behavior like disobedience, rowdiness, and overt female sexuality became status offenses and therefore crimes when committed by juveniles but not if committed by adults; and efforts to get young people out of work and into the schools, through child labor laws and the enforcement of compulsory attendance, increased in the Progressive Era. Fears about young people going astray were more vivid when lower-class youth were involved, since they were more obviously threatening—a feeling that persists in the image of lower-class youth as "social dynamite."

The social policy to cope with youth that emerged at the turn of the century was unplanned and unself-conscious, but nonetheless consistent. The essential youth policy has been the creation of public institutions, designed simultaneously to keep youth out of trouble and to prepare them for occupational roles. The expansion of the high school, the development of various training programs like vocational education, and the creation of the juvenile justice system were all responses to the "youth problem" at the turn of the century: These institutions were highly age-segregated, as befitted a separate stage of development; they were segregated by class, race, and gender, conforming to the expectations of what different groups of youth most needed; they combined programs of training with mechanisms for controlling behavior; and they reflected the assumption that training is more appropriate for young people than adult activities (employment or family life).

Ever since, the basic approach to youth problems has been the elaboration of education and training. Educational programs represent a rational response to several dimensions of the youth problems: They can be effective in giving young people a sense of purpose, in providing them with alternatives to acting out, and in giving them the values and skills necessary for adult roles. But even if programs fail to make good on their vocational promises, they may still be useful if they merely occupy students, keep them out of trouble, and try to teach them appropriate behavior. As a result, youth institutions incorporate two different and partially contradictory functions—training, or preparing students for the labor market; and warehousing, or keeping them out of the labor market. A related conflict involves independence and dependence: Youth are being prepared for independence, but in age-segregated institutions that function by limiting the independence of young people.

A final dilemma of our explicit youth policy has involved the dichotomy between work and play. Adolescents are being prepared for work, but in institutions that keep them from work. Indeed, the main idea that lay behind the condemnation of dead-end jobs and efforts to pass child labor laws was that work itself—at least the work available to teenagers—was a poor way of preparing for work. But this placed young people in institutions that—however much they might try to be like work or about work—have always been distinctly different from work settings, and have even been considered a moratorium from work. Furthermore, the schools also came to be suffused around the turn of the century with an ethic of play. This took many forms, including the pedagogical methods often associated with "progressive education" that stressed independent discovery and student-directed activities in place of the teacher-directed forms of rote learning that were more like routinized, subordinate labor. At the high school level, the development of extracurricular activities (including sports) at the turn of the century was justified in many utilitarian ways, including the need to build cooperation and teamwork, but such activities also embodied a spirit of play and quickly came to capture the greater interest of some students. The 19th century work ethic, under attack since the 1850s from critics of excessive work and from those recognizing that work itself had become degraded, was joined by a newer ethic of play that stressed the restorative powers of leisure (Rogers, 1974);

concern with expanding production gave way to fears about overproduction and underconsumption, and consumerism was born. The high school came to embody the dilemma we live with still: Most students recognize that they are in school in order to prepare for work, but their interest in studies lags far behind their interest in friends, sports, extracurricular activities, and other social aspects of high school (Boyer, 1983; National Association of Secondary School Principals, 1984). Whether work or play dominates the high school is ambiguous, and the ethic of play provides serious competition for the ethic of work in the dominant institution for young people.

THE EXPANSION OF YOUTH INSTITUTIONS: DIFFERENTIATING THE SCHOOLS

At the turn of the century, the high school was still relatively small: In 1900 only 8.5% of those 14 to 17 were in school, and college was a tiny, elite institution. A dramatic shift throughout this century has been the expansion of formal schooling, first in the high school, then in 4-year colleges after World War II, and finally with the development of the community colleges in the 1960s and 1970s. Furthermore, most of this expansion has come in public rather than private schools. The expansion of schooling, for essentially vocational reasons at each of these levels, has meant that almost all youth have become captive in institutions susceptible to public pressures, where an explicit youth policy can operate.

The expansion and differentiation of education has also created a continuum of education. This has allowed a fine differentiation of students, from high school drop-outs, to those with a high school diploma only, to those who gain access to the lower levels of higher education—the community colleges and the low-quality 4-year colleges—to those with B.A. degrees from institutions that are themselves finely differentiated by status and quality, to postgraduate education. The expansion and differentiation of institutions has facilitated the class differentiation of education as well: A vast amount of evidence confirms that high school drop-outs tend to be lower class and minority students, that working-class students are more likely to be in community colleges and the lower levels of state colleges than in state universities and private colleges, that prestigious colleges tend to have more middle-class and upper-class students than their lower-status counterparts, and that access to postgraduate education is also related to class. Differentiation has allowed the educational system to be simultaneously inclusive—even promising a spot in college to every student who graduates from high school, and apparently conforming to the ideal of equal opportunity through education—while still remaining a class-based institution.

The continuum of institutions has other implications for schooling and work, and for our explicit youth policy. Most obviously, the different levels of the education system are linked to different levels of the occupational structure, so that those who go further in school usually go higher in the rankings of earnings and occupational status. However, the link between schooling and work is, in a variety of ways, much closer at the upper levels of the educational system that at the lower levels. At the upper levels—in postgraduate education in particular, and at the high-quality 4-year institutions—the responsiveness of students to labor market conditions is relatively good. If shortages develop in particular occupations, then students respond to the higher earnings and greater employment opportunities available; conversely, enrollments decline when occupations decline, although always with a lag and always with some leeway for students who prefer certain occupations in spite of low earnings (Freeman, 1971). At the middle levels—in the community colleges (Grubb, 1986), and probably at the lower-level state colleges—enrollments are largely unresponsive to labor market conditions, and institutional rigidities are more responsible for enrollment patterns. At this level, there is substantial danger that institutions and students will over-react to trends and fads—as has happened, for example, with community college students shifting since the late 1970s into high-tech curricula (Grubb, 1984). At the high school level, there seems to be a nearly complete lack of information about labor markets, and a general ignorance of students about pathways to different occupations (Powell, Farrar, & Cohen, 1985). The historic purpose of vocational guidance—to provide students information about occupations and the preparation required—has given way to a concern among counselors with the internal procedures of the high school, leaving students no ready access to labor market information. To the extent that any occupational decisions are made at this level, they become educational decisions about whether or not to go to college, rather than decisions based on full knowledge of opportunities and requirements.

In a very different sense, the link between schooling and employment is closer at the upper levels. The overt purpose of schooling, after all, is cognitive development, not behavioral training. Jobs at the upper levels—those requiring a B.A. degree and more, for example—do tend to require various cognitive skills, including basic literacy and arithmetic skills but also the ability to be a quick learner and, for over half of such positions, advanced reading skills (McPartland, Dawkins, & Braddock, 1986). Similarly, those who hold professional positions tend to report that they received their job-related training in formal schooling, while at the lower levels of the occupational system on-the-job training is the overwhelming method of acquiring job skills. Of course, certain personal attributes—especially dependability, the proper attitudes toward work, and the ability to work well in groups—are almost universally important in employment, and education may be crucial in instilling these traits. Aside from this, however, the content of schooling at the lower levels tends to be much less relevant for unskilled and semiskilled employment[1]; at this level, schooling is vocationally useful largely as a means of access to further schooling.

In addition. for jobs requiring relatively little schooling, employers tend not to inquire about school performance (that is, grades or recommendations of teachers), perhaps because of the difficulty in getting such information in usable form from high schools; not only are students ignorant about the labor market and the requirements of work, but employers are ignorant about the capacities of their applicants. At the upper levels, with college graduates and above, this is much less true (Bishop, 1986; McPartland, Dawkins, & Braddock, 1986). One consequence of employer ignorance at the lower levels is that there is no reliable economic return to good school performance; students are rewarded for additional years of schooling, probably as a signal of reliability, but not for their actual achievements or cognitive abilities (Bishop, 1986). The lack of any return to school performance, while the return to years of schooling remains substantial, helps explain why there has been a constant escalation of years of education while the quality of schooling has tended to decline.

The loose connection between schooling and work at the lower levels of the educational system generates several problems. Most obviously, the meaning of a high school education has become unclear, at least to many students. They universally acknowledge that they are in school to gain access to decent employment, but—except for those who are bound for the better colleges—the cognitive content of the high school will not be rewarded by employers, is largely irrelevant to most jobs they are likely to get, and is much less important than skills learned on the job. For these students, the vocational promise of the high school is at best confusing, and at worst completely empty.

Of course it is this group of students—high school drop-outs and those who complete a high school diploma only, the bottom of the educational distribution—who have always been the target of our explicit youth policy. These are the students—disproportionately lower-class and minority—who are conventionally seen as dangerous, potential idlers and vagrants, threats to society, and drains on the public purse. For them, the schools have devised a series of programs designed to create a relation between schooling and work where one might not otherwise exist. At the upper levels of the educational system, where educational institutions are more clearly connected to employment, such a policy has not been necessary. The differentiation of the educational system therefore helps explain why our explicit youth policy has tended to focus on the high school, and on those lower-class and working class youth for whom socialization to work has always been the most difficult.

---

[1]See also the information in Bishop (1986): The correlations between measures of general mental ability and supervisor ratings are quite high (.56 and .58) for jobs of the highest levels of complexity, but low (.23) for jobs of low complexity.

ORIENTING ADOLESCENTS TOWARD WORK: OUR EXPLICIT YOUTH POLICY

Our explicit youth policy relevant to work encompasses programs to integrate schooling and work—vocational education, career education, counseling and guidance, manpower training programs, and work experience programs—since that integration might otherwise be loose or missing. These programs all face some common problems, especially the nature of work at the bottom of the labor market, and so they face a set of inescapable dilemmas they are powerless to resolve.

Vocational Education

Vocational education, the most obvious policy to prepare young people for work, also has the longest history. In its origins around the turn of the century, "voc ed" was designed to provide specific skill training so that those who left school and did not continue to college—the manually minded—would have employment skills to fit them for employment. The development of vocational education between 1917 and the 1960s was lackadaisical, with enrollments relatively steady and innovations relatively few; students poring into the high school did so largely to gain access to professional and managerial positions, and resistance to vocational programs preparing students for working class positions was high (Lazerson & Grubb, 1974). Since 1963, however, expanding vocational education has become one of the most popular responses to economic problems like unemployment and to social problems like the exclusion of minorities, women, and other groups from full participation in economic life (Grubb, 1978). Federal legislation was revised several times (in 1963, 1968, 1976, and 1984), and enrollments grew substantially.

High school vocational education is by far the largest program specifically concerned with work. In 1979–1980, for example, states reported about 10 million students enrolled in vocational courses; with 13.7 million high school students in fall 1979, it might appear that vocational education is relatively widespread. However, most of these students were taking a typing course or an occasional home economics course; only 30% of vocational enrollments were in programs designed to lead to employment, so perhaps one quarter of high school students were in occupationally-specific vocational programs.[2] Based on data from high school transcripts, high school graduates completed 23% of their

---

[2] These data are based on the Vocational Education Data Systems (VEDS), published in *Employment and Training Report of the President*, 1983. *The Conditions of Vocational Education*, National Center for Educational Statistics, 1981. This fraction is close to the 24% of seniors who reported themselves in a vocational track in 1980, as reported in High School and Beyond, summarized in Peng, Felters, and Kolstad (1981).

credits in vocational courses, varying from 14% among those in the college preparatory curicular to 33% for students in vocational curricula (Rumberger & Daymont, 1984). The extent of vocational training is substantial, then, but not overwhelming.

The most interesting recent development within vocational education has been its extension in the community colleges. Over the past 20 years the community colleges have expanded more rapidly than any other part of the educational system, and in the process have changed from being academic institutions preparing students for 4-year colleges into terminal vocational institutions. Perhaps as many as three-quarters of enrollments are in vocational courses rather than academic courses; in 1982 71% of degrees granted were in vocational programs, compared to 51% just 10 years earlier (Brint & Karabel, forthcoming, Grubb, 1984; Zwerling, 1976). Therefore vocational education dominates the community college much more than the high school. However, the magnitude of this vocational enterprise remains unclear, because casual enrollment and drop-out rates in these vocational programs are high.[3] The extension of vocational programs into the community colleges can be interpreted as the result of both the general inflation of the schooling system, and as a part of the differentiation of higher education (Karabel, 1974). It has also meant that vocational education now includes some semiprofessional occupations (like computer programming, many business occupations, health semiprofessionals, and engineering and science technicians) as well as the craft and industrial occupations that have traditionally dominated.

However, the skill training of vocational education has always been controversial. Despite its institutional power, voc ed has always been criticized as ineffective. Even in the 1920s, complaints arose from manufacturers who preferred to hire boys with academic training and provide them with specific training on the job, rather than hiring vocational graduates and having to train them all over again. More recent statistical evidence has confirmed that, contrary to the assumption that skill training lowers unemployment and increases wages, high school vocational programs in general confer no economic advantages on their graduates, except perhaps in some clerical programs for girls (Grasso & Shea, 1979; Meyer & Wise, 1982; Reubens, 1974; Rumberger & Daymont, 1984). For vocational programs in the community colleges the results are at least mixed (Blair, Finn, & Stevenson, 1981; Breneman & Nelson, 1981; Heinemann & Sussna, 1970; Pincus 1980; Wilms, 1974; Wilms & Hansell, 1982), possibly because their graduates are older and therefore able to obtain the adult jobs

---

[3]In 1978–1979, when total 2-year college enrollments were 4,064,382, vocational enrollments in Associate of Arts Programs were 1,959,558 and enrollments in long-term adult programs (largely technical institutes) were 969,560, suggesting that as much as 72% of enrollments were vocational. However, the 71% of A.A. degrees in vocational programs during 1981-1982 totaled only 399,717 indicating high dropout rates.

denied to teenagers graduating from high school programs. The finding that vocational programs are not especially successful has been damaging to the claim that skill training through the schools can prepare young people for work.

A related charge is that skill training is too specific, and that in a world of changing occupations and shifting job requirements students need more general skills. These criticisms emerged in major reports evaluating voc ed in 1938, in 1963, in 1968, and in 1976; the last three of these led to legislative changes designed to foster more general forms of vocational education (Grubb, 1978). More recently, the reauthorization of the Vocational Education Act in 1984 again stressed the need for broader skill training:

> In assessing the capacity of programs for special needs and the general vocational student population in meeting the general occupational skills and improvement of academic foundation, states shall assess whether the programs use problem solving and basic skills (including mathematics, reading, writing, science, and social studies) in a vocational setting. It is the intent to give a student experience in and understanding of all aspects of the industry in which the student is preparing to enter.

The charge that vocational education has been too specific indicates a special dilemma of vocational education. Specific skills are clearly distinguishable from the skills taught in the academic programs of schools, and when they result in employment the link between school and work is unambiguous. General skills, on the other hand, are less likely to be distinguishable from the academic programs, or may appear merely as watered-down versions of academic courses; if general vocational skills result in employment, the relationship between school and work may be unclear, and graduates may find employment in jobs that appear unrelated to their training. Thus vocational education has been pressed towards more specific skills to establish its vocational relevance and to distinguish itself from the academic curriculum. In addition, business people have often (though not unanimously[4]) pressed for more specific skill training, a pressure which continues now in the efforts to develop customized training and partnerships between schools and firms. The result is again to drive vocational programs education towards the specific skill training which is the least appropriate, in a rapidly changing eonomy.

In addition to giving students the skills (including the work habits) necessary for employment, vocational education has always espoused a particular attitude

---

[4]There remains a consistent voice among employers that the schools should provide general academic training and leave job-specific (or firm-specific) training to employers; see, for example, *Basic Skills in the U.S. Work Force* (New York: Center for Public Resources, 1982). My hunch is that this view predominates among large, socially conscious firms which provide their own specific training, and that the pressures for specific vocational education are more powerful at the local level from smaller firms which would like to shift their specific training costs onto the schools.

towards work itself, particularly manual and semiskilled work. The early vocational reformers insisted that vocational education would enhance the status of manual labor by restoring skill, and by eliminating the differences between manual labor and *mental* labor. The hope that education can shape the status of occupations persists; as a community college educator (Eskow, 1983) recently restated this egalitarian claim:

> We of the community colleges do not believe that there are higher and lower studies, arts that are liberal and arts that are servile—or that education for meaningful work is less worthy than education for meaningful citizenship.

In a way these hopes are pathetic: The idea that the schooling system can elevate the status of working-class occupations—which is a function of earnings, the challenge and independence of work, and other characteristics of jobs outside the control of the schools—is absurd. Yet these hopes fall squarely within the moral claims of the educational system as a response to youth problems: Vocational education has always promised to uplift large numbers of youth by giving them an alternative to idleness and vice, by training productive workers in place of those who would be underemployed, and by elevating their status so that they would be happy and productive rather than discontent or subversive.

Even when claims of skill training and the regeneration of work have failed, vocational educators have fallen back on the argument that voc ed is at least more interesting than academic education to the manually minded or those who are not academically inclined, both euphemisms for working-class youth—and thus helps to keep them in school. This is a version of warehousing, or keeping students out of the labor force in the hopes that they will learn something (if only patience) in school and not pick up the habits of sloth. The evidence suggests that students do in fact find vocational courses more interesting, although this may be because such courses are undemanding and unthreatening to students who have not done well in academic courses (Claus, 1984). However, the claim that voc ed helps keep students in school longer has no real support (Reubens, 1974), and has been countered by the evidence that vocational programs track working-class students out of academic curricula where they might continue to 4-year colleges, and thus hamper access to the best professional and managerial positions (Alexander, Cook, & McDill, 1978; Alexander & McDill, 1976). Thus even the warehousing rationale for vocational education appears to be incorrect, at least for high school programs.

Career Education

Another development, ostensibly more recent, in the efforts to prepare young people for work has been career education (Grubb & Lazerson, 1975). Both a criticism and an extension of vocational education, career education began in the early 1970s with the view that schools were doing a poor job of preparing young people for work, and proposed to orient every element of curriculum around preparation for careers—broadly defined to include "preparation for all meaningful and productive activity, at work or at leisure, whether paid or volunteer, as employee or employer, in private business or in the public sector, or in the family." While its vagueness made career education hard to implement, the early efforts concentrated on a combination of career exploration courses to familiarize students with a variety if careers and specialized skill training akin to variety of vocational training. A more radical departure from conventional school patterns was the experienced-based career education (EBCE) model, in which students would combine work and schooling, sometimes with a variety of different work placements so that career exploration could occur in a variety of jobs rather than in the classroom.

Although career educators at first tried to distinguish themselves from vocational educators, career education has much in common with voc ed. More clearly than vocational education, career education criticized the schools for segregating themselves from work and segregating young people from adults; the EBCE programs are models of how to integrate school and work. Another theme of career education has been the assertion that the schools have exacerbated the separation of mental skills from manual skills and elevated academic courses and academically-minded students over others. Like vocational education, career education hopes to elevate the status of those jobs that do not require a college degree, and thereby to remedy the perceived problem of overeducation—of too many students continuing to college. Finally, like every educational reform, career education promised (especially in its early days) to correct every social and economic crisis to which the schools could possibly be linked: unemployment and underemployment, the lag in American productivity, and the integration of pariah groups such as minorities.

Not surprisingly, career education has turned into something much more limited than its original expansive vision. Interest in experienced-based career education has dwindled, partly because of the cost of these programs but also because the educational value of these models has been unclear. Because of the difficulty of finding skilled occupations with educational potential for high school students, most EBCE placements were in the usual dead-end jobs in the youth labor market, a respite from the academic program but hardly a substitute (Farrar, DeSanctis, & Cowden, 1980). What remains of career education is largely a series of courses in career exploration, an addition to the roster of courses that crowds the high school curriculum (Cohen & Farrar, 1980). Valuable as such courses might be, given the dearth of labor market information, career education has clearly not realized its grandiose dreams of remaking the entire elementary and secondary curriculum and integrating work into schooling. Instead, a form of preparation for work has become yet another kind of coursework.

The Transition from School to Work: Counseling and Guidance

The concern with the transition from school to work—one that became prominent during the 1970s, as teenage employment increased—dates back at least to the Progressive Era. The concern about the wasted years syndrome expressed not only the fear that young people were leaving schooling without employment skills, but also that lack of information about the labor market prevented their finding work. In response, the guidance function of the schools was born. This provided testing and counseling to enable students to select courses and curricula and to facilitate a smoother transition between schooling and work.

Several problems have plagued the guidance movement since its inception (Lazerson, 1980). One involves an unavoidable dilemma—whether guidance should help fit students into available jobs and try to moderate unrealistic aspirations, or whether it should merely provide information about school and occupational alternatives and allow students to make their own choices. The first has opened guidance to charges of manipulating students, of "cooling out" students who are lower-class, minority, or female (Clark, 1960; Karabel, 1974). The approach of full information is more attractive in an egalitarian educational system, but is difficult to imagine: Full information would require education about the negative aspects of capitalist labor markets—unemployment and underemployment, dangerous work, monotonous jobs, low wages, the prevalence of dead end jobs instead of middle-class careers.

A second problem has made the model of full information impractical. The guidance function in the high school has always been underfunded, and most students have little access to guidance counselors. Furthermore, their information about occupational alternatives is generally quite limited, and most guidance involves information about courses and curricula instead of labor market opportunities. The result is that guidance has no influence at all on postschool employment.[5] Although there seems to be some improvement at the postsecondary level, it is hard to argue that guidance has lived up to its promises.

A third and more fundamental problem with counseling and information programs is the particular view of youth labor markets they embody. From the beginning, the concern over the transition from school to work viewed the job-hopping of adolescents as pathological. Implicitly, educators had in mind the middle-class career, with a period of schooling followed by a quick transition into the lowest rungs of a career without a period of search and unemployment.

[5]On the lack of labor market information generally available and the weak state of manpower forecasting, see Starr, 1982. On the ineffectiveness of guidance programs, see Hotchkiss and Dorsten, 1986.

Only a very few vocational educators—and fewer guidance counselors—accepted the view that the period of job-hopping was a temporary stage without permanent harm for most youth; not until the 1930s were there studies showing that most young people tended to settle down into permanent employment after a period of temporary youth work (Kett, 1982).

The debate over the meaning of youth jobs and youth unemployment has continued, of course. Some argue that a period of job-hopping is normal and even educational, and that public concern should be focused on only the minority of youth who seem to be unable to make the transition to adult employment (including disproportionate numbers of black and Hispanic youth). Those who see the transition to work as a serious problem have proposed remedies emphasizing guidance and counseling, labor market exchanges, and other mechanisms for providing young people with more information about labor market opportunities and the skills necessary to apply for jobs (interview skills, appropriate dress, how to fill out applications). Sometimes these efforts are school-based (of which career exploration and guidance are examples), while others are outside the school (like the proposals for the U.S. Employment Service). However, all these programs for smoothing the transition between school and work share the basic assumptions that youth unemployment is largely frictional unemployment. Under this assumption, vacant jobs and unemployed youth co-exist because of a lack of information about opportunities, and improved knowledge will automatically reduce the period between jobs and the youth unemployment rate.

The assumption that more information is better than ignorance is impossible to refute, of course. In addition, given that knowledge about work usually comes from parents (and extended family) and from the media—two sources of biased and limited information—there is a strong argument for career exploration courses and labor market information as sources of systematic information. However, although career exploration appears to increase knowledge about work, there is no strong evidence that this in turn improves labor market success (Hamilton & Crouter, 1980). Most young people who leave high school seem to shop around the labor market in an unsystematic way for a few years, taking jobs as they are offered and obtaining information about jobs from relatives and friends. Given the evidence that adult jobs are not likely to be offered to teenagers, most young people will be confined to a few stereotypical youth jobs—in fast food restaurants, gas stations, as retail clerks, doing odd jobs like babysitting and lawnmowing (Osterman, 1980)—regardless of how much information they might gain about occupations. Black and Hispanic youth face the added barriers of racial discrimination. Insufficient employment in an economy that went from 3% unemployment in the 1960s to about 8% unemployment in the 1980s was particularly serious for teenagers. Greater knowledge, even in exemplary guidance and counseling programs, cannot possibly eliminate the effects of discrimination, unemployment, and other barriers to youth.

Nonschool Training Programs: The CETA/JTPA Experience

Since the 1960s, training programs for youth and adults outside the schools have expanded. The manpower programs of the 1960s were consolidated in the Comprehensive Employment and Training Act (CETA) programs of the 1970s, and have now been superceded by the Job Training Partnership Act (JTPA), the Reagan Administration's successor to CETA. Although institutionally and politically separate from school-based training, these programs perform the same function of providing noncollege bound youth with employment skills (including both work habits and job-specific skills) to lower unemployment and smooth the transition from school to work. Typically, these programs accept only those young people in special trouble—the economically disadvantaged, school dropouts, and those unemployed for substantial periods. Therefore they are largely remedial, taking those youth who have failed in, or been failed by, the schools and trying to do for them what the schools have not done. Because of this, the task for manpower programs is in every way more difficult than the tasks the schools face.

The Great Depression, when manpower programs originated, was obviously a time of crisis requiring extraordinary measures. Direct public employment was tried for the first time, and the youth versions of adult programs, such as Youth Conservation Corps, provided some employment rather than the training that had always dominated youth policy. But even these programs were justified more for the training they provided than the employment opportunities they created. As was true for adults, the youth employment programs of the Depression were considered temporary expedients; once the Depression was over, youth policy reverted to the emphasis on training within the schools (especially in vocational educational programs) that had dominated youth policy prior to the Depression.

When manpower programs were revived in the 1960s, they were training programs rather than employment programs. A special concern with youth unemployment during the 1960s (Cohen & Kapp, 1966) survived into CETA, where the largest program—Title I training—tended to overenroll young people under age 22 (Barnes, 1978). As youth unemployment increased throughout the 1970s, alarm about young people and the possible permanent effects of unemployment mounted. The result was the Youth Employment and Demonstration Projects Act (YEDPA) of 1977, explicitly directed at youth unemployment with five programs: the Young Adult Conservation Corps, providing work on conservation projects; the Youth Community Conservation and Improvement Projects, to provide work experience on projects with some community benefit; the Youth Incentive Entitlement Pilot Project, providing wage subsidies to hire young people simultaneously enrolled in school; the Youth Employment and Training Program, providing training and other supportive services; and the Summer Youth Employment Program.

One major departure from prior practice within the CETA program was the initiation of public service employment (PSE), and YEDPA also extended employment programs in the Young Adult Conservation Corps, the Youth Incentive Entitlement Pilot Projects and the Summer Youth Employment Program. But while these programs promoted the idea that youth policy might include employment in addition to training, they did not really reshape the treatment of adolescents. Although 43% of individuals in CETA programs were in public employment positions in 1978, only 24% of youth were in such programs; the other 75% were in CETA Title I programs which provided training and counseling but not employment. Furthermore, about 80% of the employment positions available to youth (those under age 22) were summer jobs, so temporary that they can be best understood as efforts to keep troublesome adolescents off the streets rather than serious employment. Thus less than 5% of youth in CETA were in serious employment programs. YEDPA also failed to change the direction of youth policy much because two-thirds of the positions created were in the Youth Employment and Training programs (YETP) which provided training and ancillary services but not employment.[6]

The final blow to the concept of providing employment rather than training came with the Reagan Administration, which eliminated public service employment entirely. In addition, funds for training were substantially cut. In 1984 about 200,000 were enrolled in JTPA programs, many fewer than the target of 350,000 people; local programs were having trouble enrolling enough youth.[7] Compared to enrollments of over 21 million in CETA in 1981, this was a drastic reduction indeed. The Reagan changes represent extreme versions of the assumptions that have always governed out-of-school youth policy: Public efforts must remain subordinate to private labor markets; and training rather than employment opportunities are the appropriate public response to youth unemployment.

The evaluations of youth programs under CETA and JTPA reveal, as in the case of vocational education programs, distinctly mixed results. The Job Corps Program has had positive results, including widely-cited benefit-cost ratios (Long, Mallar, & Thornton, 1981). Some small, intensive demonstration projects have positive results, such as the Youth Entitlement Demonstrations (Farkas et al., 1980; Hahn & Lerman, 1984). Training seemed to have positive results, for youth as well as other groups (Taggart, 1981), although some programs were ineffective. Some were poorly implemented; others were too limited; and still others suffered from the same flaw of high school vocational educational programs: Training teenagers and then releasing them to a job market that provides teenagers only unskilled work is a basic mismatch of training and job opportunities. On the other hand, work experience programs not accompanied by

---

[6]For enrollments in different programs, see the *Employment and Training Report of the President* for 1978 and 1979.

[7]*Employment and Training Reporter,* March 11, 1984 and March 18, 1984.

training proved generally ineffective (Hahn & Lerman, 1984; Mangum & Walsh, 1980; Stromsdorfer, 1980; Taggart, 1981). These results suggest a complementarity between training and work: Not only must training be suited to job opportunities, but also work experience without training is likely to be ineffective for youth without skills.

Work Experience Programs

During the 1970s another component of an explicit youth policy developed—work experience programs combined with schooling. These too have their historical roots, especially in the continuation schools of the Progressive Era, allowing young people to combine schooling (usually vocational education) with part-time work. But the continuation schools waned, as the ideal of uninterrupted schooling followed by continuous employment became stronger.

The revival of work experience during the 1970s came from many sources, especially from a number of reports arguing that work experience would both provide appropriate socialization and reduce drop-out rates (Timpane, Abramovitz, Bobrow, and Pascal, 1976). Experience-Based Career Education, the work experience programs of YEDPA, and the practices of high schools allowing release time and credit for part-time work added to the pressures for work experience. Above all, the idea of work experience followed the practices of young people themselves, who began to participate in the labor market in ever greater numbers. The rise of work experience provides another illustration that our conception of appropriate programs for youth tends to follow rather than lead their actual behavior.

The idea that part-time work during adolescence is desirable is in one way a break with previous ideals. Work experience programs assume that work itself—rather than schooling—is the best preparation for work, contrary to the assumption of the Progressive Era that work would be detrimental to youth. Yet in another sense work experience is simply an extreme form of the assumptions embedded in vocational education. If job-related skill training is an appropriate activity for youth, then on-the-job training—if it is more effective than classroom training—must also be considered appropriate. If the problem with education has been, as vocational educators and career educators have long maintained, that schools create an artificial distance from work and segregate youth from adults, then work experience is the best way of eliminating that distance. Above all, if work has the powerful moral qualities that vocational educators have claimed, it makes more sense for students to be working rather than playing at work within artificial school settings. In this way vocational education readied the schools for work experience programs: Once it is legitimate to bring work partly into the schools, then it makes sense to do so completely.

The amount of work among teenagers, as well as anecdotes from them, suggests that the schooling solution to the transition of youth has become increasingly unpopular. Because parental incomes have risen since the 1960s, economic necessity seems not to explain the increasing work among teenagers; in addition, work during high school is less common for minority youth and lower-income white youth (Feldstein & Ellwood, 1982; Osterman 1980). The expanding materialism of youth culture may explain some increased work, but their own stories indicate that they find some meaning and responsibility in work that is denied them in school. Comments from young people reflect the sense that compared to work school is demeaning, constraining, boring:

> At school you're treated like kids, but [the students] act like kids. This year I'm expected to be more responsible, to work. You're not babies this year. People respect you [when you're working]. I like it a lot better this year. I get on better with my parents. They used to say don't come in late and don't get drunk. I felt really babied last year. Sometimes I felt like telling my teachers where to put it. They were talking to me like I was five years old. (Gaskell & Lazerson, 1980; Organization for Economic and Cultural Development, 1983)

These anecdotes suggest that many adolescents feel that work does have some of the moral attributes that many educators have claimed. Not, of course, that specific jobs are necessarily rewarding for long; the behavior of teenagers, jumping among jobs, and their own comments about the kinds of jobs they typically get suggest that teenagers have no special love for the low-skilled, routine, subordinate positions they usually get. But the idea of work, the responsibility and freedom that go with work, and the near-adult status—in contrast to the continued child-like status within high school—are attractive. The motto of many adolescents might be "work is bad, school is worse."

But adults would not (and should not) judge work experience programs by how much students like them; and so, more utilitarian and developmental concerns have emerged. One result is that work experience in high school increases employment and earning later (Corcoran, 1982; Ellwood, 1982; Meyer & Wise, 1982), suggesting that work experience is beneficial. Together with the evidence that minority and lower-income youth—precisely the groups that have the most difficulty making the transition to adult employment—tend not to work during high school, this suggests that more work experience programs should be established for disadvantaged or at risk youth.

This optimistic view of work experience would vanish if work experience tended to increase school leaving, or decreased the amount learned in school. However, moderate work does not seem to affect dropping out, class rank, or study time, and may even decrease dropping out, though a great deal of work (over 20 hours per week) does affect schoolwork (D'amico, 1984; Farkas, Smith, Stromsdorfer, Bottom, & Olsen, 1980; Steinberg, Greenberger, Vaux, & Ruggiero, 1981). These results suggest a complementarity between school and moderate amounts of work.

The evaluations of various CETA programs also seem to confirm the complementarity of work and training. In the YEDPA programs, work experience by itself did not improve either the employment or the school attendance of youth, though work experience combined with training and placement services appeared more effective (Hahn & Lerman, 1984; Taggart, 1981). Conversely, skill training to be effective requires being linked specifically to employment opportunities, and even then may be subject to decaying effectiveness (Stromsdorfer, 1980). It is important to note that work while in school seems to have positive effects although work experience in YEDPA has been ineffective; but the YEDPA programs include disadvantaged youth who have generally left school rather than middle-class youth still in school (to exaggerate the difference). These varying experiences suggest not only the power of discrimination in youth labor markets—against young people who may seem unreliable, or lack basic skills, or are minority—but also the difficulty in setting up formal remedial programs to mimic what happens informally in the youth labor market.

The greatest fears about work experience have emphasized the poor quality of youth work. If young people work in jobs with limited responsibility, routinized and unskilled tasks, capricious and demeaning supervision, and where most of their coworkers are other teenagers, then it is difficult to see how working can enhance their responsibility, skills, integration with adults, or attachment to work. As many commentators have pointed out, the moral properties of work and the attraction of the work ethic disappear when work is no longer intrinsically rewarding and challenging, when occupations do not permit continued development and mobility, and when relationships with coworkers are either degrading (as in rigid hierarchies and competitive environment) or missing (in highly automated work).

With the expansion of youth work and formal work experience programs, our youth policy has in effect turned to the unregulated labor market to socialize adolescents. Even though we do not know precisely the effects of adolescent work experiences on adult attitudes and work, the lessons of the youth labor market may provide an early, and sadly accurate, lesson about adult work.

What might adolescents learn from the youth labor market? First, they might learn that work is done for money, not for intrinsic satisfaction. Although young people report a sense of responsibility and adult participation while at work, especially in contrast to experiences in school, they also seem quite willing to leave particular jobs when other sources of satisfaction compete for attention. Steinberg et al. (1981) found that working teenagers are more cynical about work, viewing work as intrinsically unrewarding and meaningless, and cynicism is greater among youth who work longer. Of course, teenagers may view their early jobs as completely different from the jobs they expect to have later (Greenberger & Steinberg, 1981), and middle-class youth may have parents as models and other information about adult work. Still, youth work cannot possibly enhance the hopes that good work is prevalent, and may begin the long processes by which aspirations about work are reconciled to the reality.

Second, teenagers might learn that discrimination pervades the labor markets. Patterns of racial discrimination (Osterman, 1980) and segregation by gender are strong in youth labor markets. While the long-term effects of these early experiences are unclear, there is a long history of fear that black teenagers learning about racial barriers may take the alternative route of juvenile crime as the only available form of employment (Brown, 1984; Glaser, 1978; Phillips, Votey, & Maxwell, 1972). If work is the powerful socializing force that many believe, then the experiences of discrimination in the labor market should also be powerful.

Third, young people might learn that levels of unemployment in this country are relatively high. Not all youth unemployment is voluntary, after all, especially for black, Hispanic, and lower-income youth who work in smaller numbers than their middle-class, white peers. Experience seems to dictate what we consider normal: Journalists have recently come to write about unemployment rates around 7.5% as evidence of economic recovery, and the unemployment rate taken to represent the concept of full employment has climbed steadily in the post-World War II period as older versions of full employment have come to seem unattainable. It seems possible, therefore, that early experiences with unemployment prepare some youth for the lifetime of precarious employment that is common to many Americans, especially working-class Americans.

Many teenagers have antidotes to the lessons of the youth labor market. They have other models at home, or are assured that they will go to college and escape into the managerial and professional world where the quality of work, unemployment, and even discrimination are less troubling. But many others have no alternatives, and for them the youth labor market must provide early and unforgettable lessons about adult work. Whether these lessons are deplorable or merely realistic—mechanisms of cooling out, of reconciling high aspirations with the reality of the labor market—depends on one's view of whether that reality should be changed.

Of course, the labor market is not completely unregulated. Within the labor market, child labor laws have attempted to prohibit young people from working under dangerous conditions, and the minimum wage—now under attack—was instituted partly to eliminate the lowest-quality jobs and upgrade the status of labor. Many firms have experimented with efforts to improve the quality of work. Measures against discrimination exist in federal law and the Equal Employment Opportunity Commission, and macroeconomic policies and public employment programs can reduce unemployment. But these have fallen out of favor, especially under the Reagan Administration, and their effects for youth have always been limited in any case. Other policies affecting employment have been more powerful: tax incentives (including accelerated depreciation and investment tax credits) to substitute capital for labor; tax incentives for firms to locate their manufacturing abroad; and the tight monetary policy of the Federal Reserve Board, favoring the fight against inflation at the expense of employment.

While the effects of youth work are still murky, it is nonetheless clear that the old Deweyan ideal that schools could not only prepare students for work as it is, but also give them a sense of what work and life could be cannot be satisfied in current work experience programs. To give students the capacities to criticize and reshape the world they confront would require devising work experience programs selfconsciously, to promote ideals of "good work" (Stern, 1984). Such work experience would not only be intrinsically satisfying, but would also give students some measure by which they could criticize, and then remake or avoid, work of low quality.

The Shape of our Explicit Youth Policy

The explicit attempts to prepare adolescents for work in these various programs share some characteristics. They are, of course, highly age-segregated; even in manpower programs, young people tend to be in different programs than adults, and the extent of integration by age in work experience seems minimal.

Youth programs are segregated in other fundamental ways as well. Almost all of these programs are segregated by gender, because preparation for work still means different things for boys and girls. Despite fifteen years of efforts to integrate women into nontraditional programs, vocational education remains highly sex-segregated, both in the high school and in the community colleges; manpower programs and most work experience replicate these same divisions.

Our explicit youth programs are also segregated by class. It is not much of an exaggeration to claim that our youth policy is focused entirely on working-class and lower-class youth. Vocational education students have always been of lower class status than students in academic tracks, and career exploration courses appear to appeal to the same students. The efforts to smooth the transition from school to work through counseling and guidance mechanisms also focus on those who are likely to be dropouts. CETA and JTPA programs are explicitly remedial institutions and include only the most disadvantaged. While work experience among teenagers tends to be more prevalent among middle-income and white youth, those efforts to devise formal work experience programs—in YEDPA, experience-based career education, and in vocational education—naturally concentrate on the lower-class students who need such programs the most. Our policy towards middle-class youth is one of *laissez faire*, under the assumption that their parents, their success in school, and the jobs they can obtain are sufficient to prepare them for adult work roles. For lower-class adolescents the transition remains more problematic; the result has been a set of remedial programs that are, like the schools themselves, relatively class-segregated.

A third characteristic of youth programs is that they have emphasized training, rather than employment. The various efforts to move away from training and towards a greater concern with employment—in CETA, in experience-based career education, and in the potential of high school guidance to provide labor market information—have been relatively incomplete. There may be some trend to view employment more positively, especially in work experience programs. But most of these efforts are not conscious aspects of our explicit policy, but are rather the individual actions of students; the large government efforts to extend work experience have been experimental and short-lived, despite growing evidence that work and training are complementary.

The relative neglect of employment in our youth policy is curious given the fact that one of the most prominent youth problems during the last decade—unemployment—is partly a product of discrimination against youth (especially against minority youth) and insufficient labor market demand (Osterman, 1980). There is sufficient justification for our youth policy to emphasize direct intervention into labor markets, including employment creation, in addition to training. But this approach would be fundamentally at odds both with the social construction of youth as a period of preparation and with the sanctity of labor markets. The result is to generate a youth policy that tries to remedy unemployment without having any influence over the causes of the problem.

Finally, the programs of our explicit youth policy vary widely in their effectiveness. High school vocational education gives students little advantage in the job markets, despite its popularity. Community college programs may be more effective, but any positive results must be tempered by the extremely high dropout rate, and by the fact that the earnings advantage of some college is much smaller than for a B.A. degree. CETA included some highly successful programs and others that were dismal failures. Counseling and guidance within the high school are weak, and the assumption that better information about labor markets can reduce youth unemployment seems quite wrong. Work experience programs have some promise, but there remain serious questions about their effects.

But if these programs have had mixed results, the experiences of the past 2 decades have generated considerable information on which programs work and which fail. The idea of the U.S. as an experimenting society is nicely illustrated by education and training programs, whose variety constitutes a social experiment on a grand scale. Heeding the lessons of that experiment proves difficult, both because protecting turf prevents ineffective programs from being cut and because ideological resistance to any government role, by the Reagan Administration, for example, prevents even successful programs from being replicated. But the problems of youth are not going away, and for a new day the lessons of past programs can guide future policy.

DILEMMAS FOR THE FUTURE

Even in a static world, there would be a great deal to do in reshaping our youth policy. One implication of the previous section is that policies to intervene more directly into labor markets—to correct patterns of discrimination, reduce unemployment and underemployment, provide public employment where necessary, and improve the quality of work—should be developed. We have accumulated a great deal of evidence about which remedial programs are effective, and the lessons from these experiences—that intensive programs are more effective than short-term programs, that programs need to be well-managed with clear performance goals, that training and work opportunities should be coordinated—need to be implemented. The schools have recently come under intense criticism, and many reform efforts are under way.

But the world is not static. In considering our youth policy we need to examine some changes—trends both in the world of work itself, and in the conceptions of adolescence, schooling, and work that shape the social institutions of young people.

The Future of Inequality

Much of our social policy is a response to inequalities in opportunities. If inequalities become worse, then we face the prospect of youth programs trying to remedy social problems that are increasingly severe.

There is now substantial evidence that inequality in the distribution of earnings has become more serious during the 1970s and 1980s (Grubb & Wilson, 1988; Tilly, Bluestone, & Harrison, 1986; Danzinger & Plotnick, 1977; Henle & Ryscavage, 1980); many analysts are concerned that this trend will continue as well-paid manufacturing positions are replaced by unskilled service work (e.g., Kutner, 1983). Unemployment, which contributes to the inequality of earnings and to poverty rates, has been increasing throughout the post-World War II period; many fear that it will continue to increase as firms continue to export employment to low-wage countries and as other advanced countries become more competitive with American industry. Poverty rates among the nonelderly population have increased since the 1970s, because of long-term demographic and economic changes and real declines in welfare programs.

On the other hand, some observers feel that we are on the brink of another long wave (or Kondratief cycle) of economic development, stimulated in part by computer-based technologies (Freeman, Clark, & Soete, 1982). (This is a sophisticated version of technological enthusiasm, which has long claimed that technical development will create more skilled work.) Demographers project that unemployment rates are likely to fall because younger cohorts entering the labor market are smaller. These views suggest that inequalities may be less serious in the future.

If the optimists are right, the tasks of our youth policy will be easier in the next several decades, and a *laissez faire* policy may be adequate. If, on the other hand, the pessimists are correct, then education and training programs will face increasing pressures to solve the problems of unemployment, earnings inequality, discrimination patterns, declining productivity, and other problems whose causes are outside the control of social programs. In this case the *laissez faire* policies of the Reagan Administration can do little to solve the basic problems, and a new level of government programs may be necessary--industrial policies to cope with the sector-specific problems and with international competition and a coherent policy on the export of capital and employment.

New Technologies and Employment Opportunities

New technologies never lack for boosters, and those based on microelectronics and computers are no exception. Enthusiasm about high tech developments has swept many groups, including educators trying to prepare students for the world of tommorrow, pedagogues developing new methods of classroom instruction, Frostbelt states trying to rejuvenate their economies, and economic forecasters looking for new sources of economic growth and employment. The schools have responded with computer literacy courses and surging enrollments in high-tech curricula (Grubb, 1984).

Despite this enthusiasm, two issues have not yet been resolved. One issue is whether technological developments will increase unemployment, by replacing semiskilled and unskilled workers with more sophisticated machines, or whether new technologies will decrease unemployment by reducing prices and increasing demand for goods affected by technical change. There is more speculation than evidence. The fears about the effects of automation on employment in the early 1960s proved groundless because the diffusion of automation was relatively slow and because other forms of unemployment—especially caused by deficient aggregate demand—proved to be relatively more important. On the other hand, a judicious review of the recent evidence by Paul Attewell (1983) suggests that employment-destroying effects of microelectronics will probably outweigh the employment-creating effects, and simulations with an input-output model come to the same conclusions (Leontief & Duchin, 1984). Given uncertainty about how large these employment effects will be and about the speed of diffusion of new technologies, unemployment trends may continue to be dominated by other factors—inadequate demand; foreign competition and the export of jobs; and perhaps long swings in economic activity.

A second unresolved issue involves the influence of new technologies on the composition of skills. The available evidence suggests that new technologies are unlikely to increase the amount of highly-skilled work substantially. During the 1960s, when similar concerns about automation arose, technical developments tended to change skill requirements very little (Bright, 1966; Horowitz & Hernstadt, 1966). Similarly, the most widely-cited labor force projections indicate that while the growth rates of high tech jobs will be higher than average, the absolute numbers of jobs in high tech occupations will be rather small. By one moderate definition including industries, employment in high tech sectors will grow from about 6.2% of employment in 1980 to 6.6% in 1995, hardly a dramatic jump (Riche, Hecker, & Burgin, 1983). High tech occupations will grow more rapidly than others, but the numbers will still be small: Engineers will grow by about 35% between 1984 and 1995, and computer specialists will grow by 69% (compared to an average job growth of 15%), but the numbers involved—480,000 engineers and 212,000 computer specialists—amount to only 4% of the 15,918,000 new jobs that will be created. The jobs that will account for the greatest amount of job growth include cashiers, nurses, janitors, truck drivers, waiters and waitresses, and other low-tech positions (Silvestri & Lukasiewicz, 1985). Unless there are unforeseen developments or massive policy changes that are not now being contemplated, the rapid growth of high tech sectors will not be large enough to change the composition of the labor force substantially.

However, developments in high technology have captured the imagination of the public, business, students, and educators alike. The danger is that the image of such jobs may dominate the reality of service employment, generating unrealistic aspirations and unreasonable enrollments (Grubb, 1984). (Indeed, a similar problem seems to have taken place during the Progressive Era as professional employment, which accounted for only 4.2% of employment in 1900 and 5.4% by 1920, dominated the conceptions of educators and social reformers about labor markets.) It seems that the rhetoric about high tech employment helps mask the real nature of available work.

Conceptions of Schooling and Adolescence

The stage of adolescence codified in the Progressive Era was marked by a clear progression from school to work, with crucial and potentially irreversible occupational decisions made during the teenage years in the form of schooling decisions. That conception of adolescence, together with the stereotype of a troubled period, has remained relatively intact. To be sure, the period of transition is now longer because of the lengthening of schooling; and the gender-linked divisions of the Progressive Era have been softened (but hardly eroded) by the increased labor force participation of women.

However, changes in schooling and work have the potential for changing the nature of adolescence itself. Because young people now mix work and schooling much more than before, the notion of a distinct stage dominated by schooling and truncated by employment is less relevant. The idea that schooling decisions are irreversible is no longer tenable when returning to 4-year and 2-year colleges throughout the 20s and into the 30s is more common. The greater flexibility of decisions about schooling and work also has the potential for reducing the high anxiety surrounding adolescence, or for relegating that anxiety to the realm of social and sexual development. The changes in the lives of young people portend a stage considerably less distinct, less dependent on adults because of work, less anxious, but also longer than the conventional conception of adolescence.

The length of adolescence—the period before an individual achieves a completely independent economic status—has itself been a source of constant concern. The length of adolescence is a function of schooling and has increased beyond that demanded by skill requirements in the labor force as students have been driven to increase their education to improve their employability. As long as new sectors emerge with increased demands for well-educated labor, e.g., the expansion of government and services after World War II, and the current expansion of high-tech sectors, there is no problem in replenishing the demand for skilled labor. But if the process of replenishment slows or ceases, then we will face a world in which the number of well-educated workers exceeds, by increasing amounts, the jobs requiring substantial education. In fact, the process of overeducation has been underway during the post-World War II period (Rumberger, 1981), and current projections are that between 1982 and 1995, one-fifth of college graduates will get jobs not requiring a college degree (Sargent, 1984). This is a world in which the acquisition of vocational skills is no longer a serious problem of the schools, and where vocationalism, the use of schooling as a credential, and escalating levels of education and training are increasingly irrational.

There are two routes out of this vision. One is a nonvocational schooling system, one in which vocational motives have ceased to be dominant, in which vocational differentiation has been reduced, in which relevance is defined not by the requirements of labor markets but by conceptions of the well-developed individual. In fact, some of the recent commission reports appear to support a nonvocational conception of schooling, in defiance of the trend throughout the twentieth century (e.g., Boyer, 1983). The interpretation of excellence in terms of some abstract intellectual standard—rather than the requirements of labor markets—is a nonvocational conception of standards for learning. Defining equality of education opportunity with a "single standard of excellence" applied to all children (Twentieth Century Fund, 1983) is a return to older common-school ideals, where vocationally inspired differentiation is abandoned. The notion that the schools must adapt to an increasingly technological future by providing students more general skill training, purer forms of mathematics and science, and more powerful forms of thinking is similarly quite different from the vocational concept of relevance, which has stressed specific skill training and narrow preparation.

This is an attractive vision of education. It is one in which a true liberal education, an education that prepares all individuals to develop their capacities to the fullest, can emerge, in which educating individuals to the limit of their ability can have some real meaning rather than standing as mockery of what the schools cannot do. It is also a world in which the school can be left alone to do what schools seem to do best, as autonomous institutions standing somewhat apart from the rest of society rather than being forced to mimic workplaces and being freighted with the utilitarian detritus of current schooling systems. But it is also a frustrating vision, because its realization seems so difficult. There are mechanisms available to move towards this vision: stricter standards for high school (and college) graduation, more requirements for academic course work (including the humanities) at all levels, the elimination of vocational and general tracks in the high school, the elimination of vocational and professional majors in the colleges, better preparation of teachers, decreasing emphasis on preparation for careers, and efforts to monitor the tendency of employers to require higher levels of schooling. Even to mention these mechanisms is to realize that, without changing the basic purposes of schooling, such changes are difficult to realize.

An alternative future is that schooling will continue to be dominated by vocational concerns, long after most vocational instruction has become redundant. This is a much grimmer vision, one in which conflicts over access to higher levels of schooling intensify, in which educational levels continue to escalate and adolescence continues to lengthen, in which credentialism continues to undermine the academic and general content of education, in which remedial efforts (including out-of-school programs) are all the more necessary because schooling and training institutions are the only means of access to jobs. In many ways, this is a vision in which schools have become successful in their central economic mission—preparation for labor markets—but relatively unsuccessful in every other form of instruction.

The choice between these two futures is, of course, a devil's dilemma. The problem is that the first alternative tries to make schools and other youth institutions independent of labor markets, while the second subordinates these institutions completely to labor markets. In practice, we have an awkward combination of the two, with students pulled towards vocational purposes while reformers and educators try to remind us of the moral, intellectual, and political purposes of school.

There is a very different alternative, though its realization is as difficult as reforming the schools into nonvocational institutions. That is to formulate a policy around schooling and work that shapes work itself rather than schooling and training alone. Many elements of such a policy are familiar: efforts to eliminate discrimination, macroeconomic policies to ensure full employment, and public employment. Other elements—experiments to improve the quality of work, such as "industrial policy" to cope with sector-specific problems, and efforts to reduce the export of capital and employment—are still in early discussions. Such a direct approach to employment is the only way to remedy the central dilemma of our youth policy: the fact that programs for youth have always been in the weak position of responding to economic changes without having any control over those changes, and, therefore, being unable to define what our youth institutions ought to accomplish.

REFERENCES

Addams, J. (1972). The spirit of youth in the city streets. Urbana: University of Illinois Press. (first published 1909).

Alexander, K., & McDill, E. (1976). Selection and allocation within schools: Some causes and consequences of curriculum placement. *American Sociological Review, 41*, 963–980.

Attewell, P. (1983). *Microelectronics and employment: A review of the debate*, University of California, Santa Cruz.

Barnes, W. (1978). Target groups: In *CETA: An analysis of the issues*, National Commission for Manpower Policy, Special Report No. 23.

Bishop, J. (1986). *Preparing youth for employment: Does learning basic skills pay off?* National Center for Research in Vocational Education.

Blair, L., Finn, M., & Stevenson, W. (1981). The returns to the associate degrees for technicians. *Journal of Human Resources, 16,* 449–458.

Boyer, E. (1983). *High school: A report on secondary education in America.* New York: Harper and Row.

Breneman, D., & Nelson, S. (1981). *Financing community colleges: An economic perspective.* Washington, DC: The Brookings Institution.

Bright, J. (1966). The relationship of increasing automation and skill requirements. In the National Commission on Technology, Automation, and Economic Progress. *The employment impact of technological change.* Washington, D.C.: U.S. Government Printing Office.

Brint, S., & Karabel, J. (forthcoming). *The triumph of vocationalism: The community colleges and the politics of organization change.* New York: Cambridge University Press.

Brown, C. (1984). Manchild in Harlem. *The New York Times Magazine,* September 16.

Clark, B. (1960). The 'cooling-out' function in higher education. *American Journal of Sociology, 45,* 569–76.

Claus, J.F. (1984). An ethnographic investigation of attitude development in vocational education: The importance of ethnographic meaning. Cornell University.

Cohen, D., & Farrar, E. (1977, winter). Career education—Reforming school through work. *The Public Interest, 46.*

Cohen, E., & Kapp, L. (Eds.) (1966). *Manpower policies for youth.* New York: Columbia University Press.

Corcoran, M. (1982). The employment and wage consequences of teenage women's nonemployment. In R. Freeman & D. Wise (Eds.), *The youth labor market problem: Its nature, causes, and consequences* (pp. 391–425). Chicago: University of Chicago Press.

D'Amico, R. (1984, July). Does Employment during high school impair academic progress? *Sociology of Education, 57,* 152–164.

Danziger, S., & Plotnick, R. (1977). Demographic change, government transfers and income distribution. *Monthly Labor Review, 100,* 7–11.

Ellwood, D. (1982). Teenage unemployment: Permanent scars or temporary blemishes? In R. Freeman & D. Wise (Eds.), *The youth labor market problem: Its nature, causes, and consequences* (pp. 349–390). Chicago: University of Chicago Press.

Farkas, G., Smith, D. A., Stromsdorfer, E., Bottom, C., & Olsen, R. (1980). *Early impacts from the youth entitlenent demonstration: Participation, work, and schooling.* Manpower Demonstration Research Corporation.

Farrar, E., deSanctis, J., & Cowden, P. (1980). *The walls within: Work, experience, and school reform.* Cambridge: Huron Institute: ERIC document ED203 193.

Feldstein, M., & Ellwood, D. (1982). Teenage unemployment: What is the problem? In R. Freeman & D. Wise (Eds.), *The youth labor market problem: Its nature, causes, and consequences* (pp. 17–33). Chicago: University of Chicago Press.

Freeman, C., Clark, J., & Soete, L. (1982). *Unemployment and technological innovation: A study of long waves and economic development.* Westport, CT: Greenwood Press.

Freeman, R. (1971). *The market for college-trained manpower,* Cambridge, MA: Harvard University Press.

Gaskell, J., & Lazerson, M. (1980). *Between school and work: Perspectives of working class youth.* University of British Columbia.

Glaser, D. (1978). Economic and socio-cultural variables affecting rates of youth unemployment, delinquency and crime; In U.S. Department of Labor, *Conference report on youth unemployment.*

Goldstein, B., & Oldham, J. (1979). *Children and work: A study of socialization.* New Brunswick, NJ: Transaction Books.

Gottschalk, P., & Danziger, S. (1985). A framework for evaluating the effects of economic growth and transfers on poverty. *American Economic Review, 75,* 153–161.

Greenberger, E., & Steinberg, L. (1981). The workplace as a context for the socialization of youth. *Journal of Youth and Adolescence, 10,* 185–210.

Grubb, W. N. (1978, Spring). The phoenix of vocationalism: Hope deferred is hope denied. *New Directions for Education and Work, 1,* 71–89.

Grubb, W. N. (1984). The bandwagon once more: Vocational preparation for high-tech occupations. *Harvard Educational Review, 54,* 429–451.

Grubb, W. N. (1986). Responding to the constancy of change: New technologies and future demands on U.S. education; In H. Levin & R. Rumberger (Eds), *The impact of technology on work and education.* Philadelphia: Taylor and Francis.

Grubb, W. N. (forthcoming). Vocationalizing higher education: The causes of enrollment and completion in two-year colleges, 1970–1980. *Economics of Education Review.*

Grubb, W. N. & Lazerson, M. (1975, November). Rally round the work place: Continuities and fallacies in career education. *Harvard Educational Review, 45,* 451–474.

Grubb, W. N., & Lazerson, M. (1982a). *Broken promises: How Americans fail their children.* New York: Basic Books.

Grubb, W. N., & Lazerson, M. (1982b). Education and the labor market: Recycling the youth problem. In H. Kantor & D. Tyack (Eds.) *Work, youth, and schooling: Historical perspectives on vocationalism in American education.* Stanford, CA: Stanford University Press.

Grubb, W. N., & Wilson, R. (1988, May). Inequality in wages and salaries 1960–1980: The contributions of gender, race, sectoral shifts and regional shifts. University of California, Berkeley.

Hall, G. S. (1904). *Adolescence: Its psychology and its relationship to physiology, anthropology, sociology, sex, crime, religion, and education.* New York: D. Appleton.

Hamilton, S., & Crouter, A. (1980). Work and growth: A review of research on the impact of work experience on adolescent development. *Journal of Youth and Adolescence, 9,* 323–338.

Hahn, A., & Lerman, R. (1984). *The CETA youth employment record: Representative findings on the effectiveness of federal strategies assisting disadvantaged youth.* Waltham, MA: Florence Heller Graduate School.

Hawes, J. (1828). *Lectures addressed to the young men of Hartford and New Haven.* Hartford.

Heinemann, H., & Sussna, E. (1977, October). The Economic Benefits of a Community College Education. *Industrial Relations, 16,* 345–354.

Henle, P., & Ryscavage, P. (1980). The distribution of earned income among men and women, 1958–1977. *Monthly Labor Review, 10,* 3–10.

Hess, R., & Shipman, V. (1970). Early experience and the socialization of cognitive modes in children. In M. Miles & W. W. Charters, Jr., *Learning and social settings.* Boston: Allyn and Bacon.

Horowitz, M., & Herrnstadt, I. (1966). Changes in skill requirements of occupations in selected industries. In the National Commission on Technology, automation, and economic progress. *The employment impact of technological change.* Washington D.C.: U.S. Government Printing Office.

Hotchkiss, L., & Dorsten, I. (1986). *Stratification, career plans, and high school guidance.* National Center for Research in Vocational Education.

Kett, J. (1977). *Rites of passage: Adolescence in America, 1790 to the present.* New York: Basic Books.

Kett, J. (1982). The adolescence of vocational education; In H. Kantor and D. Tyack (Eds.) *Work,* youth, and schooling: Historical perspectives on vocationalism in American education (pp. 79–109). Stanford, CA: Stanford University Press.

Kohn, M. (1969). *Class and conformity*. Homewood, IL: Dorsey Press.

Kuttner, R. (1983, July). The declining middle. *Atlantic*.

Lazerson, M. (1980). Choosing our roles: American youth and guidance in historical perspective, Organization for Economic Co-operation and Development, Centre for Educational Research and Innovation Project on *The educational response to the changing needs of youth*.

Lazerson, M., & Grubb, W. N. (1974). *American education and vocationalism: A documentary history, 1870–1970*. New York: Teachers College Press.

Leontief, W., & Duchin, F. (1984). *The impacts of automation on employment, 1963–2000*. Institute for Economic Analysis, New York University.

Long, D., Mallar, C., & Thornton, C. (1981). Evaluating the benefits and costs cf the job corps. *Journal of Policy Analysis and Management 1*, 55–76.

Mangum, G., & Walsh, J. (1980). *Employment and training programs for youth—What works best for whom?*, U.S. Department of Labor, Youth Knowledge Development Report 2.2.

McPartland, J., Dawkins, R., & Braddock, J. (1986). *The school's role in the transition from education to work: Current conditions and future prospects*. Center for Social Organization of Schools, Johns Hopkins University, Report No. 362.

Meyer, R. H., & Wise, D. (1982). High school preparation and early labor force experience. In R. Freeman & D. Wise (Eds.), *The youth labor market problem: Its nature, causes, and consequences* (pp. 277–347). Chicago: University of Chicago Press.

Millar, S. M., & Harrison, I. (1964). Types of dropouts: The "unemployables". In A. Shostak & W. Gemberg, (Eds.), *Blue collar world: Studies of the American worker* (pp. 479–484). Englewood Cliffs, NJ: Prentice-lall.

National Association of Secondary School Principals. (1984). *The mood of American youth*. Reston, VA.

Organization for Economic and Cultural Development. (1983). *Education and work: The views of the young*. Paris: OECD.

Osterman, P. (1980). *Getting started: The youth labor market*. Cambridge, MA: MIT Press.

Parnes, H., & Kohen, A. (1975). Occupational information and labor market status: The case of young men. *Journal of Human Resources, 10*, 44–55.

Peng, S., Fetters, W., & Kolstad, A. (1984). *High school and beyond: A national longitudinal study for the 1980s*. National Center for Education Statistics.

Phillips, L., Votey, H., & Maxwell, D. (1972). Crime, youth, and the labor market. *Journal of Political Economy, 80*, 491–504.

Pincus, F. (1980). The false promise of community colleges: Class conflict and vocational education. *Harvard Educational Review, 50*, 332–361.

Powell, A., Farrar, E., & Cohen, D. (1985). *The shopping mall high school: Winners and losers in the educational marketplace*. Boston: Houghton Mifflin.

Ravitch, D. (1983). *The troubled crusade: American education, 1945–1980*. New York: Basic Books.

Reubens, B. (1974). Vocational education for all in high school? In J. O'Toole (Ed.), *Work and the quality of life*. Cambridge, MA: MIT Press.

Riche, R., Hecker, D., & Burgan, J. (1983). High technology today and tomorrow: A small slice of the employment pie. *Montly Labor Review, 106*, 50–58.

Rogers, D. (1974). *The work ethic in industrial America, 1950–1920*. Chicago: University of Chicago Press.

Rumberger, R. (1981). *Overeducation in the U.S. labor market*. New York: Praeger Publishers.

Rumberger, R., & Daymont, T. (1984). The economic value of academic and vocational training acquired in high school; In M. Borus (Ed.), *Youth and the labor market: Analyses of the national longitudinal survey* (pp. 157–192). Kalamazoo, MI: W. E. Upjohn Institute for Employment Research.

Sargent, J. (1984). The job outlook for college graduates through the mid-1990's. *Occupational Outlook Quarterly, 28,* 2–7.

Silvestri, G., & Lukasiewicz, J. (1985). Occupational employment projections: The 1984–95 outlook. *Monthly Labor Review, 108,* 42–59.

Starr, H. (1982). Vocational education response to skilled industrial worker shortages; In R. Taylor, H. Rosen, & F. Pratzner (Eds.), *The responsiveness of training institutions to changing labor market demands.* Columbus, OH: National Center for Research in Vocational Education.

Steinberg, L., Greenberger, E., Vaux, A., & Ruggiero, M. (1981). Early work experience: Effects on adolescent occupational socialization. *Youth and Society, 4,* 403–422.

Stern, D. (1984). School-based enterprise and the quality of work experience: A study of high school students. *Youth and Society, 15,* 401–427.

Stromsdorfer, E. (1980). The effectiveness of youth programs: An analysis of the historical antecedents of current youth initiatives. In B. Anderson & I. Sawhill (Eds.), *Youth employment and public policy* (pp. 88–111). Englewood Cliffs, NJ: Prentice-Hall.

Taggart, R. (1981). *A fisherman's guide: An assessment of training and remediation strategies.* Kalamazoo, MI: W. E. Upjohn Institute for Employment Research.

Tilly, C., Bluestone, B., & Harrison, B. (1986, December). *What is making American wages more unequal?* Unublished paper, Massachusetts Institute of Technology.

Timpane, M., Abramowitz, S., Bobrow, S., & Pascal, A. (1976). *Youth policy in transition* (Report R-2006-HEW). Santa Monica: The Rand Corporation.

Twentieth Century Fund. (1983). *Making the grade.* New York.

Wilms, W. (1974). *Public and proprietary vocational training: A study of effectiveness.* Berkeley: Center for Research and Development in Higher Education.

Wilms, W., & Hansell, S. (1982). The dubious promise of post-secondary vocational education: Its payoff to dropouts and graduates in the U.S.A. *International Journal of Educational Development, 2,* 43–59.

Zwerling, L. S. (1976). *Second best: The crisis of the community college.* New York: McGraw-Hill.

SCHOOLS AND VOCATIONAL DEVELOPMENT

3 Dreams and Aspirations in the Status Attainment Model

Alan B. Wilson
University of California, Berkeley

> *Education is the influence exercised by adult generations on those that
> are not yet ready for social life. Its object is to arouse and to develop in
> the child a certain number of physical, intellectual and moral states
> which are demanded of him by both the political society as a whole and
> the special milieu for which he is specifically destined.*
>
> *In sum, education, far from having as its unique or principal object
> the individual and his interests, is above all the means by which society
> perpetually recreates the conditions of its very existence.*
> —Emile Durkheim (1956, pp. 71, 123)

> *Insofar as individuals interact in a society or subsociety governed by an
> orientation to the future, people will identify themselves and be identified
> according to the future as they conceive it.*
> —Ralph Turner (1964, p. 211)

Although psychologists and career counselors have elaborated multidimensional
schemes for analyzing the process of career choice, matching abilities, traits, and
emerging interests of youths with the demands of jobs or modal characteristics of
adult job-incumbents, sociologists for the most part have focused on one dimension: status. This specialization of interests had its origins in the debate as to
whether the national pool of latent talent was indeed as slender as the unequal
distribution of rewards in society might suggest. A burgeoning literature
emerged under the candid rubric of "political arithmetic" (Hogben, 1938),
numerically comparing the life chances of working class youths with their more
advantaged peers. Chi-squared was an early measure of the inequality of
opportunity.

When the facts of unequal opportunities had been repeatedly documented, attention turned to the process. How do classes reproduce themselves? What, besides changes in the occupational structure, permits or facilitates upward mobility? What roles do schools play in these processes? Works such as Warner, Havighurst, and Loeb's, *Who Shall Be Educated?* (1944) and community studies of the 1950s provided insightful and poignant vignettes interpreting both transmission and mobility.

Many sociologists of the 1950s and 1960s, attached to Colleges of Agriculture while the farm population was still declining, asked why rural youths were so disadvantaged in the competition for jobs in the urban market-place. Was there a rural spirit that was slower, less driven? Or were the lower IQ scores of rural white youths due to selective and dysgenic migration as was thought to account for North-South black differentials?

Although there was still an at least implicit political concern about ascriptive nonmeritocratic impediments to equal opportunity, attention turned more and more to differential socialization and away from external obstacles. Sociologists in the late 50s and early 60s anticipated the "culture of poverty" in looking to the immediate social milieu to explain the want of motivation, effort, and ability of the individual. A causal chain leading from family, native ability, and influence of friends to school attainment and thence to career and adult status became firmly entrenched.

Particularly with the publication of Blau and Duncan's, *The American Occupational Structure* (1967), this model was formalized and quantified as a recursive path model—a unidirectional causal sequence. While Blau and Duncan dealt only with demographic data from a cross-section of adults, Sewell and his associates in Wisconsin were building longitudinally upon a study of Wisconsin high school youths initiated by Little (1958) in 1957, which included attitudinal data. During the past 20 odd years, with advances in mathematical sophistication, capacity of computers, and extensions of variables and waves of observation, a stream of ever more elaborate path models has flowed. Campbell (1983) comments:

> Since the publication in 1969 and 1970 of the basic papers on the Wisconsin status attainment model (Sewell et al., 1969, 1970; see also Sewall and Hauser, 1975), more than 500 subsequent papers have attempted to replicate, explicate, extend, or dispute the basic findings.

Throughout this sequence of elaborations of the Wisconsin model there has been a conceptual consistency that is starker in the form of path models (or systems of simultaneous equations) than in words. The models have been uniformly hierarchical in the sense of excluding any feedback loops. In most instances they have been explicitly recursive, assuming that no factors not included in the model can affect sets of dependent variables. If parental SES, IQ, friends' and teachers' expectations affect the educational aspirations of an individual, for the model to be hierarchical, his aspirations may not affect his friend's. For it to be recursive, nothing else (other than the subject's parents' SES, his IQ, and his teachers' expectations) can affect them both. Alexander & Pallas (1983) have issued a plea to "bring the arrows back in."

The purpose of this paper are twofold. The first is to explore the possibilities of relaxing those constraints on the model that seem least plausible to see whether it makes a difference. If it does, the second aim is to see how we might construe the revision.

THE WISCONSIN PANEL STUDY

The Wisconsin data are the most classic set and, of course, necessary if direct comparisons of the effects of variations of model assumptions are to be assessed. Moreover, in the most recent and intricate elaboration of the model, Hauser, Tsai, and Sewell (1983) have published sufficient data to permit remodelling without seeking access to the original raw data.

The baseline data for this study come from a questionnaire survey of all high school seniors in Wisconsin schools administered by J. K. Little (1958). Henmon-Nelson IQ score percentiles were obtained from the Wisconsin Testing Service. The rank of each student was elicited from the school he attended. In 1964 a follow-up study of a one-third subsample collected information from parents about the student's subsequent education, occupation, and whereabouts. In 1965 data were obtained from the Department of Taxation about parental income from 1957–1960. Finally, in 1975 yet another follow-up survey of the 1957 cohort was conducted. In this survey a set of parallel retrospective questions to the original 1957 survey was asked, as well as updated information on educational and occupational attainments. Table 3.1 lists the variables actually used in the present reanalysis.

Although the original sample included both sexes, much of the subsequent information was collected only from males. The sample was only statewide, and of course there have been cumulative sources of attrition through the years, but Jencks, Crouse, and Mueser (1983) have compared similar models based on these data with independent national samples and obtained only minor discrepancies.

Aside from differences in modelling, I chose to use the correlation matrix based on pairwise deletion of missing data, thus maximizing the number of cases on which each coefficient is based. Although this choice runs the danger of generating a nongramian matrix, while listwise deletion necessarily generates an internally consistent matrix, the former choice provides for each cell the better estimate of the population value and is more consistent with the maximum-likelihood approach used here.

TABLE 3.1
Observed Variables

Sym	Acronym	Number	Mean	S.D.	Source	Scale
Y_1	OCC75	3850	50.54	24.56	1975 survey	Duncan SEI
Y_2	OCC70	3701	49.43	24.65	1975 survey	Duncan SEI
Y_3	OCC64	2973	41.57	23.66	1964 survey	Duncan SEI
Y_4	ED75	3887	13.62	2.05	1975 survey	years of schooling*
Y_5	ED64	3887	13.78	1.95	1964 survey	years of schooling*
Y_6	OCCASP57	3661	48.81	27.48	1957 survey	Duncan SEI
Y_7	EDASP57	3857	0.39	0.49	1957 survey	dummy variable
Y_8	FR_ASP57	3887	0.36	0.48	1957 survey	dummy variable
Y_9	TCR_EN57	3887	0.46	0.50	1957 survey	dummy variable
Y_{10}	PAR_EN57	3887	0.59	0.49	1957 survey	dummy variable
Y_{11}	GPA54_57	3592	97.81	13.95	school records	normalized rank**
Y_{12}	IQ56	3887	101.34	14.92	Wis. Test. Serv.	Henmon-Nelson IQ
X_{13}	PAR_IN60	3540	5.02	0.72	Wis. tax records	average income***
X_{14}	PAR_IN57	3539	3.86	0.73	Wis. tax records	1957 income***
X_{15}	FA_OCC75	3800	34.66	23.30	1975 survey	Duncan SEI
X_{16}	FA_OCC57	3541	30.62	22.62	Wis. tax records	Duncan SEI
X_{17}	FA_ED75	3714	9.77	3.30	1975 survey	years of schooling
X_{18}	FA_ED57	3887	10.04	3.09	1957 survey	years of schooling
X_{19}	MO_ED75	3717	10.66	2.77	1975 survey	years of schooling
X_{20}	MO_ED57	3887	10.39	2.95	1957 survey	years of schooling

*Truncated at 17 years.
**Within-school rank normalized.
***Log of income. PAR_IN60 is log of average for 1958-60;
PAR_IN57 is for 1957 or the first available year thereafter.

THE MODEL

While using the data of the Wisconsin study, and addressing the same general questions about the relationships between home background, school experiences, aspirations, and subsequent educational and occupational attainments, both the structural model—the postulated relationships among latent variables, and the measurement model—the way in which latent variables are related to the observed variables—are quite different from previous analyses.

As has been indicated, the unidirectional causal chain of effects that has been postulated for the Wisconsin model, and, indeed, is typical of quantitative status-attainment studies, seems theoretically implausible. If, indeed, my friend's aspirations have influenced mine, I am, presumably, my friend's friend, and have, in turn, influenced his. (Or the association may merely be one of value homophily: "birds of a feather flock together.") Were my friend the subject of study, the arrow would be reversed. But clearly the effects should be, on average, reciprocal and equal in a population.

Similarly there is an enormous literature on the effects of teacher expectations. Here the observed variables are the students' reports of their perceptions of teachers' encouraging them to go to college. But certainly a student's prior achievement and his manifest motivation elicit such encouragement.

The web of nonhierarchical interrelationships among the set of endogenous variables is schematically portrayed in the path diagram in Fig. 3.1. The reciprocal causal effect between one's own and one's friend's aspirations is represented by the pair of arrows between η_6 and η_5 at the top of the figure. Similar reciprocal effects, though not necessarily of equal magnitude or even sign, are postulated between one's aspirations, teachers' encouragement, parents' encouragement, and academic achievement (represented by the pairs of arrows connecting η_5 with η_7, η_8, and η_9, respectively, in the lower left portion of the diagram).

The variables, η_5 through η_8, represent a set of interrelationships that are both synchronic and reported from the perspective of the responding student. The shared bias resulting from globalized misperception or misrepresentation is, we hope, allowed for by the correlations between errors in the observed variables, which are described below. *A priori* constraints have been imposed on the direct causal linkages among the true variables. We suppose that parents and teachers affect a student's academic achievement only through affecting his aspirations. This may not, in fact, be true. Coercion or docility may lead to compliance in the absence of internalized motivation. (However, as we shall later see, there is a strong negative correlation between the disturbances—unexplained variances—of teachers' encouragement and student achievement. While a student's good performance elicits encouragement, the converse possibly elicits nagging.) In any event, the exclusion of selected reverse arrows among this set of synchronic variables was done of necessity in order to attain identifiability. Not every possible feedback loop can be estimated simultaneously with the information available. Those that seemed theoretically compelling or most plausible were included; those that were less compelling *a priori,* albeit possible, were excluded.

The right-hand portion of the path diagram depicts the sequence of outcome variables: years of schooling ultimately attained, η_4; occupation in 1964 (7 years after the senior year in high school), η_3; occupation in 1970 (13 years after high school); and finally in 1975 (18 years after high school). This temporal sequence is treated as a causal chain. Reverse causation over time is excluded, and significant others' influence is mediated by the achievement and aspirations formed earlier.

Algebraic Model

Before presenting the way in which the exogenous parental background variables are related to this set of interrelated endogenous variables, an algebraic digression is necessary. The structural and measurement models estimated by LISREL

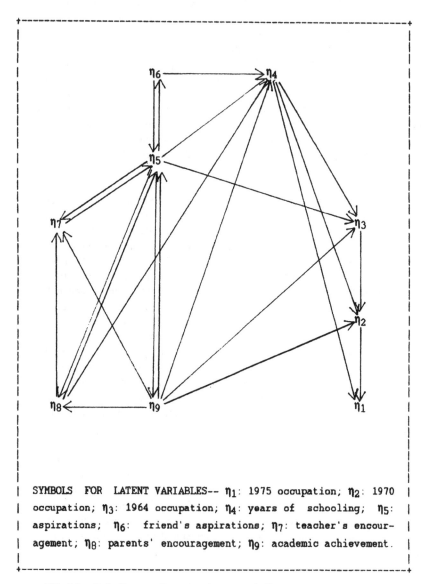

SYMBOLS FOR LATENT VARIABLES-- η_1: 1975 occupation; η_2: 1970 occupation; η_3: 1964 occupation; η_4: years of schooling; η_5: aspirations; η_6: friend's aspirations; η_7: teacher's encouragement; η_8: parents' encouragement; η_9: academic achievement.

FIG. 3.1.   Path diagram: Postulated structural effects among latent endogenous variables.

54

are ordinarily formulated in matrix form as follows (Jöreskog & Sörbom, 1981, p. I.5):

$$\eta = B\eta + \Gamma\xi + \zeta \tag{1}$$

and the measurement equations:

$$y = \Lambda_y\eta + \epsilon \tag{2}$$

$$x = \Lambda_x\xi + \delta \tag{3}$$

These equations can be equivalently recast with all variables on the left side. The structural equation becomes:

$$\begin{pmatrix} \eta \\ \xi \end{pmatrix} = \begin{pmatrix} B & \Gamma \\ 0 & 0 \end{pmatrix} \begin{pmatrix} \eta \\ \xi \end{pmatrix} + \begin{pmatrix} \zeta \\ \xi \end{pmatrix} \tag{4}$$

and the measurement equations are collapsed to:

$$\begin{pmatrix} Y \\ X \end{pmatrix} = \begin{pmatrix} \Lambda_y & 0 \\ 0 & \Lambda_x \end{pmatrix} \begin{pmatrix} \eta \\ \xi \end{pmatrix} + \begin{pmatrix} \epsilon \\ \delta \end{pmatrix} \tag{5}$$

This recasting of the algebraic model has the effect of creating augmented covariance matrices, (1) between the disturbances in the equations—the ζ's— and the exogenous variables—the ξ's, and (2) between the errors of measurement of endogenous variables—the ϵ's—and of exogenous variables—the ζ's, provided they are identifiable. Thus the set of usual constraints on simultaneous equation models, that these two sets of covariances must be zero in the population, may be relaxed if there is sufficient information to estimate nonzero parameters.[1]

The covariance matrix for the structural equation disturbances, ψ, is:

$$\text{Exp} \begin{pmatrix} \zeta\zeta' & \zeta\xi' \\ \xi\zeta' & \xi\xi' \end{pmatrix} \tag{6}$$

The covariance matrix for the uniquenesses of observed variables (measurement errors), Θ_ϵ, is correspondingly:

$$\text{Exp} \begin{pmatrix} \epsilon\epsilon' & \epsilon\delta' \\ \delta\epsilon' & \delta\delta' \end{pmatrix} \tag{7}$$

---

[1]This effectively reconstrues the import of exogeneity. Because exogenous variables are still totally determined by factors outside of the model, their unexplained variance is equivalent to the latent exogenous variables themselves—their clones, as it were. Permitting covariances between these clones and the disturbances in endogenous variables is a devious way of introducing additional causal paths from exogenous to endogenous variables outside of the coefficient matrix.

Measurement Model

Table 3.2 lists the basic statistics of the measurement model. Seven of the 13 latent variables are represented by a pair of fallible observed variables. For example, the last, ξ_{13}, mother's years of schooling, is represented by the son's report in both the 1957 and 1975 surveys.[2] (See Fig. 3.2.)

The column headed standardized relative weight, in this table indicates by an asterisk those variables that were given a normalizing weight of 1.00 in the unstandardized factor matrix to provide a metric for the latent true variable each reflects. The standardization is the product of the unstandardized weight and the estimated standard deviation of the latent variable. (For those variables with asterisks, then, it is this standard deviation.)

The rightmost column, headed communality/reliability, is one minus the variance of the estimated uniqueness or measurement error. These estimates of reliabilities for the single-variable indicators are slightly on the low side. For example, Mare and Mason (1980) estimate, for a 12th grade son, reliabilities of reporting of .92 for father's occupation, .89 for father's schooling, and .87 for mother's schooling. The zero-order correlations between the two observed measures were .72 for father's occupation, .76 for father's education, and .74 for mother's education. The lowest figures in this column, .55 each for grade point average and Henmon-Nelson IQ scores, should not be construed as reliabilities. Here communality is the more appropriate term, each variable having its specific as well as shared content.

Table 3.3 condenses information on both the model and the estimates of correlations between measurement errors. Above the diagonal are codes indicating why nonzero correlations might be anticipated between each pair of error terms. For example, the g's in the first row identify responses all derived from the same 1975 questionnaire. The i reflects the correlation between the specificity of occupational (as distinct from educational) aspirations with bias in reporting occupation.

The magnitudes of the correlations between errors that were not constrained are indicated below the diagonal by level of significance. The largest of these are between educational aspirations and ultimate educational attainment, and between IQ test scores and the set of family background variables (indicated by m's in the row labeled Y_{12}). These correlations—over five times their standard errors—clearly reflect significant association between systematic components of

---

[2]In the source data (Hauser, Tsai, and Sewell, 1983) dual indicators were reported for each latent variable. The 1975 survey elicited retrospective reports of friend's, teachers', and parents' attitudes' in 1957. These were thought to be too likely contaminated by realities of the respondent's subsequent life to reflect the same true value. Occupations in 1970 and 1975 were taken as two reports of the same midlife occupation. A retrospective report of first occupation was combined with the report of occupation in 1964 to represent early occupation.

TABLE 3.2
Measurement Model Statistics

Latent Variable		Observed Variable(s)		Standardized Relative Weight	Communality Reliability
Sym	Acronym	Sym	Acronym		
$\eta 1$	occ75	Y_1	OCC75	.93*	.86a
$\eta 2$	occ70	Y_2	OCC70	.93*	.86a
$\eta 3$	occ64	Y_3	OCC64	.93*	.86a
$\eta 4$	educ	Y_4	ED75	.92*	.85
	"	Y_5	ED64	.93	.86
$\eta 5$	asp	Y_6	OCCASP57	.87*	.76
	"	Y_7	EDASP57	.87	.77b
$\eta 6$	fr_asp57	Y_8	FR_ASP57	.88*	.77b
$\eta 7$	tcr_en57	Y_9	TCR_EN57	.88*	.77b
$\eta 8$	par_en57	Y_{10}	PAR_EN57	.87*	.77b
$\eta 9$	acad_ach	Y_{11}	GPA54_57	.77	.59
	"	Y_{12}	IQ56	.77*	.59
$\xi 10$	par_inc	X_{13}	PAR_IN60	.98	.95
	"	X_{14}	PAR_IN57	.89*	.79
$\xi 11$	fa_occ	X_{15}	FA_OCC75	.86	.75
	"	X_{16}	FA_OCC57	.83*	.69
$\xi 12$	fa_educ	X_{17}	FA_ED75	.83	.69
	"	X_{18}	FA_ED57	.87*	.76
$\xi 13$	mo_educ	X_{19}	MO_ED75	.81	.65
	"	X_{20}	M_EDS57	.87*	.76

NOTE: * Normalization constraing (unstandardized value set at 1.00)
a Error variances in self-reported occupations set equal
b Set of error variances constrained to be equal to each other

SYMBOLS FOR LATENT VARIABLES--$\eta 1$: 1975 occupation; $\eta 2$: 1970 occupation; $\eta 3$: 1964 occupation; $\eta 4$: years of schooling; $\eta 5$: aspirations; $\eta 6$: friend's aspirations; $\eta 7$: teacher's encouragement; $\eta 8$: parents' encouragement; $\eta 9$: academic achievement; $\xi 10$: parents' income; $\xi 11$: father's occupation; $\xi 12$: father's education; $\xi 13$: mother's education.

the measures not contained in the latent variables that enter the structural model. Family background is more strongly correlated with IQ than with GPA.

Drawing a complete path diagram showing all connections among variables and error terms would generate a tangled maze and require a very large sheet of paper. For those who are visually minded, however, Fig. 3.2 may be suggestive. This segment includes only two of the nine endogenous variables: aspirations, η_5, and academic achievement, η_9. Each latent variable affects two observed variables. Achievement, η_9, at the bottom, for example, affects GPA, Y_{11}, and

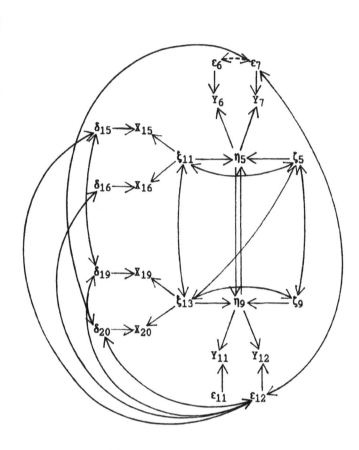

SYMBOLS FOR VARIABLES--η_5: aspirations; η_9: academic achievement; ξ_{11}: father's occupation; ξ_{13}: mother's education; Y_6: occupational aspirations; Y_7: educational aspirations; Y_{11}: grade point average; Y_{12}: Henmon-Nelson IQ; X_{15}: father's occupation reported in 1975 survey; Y_{16}: father's occupation reported on 1957 Wisonsin tax records; X_{19}: mother's education reported in 1975 survey; X_{20}: mother's education reported in 1957 survey; ζ: disturbance in equation; ε: uniqueness of observed endogenous variable; δ: uniqueness of observed exogenous variable.

FIG. 3.2. Path diagram: Details of a segment including only two endogenous variables—η_5 and η_9.

TABLE 3.3
Scheme of Covariances Among Observed Variables Uniquenesses ("Measurement Errors")
(Magnitudes Below, Interpretations on and Above, Diagonal)

		Y1	Y2	Y3	Y4	Y5	Y6	Y7	Y8	Y9	Y10	Y11	Y12	X13	X14	X15	X16	X17	X18	X19	X20
OCC75	Y_1	a	g	-	g	-	i	-	-	-	-	-	l	-	-	g	-	g	-	g	-
OCC70	Y_2	0	a	-	g	-	i	-	-	-	-	-	-	-	-	g	-	g	-	g	-
OCC64	Y_3	-	-	a	-	f	i	-	-	-	-	-	-	-	-	-	-	-	-	-	-
ED75	Y_4	*	*	-	b	-	-	j	-	-	-	k	-	-	-	g	-	g	-	g	-
ED64	Y_5	-	-	0	-	b	-	j	-	-	l	k	-	-	-	-	-	-	-	-	-
OCCASP57	Y_6	*	*	*	-	-	b	d'	d'	d'	d'	-	-	-	-	-	-	-	d'	-	d'
EDASP57	Y_7	-	-	-	8	8	-	c	d	d	d	-	k	-	-	-	-	-	d	-	d
FR_ASP57	Y_8	-	-	-	-	-	-	*	c	d'	d'	-	-	-	-	-	-	-	d	-	d
TCR_EN57	Y_9	-	-	-	-	-	-	*	-	c	d'	l	-	-	l	-	-	-	d	-	d
PAR_EN57	Y_{10}	-	-	-	-	*	-	*	-	-	c	-	-	-	-	-	-	-	d	-	d
GPA54_57	Y_{11}	-	-	-	*	*	-	-	-	*	-	b	-	-	-	-	-	-	-	-	-
IO56	Y_{12}	*	-	-	-	-	-	*	-	-	-	-	b	m	m	m	m	m	m	m	m
PAR_IN60	X_{13}	-	-	-	-	-	-	-	-	-	-	-	*	b	!	-	r	-	-	l	-
PAR_IN57	X_{14}	-	-	-	-	-	-	-	-	-	*	-	-	*	b	-	e	-	-	l	-
FA_OCC75	X_{15}	0	+	-	0	-	-	-	-	-	-	-	*	-	-	b	-	g	-	g	-
FA_OCC57	X_{16}	-	-	-	-	-	-	-	-	-	-	-	*	*	*	-	b	-	-	-	-
FA_ED75	X_{17}	0	+	-	0	-	-	-	-	-	-	-	*	-	-	+	-	b	h	g	-
FA_ED57	X_{18}	-	-	-	-	-	-	0	0	+	+	-	*	-	-	-	-	0	b	-	d
MO_ED75	X_{19}	0	+	-	+	-	-	-	-	-	-	-	*	*	*	+	-	*	-	b	h
MO_ED57	X_{20}	-	-	-	-	-	-	*	+	0	*	-	*	-	-	-	-	-	*	0	b

Note.* implies an estimate over twice its standard error
    + implies an estimate between one and two times its error
    0 implies an estimate less than its standard error
    - implies that the covariance was constrained to be zero

    a error variances in respondent's occupation constrained equal
    b unconstrained error variances--all greater than twice their
      standard error
    c error variances in ("dummy") educational expectation varia-
      bles--constrained equal
    d covariances within 1957 survey (d': insignificant)
    e covariances within tax forms
    f covariances within 1964 survey
    g covariances within 1975 survey among SES variables
    h covariances between 1957 and 1975 reports by same person
    i covariances between occupational aspirations and occupations
    j covariances between educational aspirations and schooling
    k covariances between achievement and educational variables
    l covariances admitted inductively because of magnitude
    m covariances between IQ and parental background variables
    ! not identified

IQ, Y_{12} [3] Because GPA and IQ derive from independent records, their errors are not correlated. But, as shown above, the specificity of IQ is correlated with all of the background measures portrayed on the left. The ζ's on the right represent the disturbances in the two equations that are correlated. (There may be factors not specifically incorporated into the model that affect both aspirations and achievement, e.g., good schools versus bad schools.)

The only unconventional covariances included in this diagram are those between the exogenous variables, the ξ's, and the disturbances in the equations, the ζ's. The arrow that appears on a slant between ξ_{13} and ζ_5, for example, implies that a mother's educational level may be correlated with factors not explicitly included in the model that affect a student's aspirations, such as school or neighborhood context. This seems substantively realistic, but compromises the exogeneity of the background variables as was discussed in footnote 1.

ANALYSIS

Identification

With the labyrinth of unconstrained connections between variables, the question as to whether a unique and estimable solution exists seems problematical on its face. The measurement model poses no problem. All of the postulated error terms and covariances are solvable with simple algebra except for the possible correlation between errors in reports of parental income that were derived from Wisconsin tax forms. Three covariances—those between reports of each parent's education given at different times, and those between the respondent's self-reported occupations—were fixed using supplementary data provided by Hauser et al. (1983, p. 43).

The coefficient matrix of the structural model (the augmented beta matrix described above) meets both the rank and order tests conventionally prescribed by econometricians (cf. Christ, 1966, pp. 314–331). Two circumstances make me hesitate to rely fully on this exercise. First, empirically, the partial regression of teacher encouragement on parental income is almost zero. This relation seems needed as an instrument to identify the effect of teacher encouragement on aspirations. Also the partial regression of parental encouragement on father's education is small. This too is instrumental. Second, the unconventional correlations between exogenous variables and disturbances violates the definition of an "instrumental variable" (Heise, 1975, p. 160). We rely ultimately on the facts that the LISREL program converged on a unique solution, the information matrix was nonsingular, and the covariances between estimated parameters is not high.

---

[3] All of the observed variables, Y_6, Y_7, Y_{11}, Y_{12}, X_{15}, X_{16}, X_{19}, and X_{20}, are, of course, intercorrelated. Even in this small segment of the path model, explicit representation of the initial correlations among observed variables would so overlay the diagram as to make it indecipherable.

(That these are sufficient conditions for identifiability is implied by Kendall & Stuart, 1961, chap. 18, and, but for precision errors, by Jöreskog & Sörbom, 1979 and 1981. Also see Wiley, 1973, pp. 82–83.)

Goodness of Fit

Another way of assessing the adequacy of the model is to examine how well the population covariance matrix implied by the model fits the sample covariance matrix. Figure 3.3 presents four ways of evaluating this fit. In the center of the inset is the classical ratio of chi-squared to the degrees of freedom. The value of 1.00 implies that there is a fifty-fifty chance that at least one of the 63 constrained parameters of the model diverges from the true population value—a rather indecisive statement. An anomalous feature of this statistic is that with an identical model and identical observed sample covariance matrix, the smaller the sample size, the lower the value of chi-squared would be. The larger the sample size, the more difficult it is to maintain an hypothesized model. Hoelter (1983) has suggested calculating a "critical number"—the largest sample size for which it would be possible to maintain the composite hypothesis at some selected probability level. In this case the critical number (with $z = .05$) is 3878. Hoelter suggests that for a one-group analysis, any number over 200 should be acceptable. But this is just a rule of thumb.

Jöriskog and Sörbom (1981), in the LISREL program, calculate an adjusted goodness-of-fit measure that summarizes the relative amount of variances and covariances jointly accounted for by the model. Unlike chi-squared, this measure is independent of the sample size. Its statistical distribution, however, is not known, so one can compare it only with values of the measure calculated with other models or in other studies. (The figure .993 slightly improves my batting average for large overidentified models.)

Probably the best assessment of fit comes from examining the individual cell covariances implied by the model with those observed in the sample. The qplot is a graphic display of these 210 residuals that have been normalized. Each X in the plot represents an individual residual; asterisks represent multiple observations. The closer the scatter is to a vertical line, the smaller are the residuals. The five Xs (cells) at the lower left of the scatter are the only ones more than a standard deviation from zero. Jöreskog and Sörbom (1981) suggest:

> By visual inspection, fit a straight line to the plotted points. If the slope of this line is larger than one, as compared with the 45-degree line, this is indicative of a good fit. Slopes which are close to one correspond to moderate fits and slopes which are smaller than one to poor fits. (p. III.17)

Qualitatively, then, all of these indicators suggest what might be described as a good fit. One would be far more sanguine were the set of exogenous variables more potent, more independent of each other, and more justifiably excludable as

Normalized Residuals

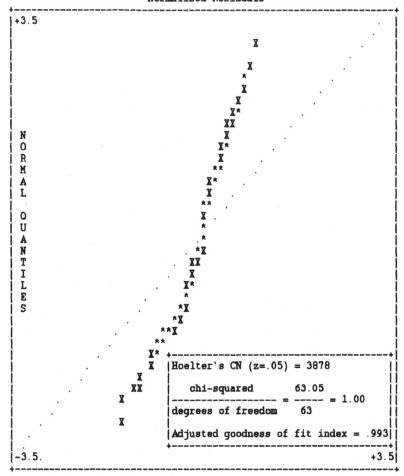

FIG. 3.3.   QPLOT of normalized residuals.

potential direct influences on at least some of the endogenous variables. This unease, however, extends to the status attainment literature in general; it is not alleviated by blithely assuming away inconvenient connections between errors or the possibility of feedback loops.

With this cavil let us finally turn to the substantive results—the parameter estimates—of the structural model. They are presented in Tables 3.4 through 3.6.

Structural Regressions

Table 3.4 shows the direct path regressions among the latent variables. These are the estimated magnitudes that are associated with the arrows in the path diagram of Fig. 3.1. The paths leading directly to the outcome variables—the occupational history and educational attainments of members of the cohort—contain no dramatic surprises. These are the first four rows of the table. The lagged effect of prior occupation has by far the largest direct impact on subsequent occupation. The leading off-diagonal figures in the first two rows, .98 and .60, estimate these direct lagged effects. The proportion of the variances in occupational status explained in the model is indicated by the R-squares in the last column of Part B

TABLE 3.4
Standardized Structural Regressions Among Latent Variables

A. Among Endogenous Variables

Sym	$\eta 1$	$\eta 2$	$\eta 3$	$\eta 4$	$\eta 5$	$\eta 6$	$\eta 7$	$\eta 8$	$\eta 9$
$\eta 1$	--	0.98*	--	-0.07*	--	--	--	--	--
$\eta 2$	--	--	0.60*	0.10*	--	--	--	--	0.14*
$\eta 3$	--	--	--	0.64*	0.09	--	--	--	0.0
$\eta 4$	--	--	--	--	0.55*	0.05	--	0.26*	0.17*
$\eta 5$	--	--	--	--	--	0.19*	0.31*	-0.81*	0.52*
$\eta 6$	--	--	--	--	0.19*	--	--	--	--
$\eta 7$	--	--	--	--	-0.19	--	--	0.18*	0.96*
$\eta 8$	--	--	--	--	1.10*	--	--	--	-0.12*
$\eta 9$	--	--	--	--	0.31*	--	--	--	--

B. Regressions of Endogenous on Exogenous Variables

Sym	$\xi 10$	$\xi 11$	$\xi 12$	$\xi 13$	R-Squared
$\eta 1$	--	--	--	--	.92
$\eta 2$	--	--	--	--	.64
$\eta 3$	--	--	--	--	.58
$\eta 4$	--	--	--	--	.58
$\eta 5$	--	0.62*	--	--	.01
$\eta 6$	--	--	0.40*	--	.28
$\eta 7$	0.0	--	--	--	.10
$\eta 8$	--	--	-0.04	--	.29
$\eta 9$	--	--	--	0.17*	.34

NOTE: * implies an estimate over twice its standard error; an unstarred nonzero number implies an estimate between one and two times its standard error;
0 (e.g., 0.0) implies an estimate less than its standard error;
- implies that a coefficient or covariance was constrained to be zero by assumption.

SYMBOLS FOR LATENT VARIABLES--$\eta 2$: 1975 occupation; $\eta 2$: 1970 occupation; $\eta 3$: 1964 occupation; $\eta 4$: years of schooling; $\eta 5$: aspirations; $\eta 6$: friend's aspirations; $\eta 7$: teacher's encouragement; $\eta 8$: parents' encouragement; $\eta 9$: academic achievement; $\xi 10$: parents' income; $\xi 11$: father's occupation; $\xi 12$: father's education; $\xi 13$: mother's education.

TABLE 3.5
Standardized Covariances Among Disturbances in Equations

Sym	Accronym	ζ_1	ζ_2	ζ_3	ζ_4	ζ_5	ζ_6	ζ_7	ζ_8
ζ_1	occ75	0.08*							
ζ_2	occ70	0.0	0.36*						
ζ_3	occ64	0.0	0.0	0.42*					
ζ_4	educ	0.0	0.0	0.0	0.42*				
ζ_5	asp	0.0	0.0	0.0	-0.23*	0.99*			
ζ_6	fr_asp57	0.0	0.04*	0.0	0.0	0.11	0.72*		
ζ_7	tcr_en57	0.0	0.0	0.0	0.0	0.0	0.0	0.90*	
ζ_8	par_en57	0.0	0.02	0.0	0.0	0.0	0.0	0.0	0.71*
ζ_9	acad_ach	0.02	0.0	0.04	0.0	0.0	0.18*	-0.40*	0.0
10	par_inc	0.03*	0.06*	0.05*	0.0	0.05	0.08*	0.0	0.0
11	fa_occ	0.05*	0.08*	0.07*	0.0	-0.10*	0.04	0.02	0.0
12	fa_educ	0.03	0.06*	0.04	0.04*	0.0	-0.10*	0.0	0.0
13	mo_educ	0.04*	0.03	0.0	0.03	0.07*	0.0	0.0	0.0

Sym	Accronym	ζ_9	ξ_{10}	ξ_{11}	ξ_{12}	ξ_{13}
ζ_9	acad_ach	0.66*				
ξ_{10}	par_inc	0.0	1.00*			
ξ_{11}	fa_occ	0.0	0.53*	1.00*		
ξ_{12}	fa_educ	0.0	0.38*	0.68*	1.00*	
ξ_{13}	mo_educ	-0.06	0.28*	0.44*	0.60*	1.00*

Notes. * implies an estimate over twice its standard error; an unstarred nonzero number implies an estimate between one and
two times its standard error;

0 (e.g., 0.0) implies an estimate less than its standard error;

- implies that a coefficient or covariance was constrained to
be zero by assumption.

The lower-right segment of the matrix is the correlation
matrix of the latent exogenous variables, ξ_{10} through ξ_{13}.

of the table—.92, and .64. The first coefficient, .98, and the associated value of
R-square, .92, seem somewhat high even for midlife stability in true occupational status. It is possible that the conservative estimates of the reliability of
these reports resulted in an over-correction for attenuation.[4]

In row 3 we see that early occupation—7 years beyond high school—is very
strongly and directly affected by years of schooling attained, with only a small
additional direct effect of aspirations. The R-square of .58 is somewhat higher,
again, than one would get with an ordinary least squares regression throwing all
prior variables into the hopper. (Cf. Sewell & Hauser, 1975, p. 100 attain an R-
squared of .43 with the same set of variables.)

[4]The uncorrected zero-order correlation between reported occupations in 1970 and 1975 was .82.

The interesting feature of this equation is that academic achievement, η_9, reflecting both GPA and IQ, has little direct effect on early occupational attainment; only an indirect effect through its impact on years of schooling attained. This finding is congruent with Bowles' and Gintis's (1975) argument that schools serve as a sorting and screening mechanism, but the merits that they ostensibly certify (in particular, scholarly ability, whether innate or otherwise) have slight intrinsic value in the market place for the mass of the labor force.

Years of schooling, in turn, in row 4, are most directly affected by the individual's aspirations, with additional incremental effects of parental encouragement and academic achievement. The latter, achievement, has additional substantial indirect effects because it shapes aspirations.

Thus far we have been tracing the typical causal chain of the status attainment process, albeit backwards from midlife to high school. Skipping down to the equation for academic achievement, shown in row 9, we see that aspirations—one's hopes or plans for the future—have the strongest direct effect upon one's

TABLE 3.6
Standardized Total Effects of Latent
Variables on Endogenous Latent Variables

A. Effects Among Endogenous Variables

Sym	η_1	η_2	η_3	η_4	η_5	η_6	η_7	η_8	η_9
η_1	--	0.98	0.59	0.41	0.30	0.08	0.09	-0.11	0.48
η_2	--	--	0.60	0.49	0.34	0.09	0.11	-0.13	0.53
η_3	--	--	--	0.65	0.43	0.11	0.13	-0.15	0.49
η_4	--	--	--	--	0.57	0.16	0.18	-0.16	0.66
η_5	--	--	--	--	-0.36	0.12	0.20	-0.48	0.59
η_6	--	--	--	--	0.12	0.02	0.04	-0.09	0.11
η_7	--	--	--	--	0.19	0.04	0.06	0.04	1.12
η_8	--	--	--	--	0.68	0.13	0.21	-0.51	0.50
η_9	--	--	--	--	0.20	0.04	0.06	-.15	0.18

B. Effects of Exogenous on Endogenous Variables

Sym	ξ_{10}	ξ_{11}	ξ_{12}	ξ_{13}
η_1	0.16	0.34	0.15	0.14
η_2	0.13	0.32	0.13	0.12
η_3	0.09	0.31	0.10	0.10
η_4	0.05	0.34	0.09	0.13
η_5	0.05	0.38	0.05	0.10
η_6	0.10	0.10	0.29	0.02
η_7	0.01	0.13	0.01	0.13
η_8	0.05	0.40	0.02	0.10
η_9	0.01	0.12	0.02	0.13

SYMBOLS FOR LATENT VARIABLES-- η_1: 1975 occupation; η_2: 1970 occupation; η_3: 1964 occupation; η_4: years of schooling; η_5: aspirations; η_6: friend's aspirations; η_7: teacher's encouragement; η_8: parents' encouragement; η_9: academic achievement; ξ_{10}: parents' income; ξ_{11}: father's occupation; ξ_{12}: father's education; ξ_{13}: mother's education.

present attainment. This was the central theme in Arthur Stinchcombe's (1964) analysis of the experience of working-class youths in Eureka, California, in which the perceived structure of future opportunities shaped present perceptions of the instrumental value of schooling. The bright future promised by one's existing (derived) position in the class structure induces diligent conformity; a bleak future leads to expressive alienation from the values and expectations of the institution designed to select the successful. Travis Hirschi (1969), too, in his study of Richmond, California, youths, found what he called "a stake in the future" to be one of the central mechanisms of social control—both facilitating school performance and containing the temptations of immediate rewards from deviant behavior. John Ogbu (1974) invokes a parallel interpretation of the lack of effort in school of black youths in Stockton, California. The historic caste-like job ceiling perceived by blacks constrains their futures, thus diminishing their present motives.

These three cited studies are exceptions to the typical placement of aspirations as an intervening variable in the attainment process, because they explicitly recognize the reciprocal feedback relationship between academic achievement and aspirations. When IQ tests are used as indicators of ability, they are most commonly construed as exogenous (cf. Sewell, 1966).

Turning now to the set of synchronic interrelationships among perceived attitudinal variables, we immediately see one reciprocal relationship whose estimates are anomalous.[5] This loop, which is marked on the table, is between parental encouragement and aspirations. It is certainly the consequence of the very weak instrumental variable affecting parental encouragement ($-.04$, the effect of ξ_{12} on η_8 in part B of the table). We need not strain our imaginations trying to overinterpret this indeterminacy. I suspect, however, that the direction of the signs is correct. In most American families, parents' hopes are raised by the manifested ambition of their offspring; youths' neglect of the pursuit of success elicits pleas for diligence.

The other coefficients in this block seem well-conditioned. Notice especially the strong effects of students' academic achievement upon both their own aspirations (.52), and upon the encouragement offered by teachers (.96). Pygmalion is reversed.

Disturbance Covariances

Table 3.5 shows the standardized covariances among the disturbances in the equations. The diagonal elements are the unexplained variances of each equation—one minus the coefficient of determination. For the set of exogenous

---

[5]A standardized regression coefficient greater than one is not plausible—not possible throughout the range of multinormal distributions.

family background variables in the lower right sector of the table, this is a correlation matrix among the estimated latent true variables. Rows 10, 11, 12, and 13 of the upper half of the table show the unconventional way in which I allowed exogenous variables to be correlated with the disturbances in the equations. Row 11, for example, shows how a father's occupation is permitted to influence his son's destiny directly even though a direct effect was excluded from the structural equation.

The largest covariance, $-.40$, between η_9—academic achievement—and η_7—teachers' encouragement—is once again probably due to the causal indeterminacy of teachers' encouragement, discussed previously.[6] The other large association, $-.23$, between aspirations and years of schooling (η_4 & η_5) might be, at least in part, explained by the "frog pond" hypothesis. It has been repeatedly shown that high aspirations are more easily maintained in a less competitive milieu (e.g., Alexander & Eckland, 1975; Davis, 1964; Wilson, 1971, 1977). This creates a self-dampening circle: High aspirations foster achievement, and a low-achieving context fosters aspirations but ultimately curtails educational advancement.

Total Effects

The direct and indirect effects of variables in the structural model are aggregated in Table 3.6.

Total effects among endogenous variables are calculated:

$$\sigma_\eta{}^{-1}[(I-B)^{-1}-I]\sigma_\eta \tag{8}$$

Effects of exogenous on endogenous variables are:

$$\sigma_\eta{}^{-1}[(I-B)^{-1}\Gamma+(I-B)^{-1}\zeta\xi'\sigma^2\xi^{-1}]\sigma_\eta \tag{9}$$

The reintroduction of effects of parental background factors in Table 3.6 (through their covariance with the disturbances in the equations) makes the process of transmission of status from generation to generation more congruent with the familiar pattern we have come to know. Substantively, an interesting pattern in the effects of parental SES is the substantially larger effect of father's occupation (column ξ_{11}) than his income or education on the son's aspirations, schooling, and occupational career.

The very large impact of aspirations (column η_5) both on subsequent career and through feeding back on high school achievement and the attitudes of significant others is clear. (The apparent negative loop of aspirations on themselves,

---

[6]Gillespie and Fox (1980) sketch a variety of potential ways in which two variables involved in a causal loop may have negatively correlated disturbance terms.

TABLE 3.7
Implied Correlations Among Latent Variables

Sym	$\eta 1$	$\eta 2$	$\eta 3$	$\eta 4$	$\eta 5$	$\eta 6$	$\eta 7$	$\eta 8$	$\eta 9$
$\eta 1$	1.00								
$\eta 2$	.96	1.00							
$\eta 3$	.74	.78	1.00						
$\eta 4$	.64	.69	.76	1.00					
$\eta 5$	.54	.57	.61	.73	1.00				
$\eta 6$	.44	.47	.45	.60	.62	1.00			
$\eta 7$	.39	.40	.43	.52	.55	.44	1.00		
$\eta 8$	.46	.48	.48	.59	.66	.54	.56	1.00	
$\eta 9$	.54	.56	.55	.67	.69	.48	.51	.52	1.00
$\xi 10$	.27	.26	.26	.29	.31	.29	.13	.31	.14
$\xi 11$	.38	.37	.37	.41	.43	.39	.22	.43	.21
$\xi 12$	.33	.33	.34	.40	.39	.37	.21	.36	.22
$\xi 13$	.26	.24	.25	.34	.33	.30	.20	.31	.21
Sym	$\eta 1$	$\eta 2$	$\eta 3$	$\eta 4$	$\eta 5$	$\eta 6$	$\eta 7$	$\eta 8$	$\eta 9$

SYMBOLS FOR LATENT VARIABLES--$\eta 1$: 1975 occupation; $\eta 2$: 1970 occupation; $\eta 3$: 1964 occupation; $\eta 4$: years of schooling; $\eta 5$: aspirations; $\eta 6$: friend's aspirations; $\eta 7$: teacher's encouragement; $\eta 8$: parents' encouragement; $\eta 9$: academic achievement; $\xi 10$: parents' income; $\xi 11$: father's occupation; $\xi 12$: father's education; $\xi 13$: mother's education.

Note. Correlations among exogenous variables were reported in Table 3.5.

$-.36$, is due to the ill-conditioned estimate of the effect of parents' encouragement.) Academic achievement in school does have substantial impact on one's subsequent career but only through its effect on years of schooling, as we saw in Table 3.4.

Comparisons with a Hierarchical Model

Tables 3.8 and 3.9 report the results of a conventional unidirectional causal model using the same data that we have been analyzing. The model is based on the "social psychological model of achievement" posited by Sewell and Hauser (1975, p. 92). There are no causal loops; significant others do not directly affect one another, but their disturbances are correlated; the respondent's educational and occupational aspirations similarly have correlated disturbances. Freeing all other coefficients in a hierarchical pattern leads to a just identified model with no degrees of freedom. (Chi-squared is zero; the model fits the data perfectly.) Also, each variable has only a single observed indicator that is assumed to be measured without error as is usual in ordinary regression analysis. The most conspicuous differences between this conventional model and the one we have been describing are the weaker determination of career outcomes (largely due to uncontrolled static in the predictor variables) and the limited importance of aspirations (because they are constrained by assumption from affecting school achievement or significant others' attitudes). Although algebraically this conventional model is much more manageable—the two-stage least squares solution being identical to the maximum likelihood solution—the model manifestly underestimates the determination of careers and implausibly excludes the interrelatedness of synchronic variables.

TABLE 3.8
Standardized Regression Coefficients Among Observed Variables in a Just-Identified Hierarchical Model Assuming no Measurement Error

Sym	Y_1	Y_2	Y_3	Y_5	Y_6	Y_7	Y_8	Y_9	Y_{10}
Y_1	--	0.67*	0.12*	0.0	0.06*	-0.04*	0.0	0.0	0.0
Y_2	--	--	0.46*	0.18*	0.07*	-0.04	0.05*	0.0	0.02
Y_3	--	--	--	0.45*	0.21*	-0.04	0.0	0.05*	0.0
Y_5	--	--	--	--	0.11*	0.26*	0.13*	0.03*	0.10*
Y_6	--	--	--	--	--	--	0.20*	0.11*	0.22*
Y_7	--	--	--	--	--	--	0.22*	0.14*	0.25*
Y_8	--	--	--	--	--	--	--	--	--
Y_9	--	--	--	--	--	--	--	--	--
Y_{10}	--	--	--	--	--	--	--	--	--
Y_{11}	--	--	--	--	--	--	--	--	--
Y_{12}	--	--	--	--	--	--	--	--	--

Sym	Y_{11}	Y_{12}	X_{14}	X_{16}	X_{18}	X_{20}	Acronym	R Squared
Y_1	0.0	0.06*	0.02	0.03*	0.0	0.02	OCC75	.70
Y_2	0.03	0.07*	0.0	0.04*	0.02	0.0	OCC70	.52
Y_3	0.02	0.05*	0.02	0.05*	0.03	0.0	OCC64	.45
Y_5	0.19*	0.08*	0.01	0.05*	0.06*	0.03	ED64	.54
Y_6	0.18*	0.13*	0.03	0.08*	0.03	0.03	OCCASP57	.44
Y_7	0.18*	0.08*	0.04*	0.05*	0.04*	0.04*	EDASP57	.48
Y_8	0.21*	0.11*	0.09*	0.13*	0.08*	0.09*	FR_ASP57	.20
Y_9	0.36*	0.10*	0.04*	0.02	0.05*	0.03	TCR_EN57	.21
Y_{10}	0.20*	0.16*	0.10*	0.13*	0.08*	0.10*	PAR_EN57	.24
Y_{11}	--	0.59*	-0.02	0.0	0.0	0.02	GPA54_57	.35
Y_{12}	--	--	0.06*	0.10*	0.13	0.12*	IQ56	.09

NOTE: * implies an estimate over twice its standard error; an unstarred nonzero number implies an estimate between one and two times its standard error; 0 (e.g., 0.0) implies an estimate less than its standard error; - implies that a coefficient or covariance was constrained to be zero by assumption.

SYMBOLS FOR OBSERVED VARIABLES-- Y1: 1975 occupation; Y2: 1970 occupation; Y3: 1964 occupation; Y5: years of schooling; Y6: occupational aspirations; Y7: educational aspirations; Y8: friend's aspirations; Y9: teacher's encouragement; Y10: parents' encouragement; Y11: grade point average; Y12: IQ score; X14: parents' income; X16: father's occupation; X18: father's education; X20: mother's education.

TABLE 3.9
Standardized Total Effects of Observed Variables on
Dependent Variables in a Just-Identified Hierarchical Model Assuming
No Measurement Error

Sym	Y_1	Y_2	Y_3	Y_5	Y_6	Y_7	Y_8	Y_9	Y_{10}
Y_1	--	0.67	0.43	0.33	0.24	0.00	0.12	0.07	0.12
Y_2	--	--	0.46	0.39	0.21	0.04	0.15	0.07	0.12
Y_3	--	--	--	0.45	0.26	0.08	0.13	0.11	0.13
Y_5	--	--	--	--	0.11	0.26	0.21	0.08	0.19
Y_6	--	--	--	--	--	--	0.20	0.11	0.22
Y_7	--	--	--	--	--	--	0.22	0.14	0.25
Y_8	--	--	--	--	--	--	--	--	--
Y_9	--	--	--	--	--	--	--	--	--
Y_{10}	--	--	--	--	--	--	--	--	--
Y_{11}	--	--	--	--	--	--	--	--	--
Y_{12}	--	--	--	--	--	--	--	--	--

Sym	Y_{11}	Y_{12}	X_{14}	X_{16}	X_{18}	X_{20}	Acronym	R-Squared
Y_1	0.21	0.34	0.09	0.18	0.11	0.09	OCC75	.70
Y_2	0.24	0.33	0.08	0.17	0.13	0.07	OCC70	.52
Y_3	0.26	0.32	0.08	0.16	0.14	0.08	OCC64	.45
Y_5	0.37	0.39	0.08	0.16	0.16	0.14	ED64	.54
Y_6	0.30	0.38	0.09	0.18	0.12	0.13	OCCASP57	.44
Y_7	0.33	0.35	0.11	0.15	0.13	0.14	EDASP57	.48
Y_8	0.21	0.24	0.10	0.15	0.11	0.13	FR_ASP57	.20
Y_9	0.36	0.31	0.05	0.06	0.09	0.08	TCR_EN57	.21
Y_{10}	0.20	0.27	0.11	0.15	0.12	0.14	PAR_EN57	.24
Y_{11}	--	0.59	0.01	0.06	0.08	0.09	GPA54_57	.35
Y_{12}	--	--	0.06	0.10	0.13	0.12	IQ56	.09

SYMBOLS FOR OBSERVED VARIABLES--Y1: 1975 occupation; Y2: 1970 occupation; Y3: 1964 occupation; Y5: years of schooling; Y6: occupational aspirations; Y7: educational aspirations; Y8: friend's aspirations; Y9: teacher's encouragement; Y10: parents' encouragement; Y11: grade point average; Y12: IQ score; X14: parents' income; X16: father's occupation; X18: father's education; X20: mother's education.

CONCLUSION

The intricate web of feedback relationships that were posited for this model have led to at least two indeterminacies in estimating coefficients. These were due to the lack of strong and independent exogenous instruments affecting parents' and teachers' encouragement, respectively. This weakness is endemic in a cross-sectional sample of youths. Perhaps teacher encouragement could be replaced by deliberate sampling of schools with sharply contrasting press-to-achieve, as Rutter, Maughan, Mortimer, Ouston, and Smith (1979) and Coleman, Hoffer, and Kolgore (1981) sought to do. (The self-selection by parents into these schools would still be confounded with school effects.) Teasing out parental press independently of feedback from the youth may be even more difficult. Contrasting samples from subcultures with strong traditions of patriarchy and filial piety (Jews, Asians) with more child-centered or *laissez-faire* families might help fix or bound the directional effects.

Despite these technical difficulties, it seems clear that the predominant imagery implicit in status attainment models, namely a unidirectional causal chain, fails to capture the large impact that a youth's perception of his future has, both on his own efforts and on significant others. A youth's aspirations have a strong impact on his persistence in school. His schooling, in turn, is the strongest known determinant of his subsequent career. But aspirations are not mere epiphenomenal reflections of the influence of significant others and innate ability. Motives and hopes are related to performance and to the expectations of others as cause as well as effect. While aspirations are moderately related to socioeconomic background, and more strongly related to school performance, they remain largely unexplained in this model. Whatever their sources, hopes for the future shape that future. Reference group theory is improved by interactional theory; both must be informed by the historical context of class, caste, and the present impact of manifest destiny.

Educators have a professional stake in understanding, if not in changing, the allocative functions of schools[7] and the stratification of opportunity[8].

REFERENCES

Alexander, K. L., & Eckland, B. K. (1975). Basic attainment processes: A replication and extension. *Sociology of Education, 48,* 457–495.

Alexander, K. L., & Pallas, A. M. (1983). Bringing the arrows back in: On the recursivity assumptions in school process models. *Social Forces, 62,* 32–53.

Blau, P. M., & Duncan, O. D. (1967). *The American occupational structure.* New York: Wiley.

[7]See, for example, Collins (1979), Dore (1976), and Meyer (1979).

[8]For a fatalistic view see Bourdieu and Passeron (1977). Bowles and Gintis (1975) are but slightly more optimistic.

Bourdieu, P., & Passeron, J-C. (1977). *Reproduction in education, culture and society*. Beverley Hills, CA: Sage.

Bowles, S., & Gintis, H. (1975). *Schooling in capitalist America: Educational reform and the contradictions of economic life*. New York: Basic Books.

Campbell, R. T. (1983). Status attainment research: End of the beginning or beginning of the end? *Sociology of Education, 56*, 47–62.

Christ, C. F. (1966). *Econometric models and methods*. New York: Wiley.

Coleman, J., Hoffer, T., & Kilgore, S. (1981). *Public and private schools: A report to the National Center for Educational Statistics by the National Opinion Research Center*. Chicago: University of Chicago.

Collins, R. (1979). *The credential society: An historical sociology of education and stratification*. New York: Academic.

Davis, J. A. (1964). *Great aspirations*. Chicago: Aldine.

Dore, R. (1976). *The diploma disease*. Berkeley: University of California Press.

Durkheim, E. (1956). *Education and sociology*. Trans. by S. D. Fox. Glencoe, IL: The Free Press.

Gillespie, M. W., & Fox, J. (1980). Specification error and negatively correlated disturbances in "parallel" simultaneous-equation models. *Sociological Methods & Research, 8*, 273–308.

Hauser, R. M., Tsai, S-L., & Sewell, W. H. (1983). A model of stratification with response error in social and psychological variables. *Sociology of Education, 56*, 20–46.

Heise, D. R. (1975). *Causal analysis*. New York: Wiley-Interscience.

Hirschi, T. (1969). *Causes of delinquency*. Berkeley: University of California Press.

Hoelter, J. W. (1983). The analysis of covariance structures: Goodness-of-fit indices. *Sociological Methods & Research, 11*, 325–344.

Hogben, L. (Ed.). (1938). *Political arithmetic: A symposium of population studies*. London: George Allen & Unwin.

Jencks, C., Crouse, J., & Mueser, P. (1983). The Wisconsin model of status attainment: A national replication with improved measures of ability and aspiration. *Sociology of Education, 56*, 3–19.

Jöreskog, K. G., & Sörbom, D. (1979). *Advances in factor analysis and structural equation models*. Cambridge, MA: Abt Books.

Jöreskog, K. G., & Sörbom, D. (1981). *LISREL V: Analysis of linear structural relationships by maximum likelihood and least squares methods*. Chicago: National Educational Resources.

Kendall, M. G., & Stuart, A. (1961). *The advanced theory of statistics. Vol. II: Inference and relationship*. New York: Hafner.

Little, J. K. (1958). *A statewide inquiry into decisions of youth about education beyond high school*. Madison: School of Education, University of Wisconsin.

Mare, R. D., & Mason, W. M. (1980). Children's reports of parental socioeconomic status: A multiple group measurement model. *Sociological Methods & Research, 9*, 178–198.

Meyer, J. W. (1977). The effects of education as an institution. *American Journal of Sociology, 83*, 55–77.

Ogbu, J. U. (1974). *The next generation: An ethnography of education in an urban neighborhood*. New York: Academic Press.

Rutter, M., Maughan, B., Mortimore, P., Ouston, J., with Smith, A. (1979). *Fifteen thousand hours*. Cambridge, MA: Harvard University Press.

Sewell, W. H. (1966). Reply to Turner, Michael and Boyle. *American Sociological Review, 31*, 707–712.

Sewell, W. H., Haller, A. O., & Ohlendorf, G. W. (1970). The educational and early occupational attainment process: Replication and revision. *American Sociological Review, 35*, 1014–1027.

Sewell, W. H., Haller, A. O., & Portes, A. (1969). The educational and early occupational attainment process. *American Sociological Review, 34*, 82–92.

Sewell, W. H., & Hauser, R. M. (1975). *Education, occupation, and earnings*. New York: Academic.

Stinchcombe, A. L. (1964). *Rebellion in a high school*. Chicago: Quadrangle.

Turner, R. H. (1964). *The social context of ambition*. San Francisco: Chandler.

Warner, W. L., Havighurst, R. J., & Loeb, M. B. (1944). *Who shall be educated? The challenge of unequal opportunities*. New York: Harper & Brothers.

Wiley, D. E. (1973). The identification problem for structural equation models with unmeasured variables: In A. S. Goldberger & O. D. Duncan (Eds.), *Structural equation models in the social sciences* (pp. 69–83). New York: Seminar Press.

Wilson, A. B. (1971). Sociological perspectives on the development of academic competence in urban areas: In A. H. Passow (Ed.), *Urban education in the 1970s* (pp. 120–140). New York: Teachers College Press.

Wilson, A. B. (1977). Education, mobility, and expectations of youths in Malaysia: In J. A. Lent (Ed.), *Cultural pluralism in Malaysia: Education, religion and social class* (pp. 58–70). De-Kalb, IL: The Center for Southeast Asian Studies, Northern Illinois University.

4 Classroom Lesson Strategies and Orientations Toward Work

Donald A. Hansen
Vicky A. Johnson
University of California, Berkeley

For over 3 decades, American education has been the target of persistent charges that it is placing our nation at risk, by failing to instill the academic skills needed by U.S. corporations to compete with foreign interests. Like the earlier accusations, the most recent blue-ribbon indictment (Gardner, 1983) was readily accepted by both politicians and educational leaders. Once again academic debate turned to charges and countercharges of who or what was responsible for the persistent decline of academic excellence.

Those closest to the problem appear to have seen it somewhat differently, however. Like everyone else, corporate employers were quick to join in the calls for educational excellence. But survey studies suggested that they saw the major failing of our schools not in academic training, but in the orientations they foster toward work. Surveying 4080 personnel managers and employers, Crain (1984) found that only 12% throught high school grades were "very important" for entry-level work, yet 94% rated dependability "extremely important." Only the most minimal of academic training appeared relevant to the majority of respondents: Basic literacy was rated as "important" by 65% and basic mathematics by 56%, but advanced skills in these areas were judged important by only 22.3% and 10.8%, respectively. Overall, Crain (1984) concluded:

> There may be a general decline in the quality of American schools—our survey doesn't address that issue. But if there is a decline, we find little evidence that it is of concern to American employers of high school graduates. (pp. 26–27)

Similar conclusions were reached in a survey of 500 human resource and public affairs executives, conducted by a nonprofit business research corporation: Although they judged the levels of learning of recent high school graduates adequate in all but one academic area (writing skills), they were troubled by deficiencies in the "willingness" of high school graduates to show up for work, to take directions, to work together, and to be responsible for their jobs (McGuire & Lund, 1984).

The employer's irritation over worker motivation seems to parallel the concerns of school administrators and teachers who decry the increasing numbers of students who seem to be indifferent to their schooling. The indifference takes various forms: Academic work is something to be endured as students await their diplomas; schooling is the rather lifeless preamble to college study; studies are the unfortunate price of participating in the social life of the school; classrooms are to be suffered simply because they are there, and no real alternatives can be seen. For a growing number the indifference is even more severe: By 1984, for example, the high school dropout rate in California had risen to 29.3% (Curtis, 1984).

Is there a relationship between these parallel observations of teachers and employers? The linkage of schooling attitudes to job performance is widely assumed, but in fact we know little of how situationally specific attitudes toward work may be, of how the differences in constraints and rewards of schoolwork compared to employment may relate to work orientations. We know even less about how the excitements and confusions of the transition from school to job may influence a change of work attitudes.

Indeed, we know little even about work attitudes of young employees today, and we are only now beginning to learn about work attitudes in the school setting. What we are learning, however, offers some promising suggestions for inquiry into how these two worlds of work may relate to one another.

Among other things, we propose in this paper that the problem is not simply that schools fail to instill effective attitudes toward work. It is also that schools often encourage students to experiment actively with irresponsibility and to adopt strategies of dealing with classroom tasks that are actively nonproductive— strategies that may carry over into the first job and perhaps beyond. Further, we argue that direct classroom efforts to strengthen work attitudes will not only fail for many students, they may even increase the problem by further encouraging active nonlearning. Finally, although we can only speculate, we suggest that much of what we are learning about nonlearning in the classroom may be directly relevant to active nonproduction in the workplace.

In the first section we consider the assumed connection of schooling attitudes and work attitudes. The second section introduces our work to date on learning strategies in the classroom, and in the following section we explore some aspects of teaching that appear to encourage active nonlearning. In the two final sections, we consider the relevance of these data and perspectives to the work setting.

WORK ORIENTATIONS IN SCHOOL AND JOB: THE ASSUMED CONNECTION

At one level of analysis, there is little difference between work in the classroom and work on the job. Both demand attention to task; both monitor, measure, and evaluate output; both reward productive effort and punish nonproductivity. Given organizational similarities, it would appear reasonable to expect that work orientations in school would readily transfer to the workplace. Closer examination suggests that beneath these surface similarities, school and work differ strikingly, especially in the rewards, punishments, and constraints they offer. Perhaps most importantly, the motive to earn money is more powerful for most individuals than is the motive to earn grades. Further, the paycheck is valuable to those who earn little, as well as to those who earn much, and even those who feel underpaid value the pay received. Grades, in contrast, may be meaningful for those who are at the top of their class, largely because grades are based on a system of internal competition. Good grades, then, enhance the ego, and promise to open doors of opportunity. For precisely the same reason, grades may have little motivating effect for those in the middle of the curve, and may even be viewed as punishment by those who fail.

Further, most schools are closer to total institutions than most corporations, and offer fewer possibilities of internal mobility, or of moving to another organization. Schools also are characterized by more consistent monitoring and evaluation, with frequent feedback to the student. This feedback can be seen to reinforce more persistently successful strategies for engaging or avoiding work. In this respect, then, schools are more constraining and controlling of day-to-day activities than are most jobs, allowing less sense of individual autonomy, more persistent rewards for successes, and more persistent reminders of failings.

Still further, schools ostensibly are dedicated to the development of the individual; the workplace, to the delivery of product or service. School administrators, at least in theory, are thus more likely to consider changing the situation to enhance the individual's experience; corporate administrators are more likely to first consider a change of personnel to enhance output. This level of analysis, then, appears to suggest that work orientations in classrooms may not transfer to the workplace.

The research literature offers little to support the view from either level. There is virtually no concrete evidence in support of a causal linkage between work in schools and on the job, nor is there evidence that suggests the lack of such a linkage. Even the popular media contradict it regularly, particularly in the perennial class reunion feature stories that revel in describing the inconsistent school and work careers of famous and not so-famous persons. The inconsistencies can be dramatic: The high school goof-off becomes a computer-world genius; the class valedictorian returns to the ten-year reunion dispirited and defeated. The media lenses also reveal less dramatic and unpublicized surprises at the class reunion: The indifferent pupil has transformed into a dedicated company man; the class grind is now unable to hold a job that demands more than minimal effort.

Despite the lack of evidence, the belief in a causal linkage is widespread, even among the professionals and businessmen who are most affected by it. Both educators and employers act as if there is no doubt at all that schools instill not only the cognitive skills but also the attitudes and habits that lead to success or failure in the world of work. Given the choice, employers hire on the assumption that graduates will be more effective and compatible with corporate life than nongraduates, even though the job demands may not require the cognitive skills represented by the diploma.

The belief that schools prepare for the world of work performance is, in fact, part of our political and academic heritage. It is shared not only by corporate heads and educational leaders, but also by social theorists of remarkably diverse commitments. It was seen in the liberal orthodoxy of the 50s and 60s, strikingly represented by Clark's (1962) *Educating the Expert Society*. In this vision, an open educational system identifies and cultivates the best and the brightest potentials of each individual child, nurturing positive work attitudes and pervasive commitments to the societal group, as well as the career flexibility needed for a rapidly changing corporate economy. Education thus becomes the key to a new age of enlightenment and equality, as it prepares the young, regardless of their origins, actively to apply their talents to the employment challenges that are opening to them.

The belief was seen as well in the radical perspectives of the 70s. These theories virtually turned the liberal arguments inside out, insisting that schools do indeed transmit cognitive knowledge, but with varying degrees of success. Far more systematically they instill attitudes toward work, including the capacity to defer gratification, to act responsibly and punctually, to bend to authority, and to tolerate impersonal bureaucracy. But in this image of education as "cultural imperialism" (Carnoy, 1974; Collins, 1979), these work orientations form part of the hegemony that veils the established power they serve. Rather than a vehicle for new enlightenment and equality, education is seen in this vision as a reactionary force that perpetuates and renews inequality, preparing individuals to set aside their own best interests as they conform to the needs of the corporate society that benefits mostly the established elite.

In a larger historical perspective, the belief is also seen in the conservative traditions of educational thought that has endured through more than two centuries of a changing American political economy. In these traditions, education is seen to prepare individuals for their future roles in life. Those who by birth or talent are destined for the most demanding leadership and executive offices are given the most rigorous and extended education, while others, destined for less demanding occupations, are educated accordingly. The image parallels the Victorian belief in the "playing fields of Eton" as the training grounds on which British public school boys attained the qualities necessary for the preeminence of British rule, not only by learning the tactics of sport, but by developing the character needed for enduring and resourceful team play.

Although these quaint conservative images have faded in both Britain and the United States, neoconservative traditions have persisted. In this country one of the more enduring versions is Bell's (1973) image of a "just meritocracy," in which exceptional endeavors are rewarded not with money or material possessions, but rather with achieved status recognition. And it is returning in the arguments of some who, despairing of the effort to bring about social change and justice through education, advocate a return to "traditional, humane justifications" for schooling:

> I think it fair to say that since societies must ration access to the most desirable jobs on *some basis,* reliance on educational credentials is probably a sensible and humane procedure. If many people who do not have such credentials could perform in a perfectly creditable manner on the job in question, restricting access to those with such credentials at least increases the likelihood that those who hold high status jobs will have been exposed to the world of ideas and the enduring values of our culture (Hurn, 1978, pp. 263–264).

Underlying such a perspective is the assumption that individuals will enter the job place at the level their education has determined, in time bringing to all levels more humanistic and cultured attitudes. This may be seen as a return to the belief in a "noblesse oblige," but in this vision the noblesse are not those who are to the "manner" born, but those who are educated to it, after being selected from among those who have the opportunity for such education.

Given the unshakability of the belief in schooling's ability to influence orientation toward work, it is tempting to conclude that problems of recent graduates in the workplace reflect the failings of schooling. It is also tempting to endorse the obvious solution: What is needed is better and/or more schooling. Again, however, data to support this interpretation are lacking. Indeed, correlational data of large scale populations suggest that such an interpretation may be invalid (cf. Coleman, 1966; Jencks, 1972).

For the present inquiry, we take at least one lesson from this history of unshakable and unsupported belief: Given available resources for data gathering, and given available methodologies for analysis, we are not likely to find convincing evidence of a causal linkage of work orientations in classroom and corporation. Nor are we likely to find evidence that will diminish belief in that linkage.

In the remainder of this paper, then, we turn attention from causes to consider the possibility that early schooling experience is simply a precursor to later orientations to work.

LEARNING STRATEGIES IN THE CLASSROOM

In opening the previous section we suggested that, although work in school is superficially similar to work on the job, on closer organizational examination they are seen to differ significantly in their rewards, punishments, and constraints. At another level of analysis, however,—that of ego functioning—the similarities of school work and real work are even more striking than their differences. In both, the individual may confront assignments that are ambiguous, inexplicit, or incomplete; in both, the individual-in-situation at times may feel incompetent or inadequate to the task; in both the task-in-situation may be of dubious value, relevance or challenge; in both, individual, task, and situation are inextricably interwoven, each with the others.

It is this level of analysis that is of concern in the present paper. Our basic argument can be put simply: Despite the organizational differences between classroom and workplace, classroom learning strategies may help predict workplace job strategies because both sets of strategies are rooted in situationally responsive ego processes that tend to persist through the developmental years and on into adulthood.

Note that these ego processes are not simply psychological or phenomenological. Rather, as Haan (1977) insists:

> Focus upon ego processes leads to concern for their situational contexts . . . because ego processes' work *is* interchange with internal and external situations, and ego processes make no sense understood in any other way. Sometimes ego processes are self-actional in reaction to situations, but their work is more often situationally interactional and transactional. (p. 5)

In our classroom research, which has been heavily influenced by both interactional sociology and developmental psychology, we have been impressed with how closely responsive psychological processes are to social situations, and we have come to see learning and nonlearning in the classroom as expressions of *situated ego-processes:*[1] Within phenomenologically similar situations, the individual tends toward consistent types of responses or strategies. In diverse situations the person will process similar levels of stress, ambiguity, or boredom in

---

[1]We have coined this term to emphasize the interplay of context and ego functioning, but the underlying conception has been actively advanced by Haan (1977).

much the same ways, and will characteristically respond with strategies that express those persistent ego processes, but in ways appropriate or responsive to the specific situation.

Ego Processes and Learning Strategies

In her seminal work on ego functioning, Haan (1977) distinguished between two basic forms of ego processes: "coping" and "defending." Although they were derived from clinical experience in psychotherapeutic settings, the concepts struck us as closely pertinent to classroom learning and nonlearning. Our classroom observations suggested a further distinction between two forms of "defending," however. One form appeared to express low levels of *self-referenced confidence;* the other, low levels of *task-referenced value.*

With hindsight we have come to recognize that we have once again discovered the motivational psychologists' distinction between expectancy and valence. Rooted in the classical work of Tolman (1932), Lewin (1935), and Hull (1943), "expectancy-valence theory" today takes a variety of forms, all of which see motivation as basically a function of two subjective factors: expectancy (the subjective probability of attaining a goal) and value (the anticipated gratification associated with that goal).[2] In Vroom's (1964) "expectancy-instrumentality-valence" formulation, for example, expectancies represent the employees' perceptions that they have the necessary abilities and role clarity to perform successfully, if they make the required effort (i.e., effort is expected to lead to successful completion of the task). For Vroom, valence essentially involves two further subjective judgments: First, that successful completion of the task will be instrumental in achieving the goals; second, that those goals relate to the satisfaction of the individual's "needs" (cf. Campbell & Pritchard, 1975).

Curiously, although expectancies and valence are clearly distinguished from one another in these theories, in each they are combined into a single dimension of motivation. That is, although the equations vary in complexity, motivation is treated as if it were a direct mathematical product of expectancy and valence (basically motivation equals expectancy times valence). As a result, these motivational theories have assumed a linear relationship between high motivation and low motivation, between high productivity and low productivity, and (by im-

---

[2]Although expectancy-valence constructs have dominated motivational theories in industrial psychology, other perspectives have also attracted considerable attention. Notably, see Porter's (1964) adaptation of Maslow's "needs hierarchy"; Herzberg's (1974) "two-factor" theory that emphasizes the importance of factors intrinsic to the work itself and argues that job enrichment will increase employee motivation; Adams' (1963) "equity theory"; Locke's (1970) "goal-setting" theory that motivation heightens the individual's consciously set goals. This latter variant of expectancy-valence theory, in contrast to some of the others, considers extrinsic reward systems (such as pay and promotion) as important to work motivation.

plication) between learning and nonlearning. The problem with such formulations has not gone unnoticed: Some years ago, in a critical review of the literature on work motivation, Laws (1978) argued that expectancy and valence must be measured independently.

This idea appears to have gone unheeded, and expectancy-valence theories have given scant attention to the difference between the non-productivity of a person who has high expectancy and low valence and that of one who has low expectancy and high valence. Our work in classrooms suggests, however, that these two conditions relate to distinctly different forms of ego defense, and that they require strikingly different interventions. Self-referenced confidence (or, more generally, expectancy) and task-referenced value (valence), that is, must be treated separately and interactively. When they are, we discover that the relationships of productivity to nonproductivity and of learning to nonlearning are decidedly nonlinear.

Learning Strategies in the Classroom

Clearly, both self-referenced confidence and task-referenced value must be conceptualized as continua. Nonetheless it can be sensitizing to treat each as dichotomous and interlinked in a simple two-by-two taxonomy. The taxonomy identifies four basic strategies of learning and nonlearning, and, we believe, of job productivity and nonproductivity (Fig. 4.1).

We have elsewhere (Hansen & Johnson, 1983) described the characteristic of these strategies, which are here somewhat restated to emphasize their potential relevance to the workplace.

Task Engaging. The task is valent, and self-expectancies are high: The individual sees relative value in the required performance and is relatively confident of his or her ability to meet its demands. In a state of situated challenge, the individual strives for an accurate understanding of the task and of the means to accomplish it, and enters into the required effort with intentionality. Ambiguity of assignment is met with efforts to clarify, interpret, and resolve. The individual attempts to makes sense of novel and unexpected elements in new situations and unfamiliar assignments by making slight adjustments in understandings of the past and in expectations of the future. This is the hallmark of effective learning and productivity, characterized by an active engagement with the task.

Task Dissembling. The task is valent, but self-expectancies are low: The individual sees a relative value in the required performance, but lacks confidence in his or her ability to meet its demands. In a situational quandary, the individual wants to perform, but is uncertain of what to do or how to do it, or whether it can be done. In the desire to succeed, to appear successful, not to fail, or at least not to appear to fail, the individual dissembles, pretending to understand, making

TASK CONFIDENCE

		HIGH	LOW
T A S K V A L U E	HIGH	(Learning Challenge) ENGAGING	(Learning Quandary) DISSEMBLING
	LOW	(Learning Bind) EVADING	(Learning Malaise) REJECTING

FIG. 4.1. Classroom lesson strategies: A taxonomy of self-reference confidence and task-referenced value.

excuses, denying, distorting, or engaging in undifferentiated thinking that includes elements that may not appear to be part of the situation. New situations and unfamiliar assignments are seen as threatening, rather than challenging, and are met with further dissembling.

Task Evading.   Self-expectancies are high, but task valence is low. The individual feels relatively confident of his or her ability to meet the demands of the assignment, but sees relatively little value in it. He or she is in a situational bind, feeling ready and able to take on a challenge, but being unable in this particular situation to identify a task of sufficient value. Constrained by the demands of the assignment and the workplace, the individual may go through the motions of task performance in an automatic fashion, usually accomplishing at least an acceptable minimum of output. But the task is neither actively engaged nor rejected: it is simply evaded. The individual is removed from the task, his or her attention is scattered, given only partially to the performance and perhaps in more important part to other competing interests such as daydreaming, distracting a neighbor, worrying about lack of money, planning a party, recalling a television drama or even mentally rehearsing another more compelling performance in an area that is found challenging. Figuratively, the individual deals with the assignment with the left hand, leaving the right hand free to deal with more important and compelling matters.

Task Rejecting.   Both self-expectancies and task valence are low: the individual lacks confidence in his or her ability and sees little value in the assigned task. He or she is in a situational malaise, neither having a clear goal or valued task, nor feeling able to secure one in this situation. In a situated state of psychological withdrawal, the individual neither actively engages assignments nor defends against them. He or she may appear passive, working within a closed system of understandings that are unresponsive to the present demands and restrictions of the situation.

In our observations of classrooms, we have seen teachers distinguish dissembling and evading from one another only rarely, and we suspect that the distinction is equally rare in the workplace. Unfortunately, when the two forms of defending are confused with one another, they are often treated in inappropriate and ineffective ways. Most frequently, the teachers in our studies would treat all lesson defending as if it were evading, even though students employed dissembling strategies far more frequently. In many work situations, of course, evading may be more common, particularly in jobs involving little novelty and considerable repetition.

The confusion of evading and dissembling is understandable, for the two often appear identical in surface-level behavior. For example, in the classrooms we studied, our observers identified at least two or three "shy" children (usually, but not always female) who "withdrew in competitive situations." Many of the teachers, schooled in the theoretical literature (e.g., Covington, 1968), told us that the withdrawal was due to fear of failure (see the description of dissembling, above). Most often, it appeared to us that the teachers were correct. In these attributions withdrawal is implicitly recognized as a situated ego-defensive strategy, rooted in low self-expectancies (dissembling).

But a person may withdraw from a situated task for quite different cognitive and emotional reasons, such as a fear of success, a belief that competition is inappropriate, a desire for conformity, or an indifference to the activity and/or its potential outcomes. Unlike the fear of failure withdrawal, which is commonly expressed in dissembling, these are seen as withdrawing by evading. (We have also seen withdrawing in our classrooms in a more passive form, in the extreme withdrawal of lesson rejecting.)

In evading, often the student simply does not respond emotionally to the demands of the lesson as strongly as she or he does to competing demands, or the the enticements of other activity. The evading may be blatant: The student may look at comic books, doodle, or pass notes, openly ignoring the lessons. The more gregarious may play up to other students, showing that they can't be bothered with the lessons because they have more important things to do, like interacting with one another. These students are often difficult to work with, for they simply find little value not only in what the teacher and the classroom do offer, but also in what they are able to offer.

Although evading is far more frequent in junior and senior high, we have observed it in the earliest years of schooling. Juan, for example, had been born in this country, yet he had learned relatively little English, even compared to his second grade classmates who had moved from Mexico only 1 or 2 years earlier.

Observational note (synopsis).   Juan was making faces at Jorge across the room, openly ignoring the English reading lesson in progress. The teaching aide went over to him and told him quietly that he'd never learn to read or write English if he didn't pay attention: he replied that he didn't need to learn to read in English because he was going to drive a garbage truck as his father does. Quite appropriately (essentially and correctly defining Juan's resistance as evading), the aide pointed out that he would have to fill out forms to get the job. The interchange ended when Juan replied that he wouldn't have to do that, because it was his father's business. Although Juan stopped distracting Jorge, he made no effort to follow the lesson.

Not all evading is so intransigent, however. The problem often is less in the student than in the lesson: Even if it is relevant to the students' interests, for example, it may demand too much effort for the expected return. Particularly in multicultural situations, it may demand actions that are inconsistent with, or even contradictory to, the student's cultural beliefs or proscriptive roles (cf. Hansen, 1986). In some cultures, for example, it is thought insulting and demeaning to offer the correct answer to a question that another child has missed (cf. Gallimore & Au, 1979; Phillips, 1972)

Of particular relevance to many jobs available to recent graduates, we observed that evading often is a response to lessons that are too easy, undemanding, and/or repetitious. It is no great surprise that even bright students in our study frequently evaded lessons. Usually they would do enough of the assignment to escape censure, most often either immediately rushing slap-dash through it, or cavalierly slashing at it during the very end of the allotted time. The major part of their attention, even while performing the lesson, was on other interests, however. With each year of elementary school, these interests were more and more of a social/sexual nature. Although dissembling remained a more common strategy, increasing numbers of students actively negotiated their ways into evading their assignments. To engage actively would be boring or less rewarding than alternate activities that relate to their emotional as well as cognitive well-being.

Dissembling also represents an active negotiation out of engaging, but the reasons for nonengaging are quite different. Although the most difficult tendencies to dissemble involve the protection of vulnerable self-conceptions, the most frequently observed instances of dissembling in our classrooms were situation-induced, resulting from simple assignment confusion. However much the children wanted to accomplish a lesson, often they were uncertain of what they were expected to do and/or of how to do it. In some instances, they seemed to be given inconsistent or conflicting demands (for examples, see discussion of "double-binds," below). Hence, they distrusted their ability to do the lesson:

Observational Note (Synopsis). For this lesson the teacher hands out a Pattern Blocks test card to pairs of Spanish-speaking children. The children are required to count out the number of blocks shown at the bottom of the card and construct a geometric pattern traced on the card using blocks of various shapes. The teacher instructs the children (in English) that they are to count out in English the number of blocks they need, and then to solve the puzzle. The children are generally inattentive, do not appear to understand the directions and begin the activity while the teacher is repeating the instructions once more. At this point the teacher reprimands one of the students.

T: "Some of you like Jose always like to grab, but you have to learn to share."

The children stumble through the exercise unclear as to the task, while the teacher emphasizes that they should count in English. Few children seem to understand, but no one asks for clarification. Through what appears to be moments of insight, a few children solve the puzzle. By watching and following those who have succeeded, others accomplish the task, but without the key element of counting in English.

Theoretical Note. This pattern has been repeated often in this classroom: ESL (English as a Second Language) lessons are marked by confusion and misunderstanding when only English is used, yet children seldom approach the teacher to ask questions. Assignment confusion seems to develop out of language confusion. When the teacher insists that students follow directions accurately, the students are placed in a learning quandary, and pretend to understand (dissemble).

In this 2nd-grade classroom, comprising mostly children from Spanish-language homes, confusion was heightened by the children's limited understandings of English. Our notes suggest, however, that assignment confusion was almost as common among the monolingual English students in our classrooms. Most often it was rooted in a problem common to all classrooms, regardless of linguistic mix: The teacher, intent on encouraging the children to practice an important skill, fails to distinguish between the difficulty of accomplishing the assignment and the difficulty of understanding it.

In the situation just described, even though the teacher's own home language was Spanish, she did not recognize that the children simply did not understand her words; her response implied that if they did not understand the assignment, it was because they were not listening closely. The solution was to repeat it, almost in the same patterns as before, again using only English to communicate the assignment, presumably because the lesson was secondarily intended to encourage the children to use English in accomplishing the assignment.

Dissembling was further encouraged in this situation by the teacher's tendency to use mild humiliation to control and encourage. One prime reason to dissemble is to avoid public humiliation, in this case the admission to self and others that one is unable to comprehend assignments or to complete tasks. This may be the beginning of an interactive process (at least in some classrooms where teachers use humiliation to control) in which children fall into trouble in part because they do not understand the basis of getting into trouble. That is, children who do not have an insight into the nature of the task they must complete may place themselves in situations in which they are likely to be humiliated, and thereby be further tempted to dissemble or even withdraw.

Clearly, not all individuals respond to assignment confusion in the same way.

Some continue to engage, attempting to make sense of the task, displaying both the value they placed on the assignment itself and retaining at least some confidence in their ability to identify what is supposed to be accomplished. Though they may be characterized as engaging in the challenges of the classroom, the challenge is not in the task assigned, but rather in the assignment itself; that is, the challenge is to identify what it was the teacher said. Another example illustrates this.

> *Observational Note (Synopsis).*   Like the others, Jaime did not understand what he was supposed to do. He first checked to see what the others were doing but no one offered ideas to copy (no one knew: Some played, some sat there, others tried their own version of the task). Jaime concentrated on the blocks and by trial and error came up with a version he thought good enough to show the teacher.
> Jaime (whispering to teacher): "Like that?"
> Teacher (apparently not hearing him; loudly): "Well, that is wrong."
> Jaime once again sat down and went on, undisturbed in appearance. He kept inquiring around, in Spanish, how to do this complicated task. Finally he had an insight, and put all his energies into the task, now seriously concentrating. Interestingly, Jaime was not able to finish the task: There weren't enough blocks for every child to complete the puzzles. Even if they all had understood the assignment, the task could not have been completed by all.

It should be emphasized that dissembling and evading may be entirely appropriate and even effective responses to specific situations. Lesson and job assignments, after all, are imposed by others, and not all are equally worthy of our energies. Some assignments may appear senseless or distasteful, some may even contradict our most basic beliefs or violate our fundamental political and moral understandings. But we are not always free to refuse overtly to accept; it may not be to our best interests to resist openly.

Each of us dissembles and evades from time to time; most of us may employ these strategies frequently in any one day. In extremely difficult situations, such as prison or a concentration camp, persistent and extreme dissembling and/or evading may forestall serious and even irreversible debilitation. In more commonplace situations, such as dealing with bureaucratic details, evading and dissembling may seem almost necessary.

Evading and dissembling also can be productive strategies. In some situations, they may contribute to subsequent effort. Calling in "sick" may allow recovery from physical or psychological fatigue that otherwise might persist; occasionally playing hookey or daydreaming may help one rest up for an unusual effort.

Evading and dissembling might also help in psyching up for a particularly intense challenge: The current assignment is given lesser attention as the individual concentrates on preparations for the coming effort. The student debater or athlete may stare blankly at the pages of the history book in the hours before competition while actively rehearsing strategies for victory. During the Second World War, the Air Force promoted a media image that they could do "the difficult immediately, but the impossible takes a little longer." Ignoring the poetic-militant license, we might suggest that the "impossible" takes longer in part because all but the most confident of engagers needs a little time in dissembling, building further confidence while pretending to others and quasi-convincing one's self that the task is already being engaged.

Dissembling also might represent playing for time, in the manner of the potential victim on the legion of late night shows who pretends compliance with the bad guys while awaiting rescue. Less dramatically, and perhaps even more frequently, the effective use of dissembling is seen in the accomplished lecturer who responds to the brilliant student's question by talking around the subject, hoping that a relevant response will soon come to mind.

The problem, then, is not that an individual dissembles or evades in some situations. The problem, rather, is that, for some, evading or dissembling becomes an habitual strategy that may be employed with increasing frequency in response to decreasing levels of situational distress or discomfort. Our research in classrooms demonstrates that both evading and dissembling can be encouraged by teaching strategies, classroom situations, and even by administrative demands and constraints. Despite the best of intentions and the most gifted efforts, one of the most fundamental lessons many children learn in the classroom is how to evade or dissemble successfully.

In the following section we identify some of the ways teachers and administrators in our study unintentionally encouraged evading and dissembling. In the final section we consider, in a preliminary way, the relevancies and implications of our work on lesson strategies for research on the job performance of young workers. In our early efforts to understand and work with evading and dissembling in the classroom we believe that there are clues to nonproductivity in the workplace, particularly among recent high school graduates.

ENCOURAGING EVADING AND DISSEMBLING

Since first identifying evading and dissembling, we have been able to observe students' lesson strategies in a total of 24 classrooms, 12 in inner-city, low income neighborhoods, 12 in schools serving middle-income communities. The great majority of the teachers and aides in these classrooms were gifted, dedicated, and effectively engaged in their work. Yet in each classroom, even those taught by the most extraordinary of teachers, both evading and dissembling were familiar parts of the school day for many children and were the habituated strategies of at least a few.

The classrooms differed strikingly in the frequency of engaging, evading, and dissembling, however. In about three-quarters of our middle-income classrooms and half of our inner-city classrooms, for example, roughly half of the students consistently engaged their lessons (with only occasional evading or dissembling). By contrast, in other classrooms, dissembling alone, or a combination of dissembling, evading, and/or rejecting were the modal strategies of the majority of students (cf. Hansen & Johnson, 1983). Our data clearly suggest that these differences cannot be understood only as artifacts of differing student populations. Rather, at least in important part, understanding of these differences must be based within the classrooms themselves.

At one level of analysis, the differences relate to variables that have little if any relevance to the workplace: Learning strategies of students clearly are influenced by such things as the content, structure, and physical presentation of the lesson. But these variables in turn relate to others that are closely paralleled in the world of work; including the structures of administrative control and teacher accountability; the physical and moral environment of the school; the morale and collective energies of students, teachers, and staff; and the political and moral activities of the surrounding community.

This statement should not be taken to mean that the person's home and community environments are irrelevant to the strategies adopted in the classroom or work setting. Neither does it indicate that the person's developmental history or physical and emotional health can be disregarded. Indeed, the major thrust of the data in our study points to the influences on learning strategies of developmental, historical, and contextual variables.

What our data do indicate is the importance of continued research that is sharply focused within the classroom and the workplace on such variables as work environments, styles of supervision, and processes of negotiation and control. For whatever the importance of historical and contextual conditions to learning and productivity, they are expressed most directly in the situated activity of the classroom and workplace.

Let us consider some of the ways this activity appears to encourage active nonlearning.

Dissembling in a Demanding Situation

Our observational data suggest that children's learning strategies may be related to their teachers' tendencies to engage, dissemble, or evade lessons and instructional interaction. The relationship is not simple and direct, however: Students are less likely to engage their lessons in classrooms where the teacher does not consistently engage, but when teachers do consistently engage, their charges do not always follow suit.

Our data suggest, rather, that consistently engaging leadership may be necessary but not sufficient to high levels of student (or worker) engaging. It is also important, then, to attend to how leaders engage, and what it is that they engage:

Actively engaging leadership can virtually force individuals to escape into dissembling or evading, or even malaise.

Elsewhere (Hansen & Johnson, 1983), we have detailed how dissembling was encouraged by a consistently engaging and demanding teacher. This talented and energetic woman appeared to be dedicated to eradicating evading in her classroom. With persistent admonitions to study in order to succeed in later life, combined with infrequent rewards, those who displayed evading were hounded into either applying themselves to their lessons or escaping altogether into lesson rejecting.

Those who tended to dissemble, however, were virtually ignored. The teacher seemed to approve of any activity that gave the appearance of lesson engaging. When dissembling was noticed, as when a student was clearly faking an answer in front of the class, it was dealt with as if it, too, was based in lesson evading. Ever alert to signs of laziness or flagging interest, the teacher treated dissembling by upping the ante, emphasizing the importance of the lesson, promising a reward, or threatening punishment. This response to displays of dissembling was common among even our most gifted teachers. Unfortunately, its effect is to encourage even deeper and more persistent dissembling, by further eroding the dissembling students' confidence.

Rejecting in an Ambiguous Situation

It is clear, then, that even an engaging teacher can unintentionally discourage students from engaging their lessons. What about teachers who themselves evade and dissemble? We suspect that such teachers persistently discourage engaging, at least in some students. To date, we have observed only five classrooms in which the teacher fairly frequently failed to engage actively in the teaching effort. In these five rooms, however, we also found the lowest proportions of students who consistently engaged their lessons.

This linkage of teachers' to students' task strategies is illustrated by the case of a second-grade teacher who was exceptionally warm and empathic, but prone to dissembling. Frequently assigning independent work, the teacher often sat at a desk at the front corner of the room, looking busy but usually doing little. When she did interact with individual children, she often deflected their focus from their lessons with pleasant but irrelevant conversation.

Given this teacher's warmth and appreciation of lessons well done (and even those not so well done), it is understandable that a relatively high number of her students were observed to be engaging. What was surprising was the relatively few who were dissembling and evading, and the exceptionally high number who were observed to reject most frequently. The clue to this pattern is only partly in the teacher's inconsistent engaging: In this case we see the importance of looking at what was engaged and how.

Although this teacher tended to dissemble, she seemed insensitive to the nature of her students' dissembling, sometimes treating it as if it were evading, at other times as if it were engaging. Further, she often responded to risk taking, which can be a particularly effective component of lesson engaging, as if it were evading. Any behavior that was thought to be nonengaging was dealt with through direct imperatives ("you must do it"), and/or public humiliation.

Thus, despite her warmth and relaxed manner, this teacher presented an ambiguous system of rewards and punishments. Usually good work was rewarded, but sometimes it was ignored. Often, questionable responses were rewarded as well, as the teacher mistook dissembling for engaging. Not surprisingly, students often were unsure of what they had done to gain the teacher's praise. Most troublesome to the students, however, was the ridicule and humiliation that could follow attempts to engage, as the teacher mistook them for evading.

A further aspect of this situation compounded the students' dilemma: Assignments often were unclear or ambiguous. This is succinctly illustrated in the following observation, describing one of the many times that assignment confusion in this classroom clearly led to lesson dissembling. In this instance, we also see what can happen when dissembling is mistaken for evading: The teacher, apparently hoping to shame the student into applying himself, employs humiliation, and the student simply gives up (a rapid devolution from dissembling to learning malaise and lesson rejection).

Observational Note.   The children were assigned a rather complex puzzle. . . .
The teacher gave a brief explanation (in English) of what she wanted. Soon it became evident (to the observer) that the children did not really understand what was expected of them. Some, as for example Pablo, just stared at the blocks and played with them, not at all doing his task. The teacher turned to him with a dry, cutting voice:
Teacher: "This boy is not supposed to be doing this."
The teacher explained the task to him again. Pablo tried once again, and once again failed.
Teacher (loudly): "You are not listening!"
The other children appeared equally unsure of what they were to do. Some eventually developed an insight into the nature of the task through trial and error. . . . Others looked around and only after seeing what other children were doing had an insight into the assignment.

Theoretical Memo.   The following sequence has been frequently observed in this room:

1. The assignment is made in brief, dry fashion.

2. Children do not understand the nature of the assignment.

3. Children either daydream, look around impatiently, or practice trial and error.

4. Once they develop an insight (either from within or by watching others), some children enthusiastically concentrate on their work and complete the task.

Those who do not develop an insight either sit there daydreaming (malaise?) or simply play with their blocks.

In this classroom, those who do play often get yelled at (e.g., 'This boy is not . . .') which often seems to further turn off the child. This was clearly seen in Pablo's denial of even pretending to follow the teacher when she offered a second explanation.

Strategies of Nonlearning as Responses to Double-binds

Another of our 2nd grade classrooms illustrates a fundamental problem that was seen in all of our rooms: Students and teachers were caught in double-binds that locked them into nonproductive behavior patterns and interchanges. In this room, the binds were more pervasive than most, and the teacher vacillated frequently between evading and engaging. As in all of our inner-city classrooms, a significant number of children tended to dissemble. In this room, however, disproportionate numbers tended to evade and reject; little more than one-fourth could be characterized as fairly consistently engaging.

We have characterized evading as a response to a bind: The individual feels capable of doing what is demanded, but would rather not. To escape the bind the individual evades the demand by doing something more compelling, more interesting, or simply less demanding. Often the evading is not overly risky: If the demands to perform increase, the individual can abruptly turn to the task and avert punishment.

A double bind is not so easily handled however. Unlike a simple bind, in a double bind the person is expected to do two things that are incompatible. To honor one expectation is to dishonor the other. The risks imposed by double binds often are inescapable, particularly if the conflicting demands come from two sources (split double bind), such as teacher vs. parent, or union vs. employer. Faced with conflicting demands the person will be damned no matter which is engaged, and may be doubly damned if both are evaded. On the job, workers often face such binds, in conflicting demands to produce and perform and at the same time act ethically toward customers or responsibly toward fellow workers.

It is not only students and workers who suffer double binds. The teachers in our study were often caught in such binds, as are many supervisors and midlevel administrators. For this teacher, the split double bind took a form familiar in the corporate world, involving a conflict of administrative process and professional commitment. The teacher was committed to encouraging social and academic competence in her class of ethnic minority children. She knew that the principal, who shared the commitment, also believed that competence required confidence and self-esteem, which for minority children in turn required knowledge of, and pride in, their home cultures.

Many other teachers in our study faced similar situations, which they resolved more or less successfully. This teacher faced an additional problem, however: As a teacher in a bilingual program, she was bilingual and bicultural, but not in the first language or culture of any of her students. Lacking knowledge of any of the varied languages and cultures they represented, she believed that she could satisfy the principal's expectations and her own professional commitments, but only if she devoted all of her energies and all available class time to the effort.

. That was only one side of this teacher's pervasive double-bind, however. For she also recognized that what really counted in evaluating teachers in bilingual classes were the annual district tests of improvement in basic skills. But to teach these skills to her children was also a monumental task. Limited in her own knowledge of English usage, flawed in her grammar and syntax, and faced with students who were quite limited in language skills (even in their home language), the job of teaching the full range of functional literacy and numeracy skills would again demand all of her energies and class time. To satisfy the principal and her own professional commitment, then, would mean that she would not meet the administrative measure of her competence: Her children would not do well on the district tests, and she would be considered a poor teacher by everyone, including the principal.

Her resolution was to teach for the tests, evading all but the most minimal bicultural exercises and lessons designed to enhance minority children's esteem. Little time remained for more substantive lessons, as she drilled the children over and over on the same exercises, until they could answer the questions that would appear on the test forms. The strategy had worked in past years: The teacher was proud of her classes' test scores, explaining that it was especially important that minority students not have the stigma of poor test performance on their records. Not only that, she implied, the scores showed that they had a good teacher.

In our independent testing of the children's English skills, this class did in fact do relatively well on the more rote language tasks, such as word recognition and vocabulary. The teacher's strategy appears to have succeeded at a price, however: Scores were correspondingly low on the more demanding skills such as text comprehension. Not only that, the students were often bored with the rote lessons, and rarely dissuaded from their tendencies to dissemble, evade, and reject. A great deal of time and energy were spent on controlling the class as a whole, but the teacher, intent on leading the class through flash card exercises and group recitations, monitored individual responses only sporadically.

Another price of this strategy for resolving the double bind surfaced as the school year progressed: The teacher felt that her professional commitments were being neglected; her abilities were not being used fully, and she was not being allowed to tap the children's real capacities for learning. Although she did not use the terminology, the teacher herself saw much of her classroom life as enmeshed in a complex of double binds, which at times she felt virtually forced into translating directly into a double bind on her children.

Many double binds are not as overt and transparent as the one described here,

which involved fairly clearly articulated job expectations. Other demand conflicts are only implied in the behavior and attitudes of the participants or in the
ways the situation is structured. That is the kind of bind we saw most commonly
in all of our classrooms, including this one.

In all of the classrooms we have observed, the children were persistently
admonished to learn, but in this one the teacher's actions often implied, "but not
too much or too fast." In every classroom, students who finish an assignment
early may be told, now and then, to sit quietly until the others finish. This is no
great problem if the child must simply wait five or ten minutes once in a while;
the message is one that all of us face from time to time, to "hurry up and wait."

In this class, however, the message was reinforced repeatedly for a few
industrious students; even when they asked for the additional work they would be
told to be quiet and wait, and at times the waiting period was extended. In the
most extreme case we observed, a bright and engaged student, who had finished
the independent reading assignments for the year, asked to be given the next
level textbook. He was told to wait until next year, even though there were four
weeks of school left. When he asked why, the teacher explained, "If you study
the next level now, what will you study next year?" She offered no options, and
the student was left to his own devices.

The teacher's explanation at first puzzled us; it appeared callous and arbitrary.
In discussing the situation with her during lunch break, however, it became clear
she felt caught in another double bind. Professionally, she realized that if the
child did not go on to the next level valuable time would be wasted and the child
would probably be a discipline problem for the rest of the year. Yet if she
allowed the child to go on to the next level, next year's teacher would be vexed
with her, and probably complain to the principal, because the student "will say I
already did that" and the student will be out of sync with the rest of the class.

In resolving this double bind, however, the teacher unwittingly created another one for the student. For the message, "hurry up and wait," tells the student
more than the teacher seemed to recognize. To be sure, to the student the
message means wasted time, boredom, and the risk of being disciplined, but it
conveys something of more enduring significance, not only to the individual
student, but to the entire class.

Whatever words are used, the teacher's behavior says that these students need
not try so hard; no one expects much of them, and limited expectations should be
accepted. To exceed those limitations is only to make trouble for the teacher and
the rest of the class, and whatever extra they may learn or accomplish simply
isn't worth it. For many children such a message is a threat to self-esteem, for it
tells them the teacher does not think they are worth challenging, or that they
cannot really go beyond the set limits.

Even for those whose self-esteem is not so vulnerable, however, the message
is frustrating: They are told to work hard, but when they do they are told not to.
This situation represents one of the tightest double-binds imaginable: A single

authority tells the individual both to do something and not to do it. Unlike a split double bind, the individual cannot even choose which authority to honor: No matter what is done the single authority will be violated. The result, most often, is evading, and if that brings punishment from the authority (even mild censure: "Why can't you fit in better?"), withdrawal and malaise may follow.

Clinical and experimental literature attest the personal price of enduring pervasive double binds: frustration and anxiety, increasing unpredictability, hostility and aggressive behavior, and gradual withdrawal into a state of helplessness and hopelessness. This devolution under continuing and pervasive double binds appears to us as an extreme example of the transition from engaging to evading and on to malaise.

In short, whatever the sources of the conflicting demands, double binds appear to be exceptionally destructive of productivity, encouraging evading and malaise even in highly motivated individuals. The relevance of this discussion to the workplace should be obvious, for both double binds and split double binds are familiar parts of many corporate settings. So, too, are the other examples of situated nonproductivity in the classroom that have been presented in this section. We turn, then, to some of the relevancies and implications of our work for research on work orientations in the corporate world.

CLASSROOM LEARNING STRATEGIES: IMPLICATIONS FOR THE WORKPLACE

In the second section, we suggested that the adolescent's orientations to classroom lessons may be precursors of the young adult's orientations to work. The ensuing discussion allows us now to make our meaning more specific: Strategies of dealing with classroom assignments—and especially strategies of evading and dissembling—can help us predict tendencies to adopt nonproductive work strategies, but only if the workplace is similar to classrooms in specific situational qualities that relate to the interplay of self-expectancy and task-valence.

Classroom Strategies and Early Job Performance

Our perspective on situated ego functioning suggests a parsimonious, though partial, interpretation of both the continuities and discontinuities between classroom learning strategies and work strategies (which were discussed in the opening section). To put it in most simple formula, it is persistent ego functioning that helps most to explain continuities of work strategies across time and place; it is situational and task dissimilarity that helps most to explain the discontinuities. Whether it is in the classroom or on the job, if stressed, confused, or bored, one individual may tend to engage more actively in the task, another actively to evade, and a third to dissemble. A few may simply withdraw.

Even given closely similar situations, however, the persistence of ego-functioning over time is far from perfect. The influence of maturation and development on ego functioning remains unclear and to date has been given little research attention. Further, Haan's (1977) work suggests that individuals can learn and be taught to recognize and to some degree control their tendencies to dissemble and evade in difficult situations. A corollary to this clinical insight has been particularly important to the present paper: Individuals can also learn and be taught to dissemble and evade in difficult situations. The teaching, moreover, may be unintended. Teachers who do emphasize responsible work habits and the value of effort and achievement may, by that very emphasis, encourage students to practice these strategies of active nonlearning. Even responsible and ambitious graduates, then, may enter the workplace practiced and skilled in responding to difficult or uninteresting work situations with dissembling or evading.

The question, then, is whether those skills in fact transfer to the workplace. It is reasonable to *suspect* that they do. For one thing, when similar strategies successfully avert ego threat, strain, or confusion in a variety of situations, the tendency toward adoption of those strategies can be expected to grow habitual. It is also reasonable to expect that the longer a habitual strategy persists, the more deeply it is ingrained in the individual's repertoire and the more likely it is to be employed in subsequent situations. Further, it is likely that success generalizes: The strategy that has become habitual in a wide range of similar situations eventually may be employed in situations of decreasingly similar character.

It is particularly reasonable to hypothesize a variety of linkages between lesson strategies in the classroom and work strategies in early employment. For example:

> The longer defensive and nonproductive lesson strategies are employed in the school years, the more likely they are to surface in a new job, particularly in situations the individual finds stressful, threatening or confusing.

> The more habituated and persistent across classroom situations the defensive and nonproductive lesson strategies, the more strongly they will predict work strategies in early employment, despite differences in situated motivating factors.

> The earlier defensive lesson strategies are adopted in schooling and the more successfully they are practiced through schooling years, the more strongly they will predict nonproductive strategies in early employment.

In general, then, it is reasonable to hypothesize that early classroom learning strategies may help predict the individual's tendencies to engage, dissemble, or evade in difficult workplace situations, particularly in early employment. Such hypotheses are based on speculative interpretations, however. Considerable development is needed before they might serve even as sensitizing possibilities in research studies of classroom-workplace continuities and discontinuities. The claim that orientations to classroom lessons are in some ways precursors of orientations to work remains just that: a claim, neither supported nor refuted—indeed, not even addressed—by research data or other systematic evidence.

There is another reason why employers and students of work orientations might give their attention to work on classroom learning and nonlearning, however. For whether the tendency to employ these strategies transfers from one situation to another, or whether there is in fact a persistence of ego functioning, it is clear that dissembling and evading are common strategies not only in the classroom, but also in the workplace.

Evading and Dissembling in the Workplace

Our study of nonlearning neither supports nor questions the claim that contemporary schools are failing to train students in positive work habits and attitudes. Nor was it designed to address it. But our work does suggest that the claim is simplistic. For it appears that productive work strategies—at least in the classroom—relate in important part to the ways the work situation is structured, monitored, and evaluated.

Assignment confusion, for example, is endemic in classrooms, where children and teachers are expected to change focus and activity frequently. But it is also common in the workplace, particularly among newly hired employees, and among experienced workers who are asked to do more than rote and routine tasks. Indeed, the less rote and routine the task, the more likely is dissembling due to a lack of confidence in one's ability to match its demands.

Our work, then, raises the possibility that employers might look for the sources and precipitants of nonproductive work strategies not only in the schools, but also in the workplace. For example, it is often assumed that employers do their best to correct the mistakes of the schools; our work raises the possibility that in doing their best, employers may inadvertently encourage dissembling and evading on the job. Just as teachers, principals, and school boards may unintentionally encourage nonproductive strategies, so might job supervisors and the executives who help structure the work setting.

The examples presented in this paper suggest a few of the many ways supervisors and administrative policies can encourage the adoption and practice of nonproductive work strategies. Our data on schools raise the possibility that employers and workers may unintentionally collaborate to discourage productivity and performance on the job. Supervision and control, in particular, can encourage such habits, particularly if the ego processes underlying the nonproductivity are misdiagnosed. For supervision that might be most effective in encouraging the evader to accept the challenge of the task may precipitate those who dissemble into further dissembling and even on toward withdrawal and resignation.

From a more optimistic perspective, the capacity of the individual to learn to engage tasks more effectively in difficult situations suggests that dissembling and evading on the job—whatever their genesis—can be reversed by situational and interactional interventions. Although we have not yet addressed research specifically at such interventions, in our current work we are beginning to identify some teaching interventions that might encourage and allow the student to turn from evading and dissembling to more effective learning strategies.

It is possible, of course, that what we are learning about responses to task assignments and supervision in classroom settings is specific to the teacher-student relationship and of little relevance to the workplace. The history of ideas in social psychology and small group processes suggests otherwise, however. This level of inquiry has proven to be a robust traveller from setting to setting, and what we learn about task dissembling and evading in one setting could well inform us about the other.

REFERENCES

Adams, J. (1963). Towards understanding of inequity. *Journal of Abnormal and Social Psychology, 63*, 442–436.

Bell, D. (1973). *The coming of post-industrial society.* New York: Basic Books.

Campbell, J., & Pritchard, R. (1975). Motivation theory in industrial and organizational psychology. In M. Dunnette (Ed.), *Handbook of industrial and organizational psychology.* Chicago: Rand-McNally.

Carnoy, M. (1974). *Education as cultural imperialism.* New York: McKay.

Clark, B. (1962). *Educating the expert society.* San Francisco: Chandler.

Coleman, J., et al. (1966). *Equality of educational opportunity.* Washington, DC: United States Government Printing Office.

Collins, R. (1979). *The credential society: An historical sociology of education and stratification.* New York: Academic Press.

Covington, M. (1968). Promoting creative thinking in the classroom. In H. Klausmeier & G. O'Hearn (Eds.), *Research and development* (pp. 22–30). Madison, WI: Educational Research Services.

Crain, R. (1984). *The quality of American high school graduates: What personnel officers say and do about it.* Washington, DC: National Institute of Education.

Curtis, D. (1984, December 14). Tough new goals set for state high school. *San Francisco Chronicle.*

Gallimore, R., & Au, R. H-P. (1979). The competence/incompetence paradox in the education of minority children. *The Quarterly Newsletter of the Laboratory for Comparative Human Cognition, 1*, 32–37.

Gardner, D. (1983). *A nation at risk.* New York: Carnegie.

Haan, N. (1977). *Coping and defending: Processes of self-environment organization.* New York: Academic Press.

Hansen, D. (1986, December). *Sociocultural stress and lesson strategies: Families, classrooms and language-minority students.* Paper presented at American Anthropological Society meetings, Philadelphia.

Hansen, D., & Johnson, V. (1983). *Locating learning: The social contexts of second-language acquisition.* Washington, DC: National Institute of Education.

Herzberg, F. (1974). *Work and the nature of man.* Cleveland: World.

Hull, C. (1943). *Principles of behavior.* New York: Appleton-Century.

Hurn, C. (1978). *The limits and possibilities of schooling.* Boston: Allyn and Bacon.

Jencks, C. (1972). *Inequality: A reassessment of the effect of family and schooling in America.* New York: Basic Books.

Laws, J. L. (1978). Work motivation and work behavior of women: New perspectives. In J. Sherman & F. Denmark (Eds.), *The psychology of women: Future directions in research.* New York: Psychological Dimensions.

Lewin, K. (1935). *A dynamic theory of personality.* New York: McGraw-Hill.

Locke, E. (1970). Job satisfaction and job performance: A theoretical analysis. *Organizational Behavior and Human Performance, 5,* 484–500.

McGuire, E., & Lund, L. (1984). *The role of business in precollege education.* Washington, DC: The Conference Board.

Phillips, S. (1972). Participant structures and communicative competence: Warm Springs children in community and classrooms. In C. Cazden, V. John, & D. Hymes (Eds.), *Functions of language in the classroom.* New York: Teachers College Press.

Porter, L. (1964). *Organizational patterns of managerial job attitudes.* New York: American Foundation for Management Research.

Tolman, E. (1932). *Purposive behavior in animals and men.* New York: Appleton-Century-Crofts.

Vroom, V. (1964). *Work and motivation.* New York: Wiley.

5 Cultural Boundaries and Minority Youth Orientation Toward Work Preparation

John U. Ogbu
University of California, Berkeley

INTRODUCTION: THE PROBLEM

Transition from adolescence to adulthood in contemporary societies is generally recognized as a difficult and complex task for young people. One area of major concern is the youths' ability to join the labor force and function as productive members of their society. In the last three decades this problem has received increasing attention from both policymakers and researchers in the United States and other industrial societies (Betsey, Hollister, & Papgeorgiou, 1985; Jenkins, 1983) because of its growing magnitude.

In the United States the problem of youth unemployment has been getting worse since the late 1940s. As Hahn and Lerman report (1985), the youth (16–24 years-of-age) unemployment rate was more than double that of adults (25 years and over) between 1947 and 1957. The problem grew worse in the 1960s, increasing from 8.2% to over 10%, while adult unemployment rate averaged just about 3.5%. Yet the 1960s was a period of rapid economic growth. With the economic recession of the 1970s, youth employment prospects continued to worsen, so that the unemployment rate among teenagers averaged about 12.6% during the decade. In 1984 youth unemployment rose to about 24.5%, more than double the adult unemployment rate.

The unemployment rate is high for all American teenagers, but it is exceptionally high among minority teenagers, such as American Indians, black Americans, Mexican Americans and Puerto Rican Americans. Furthermore, the gap between white and black youths in unemployment rate has been widening since 1955. Among black youths, especially, the unemployment rate reached almost 50% in 1982. In 1984 it declined slightly to just under 43% whereas the unemployment rate for all teenagers declined to 18.9%. It should be noted that the increasing unemployment rate of minority youths occurred during the period when many intervention programs were initiated for the "disadvantaged" youths, i.e., since the 1960s (Ogbu, 1981a).

In this chapter I focus on black American youths. I first note some of the conventional explanations of youth unemployment problems, namely, the supply-side explanation and the demand-side explanation. I argue that the two sides of the problem are interrelated. The purpose of the chapter is, however, to shed some light on some puzzles in the study of the education of black youths: the paradox of high educational aspirations but low academic performance; the lack of the same strong correlation between SES and academic achievement that is found among white youths; the distinctive feature of black youths' "resistance" to schooling; and the distinctive features of the cultural differences that affect black children's schooling. Specifically, I argue that events which have happened and, to some extent, continue to happen to black Americans or the "collective problems" faced by blacks, have led them to make certain culturally patterned responses or "collective solutions". The latter are an important source of influence on black youths' perceptions of, and responses to, schooling, and thus distinguish their school experience from the school experience of white youths as well as from the school experience of other minority youths, particularly the school experience of immigrant minority youths.

SOME CONVENTIONAL EXPLANATIONS OF MINORITY YOUTH UNEMPLOYMENT

There is no agreement among researchers and policymakers as to whether the causes of minority youths' increasing unemployment problems lie primarily on the supply side or on the demand side of the labor market. Both sides are undoubtedly implicated. My own research suggests that some reciprocal effects exist between the two sides of the labor market forces, especially between minority youths' and minority people's employment opportunity structure on the one hand and preparation of minority youths for the labor market on the other (Ogbu 1974). This chapter focuses on such a reciprocal relationship, based partly on my longitudinal ethnographic study in Stockton, California.

Minority Youths' Education and Unemployment

The relationship between the education and unemployment of minority youths has at least two aspects. One is the possibility that the youths are not adequately prepared to enter and participate in the labor force. For instance, minority youths may not have graduated from high school or from other appropriate terminal educational institutions. Thus, a number of studies indicate that the unemployment difficulties of minority youths are partly due to inadequate education. These studies suggest that a greater proportion of black youths do not complete high school; they further show that the quality of education received by black youths is probably lower than the quality of education received by white youths. It appears that black youths do not read, write, or compute as well as white youths do, according to a nationwide test of basic skills administered to 17-year-olds (National Assessment of Educational Progress, 1976) Furthermore, some studies show that among black youths, those with education similar to white youths may do as well as the whites in the labor market and, in the inner city, it has been found that black youths with better academic records do better than their peers in the labor market.

But it has also been noted that these differences in educational attainment and quality of schooling do not satisfactorily explain the increasing gap in unemployment rates between black and white youths. One reason is that the unemployment gap has been rising even though the education gap has not been increasing. Moreover, correlational studies reveal contradictory results. Some studies show, for instance, that the relationship between education and employment status is weaker for black youths than for white youths. It is true that proportionately more black youths than white youths drop out of school; and it is true also that school dropouts have more difficulty getting jobs than high school graduates. But these observations do not explain the following pattern of events that occurred in October of 1982: Only 29.1% of black high school graduates were employed, compared to 66.5% of the whites; only 14.8% of black high school dropouts had jobs, compared to 42.9% of the whites; and a black high school graduate was more likely to be unemployed (58%) than a white high school dropout (36%). Even black college graduates fared less well in the labor market than white high school graduates: Among black college graduates 23.9% were unemployed, compared to 21.4% of white high school graduates (Children's Defense Fund, 1984). There is also ample evidence that historically black youths have fared less well than white youths in the labor market, just as black adults have fared less well than white adults, at any given level of educational attainment.

Nevertheless, it is more difficult for black youths who drop out of school to find and hold jobs with good wages. And proportionately more black youths do drop out of high school. Moreover, the quality of education received by black youths appears to be lower than that of the white youths, as, for example, indicated by the results of tests of basic skills. Thus, we can assume that to some degree many black youths come to the labor market educationally less prepared compared to white youths.

Class, Culture, and Minority Education

There are many competing explanations of the failure of black youths to obtain adequate education for labor force participation. I have summarized some of these explanations elsewhere (Ogbu 1978, 1984) Of particular interest here are those that emphasize socioeconomic backgrounds, the resistance of the working class, and the cultural differences.

Correlational Studies.   Correlational studies deal with the relationship between children's socioeconomic background factors and their school adjustment and performance. It is often assumed that lower-class children generally do less well in school because they lack the ability (i.e., do not have appropriate IQ test scores) or because their families do not know how to prepare them effectively for school adjustment and academic success. Using SES as a measure of class membership, most black youths are usually classified as belonging to the lower class, and their school adjustment problems and lower academic performance are attributed to their lower-class background (see Coleman et al., 1966).

But these correlational studies fail to explain why black youths do not perform like white youths of similar social class background. Consider, for example, a report on the test scores of black and white candidates taking the SAT test in the 1980–1981 season, as reported in the *New York Times* of October 24, 1982 (Slade, 1982). Black candidates from homes with annual incomes of $50,000 or more had a median verbal score of about the same level as white candidates from homes with average annual incomes of $13,000 to $18,000. Furthermore, black candidates from homes with average annual incomes of $50,000 or more had a median math score slightly below the median math score of white candidates from homes with average annual incomes of $6000 or less. Another example is reported by Kristen Anton, who studied the academic records and college admissions of some 4000 California high school graduates of 1975. She found that among blacks and chicanos, "children from affluent and well-educated families are not benefiting from their parents' achievement and, like children from poorer families, have trouble getting into college" (*Oakland Tribune,* Aug. 7, 1980, p. 1).

Still another example comes from a study of a Southeastern suburban elementary school located in an area where black households had higher educational attainment, better job status, and higher income than white households; yet, the academic achievement of black children lagged behind that of the whites (Stern, 1986). Specifically, the study found that in terms of socioeconomic status, about twice as many black adults as white adults held college degrees, and about one-and-a-quarter as many blacks as whites had high school diplomas; there were one-and-a-half times as many blacks as whites holding managerial and professional jobs, and black unemployment was almost the same as white unemployment; the average annual income of a black household was about 39.1% higher than the average annual income of a white household, a difference of about $10,000 per household in favor of blacks. "In sum," the study concludes, "the majority of black parents sending their children to (the) elementary school were of higher socioeconomic status than their white neighbors, to the extent that they had white neighbors." But in spite of the middle-class status and the affluence of their families, black children, who made up 80% of the school population, lagged behind their White peers in the school district in academic achievement. Thus, in 1980–81, the 3rd grade students at the elementary school scored at 2.6 grade equivalent level or about 30th percentile nationally, whereas the county or school district average was about 3.1 grade equivalent level. In the same year, the 5th grade students at the elementary school scored at 4.7 grade equivalent level or about 38th percentile nationally, whereas the school district average was 5.2.

Other studies point to similar lower performance of black students from various social class backgrounds when compared to their white counterparts (see Haskins, 1980; Jencks, 1972; Jensen, 1969, 1980; Oliver et al., 1985; U.S. District Court for Northern California, 1979; Wigdor & Garner, 1982). Data from a recent ethnographic study of a black high school in Washington, D.C. show clearly that middle-class as well as nonmiddle-class black students are not doing well in their courses (Fordham & Ogbu, 1986). It is thus evident that middle-class blacks are not making it in school like their white middle-class counterparts.

Class Resistance Studies.   Of late some studies have tried to explain black school performance as a consequence of class resistance. Resistance theory emphasizes the perceptions and responses of subordinate groups and, in the field of education, elements of opposition in their relationship to "the system," i.e., the educational system. The problem, according to the resistance theory, lies essentially in the conflict relationship between lower-class or working-class children, on the one hand, and the schools controlled by the middle class or the elites, on the other.

The theory of resistance in education was initially formulated and applied to working-class youths in Europe. Briefly, based on his ethnographic study of working-class youths in Britain, Willis (1977) postulated that working-class youths consciously reject the meaning and knowledge taught by the schools and turn to working-class adults as a source of materials for resistance and exclusion. That is, they repudiate the school by forming countercultures that eventually impede their school success and upward social mobility through employment in the more desirable sector of middle-class types of jobs.

The resistance theory sheds some light on the school behavior of some black children as one source of their poor school performance. Studies of American Indian and Mexican-American students at elementary and high school levels suggest that these students also manifest both resistance and opposition to school culture. Some studies (e.g., Erickson & Mohatt, 1982) show that the minority children consciously and unconsciously insist on retaining their own cultural beliefs and behaviors rather than accept school norms and practices that they certainly know to be the basis of teaching and learning. Moreover, not only are the minority children unwilling to adopt the standard procedures of the school and classroom, they sometimes band together in an organized opposition against the teacher (Foster, 1974; Philips, 1972, p. 376). And there is evidence that students who try to adopt the standard procedures of the classroom or who try to cross "cultural boundaries" may experience negative sanctions from their peers (Fordham & Ogbu, 1986; Petroni, 1970; Philips, 1972; Wax, 1970, 1971).

But the resistance of black/minority students cannot be equated with the resistance of white working-class youths for at least two reasons. One is that black youths do not consciously reject school learning and knowledge. Instead, black youths say emphatically that schooling is important and, even though they may say that the school kowledge is whiteman's knowledge and not theirs, they want to get an education in order to escape from poverty and other problems plaguing their ghetto community (Weis, 1985). In spite of this belief in education, though, many black students do not do well in school; and they fail to use education effectively to achieve upward social mobility or to move out of the ghetto. Indeed, the paradox is that black youths affirm education and schooling, desire to do well in school, but in actuality behave in ways that result in poor school performance. Black youths often express their contradictory behavior by their excessive tardiness, lack of serious attitudes toward their schoolwork, lack of serious effort or persistent effort to do schoolwork, excessive use of drugs among older students, and the like (Ogbu, 1974, 1977; Weis, 1985).

The second reason is that the resistance of Black youths is not caused primarily by their response to the regularities of the school and classroom, as was suggested by Weis (1985). She says that black youths behave the way they do because they understand the collective conditions of black people in America and because they know that they are receiving an inferior education that cannot improve their existence or status. She notes that it is primarily through their day-to-day interactions with the school and classroom regularities that they form their counter or oppositional culture, which, in turn, enables them to understand how the system works and learn to enact their contradictory behaviors. I doubt that black youths form their counter or oppositional culture mainly because of the way they are treated in school or because of classroom requirements. The data from the case study presented later in this chapter and from other studies suggest that black youths bring their opposition or resistance to standard practices and rules of the school from the community *and* that the resistance they learned as they grew up in the community developed in the course of the history of black Americans as a collective response to their treatment by white Americans.

Cultural Differences And Conflict Studies.   Anthropologists have been less concerned about the effect of social class differences on minority education and more about the effect of cultural differences broadly defined. In fact, it can be said that the main assumption underlying various anthropological explanations is that the problem is *caused* by cultural differences and cultural conflicts. Anthropologists claim that cultural conflicts occur in schooling when children with different cultural backgrounds attend school or are educated in a different culture, i.e., receive their education in a culturally different learning environment from the one familiar to them at home. In such a learning situation the children from the different backgrounds have difficulty acquiring the content and style of learning presupposed by the curriculum materials and teaching methods (Philips, 1976). Cultural conflicts occur when nonWestern children attend Western-type schools as well as when immigrant children, minority children, and lower-class children attend schools controlled by middle-class members of the dominant group in an urban industrial society like the United States (LaBelle, 1976).

The conflict may be in language and communication, cognition, social interaction, values, or in teaching and learning techniques. It is often assumed, if not asserted, that the conflicts in a particular domain of inquiry studied by a given investigator is *the cause* of the children's academic and/or social adjustment difficulties in school. For example, it has been claimed that Puerto Rican children living on the mainland experience learning difficulties because they do not interpret eye contact in the same way as do their white teachers (Byers & Byers, 1972); that Oglala Sioux Indian children's learning difficulties stem from the fact that they experience cultural miscommunication in their relationship with white teachers: The Indian children resist teachers' attempt to teach them because the structure of teacher-controlled exchange or communication is foreign and uncomfortable to them (Dumont, 1972); that Warm Springs Indian children in Oregon fail to learn successfully under white teachers because the rules that govern the use of speech in their community are different from those used or expected by white teachers (Philips, 1972); that native Hawaiian children do not learn to read unless teachers employ a talk story format or style that is indigenous to their culture (Au, 1980); and that black children do poorly in school because of conflict in learning style (Boykin, 1980, 1986).

There is no question that cultural differences and cultural conflicts are real and cause real difficulties in school learning for nonWestern children in Western-type schools, and for lower-class and minority children in the public schools in the United States (Gay & Cole, 1967; LaBelle, 1976; Lancy, 1983; Musgrove, 1953). But there is some reason to be skeptical about any generalization that the cause of persistent disproportionate school failure rates of black and similar minorities lies in conflicts in cognitive style, communication, social interaction, or techniques of teaching and learning. In the first place, the cultural conflict explanation appears to have been offered long before anthropologists carried out ethnographic research on schooling. Furthermore, proponents of the cultural conflict explanation do not explain why the posited conflicts do not adversely affect all minorities but only some (Ogbu, 1982 a, 1985). Why, for instance, do some minorities cross cultural/language boundaries and learn more or less successfully? And why do some other minorities with similar cultural and language differences have greater difficulty crossing cultural/language boundaries? By and large, the proponents of the cultural conflict explanation have yet to address the issue of variability in minority school performance.

Another difficulty with the cultural conflict explanation is that it lumps together all cultural differences, suggesting that they cause the same problems. But there appear to be different types of cultural differences that have different implications for schooling, as I try to show in the next section.

There I present a theoretical framework for understanding minority students' school orientation and its influence on school outcomes, as well as the community factors that shape the school orientation. My presentation focuses on one of three sources of sociocultural factors affecting the school performance of minority children. The other two are societal and school factors of which I have written extensively (see Ogbu, 1974, 1977, 1978, 1982b, 1986a, 1986b). My analysis here should, therefore, not be read as blaming the victim; nor should it be interpreted as absolving American society and the public schools of their responsibility to provide blacks and similar minorities with meaningful and effective education.

YOUTH ORIENTATION TOWARD SCHOOLING: A CULTURAL-ECOLOGICAL FRAMEWORK

We need a theoretical framework that will explain why black youths do not perform in school like white youths of similar social class background, why working class black youths seem to desire education but *resist* behaving in a manner conducive to school success, and why cultural conflicts as well as the teaching and learning problems they cause appear to be disproportionate and persistent among blacks and similar minorities but not among some other minorities. Furthermore, we need a framework that will shed some light on the phenomenon of high educational aspirations of black youths coupled with their low academic achievement. I am suggesting here such a framework, namely, a cultural-ecological framework.

Cultural-ecological framework embodies the reciprocal relationship between societal opportunities and rewards for education, on the one hand, *and,* on the other, the efforts expended by groups and individuals to pursue educational credentials for labor force participation and remuneration. One of its distinguishing features is the notion of a folk theory of success or getting ahead, i.e., people's *status mobility system* (LeVine, 1967). Members of a society or its segments tend to share a theory of getting ahead based on their past and present experiences. That is, they have a cultural knowledge and a belief system about how one gets ahead, however they define getting ahead. A status mobility system works if the folk beliefs supporting it are confirmed by actual experiences of members of the society or group. Thus, the folk system or status mobility system works when a large proportion of the people have, for example, found jobs and earned wages commensurate with their educational credentials. Such experiences constitute a social recognition of, and reward for, individual educational efforts. Such recognition and reward tend to generate and reinforce positive evaluation of educational pursuits, including efforts to maximize test scores. Cultural recognition and rewards also motivate parents and other childrearing agents to train children to behave in a manner that will maximize academic achievement. These orientations and behaviors are "cultural" in the sense that members of the society or its segment consciously or unconsciously come to perceive and respond to schooling in the manner believed to maximize school success and thereby increase their chances for employability and advancement on the job. These commonly held assumptions (or native theory) of how one gets ahead are the cognitive basis of parents' behaviors in training children as well as striving for self-advancement.

In a racially stratified society, the status mobility system or folk theory of success of the subordinate racial group, like black Americans, differs from the folk theory of success of the dominant group for at least three reasons. One is that there usually exist *a job ceiling* and other barriers that limit the access of the minorities to jobs, wages, and other societal benefits of formal education. A job ceiling consists of formal statutes and informal practices used by white Americans to limit the access of minorities to desirable occupations, to truncate their opportunities, and to channel narrowly the potential returns the minorities can expect from their education (Mickelson, 1984; Ogbu, 1978). A job ceiling is no mere construction of the minorities; it is real. Consider the case of AT & T that was settled in 1974 by the Equal Employment Practices Commission. The giant company had been saving about $362m a year by not paying black, Hispanic, and female employees what they would have earned on the basis of education and ability if they were white males (DeWare, 1978). Whites have used the job ceiling historically to prevent blacks from competing freely for desirable jobs and other rewards of education.

Second, white employers often required *additional qualification* from blacks besides school credentials when they applied for jobs or promotions. For example, in the past, white employers and supervisors required blacks seeking employment, promotion, or public office to "uncle tom" or assume the role of dependent, compliant client in a kind of patron-client relationship. I have suggested elsewhere (Ogbu, 1978, 1984) that this kind of treatment or expectation makes Blacks frustrated, bitter, and resentful; it forces them to search for alternative strategies for self-betterment and subsistence, and to fight continually against the system. All these responses, in turn, reinforce a divergent folk theory of making it.

A related development is that black Americans and similar minorities who face a persistent job ceiling tend to develop *an institutionalized discrimination perspective* or a belief that they cannot advance into the mainstream like the whites by merely adopting rules of behavior for achievement and the cultural practices that work for White people. As a result, the minorities spend a good deal of time and effort attacking such rules of behavior for achievement or such criteria of selection for jobs and other societal positions defined by white Americans. The folk theory of the minorities also includes some of the alternative strategies that are not necessarily approved by white people, as well as some alternative strategies of making it that may actually impede the chances of the minorities to make it through school and mainstream employment.

The job ceiling and the folk theory of getting ahead it generates affect the schooling of blacks and similar minorities adversely in a number of ways. In general, the job ceiling and the folk theory tend to discourage the minorities from working hard in school. This is partly because of a long history of unmet expectations which makes some members of the group become disillusioned and doubtful about the real value of schooling. In other words, *the way the minorities perceive the job ceiling against them as a group affects their individual perceptions of schooling and responses to schooling. Such a situation develops from a collective historical experience.* One can better understand this problem by comparing black and whites as Shack (1970) has suggested. He says that in the absence of a job ceiling among whites, they have been able to receive adequate payoffs for their educational efforts, i.e., the fact that white Americans have historically been able to find jobs and receive wages and promotions on the job proportional to their educational credentials and individual ability has enabled them to develop "effort optimism" toward schoolwork. This development is embodied in the white maxim, "If at first you don't succeed, try, try, again." Because of a job ceiling, blacks have had a contrary experience that has taught them that jobs, wages, and promotions are not necessarily based on educational credentials and individual ability and effort. Consequently, blacks have not developed the same kind of "effort optimism" as whites toward schoolwork. Rather the kind of attitude they developed as a consequence can be seen in the opposite maxim, "What's the use of trying" (see also Dollard, 1957; Frazier, 1940; Ogbu, 1974, 1977; Schulz, 1969). I suspect, therefore, that one consequence of the job ceiling is that blacks do not appear to have developed a strong academic tradition.

The job ceiling and folk theory of making it affect the schooling of black youths in other ways. One is that as Black children get older and become aware of their limited future opportunities for mainstream employment, they also become aware of some people in their communities who have made it through survival strategies and without good school credentials or mainstream jobs (Bouie, 1981; Ogbu, 1974). Their observations may lead them to divert their time and effort into nonacademic activities that may come to compete with schooling. Furthermore, the survival strategies may also promote attitudes and behaviors that are not compatible with school-required attitudes and behaviors (Ogbu, 1982a).

One may gain some idea about how black youths' perceptions of opportunity structure, particularly in the inner city, affect their orientation toward schooling from Dearich Hunter's article "My Turn," in *Newsweek,* August 18, 1980. Hunter is a 15-year-old high school student from Wilmington, Delaware, who has also lived in Brooklyn. In the article he describes several categories of inner-city black teenagers. The "rocks" are the majority who have given up all hope of making it in the mainstream economy by means of school credentials. Consequently, they have stopped trying to do well in school. They do not bother to look for work because not even their parents can find work. The "hard rocks," Hunter says, are "caught in a deadly, dead-end environment and can't see a way out, a life that becomes the fast life or incredibly boring—and death becomes the death that you see and get used to every day." The "ducks" are the few who still believe that they can make it by succeeding in school. The "ducks," unfortunately, often become the target of ridicule and rip-off by the "hard rocks." And a "hard rock" who tries to change, to become one of the "ducks," usually falls into the category of "junkies." For, often, those attempting to change find themselves abandoned and despised, eventually becoming drug addicts. Thus, we can see the job ceiling not only discourages blacks from developing a strong tradition of pursuit of academic success as a cultural norm, it also creates disillusionment that discourages black youth from maximizing their school efforts (Ogbu, 1983b; 1984b).

The situation is paradoxical, however, for when blacks are questioned directly they usually respond like white Americans, namely, that to get ahead one needs a good education. On the other hand, other evidence suggests that they do not really believe that they have an equal chance with white Americans to get ahead through education. One such evidence is the type of writing by Hunter (1980) cited earlier, as well as autobiographies. Another is that blacks tend to reject or attack both the criteria by which academic achievement is measured and also the use of qualifications or measures as criteria for employment in some situations. Furthermore, observations indicate that black youths do not work hard enough in school to get the education that will help them get ahead when they finish school. Still another evidence is that blacks tend to employ a variety of techniques, often through collective struggle, to remove, reduce, or circumvent the barriers in opportunity structure. Moreover, blacks, as noted earlier, have developed a variety of survival strategies to compensate for apparent lack of equal opportunity for equal and fair competition in mainstream economic and other institutions. Finally, there is increasing ethnographic evidence that some black students who try to do well in school experience both social and psychological pressures strong enough to discourage them, a matter I will take up in the next section.

This paradoxical situation means that it is difficult to correlate black youths' aspirations with their actual academic efforts and outcomes, and that it is difficult to explain their academic behaviors and outcomes merely in terms of cultural differences and cultural conflicts. How, then, does one explain the paradox? I suggest it is first necessary to understand that there are different kinds of minority status with different interpretations and acceptance of attitudes and behaviors associated with mainstream school learning. Black Americans represent one such type of minority status.

Involuntary Minority Status, Culture, and Resistance

I have suggested elsewhere that one important prerequisite for understanding the school performance differences among minority groups is to recognize that there are *different types of minority groups* (Ogbu 1978, 1983a, 1985a, 1987b), with *different types of cultural differences* (Ogbu 1980, 1982, 1985a), and with *different types of social or collective identities* (Ogbu 1981b, 1982, 1984, in press-a, in press-b). Black Americans, like American Indians, Mexican Americans in the Southwestern United States, and Native Hawaiians, are *involuntary minorities* or *castelike minorities*. In contrast to *immigrant minorities, involuntary minorities* were initially brought into the United States involuntarily through slavery, conquest, or colonization. Thereafter they were relegated to menial positions and denied true assimilation into mainstream society. In the case of Mexican Americans, those who later immigrated from Mexico were assigned the status of the original conquered group with whom they eventually came to share the same sense of peoplehood.

Involuntary minorities develop a cultural system characterized by a divergent folk theory of getting ahead, an oppositional or ambivalent cultural/language identity, an oppositional or ambivalent cultural frame of reference with emphasis on style or meaning rather than content, and a distrust for the dominant group and the institutions they control. Involuntary minorities develop this distinctive cultural system *after* they have been forced to assume their minority status through conquest, slavery, or colonization. I have already discussed black American folk theory, the job ceiling and other barriers that generated it.

Involuntary minorities develop oppositional cultural or social identity *after* they have been forced into their minority status. They do so in response to the discriminatory political, economic, social, and psychological treatment they experience at the hands of the dominant group. The treatment may include deliberate exclusion of the minorities from true assimilation or the reverse, forced assimilation (Castile & Kushner, 1981; DeVos, 1967, 1984; Spicer, 1966, 1971). The minorities also develop the oppositional identity because they realize that their treatment or oppression is collective and enduring. They tend to believe that they cannot expect to be treated like the whites regardless of their individual differences in ability, training, or education, differences in place of origin or residence, or differences in economic status or physical appearance. Furthermore, these minorities know that they cannot easily escape from their birth-ascribed membership in a subordinate and disparaged group by "passing" or by returning to "a homeland" like the immigrants (DeVos, 1984; Green, 1981).

New and reinterpretations of cultural forms, symbols, and behaviors begin to emerge *after* the minorities have become subordinated. These developments enable the minorities to cope with their subordination. The new cultural developments or ''secondary cultural differences'' (Ogbu,1982a) combine with the oppositional cultural identity to create cultural boundaries that are not easily crossed by the minorities. One of the main features of the secondary cultural differences or cultural coping mechanisms is *cultural inversion*, a tendency for the minorities to define certain forms of behavior, events, meanings, and symbols as *not appropriate* for them because these are characteristic of white Americans. At the same time the minorities define other forms of behaviors, events, meanings, and symbols (usually the opposite) as more appropriate for them because they are not characteristic of white Americans. Thus, the minorities consider certain attitudes and behaviors appropriate for themselves in opposition to the preferences and practices of white Americans or dominant-group members. *From the point of view of the minorities, cultural inversion results in the emergence and co-existence of two opposing cultural frames of reference or cultural ideals orienting behavior, one appropriate for the minority-group members, the other appropriate for white Americans.* The minorities' cultural frame of reference is emotionally charged because it is intimately related to their collective identity. Consequently minority-group members who try to behave like white Americans or who try to cross cultural boundaries, to ''act white'' in forbidden domains may face opposition both from their peer group members and from within, the latter because of ''affective dissonance'' (DeVos, 1984).

Oppositional identity and oppositional cultural frame of reference affect black youths' transition from school to work because they discourage the youths from adopting the rules of behavior for achievement and the cultural practices that enhance academic success which they consider ''white.'' More specifically, the oppositional process arising from cultural identity and cultural frame of reference interferes with the process of black youths' schooling because black youths tend to equate school learning with learning the white American cultural frame of reference and tend to equate following the standard practices and related activities that enhance social adjustment and academic success with acting white. And they interpret such school learning and behavior, consciously or unconsciously, as threatening to their own culture, identity, and language. For this reason, black youths face both social (peer) and psychological pressures if they try to adopt conventional classroom and school attitudes and behavior practices conducive to school success (see Fordham & Ogbu, 1986; Ogbu, 1983b). These pressures discourage bright black youths from adopting serious attitudes toward school and from working hard in school. The dilemma of black youths is that they have to choose between acting white (i.e., adopting appropriate attitudes and behaviors or school rules and standard practices that enhance academic success but that are perceived and interpreted by their peers as typical of white Americans and therefore negatively sanctioned) and acting black, (i.e., adopting attitudes and behavior practices that their peers consider appropriate for blacks but that are not necessarily conducive to school success).

There thus coexist in the black community two opposing cultural frames of reference, one appropriate for blacks; the other appropriate for Whites. From the point of view of the black cultural frame of reference, school learning—the adoption of attitudes and behaviors that enhance academic success—falls within the white cultural frame of reference. Therefore, it does not receive the kind of social and psychological support, albeit unconsciously, that blacks give to attitudes and behaviors within the black cultural frame of reference. Black children acquire the black cultural frame of reference as they grow up in their community; they also acquire the social and psychological evaluation and responses of blacks to the white cultural frame of reference, including the equation, albeit unconsciously, of school learning with the learning of white cultural frame reference. Therefore, when black children begin school they bring with them the potential for resistance, and the latter becomes manifest in the course of their school career as they get older and acquire more of their cultural frame of reference as well as encounter unpleasant experiences in school.

Finally, involuntary minorities distrust white Americans and the public schools they control. In the case of black Americans, there are many episodes throughout their history that appear to have left them with the feeling that white Americans and the public schools cannot be trusted (Ogbu,1985b). Inner-city blacks in particular do not trust the schools to provide their children with the right education. This distrust arises from perceptions of past and current treatment of black children by the schools as discriminatory, enduring, and more or less institutionalized. The discriminatory treatment is, of course, not merely a construction of the minorities; it has been documented in several studies and throughout the United States as well as throughout the history of black education (see Bond, 1966; Kluger, 1977; Ogbu, 1978; Weinberg, 1977). Not only are blacks skeptical that the public schools can educate their children adequately, they also do not readily accept school rules of behavior and standard practices, nor do they interpret them as white Americans do. I suggest that the distrust of white people and the public schools they control, as well as the skepticism of blacks over the appropriateness of the school rules and standard practices, probably make it even more difficult for black parents and community to teach their children effectively to accept, internalize, and follow the school rules and standard practices that lead to academic success. I also suggest that the distrust and skepticism probably make it more difficult for black children than for white and immigrant minority children, especially as black children get older, to accept, internalize, and follow the school rules and standard practices (Ogbu 1984a).

The cultural differences that black youths encounter in school are thus distinctive, communally based, and rooted in black people's responses to historical subordination by white Americans. School experience is important in their manifestation, but their historical and communal roots should be recognized, as should their role in boundary-maintenance. They are a part of the cultural curriculum that black children learn in the community as they grow up *qua* involuntary minority children. Elsewhere (Ogbu, 1988) I have also suggested that the features of the secondary cultural differences of black Americans and other involuntary minorities make the cultural differences the children of such minorities encounter in school different from the cultural differences encountered in school children of immigrant minorities and probably other nonmainstream people. Furthermore, the distinctive cultural differences of involuntary minorities (e.g., black youths) cause teaching and learning problems that are more persistent (partly because they are not well understood) than the cultural differences of other minorities.

In summary, the experience of black Americans as an involuntary minority group in the labor market and in the society of the United States in general has led them to evolve a cultural system with a folk theory of getting ahead which, in turn, has not led to the formation of a strong tradition of academic work or academic effort optimism. Their experience has led them to develop an identity system and a cultural frame of reference that encourage black youths to perceive and interpret school learning as a subtractive process, as a threat to their own sense of identity and security, and to develop distrust for white Americans and the public schools they control, making it difficult for black youths to accept, internalize, and follow school rules and standard practices conducive to school success. These "community forces," as I call them, which black children bring to school—a folk theory of getting ahead, an oppositional identity and cultural frame of reference, and a distrust of the system and those who control it— developed as a collective adaptation or response to the social realities of black people in America. They exist in the community and are learned by the children naturally in the course of their normal development. Black individuals vary in their degree of involvement in this collective adaptation; and segments of the black community may also vary in this respect.

To conclude this section I would like to address again the issue of class and education among contemporary black Americans. It is generally agreed that there is now a substantial middle class among blacks. This fact has led some to argue that the problem of low school performance is the problem of lower-class or "underclass" blacks, not that of the middle class. They further argue that middle-class blacks are now making it in school and society as do their middle-class white counterparts, while "underclass" blacks are not making it just as "underclass" whites are not making it. From this point of view, the analysis I proposed in this chapter is applicable to the black "underclass" and not to the black middle class (Bond, 1981; van den Berghe, 1980; Wilson, 1980). However, although these critics rightly point to the growing number of blacks in traditionally white middle-class jobs, the flight of middle-class blacks into the suburbs, and the increasing enrollment of middle-class black children in magnet and selective schools, suburban schools, and private schools, they do not present evidence to show that black children in such schools are performing as do their white peers. I do not deny that among blacks as among whites, middle-class children do better in school than lower-class or "underclass" children of the same racial group. But evidence shows that black middle-class children are not necessarily doing as well in school as their white middle-class counterparts nationally (Heller, Holzman, & Messick, 1982; Slade, 1982), in affluent suburbs (Fairfax County Public Schools, 1985; Montgomery County Public Schools, 1984; Stern, 1986) and in the inner city.

The assumption that middle-class black youths are doing as well in school as their white middle-class counterparts because blacks now have more opportunities to attain traditionally white middle-class jobs, earn high wages, live in white suburbs, and send their children to school outside the inner city, is based on a misunderstanding of racial stratification. The misunderstanding lies in interpretation of racial stratification as involving only instrumental barriers (e.g., a job ceiling) that relegate racial minorities to low socioeconomic status. Proponents of this instrumental interpretation assume that when the job ceiling and related barriers are relaxed or removed so that the minorities have more opportunities to achieve middle-class jobs, wages, and residence, then blacks will begin to behave like their white counterparts in school, on the job, and in general. But the change is not that simple or straightforward because there is yet another dimension of racial stratification, the expressive component, that is not a part of the changes on which the critics base their evaluation. The expressive component of racial stratification includes the oppositional cultural identity and cultural frame of reference discussed earlier. It is not only the proponents of instrumental interpretation who do not recognize the expressive components; policymakers and reformers also do not and, thus, never make them a part of their agenda for change. Nor do the expressive factors, the oppositional identity and cultural frame of reference, trust, etc., disappear simply because of increased opportunities for blacks to hold professional jobs, earn more money, live in white suburbs, and send their children to better schools and to schools outside the inner city. Those factors may help to some degree. But there is some evidence that black middle-class children outside inner-city schools continue to be affected by the burden of acting white, as well as evidence that blacks who have made it in school and are now situated in what were traditionally white positions in the corporate economy and mainstream institutions continue to be affected by the burden of acting white. That is, evidence suggests that even today the oppositional process or the expressive dimension of racial stratification persists and cuts across social class boundaries among black Americans (Ogbu, 1988; see also Baker, 1984; Campbell, 1982; Davis & Watson, 1983; Mitchell, 1982, 1983; Taylor, 1973).

What I would like to emphasize in concluding this section is, however, that the ultimate source of the community forces or cultural influence on black youths' school performance discussed in this chapter, both instrumental and expressive, lies in the job ceiling and other discriminatory treatment of black Americans by white Americans. The job ceiling and other discriminatory treatments shaped the perceptions and responses of blacks for many generations. The

cultural or community influences described in this section, including disillusionment, opposition, cultural conflicts, and distrust, do not, therefore, merely originate from the childrearing practices of black families; they do not originate
merely from black children's encounter with the schools, although how black
youths are treated by the schools is important. The family and peer groups are
also important in facilitating the development and manifestations of these community forces. In the case study that I describe next, I show how these community forces produce the paradox of high educational aspirations and low school
performance in a local community.

THE STOCKTON, CALIFORNIA, EXAMPLE

Background

I began the study reported here in 1968 with about 730 black, Chinese, Filippino,
Mexican-American, and white children from kindergarten through grade 12. The
ethnographic study covered a high school, a junior high that fed it, and an
elementary school serving the junior high school. Many school personnel in each
school, as well as in the school district, were interviewed. In the community, I
interviewed parents, other adults, and students. In addition to the interviews, I
collected quantitative as well as qualitative data about the community and the
schools. Although the initial study was concluded in 1970, I continued to update
through occasional field visits for specific events and through supervision of 4
doctoral dissertations by native Stocktonians who studied with me at Berkeley or
some nearby university.

Following the graduation from high school in 1981 of the children who were
in kindergarten when I began the study in 1968, I returned to Stockton in 1982 to
study the overall academic career of the entire sample and their transition from
school to work and adulthood. I was able to interview, or obtain data on, about
315 of the original sample. The study in 1982 included transition to labor force
because I had earlier studied the educational and occupational aspirations and
expectations of the older students and their parents. The following analysis is
primarily about black Americans, although I will occasionally compare them
with other groups.

The Paradox of High Aspirations and Low Accomplishments

Aspirations. In 1969, blacks in Stockton had relatively high aspirations for
both school credentials and future occupations. Most youths interviewed wanted
more education than their parents had attained. Indeed, when questioned specifically, black youths said they would not be content with their parents' levels of

education. Black teenagers also wanted better jobs than their parents had. Most of them said they did not want the unskilled and semiskilled jobs held by their parents. They wanted white-collar and professional jobs instead.

Accomplishments. Despite their declared intentions, there were indications in 1969 that the youths might not go as far as they said they would in school. In both classroom grades and in the results of state-mandated tests, the children were doing considerably worse than other ethnic groups (Ogbu, 1974, 1977). My initial doubt about black youths being able to achieve their educational goals was largely confirmed in the restudy in 1982. A large proportion of these youths did not graduate from high school. As for employment, their status in 1982 did not reflect their aspirations in 1969–70 (Ogbu, 1984b, 1986b). Many of them had not even succeeded in joining the labor force at all as they were unemployed, on welfare (in the case of females), or in jail (in the case of males). Of those who had died, some were reported to have died from auto accidents or in the commission of a crime. On the other hand, among the black youths gainfully employed, the proportion was smaller than those who graduated from high school. This was true for both males and females.

Apart from high unemployment, those employed held mostly menial jobs, i.e., unskilled and semiskilled jobs (Ogbu, 1986b). Looking back at the youths' aspirations in 1969, it was clear that in 1982 they had not come close to realizing what they wanted to achieve in the labor force. For example, although 42% desired professional, managerial, and supervisory jobs, very few were holding such positions in 1982. Many were holding the same kinds of jobs that their parents had, which they had said they did not want.

I now turn to examine the reasons for the poor school performance of black youths, the first setback in their transition from school to work. I will first briefly summarize how the wider community of Stockton and its schools contributed to the problem. Then I take up some of the immediate causes of the youths' relative lack of school success, namely, their failure to take their schoolwork seriously, to devote adequate time to doing their schoolwork, to work hard, and to persevere. My main objective in the following pages is to examine the historical, structural, and collective or community forces that caused the youths not to take their schoolwork seriously, not to devote enough time to their schoolwork, not to work hard, and not to persevere, in spite of their expressed desire to do well in school in order to get good jobs when they finished school.

Causes of the Paradox

Three sources of observable factors adversely affecting black students' school performance in Stockton are the treatment of blacks by the wider Stockton community, the treatment of blacks by the local schools, and the responses of blacks to their treatment by the schools and the city. I have described the societal and school treatment or forces in detail elsewhere (Ogbu 1974, 1977). Here I focus only on selected societal and school forces, on black responses, and on the effects of such responses on black youths' perceptions of and responses to schooling.

Residential Segregation and Inferior Education.   From the time that blacks first settled in Stockton in the mid19th century, they were segregated residentially and forced to live in less desirable neighborhoods. This was not because blacks could not afford to rent or buy homes in better neighborhoods. A study by two sociologists in a local university (Meer & Freedman, 1966) found that in 1963, black professionals, including teachers, lawyers, social workers, doctors, and others, had an average annual family income far above the city average and had more education than the average white Stocktonian. Yet the blacks were not allowed to buy homes in the more desirable parts of the city occupied by whites (see also Ogbu, 1977). During my initial study, both black and white informants said that it was still difficult for middle-class blacks to obtain mortgage loans if they wanted to buy homes in predominantly white neighborhoods (Ogbu, 1974, p. 44; 1977, p. 10).

Black education has historically been segregated and inferior to white education in Stockton partly because of residential segregation. Various devices were used to reinforce segregated neighborhoods (Ogbu, 1974, 1977, 1986b). For example, in 1969, local whites opposed a plan to integrate the public schools by busing, saying that they favored integration through neighborhood integration. But they also voted against Proposition 14 for open housing by a margin of 2 to 1. In 1970, they opposed a plan to build low-cost housing outside the central city and in predominantly white neighborhoods.

Further, to keep blacks and whites residentially segregated, local officials in charge of federal housing programs appeared to administer housing subsidies and related assistance in a manner that reinforced the residential segregation. The mechanism was to assign leased housing and subsidized apartment rentals to blacks and whites in separate parts of the city and county. The following excerpt from an interview with a black school administrator involved in a collective struggle against residential segregation reveals how blacks perceived and interpreted the action of the housing authority. In my interviews I found that such perceptions and interpretations cut across class among local blacks.

Informant: . . . The federal government sponsors all low-rent housing, you know. The federal government says you cannot discriminate in any way. If you go out and apply, your name goes—they put your name down. The next person comes, he applies, you know, his name goes down. We cannot discriminate in any way (according to the law). Now, in order to get around this thing (i.e., prohibition against discrimination), we have one housing authority in San Joaquin County. One! That takes care of San Joaquin County. We have homes in Tracy, Thornton,—

Anthropologist:	Lodi?
Informant:	No, not Lodi. We have the Camps, though, the Horney Lane Camp for migrant farmworkers. We have Conway Homes, Sierra Vista Homes, and we have the leased housing. One housing authority, though, one housing authority in charge of this whole thing. In order to keep black, white, middle class or middle or whatever you want to call it, what we do is, uh! we have offices for applicants at each location. Now, you know that no white (person) is going to go out there to Sierra Vista (to apply). It's strictly gonna be blacks. In Sierra Vista (apartments) we have out there 390 black families out of 400. Well, there's 35 white families out there. (But) in leased housing under the same program— this is where you have homes now (as opposed to apartments), you know, scattered throughout the district, uh! out of 600 homes, 560 (are) white.
Anthropologist:	Really?
Informant:	Yeah. But we have one housing authority. And what would be wrong with havin' all these applicants come to one central place and apply, so you (can) put the, you know, white, black, white, black, and then when you take the next vacancy occurring, here it is. "If you want this house, you get it. If you don't want it, we can't make you take it." You can go back to the bottom of the list. We could, we could do a lot by eliminating our ghettos out at Sierra Vista. But we don't want to hurt anybody, though, see? Whites don't want to live out there (in Sierra Vista). But they want this $50 a month rent (subsidy), though— to keep blacks out there. Let us have the scattered housin', the leased housin', the homes, so that nobody will know I'm on welfare and nobody'll know. We have some people livin' in (some) 150 (houses) which would cost—it would cost them $150 to $200 a month at fair market value, but they don't pay for that.
Anthropologist:	You know—
Informant:	Yeah! Fifty-four dollars.—Now, we have—there's 600 and some whites on leased housin'; we have a hundred blacks (on leased housing, too). Now, if you look at the map for the leased housin' (showing the map to the anthropologist), you know, we have a map (to monitor what is going on; that is, for) every house that is under leased housin' we have a little red flag. We also have, uh! a racial break-down of this. We have all the blacks in one little area. It's not scattered. The blacks are not scattered. They're in that one little group. These things—it's just terrible. We have created it.—our government, our agencies— HUD set up this program. Well, we want to integrate, and we're gonna scatter housin', put these families all out there. What do we do? Give these middle-class whites first options on these (leased) houses, give em $200 home for $54 a month. There has to be something wrong when you have 600 white families on leased housin', 35 (white) families in Sierra Vista (apartments). (Then) in Sierra Vista (apartments) you have 390 black families, in Sierra Vista, ghetto construction-type homes and 100 black families on leased housin'. And out of these 100, they're all bunched in one area.

Black Stocktonians believed that they were forced to live in inferior and segregated housing; they also believed that with inferior and segregated housing came inferior and segregated education. Therefore they constantly were engaged in a collective struggle against both until 1977 when the courts declared in their favor and ordered the public schools integrated. The collective struggle against segregated and inferior housing and education indicates the differential perceptions of blacks and whites in Stockton. These differences in perceptions and interpretations of how the system worked or should work contributed to the formation of the folk theory of getting ahead of local blacks, as well as to the evolution of a number of survival strategies among them.

Job Ceiling.   Blacks in Stockton have also faced a job ceiling since their arrival in the city (Ogbu, 1977). The first blacks worked as sailors, shopkeepers, cooks, carpenters, and muleteers in gold mines (California Fair Employment Practices Commission, 1972, p. 2). During the next 100 years blacks did not rise above menial tasks because of the job ceiling. Labor shortages during World War II resulted in a slight rise in their job status. They kept some of the gains after the war (Model City Correctional Project, 1967), but made no further advances. In fact, the situation probably grew worse, prompting school personnel writing about black school dropout in 1947 to comment that blacks were "at best greatly restricted in their field of occupational endeavors, and are subject for the most part, to less desirable social environment" (Stockton Unified School District, 1948). The job ceiling kept black occupational status remarkably low until the mid1960s (see Ogbu, 1977). For example, it required pressures from the black community for the school district to hire its first black teacher in 1947 (Sandelius, 1963). My interviews with several black college graduates revealed that many had been denied employment in the school district and other local establishments because their spouses were already employed and therefore they "did not need to work." I have summarized elsewhere (Ogbu 1974, 1977) the local job ceiling against blacks and the changes occurring during my study.

Inadequate Educational Payoff.   Because blacks were restricted to unskilled labor to a greater proportion than whites, they remained poorer. They were subject to seasonal and intermittent employment, and their unemployment rates always far exceeded those of white Stocktonians. In 1960 and 1970, for instance, the unemployment rates for black males were twice those of white males; the rates for black females were worse: more than five times those of white females (Ogbu, 1974, p. 49; South Stockton Parish, 1967). As a result of their unemployment and underemployment, blacks averaged only a $4279 median family income in 1960, compared to the city median family income of $6059; in 1970, the median family income of blacks was only $6021, compared to the city median family income of $9,533. The increasing gap in income was occurring in spite of a narrowing gap in education.

The lack of fit between black educational attainment and income was clearly evident when blacks and whites from the same census tracts were compared. Of the 13 census tracts for which data were available by race in 1969, there were 10 in which blacks had substantially higher median years of schooling than the general population. In 7 of the 10, blacks had substantially lower median family income in spite of their higher educational attainment. Only in the remaining 3 census tracts did the median family income of blacks exceed that of the total population, as did their educational attainment level. And in only one of the 13 census tracts did blacks have a higher median family income even though their median years of schooling was lower. This anomaly was due to the fact that black professionals, including morticians, building contractors, preachers, and the like, were concentrated in this census tract (over 45% blacks here reported being in this occupational category) (Ogbu 1977, p. 9).

Black Response to Job Ceiling and Related Barriers

What was the impact of the job ceiling on black folk theory of how to get ahead in Stockton? What was the impact on how local blacks actually strove to get ahead? And how did the latter affect their quest for education? It was not uncommon when questioned about what a person should do to get ahead in Stockton for a black informant to advise that the person should get as much education as possible. Black parents admonished their children to get an education so that they could get good jobs or get ahead. Thus, it seemed that black parents shared with white middle-class parents a folk theory that had as its injunction, "Go-to-school-to-get-a credential-to-get-a-job." But it would be an error to rely solely on black verbalization of what appeared to be an American societal ideal or their own desire.

One gains a closer understanding of black folk theory of making it in Stockton by observing what they actually did, as well as by listening to their remarks about problems of getting ahead at public meetings and in nonformal interviews. Data from these sources suggest that black Stocktonians did not believe that the white folk theory of success or the societal ideal worked for them to the same extent that it worked for whites. To shed some light on black folk theory I first discuss what they thought about their chances of success when they contested with whites in an economic system or other spheres controlled by white people; then I describe one example of how they attacked the rules or employment selection criteria established by whites. The latter action also indicated that blacks did not accept such rules for joining the labor force.

Stockton blacks believed that they had less chance of being hired for a job when they competed with whites with similar educational qualification and ability. For a black person to be hired he or she must be "twice as good" or "twice as qualified" as the white, according to informants. Because they saw their opportunities as more limited in comparison with opportunities for whites, blacks would agree with the following opinion expressed by a Mexican-American parent who said that although education was important for getting jobs, it was not enough. For a minority applicant to be hired over a white competitor, he said, "You (i.e., the minority applicant) have to show that you are better than the white man. And if you were going to take a test or if you are going to interview for a job, your test (score) has to be far better than the superior's—which is supposed to be the white man. Otherwise, they won't even look at you; they won't even hire you." Based on shared knowledge and experience, blacks believed that they would not make it or compete successfully with whites by simply adopting the rules of behavior for achievement that worked for white people (Ogbu, 1974).

Blacks went beyond believing that the same rules did not work for them; they worked to change those rules. Thus they tried to change the criteria and selection procedures for employment in the civil service and in the private sector which were established by white people. Let me describe one example.

White Stocktonians attributed the employment problems of blacks to their lack of "qualification." But in the case described here it is evident that whites and blacks (as well as Mexican Americans) perceived the qualification problem differently. Whites said that more blacks did not participate in the labor force above the job ceiling because they were not qualified; by this the whites meant that blacks competing for jobs with whites did not have the same kind of school credentials that whites had or that blacks did not do as well as the whites when they took employment tests. Blacks, on the other hand, claimed that many whites would not hire them even if they had the same school credentials or passed the job examinations. Throughout my fieldwork the problem of qualification was widely discussed and these discussions revealed the different views of whites and blacks. One event organized by the city council highlights the problem of qualification and the contrasting views.

Blacks and Mexican Americans complained at several city council meetings that they were systematically excluded from city jobs. They specifically claimed that requiring candidates for city jobs or for promotions to pass standardized examinations effectively excluded them because "the tests are biased." They pointed out that because of biased tests only 30 of the 886 city employees as of March 1969 were black, and the figure for Mexican Americans was not much higher.

Following repeated allegations, the city council set up a "workshop in equality" to study the problem. Testimonies and documents presented at the workshop showed that in 1935 the city charter stipulated that the examination for city jobs could be oral or written; during my study the examination was mainly written. Candidates, according to the charter, should be tested for physical or mental abilities, but the test should be job-related. To become eligible to take the test, candidates must have attained a certain level of formal education; and to be eligible for a job after the test, the person must score at least 95 on the revised edition of the Army Alpha test. There were later changes in the requirements. For example, the Army Alpha test was no longer used by 1969; a candidate was required only to obtain 70% on each part of the examination and in the overall test to qualify for a job; war veterans were to obtain 65%, or 60% if disabled.

City officials and some whites justified the test, saying that it provided an objective criterion for selecting the best qualified candidates for city jobs; that using test scores to select city employees eliminated politics from civil service, ensured that best qualified people were hired, and thus enabled the city to maintain a high standard of civil service. City officials acknowledged that minorities usually did less well on the test but this, according to them, was due to their "disadvantaged" cultural backgrounds, family patterns, or personality factors. They said that the city was willing to establish remedial programs to help the minorities prepare for the civil service test.

The minorities, on the other hand, argued that the test was culturally biased; that the required score of 95 to 110 points excluded the average person from getting city jobs; and that minorities who failed the test for some city jobs got the same jobs in the private sector and did them successfully. They alleged that both city and county officials used prisoners (many of them minorities) who had not taken civil service tests to do some city jobs that ordinary citizens did not get because they failed written examinations. The point to stress is that the dismal performance of minorities in employment appeared to provide an objective support for the job ceiling, thereby reinforcing white stereotypes concerning the intellectual inferiority of blacks. For their part, blacks saw the tests, as indeed they tended to see all tests given by whites, not as a device to enable them to get jobs or get ahead but rather as a device to keep them down; that is, as a device for excluding them from gainful employment, especially above the job ceiling. The impression gained from discussing the problem of qualification and testing with local black students, parents, and other community members was that they more or less went to take tests given by white people with a great deal of fear and suspicion.

In summary then, this attempt by blacks (and Mexican Americans) to change the selection criterion for employment reveals something of their folk theory of getting ahead. Stockton blacks believed that employment tests were designed to prevent them from getting jobs, that the tests were not necessarily a way to qualify for employment or to measure one's ability to do a job. Because of many personal encounters they appeared to have had with job discrimination and because of shared community knowledge of such discrimination, blacks developed a collective distrust of the rules or criteria for employment established by white Stocktonians, including employment tests.

Folk Theory of Getting Ahead and Schooling

One way in which the job ceiling and the folk theory of getting ahead it generates affected the schooling of black youths in Stockton appeared to be to discourage them from maintaining serious attitudes toward their schoolwork and from investing adequate time and effort to do their schoolwork. I have summarized my observations on these matters elsewhere (Ogbu, 1974): The children lack serious attitudes and effort toward their schoolwork at home, in the community, at school, and in the classroom. They manifest this orientation by their excessive absenteeism from school and classes, by their reluctance to do their schoolwork when present, by their disruptive behaviors in classroom and so on. Interviews showed that students' educational and job aspirations did not necessarily influence their school attitudes and behaviors. How did the job ceiling and the folk theory of success discourage serious academic attitudes, hard work and perseverance among black youths in Stockton?

I have already noted that when questioned directly, black parents and other adults said that to get a good job one needed a good education. But their various behaviors cast doubt on the seriousness of such a statement. Similarly, parents admonished children to get a good education in order to get a good job. They told them that they valued education and encouraged them to go to school and do well. But these same parents did not necessarily teach their children the appropriate or serious attitudes, the habits of hard work and perseverance conducive to school success. And it appeared that they failed to teach these attitudes and behaviors because black experience with the job ceiling did not permit them to develop these qualities as a part of their cultural tradition. That is, since blacks had not historically experienced good payoffs for their education due to the job ceiling, black families did not develop a tradition of inculcating in their children strong concrete academic beliefs, attitudes, and persevering effort conducive to school success. Nor did black youths encounter concrete experiences as they grew up that would promote such beliefs, attitudes, and effort. That is, because of the job ceiling, blacks historically did not get jobs and wages commensurate with their school credentials. And because of this collective experience, many black families did not have a history that provided concrete evidence that one needed an academic success or school credential to enter or maintain middle-class status, or that pursuing academic success actually brought benefits (e.g., jobs, wages, social recognition) that would outweigh the cost and risks involved (Mickelson, personal communication; Ogbu, 1974). In the absence of the concrete experience in their own lives and family histories, black parents did not seem to be oriented culturally toward showing their children how to succeed in school.

In addition, the parents appeared to be giving children contradictory messages about education. On the one hand they strongly admonished them to get a good education in order to get good jobs. On the other hand they also taught the children that Stockton did not reward blacks and whites equally for similar educational accomplishments. Black parents conveyed this message subtly and unknowingly when they talked about their own personal experience and frustrations due to the job ceiling and other barriers, or when they talked about similar experiences and frustrations of relatives, friends, neighbors, and other members of the black community. The actual texture of black parents' lives and the lives of other adults in the community with histories of unemployment, underemployment, and discrimination probably conveyed a powerful message that counteracted parents' verbal encouragement. Thus, although in the early years, black children accepted their parents' view of schooling, they would later begin to question it as they became aware of the job ceiling and related barriers.

Apart from the subtle messages conveyed unknowingly by parents, black children also learned about the job ceiling from older siblings, relatives, and other adult members of the community (Ogbu, 1974, p. 100). They further learned about it from observing public demonstrations for more jobs and better wages and from the mass media. There were several such demonstrations against local business establishments and against the school system itself a few years before my research began as well as during and after my study. From exposure to the community knowledge of, and beliefs about, the job ceiling from these sources, even very young black children would begin to form their image of the connection or lack of it between school success and black ability to get a good job; they would also begin to learn to believe, like older blacks around them, that their chances of getting ahead with school credentials were probably not as good as the chances of white children. As they got older and experienced personal frustrations in looking for part-time or summer jobs, their unfavorable perceptions and interpretations of their future opportunities relative to white opportunities would become even more crystalized and discouraging. Although their perceptions and interpretations might be incorrect, such as that employment opportunities were unlimited for their white peers, their unfavorable comparison would lead to increasing disillusionment about their future and to doubts about the value of education or schooling. As a consequence, the children increasingly ignored their parents' advice to take their schooling seriously, to work hard, and to do well in school.

The development of black adults' folk theory of getting ahead was partially revealed in my interviews with some 75 black and Mexican-American youths in 1969 and 1970. Many of these youths believed that white youths were more serious about schooling and did better in school because "they know that they have more opportunities in society." The informants said that blacks, in contrast, gave up too soon because they realized that they did not have the same opportunities after graduating from high school. As one student remarked, "The Anglos work harder because they believe that they are the head of every business in the U.S." This student went on to add that "most Anglos don't give minority groups any chance or opportunities" (Ogbu, 1974, pp. 93–97). On the whole, the youths, like their parents, held contradictory beliefs and attitudes about schooling and its connection or lack of it with future employment. But it appeared that what actually influenced their school behaviors were the concrete beliefs and attitudes derived from collective experience and perceptions of discrimination or exclusion due to the job ceiling.

Survival Strategies.

Attempts to change the rules for employment that blacks believed worked against them were but one way one gained some insight into the folk theory of success of Stockton blacks. Some further knowledge about the folk theory was gained by studying black survival strategies under the job ceiling. Some survival strategies such as collective struggle or civil rights activities and clientship or uncle tom-ming served to break, raise, or circumvent the job ceiling and enabled blacks to advance within the system controlled by whites. Examples of collective struggle were the boycotts of white businesses and white controlled public schools that took place between 1967 and 1973. Briefly, in 1967 the Black Unity Council, a civil rights organization, organized a boycott of major white business establish-ments, including J.C. Penney. Following this, the white businesses began to hire blacks as sales and clerical workers for the first time. In 1969, Ebony Young Men of Action issued a threat of boycott to several other major businesses that had hiring and promotion practices that adversely affected blacks and other minorities. In response, the businesses entered into negotiation and subsequently hired about 390 blacks and other minorities for the first time or in positions where minorities never worked before. Some firms also promoted minorities to positions they had never held. It should be noted that collective struggle includes any collective action against the system, such as the rioting against the school system which took place in 1969. Although not legitimated by white people, such events often increased the pool of jobs and other resources available to blacks. Thus, following the school riot in 1969 the School District increased the number of black and Mexican-American school administrators, teachers, and counselors and made other changes demanded by the minorities.

Clientship was another strategy that conveys important information about how blacks thought they could get ahead under the job ceiling. Blacks have learned through generations of experience that one key to advancement even in that part of the universe open to them is through white favoritism, not merit. They also learned that the way to solicit that favoritism is by playing some version of the old Uncle Tom role, being compliant, dependent and manipulative. Black Stock-tonians played this role in their relationship with individual whites and white organizations, and white controlled public institutions. They employed clientship to get ahead quite commonly. I have described some examples of this strategy elsewhere (Ogbu, 1981a). In general I found that both whites and blacks tended to assume that successful black persons and blacks in high social, political or occupational positions attained their positions by playing the uncle tom role.

Some blacks resorted to hustling and pimping as coping mechanisms. Hus-tling is a technique of exploiting interpersonal relationship for material and nonmaterial benefits. It appeared to be used primarily to exploit nonconventional resources or street economy. Some informants considered hustling a legitimate thing for blacks, arguing that whites were against it because it is a black thing.

They admired hustlers partly because a hustler worked for himself and not for white people. This attitude is reflected in the following excerpt from an interview with a high school student and his mother:

Student: They say that the hustler is no good.

Mother: But he's Black.

Student: This is good, you know; this is all he can survive. I am not going to say that this is all he can survive, but then, if he's got to survive somewhere, I mean, you know, toughest way, he's going to do it. And this is what I'm saying. He uses his head—.

Mother: *And not the whiteman's head.*

Student: See? And as far as I am concerned, this is good because he is doing his own thing. *He is not doing the whiteman's thing.*

Anthropologist: All right. Would you recommend that many of us go into pimp business? Or, hustling business? That is, Black business?

Student: Wait! If this is your own thing, do it.

Mother: In other words, he is saying, "If this is what you want to do, you do it, *and not do what the whiteman wants you to do.* Because this is the way it has been from generation to generation (i.e., the white man has been telling the Black man what to do).

In summary, from individual and collective encounters with the job ceiling and other barriers, black Stocktonians had come to believe that the way to get ahead was different for blacks and whites. In other words, they developed a folk theory of getting ahead that in important respects differed from the white folk theory and that included survival strategies not necessarily approved by white people. But the difference in the folk theory was not always evident from verbal replies to questions about how a black person got ahead because blacks tended to give the same responses as whites, namely, that the black should get a good education to enable him or her to get a good job. To learn what black Stocktonians really believed about getting ahead it was important to listen to their public and private discussions of the problems they faced when they tried to get a job, to get a loan to start a business or buy a home in a white neighborhood. Further knowledge about their theory of getting ahead came from observing their efforts to change the rules of the game established by white people and from observing their strategies used to satisfy their material and other wants outside the domain controlled by white people.

The survival strategies—collective struggle, clientship, hustling and the like—may increase access to conventional or mainstream resources, but they also appeared to promote some attitudes, skills, and behaviors that were not necessarily conducive to academic success. Although I did not conduct a systematic study of the effects of the survival strategies on schooling I will speculate on some possible contributions they may make to the academic problems of black youths, including the youths' lack of serious attitudes toward schoolwork, lack of sufficient time devoted to schoolwork, and lack of perseverance, as well as some tendency toward disruptive behavior in school.

However, before I proceed I want to state emphatically that I do not say or imply that the survival strategies are wrong, that they were not useful or needed, or that they were the main cause of black youths' school problems. What I want to say is that in addition to their valuable contributions to the survival and advancement of black Stocktonians under the job ceiling and related barriers, the survival strategies also contributed to the school problems of black children.

Collective struggle, whether legitimated by white Stocktonians as civil rights activities or not, tended to increase access to jobs, housing and other resources. This motivated some black youths to try to do well in school (Ogbu, 1974). But this strategy also appeared to teach other black youths that it was the system that caused high unemployment and other problems faced by black Stocktonians; and eventually the youths learned to blame the system, including the schools, for their own academic failures. Some youths used this to rationalize their low school performance when, in fact, they failed because they did not work hard. As noted earlier, in Stockton, black children had ample chance to witness collective struggle before, during, and after my initial fieldwork of 1968–1970. These struggles included the organized school boycott of 1967, and the boycotts of local white businesses the same year. Each resulted in employment gains for blacks and other minorities. There were also organized protest against discrimination in housing, as well as against school segregation.

Clientship or uncle tomming taught the children that favoritism, not merit, was the way to get ahead and that one gained white favoritism by being dependent and manipulative. The children learned manipulative attitudes and behaviors used by their parents in dealing with white people and white–controlled institutions. When the children applied these manipulative attitudes and behaviors to classroom and school situations they were often incompatible with demands of teaching and learning effectively. This resulted in difficulties and disruptions adverse to the children's academic performance.

Hustling and related strategies might also adversely influence black youths' academic attitudes and efforts in at least three ways. One is that the reverse work ethic of hustling insists that one should "make it without working," especially without working for white people. Something of this attitude was expressed in the excerpt from the interview with a high school youth and his mother. Other researchers (e.g., Foster, 1974) have reported that black children with hustling orientation feel that doing schoolwork is "doing the whiteman thing." Second, the assumption that every social interaction is an opportunity to manipulate other people for some personal exploitation might also adversely affect the youths' schoolwork. Some youths who played the manipulative game with teachers or classmates caused disruptions detrimental to learning in the classroom. Finally, although most black youths do not become hustlers or pimps (Perkins, 1975), for some youths hustling presents an attractive alternative strategy to schooling.

Conflict, Distrust, and Acceptance of School Rules and Standard Practices

One prominent feature of the relationship between blacks and whites as well as the relationship between blacks and the schools controlled by whites was conflict. The two racial groups in Stockton continually fought over education, jobs, crime and justice, housing, and the like. I have previously discussed black boycotts of white businesses because of discrimination in employment and promotion. I have also noted black complaints about treatment by the local federal housing authority. What I should add is that in 1963 when black families first moved into white neighborhoods, whites dumped garbage into the yards of the black families (Ogbu, 1977). Conflicts over education dated back to mid-19th century (1863–1879) when Stockton's public schools excluded blacks and Indians. After blacks won admission into the public schools through state legislative action, the conflicts shifted to issues of segregated and inferior education, and the segregation aspect was not settled until the courts decided in favor of blacks in 1977. During my research, conflicts over segregation and busing, as well as over school curriculum, textbooks, school meals, tracking, and disciplines often drew large attendance to school board meetings and other settings and were widely publicized by the mass media.

Stockton's blacks, like blacks in other parts of the United States, interpreted segregated and inferior education as a deliberate design by white people to prevent them from qualifying for more desirable jobs open to whites. One result of the persistent and pervasive conflict was that blacks developed a deep distrust for whites and the public schools controlled by the latter.

The conflicts between blacks and whites and the distrust growing out of the conflicts adversely affected the academic orientation and efforts of black youths. The children were fully aware of the conflicts and that their parents and other members of their community distrusted the schools and school officials: They learned about these matters from family discussions and community gossip; they observed them in public demonstrations; and they even participated in the demonstrations against the schools, for example, during the school boycott of 1967 and the high school riot of 1969. Even black school employees who were generally bitter and frustrated communicated the tension and distrust to black children in many subtle and sometimes not-so-subtle ways. It seems reasonable to assume that the conflict and distrust in these relationships might make it difficult for blacks to teach their children and for black children to acquire the beliefs, values, and attitudes that supported the schools as a societal institution. Specifically, my observations lead me to conclude that it was difficult for black children to accept, internalize, and follow school rules of behavior for achievement because of the conflicts and distrust between blacks and the schools.

I found that black children were generally skeptical about what schools taught them about American economy, polity, and history. Take, for example, an incident that took place at a public meeting following the high school riot in 1969. The hero of the occasion was a black youth who had been in and out of jail several times. He was holding a high school history textbook, *The Land Of The Free.* As he strolled from one end of the platform to the other he asked the teachers in the audience if they ever thought while teaching their classes made up of mostly minority students what the title of that book meant to blacks and other minorities in their classes. The youth was cheered loudly by students and parents alike as he repeated the question over and over. Apparently, not only did other black and minority students agree with him, but black and other minority parents also agreed that the school textbook did not represent social reality as they experienced it.

In sum, it seems that it would be difficult for black youths to accept and internalize school rules of behavior for achievement and to follow the standard school behaviors under the situation just described.

Oppositional Identity, Oppositional Cultural Frame of Reference and Schooling

I suggested earlier in this chapter (see also Ogbu, 1984) that in addition to the instrumental responses (e.g., folk theory of getting ahead, survival strategies, etc.) to the job ceiling and related barriers, black Americans have also forged a collective social identity in opposition to white identity, and a kind of oppositional cultural frame of reference. These phenomena were also present in Stockton. Other kinds of treatment contributed to promote the formation of oppositional process in the black-white relationship in Stockton. The most prominent, both historically and during my study, was the stereotyping of low-income blacks (which would include most blacks in the city) as "nontaxpayers" (Ogbu, 1974, pp. 49–57). Low-income blacks, like everyone else, of course, paid *property tax* (if they owned homes) and *income tax* (if they worked and earned wages) as well as *sales tax;* but they were often publicly referred to and treated as nontaxpayers. In local white folk classification, a taxpayer was one who not only paid taxes (property, income, sales), but also was publicly acknowledged to be a taxpayer. And to be so recognized a Stocktonian needed to live in a neighborhood (1) with few or no welfare recipients, particularly those receiving Aid to Families with Dependent Children or AFDC, and (2) with high assessed property values. The nontaxpayer was a person who lived in a neighborhood (1) with many welfare recipients, (2) with low assessed property values, or (3) was himself or herself a welfare recipient. Most blacks lived in such nontaxpayer neighborhoods and would, therefore, qualify as nontaxpayers. Generally nontaxpayers were regarded and treated as imcompetent and dependent people who made little or no useful contributions to the cost and responsibility of running city government and its social services, like education. Instead, taxpayers carried the financial burden and social responsibility. It was no wonder that since 1850, taxpayers in Stockton have from time to time protested against "high and unjust taxation" (Ogbu, 1974, pp. 51–52). There was an elaborate news coverage of the interests and opinions of taxpayers in the local newspapers, radios, and television; news about nontaxpayers also occurred frequently but it was usually about "their problems," with particular emphasis on nontaxpayers violations of the law, their family and other crises, and what taxpayers were doing to help or rehabilitate them.

Another characterization was that blacks as nontaxpayers "resisted assimilation" into the "mainstream culture." That is, they were unwilling or unable (if left on their own) to adopt values that would transform them into taxpayers and more "useful citizens." A survey of churchgoing taxpayers found that 62% thought that nontaxpayers "are stupid, narrow in their view, intolerant, lacking in imagination, lacking in curiosity, and lacking in ambition." Taxpayers also regarded them as "immoral and dirty," selfish and "not willing to improve their own situation" (Hutchinson, 1965, p. 4).

Still another characterization worth mentioning was that nontaxpayers were caught in a "welfare cycle" (Ogbu, 1974, pp. 181–182; 1977, p. 24). That is, white Stocktonians thought that black parents on welfare were not able to raise their children to be self-supporting adults. As a result their children grew up also to become welfare recipients who, in turn, raised their children to be welfare recipients. At the time of my initial study, taxpayers were considering various measures to break the welfare cycle. In one program, called *Happy Birthday,* black mothers would be trained from the time their children were born to raise their children like white middle-class parents raised their own children. It was reasoned that this would enable black children to succeed in school, get jobs as adults, and stay off welfare (Stockton Unified School District, 1968). One elementary school developed a program whereby white middle-class families "adopted" the families of its black and Mexican-American students. According to the school, the white families would help the children in the adopted families develop better attitudes about themselves and their chances of succeeding in school and later adult life.

The formation of black collective or social identity derived from their collective response to the job ceiling and related barriers as well as their responses to their denigration as a people and the denigration of their culture by white Stocktonians. Local blacks thought that their identity was not merely different but oppositional to white identity, and they perceived their culture to be in many respects opposite to white culture. Some informants said that the two racial groups lived in mutually exclusive worlds. Culturally there was a white way and there was also a black way. Some ways of behaving were acceptable and defended as black because they were not white, especially if white people condemned such behaviors. For example, as noted earlier in an interview excerpt, hustling was defended by a youth and his mother as the black thing that was being condemned by white people.

Black people were expected to stick together against whites, especially in times of crisis or when a black ran for a public office against a white. The latter was brought home to me in 1969 during the campaign for election to the County Board of Supervisors. I had taken my 74-year-old landlord to a meeting of Black Unity Council, not knowing that he was not acceptable to those in attendance because he campaigned for a white candidate running against a black. His presence changed the orientation of the meeting as speaker after speaker condemned him for being "the white people's nigger." After half an hour of such uncomplimentary speeches, my landlord left. When I returned from the meeting later we had a long discussion about black-white relationship in Stockton and during the discussion he explained why he campaigned for the white candidate even though *he was expected to support the black candidate.*

The elements of opposition—identity and cultural frame of reference—resulted more or less in an equation of school learning with the learning of white cultural frame of reference which, to some black youths was unacceptable. The school curriculum was equated with white culture; and doing schoolwork was interpreted by some as doing the whiteman thing, as acting on whiteman's orders rather than doing something by choice. It was also believed by some that school knowledge was whiteman's knowledge, not black knowledge, so that although it was necessary to learn it to get school credentials for employment, blacks could not really identify with it. This definition of school knowledge as white knowledge, not black, is illustrated in the following interview excerpt:

Mother:	Them books. Them books. Them lily white books. (Laughter). Them lily white books. Change them books. Do you know, let me tell you, John. Do you know what? You can go, say, the last year, two years, you can go to town, to J.C. Penney's, and so on and you can see Black statues in the windows. Show me a book that you can pick up and say it is about Black people.
Anthropologist:	Well, you can come to George Washington School and I will show you many of them.
Mother:	Yes, but that's just—Were they there last year?
Anthropologist:	I don't know but at least we are getting them now. We are getting them now in school.
Mother:	But you asked me what you can do to change?
Anthropologist:	Yea.
Mother:	But do every classroom have Black books? You can read that Cortez conquered—whatever Cortez conquered. You can read about that but you can never read nowhere where Black man conquered nothing. You know that's a lie. You know, you know they even told me Tarzan was Black and do you know I was grown with 7 kids before I ever learned that Tarzan was Black? He was raised and born in Africa.
Anthropologist:	Really?
Mother:	And when you look on television what do you see? Black Tarzan swinging on the tree?
Son:	I had a good point a while ago. . . .

Mother: But this is true. You don't see Black something. But you see they have, they got it now. But last year they didn't have them.

Son: This is what it is.

Mother: You got your point?

Son: No. This is not the point. Now, the whiteman like I say, will not teach you something where he will hurt himself. He is not going to do this. And he is not going to fully teach you. I mean—they might bring out a book that will tell you something about Black history but then he's going to kind of mix it up and make it sound as though the whiteman was good. Like they always said it was a whiteman that was there when a Blackman invented something, see? First, they said the whiteman invented something but it was the Blackman that was with him. But now they sort of change it saying the the Blackman invented it but it was the whiteman that helped him. See? It changed so that the whiteman always helped him. See? The whiteman always won.

Mother: Like the blackman never do nothing for himself.

Son: That's it.

Anthropologist: You know, as you go higher in your education you will find that there are some books written by Black people and that they didn't change things the way you have been pointing out.

Mother: But wait, John. Let me ask you something: Is it better for him (pointing to her son) to learn when he goes to college or learn before ever, before he flips off the ground? Why hang yourself before you know that if you kick long enough you're going to hang yourself? Why don't they reverse it? If they reverse it and let them know while they are in grammar school about the Black people? Why does he have to go to college to learn about his own culture?

Son: Why should I go to college to learn about my own culture? Yea!

Mother: He's bitter about the time he gets to college. He's a militant by the time he gets to college.

Son: Why did they keep, like I say, they kept you down for so long.

Mother: That is why we don't have many more Blacks and Mexican Americans going to college. Because by the time they make it to college they're so fed up and so, they've been kicked so long that by this time they say, "Forget it." They don't have patient to fight some of them. They don't have much face to fight harder.

Anthropologist: The Mexican Americans?

Mother: The Blacks.—I am more concerned about the Blacks. This is what I am saying about the Blacks. The Mexican Americans have got somewhere. They read about themselves, not everyday. But every now and then they read about what Mexicans did. They're going to read he fought some Indians somewhere, you know. He's going to read every now and then, But the black he never did read something. Just like they say, Columbus discovered America. He didn't. The Blackman did. He had nothing to do with it.

Son: He! Wait a minute, (He mentioned some other discovery which he claimed wasn't made by the whiteman, but it was mostly unclear).

Mother:	No. They just accidently stumbled upon it.
Son:	America was already here, it was already occupied by the Indians. How are they going to discover it?
Anthropologist:	Well, it is the same way they claimed to have discovered Africa. We were there all the time, you know?
Son:	How are they going to discover something?
Mother:	You see what I am saying is that they said that they discovered it while nobody discovered it but them before the Indians got here. But still they say the whiteman did it. Columbus did it but all the books that I have, I was grown up before I found out that it wasn't; it was a black man and he looked through that thing and they accidentally went into the place they called America while they were going somewhere else.
Son:	Have you ever noticed this, that when a Blackman wants something he asked a whiteman and the whiteman says no, he can't have it at the time. But then when the whiteman say this is what the black people need he give it to him, but then when a Black person asks for something that he wants they don't want to give it to him. Have you noticed that?

On the whole, it seemed that black youths (and some of their parents) regarded school learning as a one-way acculturation process. They did not appear to distinguish clearly between learning the school curriculum and practicing the standard attitudes and behaviors that enhance academic success for credentials from learning and practicing white attitudes and behaviors perceived as threatening or displacing their black identity, culture, and language. School knowledge (in various subject matters) was whiteman's knowledge, not black; doing schoolwork was carrying out tasks predetermined by the whites, and not a matter of self-determination by blacks. This contrasts with hustling where the black hustler is "doing his own things, not the whiteman's thing." Thus, the oppositional process makes it difficult to cross cultural boundaries in the educational context even by those who desire academic success and have the ability. Those who adopted the attitudes and behaviors enhancing school success and those who succeeded faced social pressures and accusations of "acting white," and being "uncle toms."

CONCLUSIONS

This chapter has examined the education of black youths, their preparation for labor force participation. It has shown that in a community like Stockton, California, black youths are not as successful in school as one might have expected, judging from their expressed desire to obtain a good education for future employment. A major reason—but not the only one—for their relative lack of school success is the type of cultural orientation they bring to school, i.e., the folk model or their understanding of "social reality," which embodies elements of their theory of how black people get ahead, their survival strategies under a job ceiling, distrust for white people and the schools they control, as well as oppositional identity and cultural frame of reference.

Black children's cultural orientation is different from white children's cultural orientation and it is different from the cultural orientation of minority children who are of immigrant origins (Ogbu,1984a,1987). But black cultural orientation is not different because black families use different childrearing practices in raising their children; it is not merely a product of black youths' encounter with the schools, although the schools play a part in shaping it. Rather, black children's cultural orientation is a product of the collective experience of black people in the labor force and other domains, past and present. It exists in the community and is learned in the community as the children grow up. It cuts across social class, although it is not shared to the same degree by everybody and by every group. But it appears to be a factor that accounts for the lack of similar correlations in comparative studies of blacks and whites. It also appears to differentiate the resistance of black youths from the resistance of white working-class youths to schooling.

REFERENCES

Au, K. H. (1980). Participant structure in a reading lesson with Hawaiian children: Analysis of a culturally appropriate instructional event. *Anthropology and Educational Quarterly, 11*, 91–115.

Baker, H. A. (1984). *Blues, ideology, and Afro-American literature: A vernacular theory.* Chicago: University of Chicago Press.

Betsey, C. L., Hollister, R. G., Jr., & Papgeorgeiou, M. R. (Eds.). (1985). *Youth employment and training programs: The YEDPA years.* Washington, DC: National Academy Press.

Bond, G. C. (1981). Social economic status and educational achievement: A review article. *Anthropology and Education Quarterly, 12*, 227–257.

Bond, H. M. (1966). *The education of the Negro in the American social order.* New York: Octagon.

Bouie, A. (1981). *Student perceptions of behavior and misbehavior in the school setting: An exploratory study and discussion.* San Francisco: Far West Laboratory for Educastional Research and Development.

Boykin, A. W. (1980). *Reading achievement and the sociocultural frame of reference of Afro-American Children.* Paper presented at NIE Roundtable Discussion on Issues in Urban Reading, No. 19–20, Washington, DC.

Boykin, A. W. (1986). The triple quandary and the schooling of Afro-American children. In U. Neisser (Ed.), *The school achievement of minority children: New perspectives* (pp. 57–92). Hillsdale, NJ: Lawrence Erlbaum Associates.

Byers, P., & Byers, H. (1972). Nonverbal communication and the education of children. In C. B. Cazden et al. (Eds.), *Functions of language in the classroom.* New York: Teachers College Press.

California, State of (1972). *City of Stockton: Affirmative action survey.* Sacramento: The California Fair Employment Practices Commission, unpublished manuscript.

Campbell, F. (1982). Black executives and corporate stress. *The New York Times Magazine,* Dec. 12, pp. 1–42.

Castile, G. P., & Kushner, G. (Eds.). (1981). *Persistent peoples: Cultural Enclaves in perspective.* Tuscon: University of Arizona Press.

Coleman, J. S., Campbell, E. R., Hobson, C. J., McPartland, J., Mood, A. M., Wernfield, F. D., & York, R. L. (1966). *Equality of educational opportunity.* Washington, D.C.: U.S. Government Printing Office.

Davis, G., & Watson, C. (1983). *Black life in corporate America: Swimming in the mainstream.* Garden City, NY: Anchor Books.

DeVos, G. A. (1967). Essential elements of caste: Psychological determinants in structural theory. In G. A. DeVos & H. Wagatsuma (Eds.), *Japan's invisible race: Caste in culture and personality* (pp. 332–384). Berkeley: University of California Press.

DeVos, G. A. (1984, April). *Ethnic persistence and role degradation: An illustration from Japan.* Prepared for the American-Soviet Symposium on Contemporary Ethnic Processes in the USA and the USS. New Orleans.

DeWare, H. (1978, July 4). Affirmative action plan at AT&T is permitted. *The Washington Post,* pp. A1, A7.

Dollard, J. (1957). *Caste and class in a southern town* (3rd ed.). Garden City, NY: Doubleday Anchor Books.

Dumont, R. B., Jr. (1972). Learning English and how to be silent: Studies in Sioux and Cherokee classrooms. In C. B. Cazden et al. (eds.), *Functions of language in the classroom.* New York: Teachers College Press.

Ellwood, D. T., & Wise, D. A. (1983). Youth Employment in the 1970s: The Changing Circumstances of Young People.'' In R. R. Nelson & F. Skidmore (Eds.), *American families and the economy: The high costs of living* (pp. 59–108). Washington, D.C.: National Academic Press.

Erickson, F., & Mohatt, J. (1982). Cultural organization of participant structure in two classrooms of Indian students. In G. D. Spindler (Ed.), *Doing the ethnography of schooling: Educational anthropology in action* (pp. 132–175). New York: Holt.

Fairfax County Public Schools (1985). *Annual report on the achievement and aspirations of minority students in the Fairfax County Public Schools, 1984–85.* Fairfax, VA: Fairfax County Public Schools, Office of Research.

Fordham, S., & Ogbu, J. U. (1986). Black students' school success: Coping with the ''burden of 'acting white'.'' *The Urban Review, 18*(3).

Foster, H. L. (1974). *Ribbin', jivin', and playin' the dozen: The unrecognized dilemma of inner-city schools.* Cambridge, MA: Ballinger.

Frazier, E. F. (1940). *Negro youth at the crossways: Their personality development in the middle states.* Washington, DC: American Council on Education.

Gay, J., & Cole, M. (1967). *The new mathematics and an old culture: A study of learning among the Kpelle of Liberia.* New York: Holt.

Green, V. (1981). Blacks in the United States: The creation of an enduring people. In G. P. Castile & G. Kushner (Eds.), *Persistent peoples: Cultural enclaves in perspective* (pp. 69–77). Tucson: University of Arizona Press.

Hahn, A., & Lerman, R. (1985). *What works in youth employment policy? How to help young workers from poor families.* Washington, DC: National Planning Association.

Haskins, R. (1980). *Race, family income, and school achievement.* Unpublished manuscript.

Heller, K. A., Holtzman, W. H., & Messick, S. (Eds.). (1982). *Placing children in special education: A strategy for equality.* Washington, DC: National Academy Press.

Hunter, D. (1980, August 18). Ducks vs. hard rocks. *Newsweek,* pp. 14–15.

Hutchinson, E. W. (1965). *Stockton church metropolitan strategies: Parish studies report.* Appendix A., Characteristics of the Stockton Metropolitan Area. Mimeo.

Jencks, C. (1972). *Inequality.* New York: Harper and Row.

Jenkins, R. (1983). *Lads, citizens, and ordinary kids: Working-class youth life-styles in Belfast.* London: Routledge and Kegan Paul.

Jensen, A. R. (1969). How much can we boost IQ and scholastic achievement? *Harvard Educational Review, 39,* 1–123.

Jensen, A. F. (1980). *Bias in mental testing.* New York: The Free Press.

Kluger, R. (1977). *Simple justice.* New York: Vintage Books.

LaBelle, T. J. (1976). Anthropological framework for studying education. In J. I. Roberts & S. Akinsanya (Eds.), *Schooling in the cultural context: Anthropological studies of education.* New York: David McKay.

Lancy, D. F. (1983). *Cross-cultural studies in cognition and mathematics.* New York: Academic Press.

LeVine, R. A. (1967). *Dreams and deeds: Achievement motivation in Nigeria.* Chicago: University of Chicago Press.

Meer, B., & Freeman, E. (1966). The impact of Negro neighbors on white homeowners. *Social Forces, 45,* 11–19.

Mickelson, R. A. (1984). *Race, class, and gender differences in adolescent academic achievement attitudes and behaviors.* Unpublished doctoral dissertation, Graduate School of Education, University of California, Los Angeles.

Mitchell, J. (1982). Reflections of a Black social scientist: Some struggles, some doubts, some hopes. *Harvard Educational Review, 51,* 27–44.

Mitchell, J. (1983). Visible, vulnerable, and viable: Emerging perspectives of a minority professor. In *Teaching minority students.* New Directions for Teaching and Learning, No. 16, pp. 17–28. San Francisco: Jossey-Bass.

Model City Correctional Project (MCCP) (1967). *Socioeconomic investigation of San Joaquin County* (Appendix Report). Stockton: Institute for the Study of Crime and Delinquency. Mimeo.

Montgomery County Public Schools. (1984). *A study of children at-risk: A report by the Citizen's Minority Relations Monitoring Committee on the Montgomery County (MD) Board of Education and the Montgomery Country Public Schools for 1982–83.*

Musgrove, R. (1953). Education and the culture concept. *Africa, 23,* 110–126.

National Assessment of Educational Progress. (1976). *Survey of functional literacy.* Washington, DC: Office of Education, Department of Health, Education, and Welfare, U.S. Government Printing Office.

Oakland Tribune. (1980, August 7). U. C. Study on minorities in college, p. 1.

Ogbu, J. U. (1974). *The next generation: An ethnography of education in an urban neighborhood.* New York: Academic Press.

Ogbu, J. U. (1977). Racial stratification and education: The case of Stockton, California. *ICRD Bulletin, 12,* 1–26.

Ogbu, J. U. (1978). *Minority education and caste: The American system in cross-cultural perspective.* New York: Academic Press.

Ogbu, J. U. (1980). *Cultural differences vs. alternative cultures: A critique of discontinuity hypothesis in classroom ethnographies.* Paper presented at a symposium, "Beyond the classroom." Annual Meeting, American Anthropological Association, Washington, DC.

Ogbu, J. U. (1981a, March) *Transition to adulthood: Minority youth, schooling, and employment in cross-cultural perspective.* Paper prepared for Round Table Discussion on the Human Dimension of International Development, Center for International Studies, Duke University, Durham, N.C.

Ogbu, J. U. (1981b, winter). Racial stratification and IQ. *Partnership.*

Ogbu, J. U. (1982a). Cultural discontinuities and schooling. *Anthropology and Education Quarterly, 13,* 290–307.

Ogbu, J. U. (1982b). Equalization of educational opportunity and racial/ethnic inequality. In P. G. Altbach, R. F. Arnove, & G. P. Kelly (Eds.), *Comparative education* (pp. 269–289). New York: Macmillan.

Ogbu, J. U. (1983a). Minority status and schooling in plural societies. *Comparative Education Review, 27.*

Ogbu, J. U. (1983b, October). *Crossing cultural boundaries: A comparative perspective on minority education.* Paper presented at a symposium, "Race, class, socialization and the life cycle," in honor of Professor Allison Davis, University of Chicago.

Ogbu, J. U. (1984a). *Understanding community forces affecting minority students' academic effort.* Prepared for the Achievement Council of California, Oakland, CA. Unpublished manuscript.

Ogbu, J. U. (1984b). Investment in Human Capital: Education and Development in Stockton, California, and Gwembe, Zambia. In J. Glazier et al. (Eds.), *Opportunity, constraint, and change: Essays in honor of Elizabeth Colson,* Special Issue: *Kroeber Anthropological Society Papers,* nos. 63 & 64 (pp. 104–114).

Ogbu, J. U. (1985). Research currents: Cultural-ecological influences on minority school learning. *Language Arts, 62,* 860–869.

Ogbu, J. U. (1985b). *Schooling in the ghetto: An ecological perspective on community and home influences.* ERIC ED 252 270.

Ogbu, J. U. (1986a). Class stratification, racial stratification, and schooling. In L. Weis (Ed.), *Race, class, and schooling* (pp. 6–35). Special Studies in Comparative Education. Comparative Education Center, State University of New York at Buffalo, #17.

Ogbu, J. U. (1986b). Stockton, California, revisited: Joining the labor force. In K. M. Borman & J. Reisman (Eds.), *Becoming a worker* (pp. 29–56). Norwood, NJ: Ablex.

Ogbu, J. U. (1987a). *Identity, cultural frame, and schooling among involuntary minorities.* Working Paper #4. Department of Anthropology, University of California, Berkeley.

Ogbu, J. U. (1987b). Variability in minority school performance: A problem in search of an explanation. In E. Jacob & C. E. Jordan (Eds.), *Explaining the school performance of minority children.* Special Issue, *Anthropology and Education Quarterly,* 18(3):312–334.

Ogbu, J. U. (1988). Diversity and equity in public education: Community forces and minority school adjustment and performance. In R. Haskins & D. McRae (Eds.), *Policies for America's public schools: Teachers, equity, and indicators* (pp. 127–170). Norwood, NJ: Ablex.

Oliver, M. L., Rodriquez, C., & Mickelson, R. A. (1985). Brown and black in white: The social adjustment and academic performance of chicano and black students in a predominately white university. *The Urban Review, 17*(2), 3–24.

Perkins, E. (1975). *Home is a dirty street: The social oppression of black children.* Chicago: Third World Press.

Petroni, F. A. (1970). "Uncle Toms": White stereotypes in the black movement. *Human Organization, 29,* 260–266.

Philips, S. U. (1972). Participant structure and communicative competence: Warm springs children in community and classroom. In C. Cazden, D. Hymes, & W. J. John (Eds.), *Functions of language in the classroom* (pp. 370–394). New York: Teachers College Press.

Philips, S. U. (1976). Commentary: Access to power and maintenance of ethnic identity as goals of multi-cultural education. In M. A. Gibson (Ed.), *Anthropological perspectives on multi-cultural education.* Special Issue, *Anthropology and Education Quarterly, 7,* 30–32.

Rees, H. E. (1968). *Deprivation and compensatory education: A consideration.* Boston: Houghton Mifflin.

Sandelius, S. E. (1963). *Employment of certificated personnel of ethnic minority groups in Stockton Unified School District, 1947–1962.* Unpublished M.S. thesis, University of the Pacific, Stockton, CA.

Schulz, D. A. (1969). *Coming up Black: Patterns of ghetto socialization.* Englewood Cliffs, NJ: Prentice-Hall.

Shack, W. A. (1970). *On Black American values in white America: Some perspectives on the cultural aspects of learning behavior and compensatory education.* Paper prepared for the Social Science Research Council: Subcommittee on Values and Compensatory Education, 1970–71.

Slade, M. (1982, October 24). Aptitude, intelligence or what? *New York Times*.

South Stockton Parish. (1967). *A statistical study of South and East Stockton*. Stockton, CA. Mimeo.

Spicer, E. H. (1966). The process of cultural enclavement in Middle America. *36th Congress of International de Americanistas, Seville, 3*, 267–279.

Spicer, E. H. (1971). Persistent cultural systems: A comparative study of identity systems that can adapt to contrasting environments. *Science, 174*, 795–800.

Stern, S. P. (1986, December). *School imposed limits on Black family "participation": A view from within and below*. Paper given at the 85th Annual Meeting of the American Anthropological Association, Philadelphia.

Stockton Unified School District. (1948). *Community survey: In-school youth*. Stockton, CA: Research Department, Stockton Unified School District.

Stockton Unified School District. (1968). *Assisting parents to promote school success: A proposal*. Stockton, CA: Federal Project Office, Stockton Unified School District.

Taylor, S. A. (1973). Some funny things happened on the way up. *Contact, 5*, 12–17.

U.S. District Court for Northern California. (1979). *Larry P. vs. Wilson Riles: Opinion*. San Francisco: Unpublished document #C-71-2270RFP.

van den Berghe, P. (1980). A review of minority education and caste. *Comparative Education Review, 24*, 126–130.

Wax, R. H. (1970). The warrior dropout. In H. M. Lindquist (Ed.), *Education and the process of cultural transmission* (pp. 207–217). Boston: Houghton Mifflin.

Wax, M. L. (1971). *Indian Americans: Unity and diversity*. Englewood Cliffs, NJ: Prentice-Hall.

Weinberg, M. (1977). *A chance to learn*. New York: Cambridge University Press.

Weis, L. (1985). *Between two worlds: Black students in an urban community college*. Boston: Routledge and Kegan Paul.

Wigdor, A. K., & Garner, W. R. (Eds.). (1982). *Ability testing: Uses, consequences, and controversies*. Washington, DC: The National Academy Press. Part 11: Documentation.

Willis, P. (1977). *Learning to labor: How working-class kids get working-class jobs*. New York: Columbia University Press.

Wilson, W. J. (1980, June). *Race, class, and public policy in education*. Lecture given at the National Institute of Education, Annual Vera Brown Memorial Seminar Series, Washington, DC.

6

Career Development in Adolescence: Theory, Measurement, and Longitudinal Findings

John O. Crites
Northwestern University

This chapter presents the conceptual, psychometric, and empirical contributions of a group of theoreticians and researchers gathered together under the leadership of Donald E. Super in the early 1950s at Columbia University. In response to a study conducted by Ginzberg, Ginsburg, Axelrad, and Herma (1951), which proposed a developmental schema of career decision making, but which was based on *cross-sectional* data, Super (1955) launched the Career Pattern Study, a 20-year *longitudinal* investigation of career maturity from the 9th grade to age 35, which initiated several other projects focused on age related trends in vocational behavior. Among these was that of the writer (Crites, 1964, 1973, 1974b, 1978), who constructed a standardized inventory to measure the various dimensions of career maturity and who traced changes in the scores on this instrument (*Career Maturity Inventory*–CMI) across the period from grade 7 to grade 12 for both males and females. In the discussion that follows, the "Concept of Career Development" is first explicated, then the "Measurement of Career Development" is presented, with a final section on the "Results from a Six-Year Longitudinal Study of Career Maturity."

CONCEPT OF CAREER DEVELOPMENT

As recently as 25 years ago, the concept of career development was largely unknown and unarticulated, although it had been presaged by Carter's (1940) conceptualization of the formation of career attitudes in adolescence and Super's (1942) use of life stages in the analysis of career exploration and establishment. The prevailing views of career behavior before the 1950s were almost entirely nondevelopmental. They characterized career decision making as a time-bound, largely static event that occurred at the crossroads of life, usually upon high school graduation, when an adolescent did a self-assessment, analyzed the world of work, and then decided what to do. Seldom was attention given to either the antecedents or the consequences of the choice act. It was assumed that career choice was a more or less isolated experience in the ongoing life activities of the individual, having little or no effect upon subsequent success and satisfaction. The choice act was epitomized in the guidance literature of the 1930s and 1940s by the picture of a young man or woman standing at the junction of several career paths, deliberating about which to follow. This cross-sectional, ahistorical concept of career choice dominated vocational psychology for several decades (Crites, 1965). It was institutionalized and perpetuated by the construction of a host of trait-and-factor measures (aptitudes, interests, and personality characteristics) designed to facilitate the process of "matching men with jobs" (Crites, 1969). This model of career choice and the practice of a rationalistically oriented career counseling built upon it (Hahn & McLean, 1955; Williamson, 1939) still persists; but it is in an incipient decline and is being challenged by contemporary emphasis upon career development.

These newer ways of conceptualizing the young person's relationship to school and work had their origins in a recognition of the developmental context within which the processes of learning and decision-making occur. What has been called "vocationalization" (Crites, 1958, 1969; Herr & Cramer, 1972) encompasses the experimental and temporal span of the childhood and adolescent years when the "greening" of the individual vis-a-vis the world of work takes place. Ginzberg, Ginsburg, Axelrad, and Herma (1951) were among the first (cf. Dysinger, 1950; Super, 1953) to observe that the choice of an occupation is a process, not simply a one-time event, which extends approximately from age 10 to age 21 and which progresses through differentiable periods of deliberation, culminating in a more or less satisfactory and satisfying compromise between personal needs and occupational realities. Super (1955, 1957) elaborated on this theory of career development and introduced the concept of career maturity to denote "the place reached on the continuum of vocational development from exploration to decline" (Super, 1955, p. 153). He hypothesized five dimensions along which career maturation proceeds: (1) Orientation to Vocational Choice; (2) Information and Planning; (3) Consistency of Vocational Choice; (4) Crystallization of Traits; and (5) Wisdom of Vocational Preferences. An individual's career maturity can be defined by his or her standing along these dimensions in relation to either chronological age and expected life stage or the behavior of others coping with the same developmental tasks (Super, Crites, Hummel, Moser, Overstreet, & Warnath, 1957).

To cast Super's dimensions of career maturity into a conceptual framework that has heuristic value for measurement and theory as well as subsumptive utility for comprehending research findings, Crites (1965, 1974a) proposed the model shown in Fig. 6.1. Its formal characteristics have been extrapolated from a schema suggested by Vernon (1950) for the structure of intelligence, in which the lowest level includes the operationally defined variables of interest; the intermediate level represents group and dimensional factors constituted from the interrelationships among the variables; and the highest level is defined by the common variance among the group factors. In other words, the model is a hierarchical one based on the assumption that the factorial structure of the correlations among variables and groups is oblique rather than orthogonal, although it has been hypothesized that developmentally the trend should be toward greater differentiation of specific behaviors (Crites, 1974a; Super & Overstreet, 1960). Substantively, the model has been derived from Super's (1955) original dimensions of career maturity, with certain emendations and additions. The Consistency of Career Choices and Realism of Career Choices groups are much as they were first proposed, with certain changes to reflect more recent thinking on the variables that contribute to these factors. The Career Choice Competencies and Career Choice Attitudes groups were formulated from Super's Orientation to Vocational Choice, Information and Planning, and certain components of the Crystallization of Traits dimensions, as well as from concepts proposed by other theorists (Crites, 1964).

An increasingly useful and meaningful distinction among the dimensions in the model of career maturity—one which was not previously explicitly articulated—is that between career choice *content* and career choice *process* (Crites, 1974a). The former encompasses the Consistency of Career Choices and Realism of Career Choices factors in the model (Fig. 6.1). To define these dimensions operationally, it is necessary to elicit a career choice from an individual. A question like, "Which occupation do you intend to enter when you have completed your schooling or training?" (Crites, 1969, p. 139) is asked, and, if the individual has made a choice, an occupational title, e.g., machinist, copywriter,

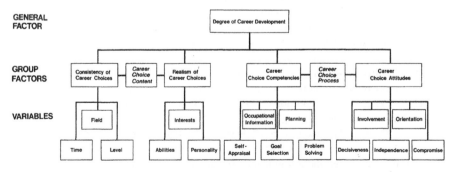

FIG. 6.1. A model of career maturity in adolescence.

or dancer, is given in response. This is career choice *content*. In contrast, career choice *process* refers to the variables involved in arriving at a declaration of career choice content. These variables include the group factors of Career Choice Competencies and Career Choice Attitudes in the model of career maturity. Obviously, they cannot be explicated without some confounding with career choice content, which accounts for a portion of the interrelationships between the variables. However, process and content are largely distinct, much as the assembly line and the product are.

CONTENT OF CAREER DEVELOPMENT

Consistency of Career Choices

In Fig. 6.1, the Group Factor termed Consistency of Career Choices refers to two criteria: First, if an adolescent has more than one career choice, then these should be consistent with respect to occupational Field and Level, in a classification schema that includes both these dimensions, such as Roe's (1956). For example, if an individual has two choices, physician and biochemist, they would be consistent, because they are in the same Field (science) and at the same Level (1– professional). However, if one choice is physician and another tool-and-die maker, which is in the technological Field and at Level 4 (skilled), then the choices would be inconsistent, the underlying assumption being that these inconsistent choices involve quite different interests and aptitudes. The principle is that consistent choices reflect greater awareness and knowledge of one's vocational capabilities. Other things being equal, the greater the consistency of an adolescents' career choices at any given time, the greater his or her career maturity.

It is important to note the qualification *at any given time*, because the consistency of career choices can obviously change from one period (or stage) of adolescent career development to another. Inconsistent choices can become more consistent, and consistent choices can become inconsistent. There is evidence (see below) that adolescent females often change what are consistent choices at the beginning of junior high school, i.e., the choices generally agree with each other and presumably with aptitudes and interests, to choices that conform more with the impact of the socialization and sex-stereotyping processes during the high school years. A disproportionate number change their career choices to typing, teaching, and homemaking, even though they may be qualified for other occupations. Conversely, inconsistent choices may change to consistent ones. In a study of the changes in career choices of 109 boys between grades 8 and 11, Holden (1961) found that the 8th graders who aspired to occupations considerably above their level of aptitude lowered the level of their career choices as 11th graders to agree more closely with aptitude. Thus, consistency of career choices through adolescence appears to be an exogenous variable that directly affects their realism—they become more or less realistic over time.

Realism of Career Choices

By realism of career choice is usually meant agreement of the individual's aptitudes, interests, and personality characteristics with those required by the chosen occupation. Minimal levels of both general and special aptitudes are necessary for successful performance of the job duties and tasks of most occupations (Super & Crites, 1962). Other things being equal (e.g., employment opportunities), the greater the match between the individual's aptitudes and those demanded by occupations, the greater the probable success in the chosen career (Lofquist & Dawis, 1969). Likewise, to the extent that an adolescent's vocational interests are similar to those of most members of an occupational group, the greater the chances of job satisfaction, the complementary outcome to success in the career adjustment process (Holland, 1985). On the other hand, despite the persistent assumption that personality characteristics (such as traits or needs) are related to career choice and adjustment (Lofquist & Dawis, 1969; Roe, 1956), the evidence is more clinical than empirical, with the exception of the facility to get along with others. There is considerable documentation (Henchley, 1981) that the single most critical factor in job *failure* is inability to get along with others. And, contrary to common misconception, it is not the aggressive employee who fails as much as it is the nonassertive one, who is passed over for promotion or released during an organizational down-sizing, because his or her competence is largely unknown to his or her supervisors.

That realism of career choice is related to not only job success and satisfaction after occupational entry, but also to career development during adolescence has been well-established (Crites, 1978; Westbrook, 1976a, 1976b). Also well-established is the *increasing* realism of career choice from early to late adolescence (Crites, 1969). As would be expected theoretically (Super & Overstreet, 1960), adolescents become more realistic in their career decision making as they mature. When they reach the end of adolescence, on the average, they are both more realistic and career-mature than they were at the beginning. Hence the relationship of Realism of Career Choices and Career Maturity (Attitudes and Competencies) shown in the hierarchical model in Fig. 6.1. The Career Choice Content factors (Consistency and Realism) are interrelated in the range .40–.60, as are the Career Choice Process variables, but the cross-correlations between Content and Process are in the .30s. These correlations represent the hierarchical structure in late adolescence, whereas it is less differentiated in early adolescence (Crites, 1978; Crites, Wallbrown, & Blaha, 1985), as the next section on career maturity brings out.

MEASUREMENT OF CAREER DEVELOPMENT

Theoretical Issues

Assessing career development not only poses the traditional psychometric problems encountered in the quantification of any variable, e.g., reliability and
validity, but also introduces conceptual and methodological issues that are pecu-
liar to the measurement of variables hypothesized to change over a period of
time. More specifically, these include the following:

- necessary conditions for measuring a developmental variable,
- appropriate psychometric paradigm for constructing indices of development,
- test construction methodology best suited for developmental assessment
  devices.

A discussion of these issues and of proposed resolutions of them provides a
background against which the specific features of appropriate measures can be
described.

Implicit in the concept of career development is the assumption that vocational behaviors mature over time in a systematic fashion. Ginzberg et al. (1951,
p. 186) specify that the process of career decision making is "largely irreversible," and Super and Overstreet (1960) state that it is characterized by increasing
goal-directedness, realism, and independence. In early work on the measurement
of career development, it was assumed that the implication of this conceptual
model was a linear (or at least monotonic) process of change in vocational
behaviors over time. In other words, the constraint was introduced that, if the
trends were not either linear or monotonic, they could not be considered as
developmental. Recent theory and research have seriously questioned this assumption, however, and have occasioned a revision of it. Baltes and Goulet
(1970, p. 10) observe that: "The only major criterion that seems necessary to
define developmental change is whether there exists a systematic age-functional
relationship (Kessen, 1960; Spiker, 1966) from birth to death, whatever the
shape of this relationship (linear, nonlinear, increasing, decreasing, U-shaped,
inverted U-shaped, etc.) may be." There appears good reason, therefore, to
adopt a less restrictive definition of developmental phenomena for at least some
purposes.

The obvious measurement model to fulfill this condition would be the age-
scale methodology of test construction used in the Stanford-Binet, in which items
are selected and allocated to age groupings according to the criterion of percent
passing at each successive level. This procedure has the advantage of including
only items that are age-related; however, it has the disadvantage of lack of
comparability of scores and dispersions at different age levels (Crites, 1961).

The alternative point-scale model, which measures the same behaviors with fixed variance regardless of age, exemplified by the Wechsler Adult Intelligence Scale, avoids this problem but generates another: the typical low validity of rationally derived scoring keys. Instruments constructed by this test methodology are not necessarily related to time or any other variable. A possible solution to this dilemma can be found in combining certain features of age-scales and point-scales into a composite measurement model. According to Crites (1961):

> From the age-scale this model incorporates a scoring key derived from item responses which differentiate between older and younger age groups within a given vocational life stage. . . . From the point-scale the proposed model follows the practice of constructing norms for each age level rather than using quotients based upon age ratios. In other words, an individual's peer group, not his [or her] age, is the reference point for evaluating his [or her] career maturity (p. 258).

Using this model, a scale can be constructed in which the items are not only related to time but also comparable from one unit of time to another (Crites, 1974a).

Still another problem remains, however, in the assessment of career development: How can a measure be constructed that is not only empirically related to time but also composed of theoretically meaningful item content? Not infrequently, inventories or tests that are developed empirically through the differentiation of criterion groups, such as the Minnesota Multiphasic Personality Inventory (MMPI) or the Strong Vocational Interest Blank (SVIB), include items that make little psychological sense. Thus, some MMPI items, such as ''I think Washington was greater than Lincoln,'' are empirically valid but theoretically barren. To attain both empirical and theoretical usefulness in a measure of career development, it is necessary to combine the rational definition of item content with the empirical derivation of the scoring key (Crites, 1961, 1965, 1974a). The procedure to follow to achieve this combination is:

1. Write items that are theoretically relevant to the construct of career maturity (see Fig. 6.1) and also linguistically representative of the verbal vocational behavior of adolescents.

2. Select items as indices of career maturity that differentiate among age and grade levels in adolescence in a systematic way.

3. Conduct research on the psychometric characteristics of the selected items. These characteristics include internal cosistency, response bias, stability, and validity.

The product of this combined rational-empirical test methodology is a measure of career development that has both psychological salience and psychometric significance.

Construction of the Career Maturity Inventory

In constructing the Career Maturity Inventory (CMI), every effort has been made to follow these desiderata for measuring career development. The combined rational-empirical test methodology has been used throughout as a measurement model for designing and developing the CMI. How this model has been applied generally in formulating a blueprint for the CMI is discussed with reference to:

- accumulating a universe of item content,
- conceptualizing a sampling plan for data collection, and
- defining a psychometric terminology that is consistent with theoretical concept.

The point of departure for constituting a universe of item content for the CMI was an enumeration of the central concepts in contemporary career development theory (Crites, 1964) and their synthesis into a model of career maturity (Fig. 6.1). Because operational definitions for the content dimensions of consistency and realism in career choice were already available (Crites, 1969; Super, 1955), the CMI was conceived to measure the process dimension subsumed by the Career Choice Competencies and Career Choice Attitudes group factors. Content for the multiple-choice items of the Competence Test was developed in two ways: First, item stems were written to describe realistic problems, plans, or jobs of hypothetical persons. Subject matter was drawn from counseling case records, personal experiences, biographies, occupational information pamphlets, and other real-life sources. Second, item alternatives were based upon the responses of groups of students to open-ended forms of the item stems (cf. Cook, 1951, 1958). The participating groups (average N = 30) were students in grades 7 through 12 in the Cedar Rapids, Iowa, school system. The students' responses were classified and edited to create the experimental form of the Competence Test. Similarly, item content for the Attitude Scale has been taken from everyday situations. A pool of approximately 1000 items was accumulated from attitudinal statements made by clients in the course of vocational counseling over a period of 5 years. These verbalizations were recorded on magnetic tape or in casenotes and edited for inclusion in the CMI. In short, the principle applied in collecting item content for both the Competence Test and the Attitude Scale of the CMI has been to make it as realistic as possible, consistent with the theoretical definitions of the variables in the model of career maturity (Fig. 6.1).

The sampling plan for collecting standardization and scoring-key data on the CMI evolved from a combination of cross-sectional and longitudinal designs for studies of developmental phenomena (Crites, 1974a). Figure 6.2 shows the sampling plan that was used across grades 5 through 12 (and the corresponding age groupings from 11–5 to 17–6) for the CMI Attitude Scale. Subjects were first tested cross-sectionally within the age/grade levels at the same time. They

148

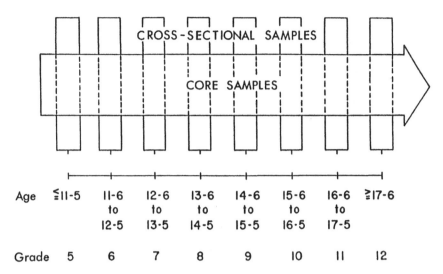

FIG. 6.2. Sampling plan for collecting data on the CMI attitude scale.

were then retested each succeeding year until the original 5th grade students (11–5 age group) were in the 12th grade. The Core samples are defined, therefore, as those students who were tested on consecutive occasions from the time data collection began until they were graduated from high school. This combined cross-sectional/longitudinal design has distinct advantages over either the cross-sectional or the longitudinal methods of collecting developmental data (Crites, 1974a); but it has an obvious disadvantage—it takes time. To shorten the period over which data must be collected before longitudinal analyses can be made, a new design was formulated for collecting data for the CMI Competence Test. Based on a model proposed by Schaie (1965, 1970), it constructs a composite longitudinal gradient from observations at only two points in time, given empirical confirmation of one assumption. Grades 5 through 12 can be tested, for example, and then retested 1 year later. The means on test and retest at each grade level can be compared statistically. If they do not differ significantly, it can be assumed that the samples are from the same population. They can then be combined, as indicated in Fig. 6.3, to form a composite longitudinal gradient.

Using samples from the longitudinal data collected on the Attitude Scale, Form A-1, Meade (1974) empirically tested the feasibility of constructing a composite longitudinal gradient. He randomly selected 150 students tested in 1964 and 1965 and combined them, as shown by the interlocking design in Fig. 6.3, into a composite longitudinal gradient. The latter was next compared with the actual longitudinal gradient, based on 150 students who had been repeatedly tested with the Attitude Scale, Form A-1, from grade 7 through grade 12. Statistical analysis of these data, with sufficient power to detect 2 raw score point

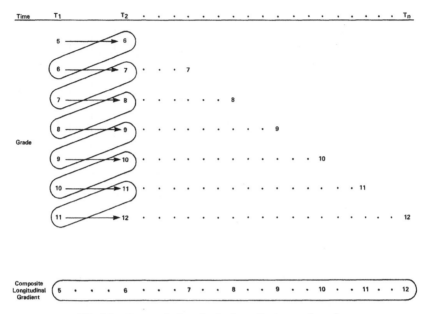

FIG. 6.3. Composite longitudinal gradient sampling plan.

differences between means, yielded significant deviations ($p<.01$) in the curves at the 10th and 12th grade levels. However, these differences (1.42 and 1.45 respectively) were relatively small as compared with the average yearly increases (2 raw score points). Moreover, a further trend test on the same data indicated that they were both linear. In other words, essentially the same conclusion, with one possible exception, about the maturation of career attitudes would have been drawn from the composite gradient as from the actual longitudinal gradient. The exception, contingent upon further confirmation, is that the differences between the curves for grade 10 and grade 12 may be psychologically expected ones (Rathburn, 1973), but if they are not, then the composite gradient has much to recommend it. Plans are to test it further, in research on the Competence Test as well as the new Attitude Scale, Counseling Form B.

More recent research has focused upon the fitting of the Model of Career Maturity depicted in Fig. 6.1 to empirical data. Using data from a rural sample of 312 9th graders from central North Carolina and 200 vocational-technical students from the same region, Westbrook, Cutts, Madison, and Arcia (1980) attempted to test the Model, using a principal-axes method of factor analysis, which *cannot* yield an hierarchical structure. In other words, they used an inappropriate statistical technique to test the Model, and not surprisingly found no support for it. In a reanalysis of *their* data with Wherry's (1984) hierarchical method of factor analysis, which *is* appropriate for testing the Model, Crites,

Wallbrown, and Blaha (1985) found the expected structure. Wallbrown, Silling, and Crites (1986) then replicated these results on the national normative sample for the Career Maturity Inventory from grade 6 through grade 11. The data supported not only the hierarchical structure of career maturity indicated in Fig. 6.1, but also the hypothesized developmental trend from less to more differentiation during adolescence. It can only be concluded that adolescents do mature in their attitudes and competencies in making career choices. But, this conclusion is based upon cross-sectional data. In the following section, longitudinal findings are reported that are corroborative and that also reveal highly significant gender differences in the career development of adolescents.

RESULTS FROM A SIX-YEAR LONGITUDINAL STUDY OF CAREER MATURITY

The Rathburn (1973) study utilized longitudinal data collected with the original Attitude Scale (Form A-1), following the sampling plan shown in Fig. 6.1, which was a combined cross/cohort-sequential design (Schaie, 1965). In the academic year 1961–62, all of the students in the junior and senior high schools of Cedar Rapids, Iowa, were administered the Attitude Scale and were retested each subsequent spring, on or about May 1st, so that by 1969 scores on approximately 10,000 students had been generated. Because the testing was cross-sectional as well as longitudinal, the data could be cast into the schema presented in Table 6.1. It makes possible a variety of statistical analyses that cannot otherwise be conducted on just cross-sectional *or* longitudinal data. Among these are analyses of (1) behavioral changes over time *within* a cohort, (2) differences *between* cohorts in behavioral changes, and (3) interaction of cohorts with time, which, if significant, might indicate that either behavioral changes occur at varying rates in different cohorts or there is a confounding with environmental change.

To pursue these analyses with the cross-sectional and longitudinal data on the Attitude Scale, samples of 100 males and 100 females were randomly selected from the 461 students on whom scores were available for every year between the 7th and 12th grades. That is, for each student there were 6 repeated measures for the period between grades 7 and 12 (see Table 6.2). A multistage statistical analysis of these data was performed, the first phase being an ANOVA of grade and sex to determine any possible differences in career attitudes on these two variables. The F tests for both were significant at the .01 level. Next, trend analyses for males and females separately across grades were conducted, the purpose being to test whether or not the curves in career attitude maturity were increasing linear functions of time. For the males, the linear and quadratic components were significant at the .01 level; and for females, these components plus the cubic were significant at the same level. It was concluded that for both

TABLE 6.1
Schema for Research Designs Corresponding to Schaie's General Model
of Developmental Research [a],[b]

Cohort	Time of Measurement														
Year of Birth	'56	'57	'58	'59	'60	'61	'62	'63	'64	'65	'66	'67	'68	'69	'70
1946						15									
1947						14	15								
1948						13	14	15							
1949						12	13	14	15						
1950	6	7	8	9	10	11	12	13	14	15					
1951		6	7	8	9	10	11	12	13	14	15				
1952			6	7	8	9	10	11	12	13	14	15			
1953				6	7	8	9	10	11	12	13	14	15		
1954					6	7	8	9	10	11	12	13	14	15	
1955						6	7	8	9	10	11	12	13	14	15
1956							6	7	8	9					
1957								6	7	8					
1958									6	7					
1959										6					

[a]Entries represent ages corresponding to each combination of cohort and time of measurement.

[b]In this table, cohort-sequential design is represented by the cells included within the horizontal parallelogram; time-sequential design is represented by the cells within the vertical parallelogram; cross-sequential design is represented by the cells included within the square. The design used in the Vocational Development Project is represented by the triangle.

sexes the trends were nonlinear. To identify where these departures from linearity were between the two groups, t-tests comparing males and females in each grade were run. The results indicated sex differences at every grade level, except the 7th. In other words, males and females were essentially equivalent in their career attitude maturity at the beginning of the junior high school years, but as career development progressed the females matured at a faster rate than the males, and the differences between them became increasingly apparent.

These trends in the maturity of career attitudes are depicted graphically in Fig. 6.4, which shows the generally higher profile elevation on the CMI for females after the 7th grade. Also of considerable interest are two other characteristics of these curves. First, note the dip between the 9th and 10th grades for both males and females. This time marked the transition for these students from the familiar, and presumably less threatening, environment of junior high school to the unknown, and potentially threatening, environment of senior high school. Because the CMI-Attitude Scale has been shown to be related to general adjustment status, it can be hypothesized that this discontinuity in career development reflects the shock that is often occasioned by moving from a secure to a strange environment. Second, note a comparable dip for males, but not females, in the

12th grade. This phenomenon appears to be what has been termed "regression in career development at a choice point." Again, on the threshold of leaving a relatively nonthreatening world to enter a possibly hostile one, males regress in the maturity of their career attitudes to an earlier point in development, approximately equivalent to their status in the 10th grade. This existential condition evidently was more marked for males than females in these samples at the time (Spring, 1969), because more of the former were closer to the reality of having to support themselves economically or train themselves vocationally for gainful employment.

The implications of these findings for theory construction, further research, and counseling practice are manifold. Theoretically, not only is it clear that there are sex differences in career attitude maturity, but it is equally well-established that a linear model of career attitude development is not a viable one. It does *not* fit the longitudinal data that it was intended to explain. Similarly, research on career attitude maturity in adolescence must take into account the impact of environmental factors upon the course of career development, particularly the school and the peer culture as the principal agents of socialization and voca-

TABLE 6.2
Data Design for Trend Analyses of Male and Female Career Attitude Maturity in Grades 7 Through 12

	Subjects	7	8	9	10	11	12
	1						
	2						
	.						
MALES	.						
	.						
	.						
	100						
SEX	1						
	2						
	.						
FEMALES	.						
	.						
	.						
	.						
	100						

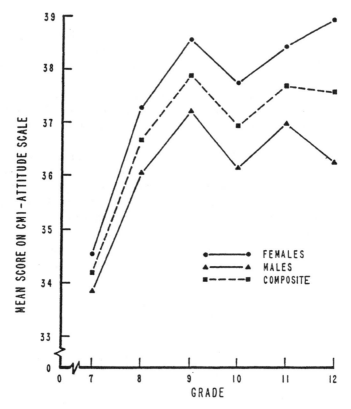

FIG. 6.4. Profile of CMI attitude scale score means across grades.

tionalization during these years. Finally, career counseling would appear to be particularly critical for both males and females at the beginning of senior high school to assist them in making the transition from junior high school, as well as in the 12th grade, when they are faced with uncertain prospects in the future.

REFERENCES

Baltes, P. B., & Goulet, L. R. (1970). Status and issues of a life-span developmental psychology. In L. R. Goulet & P. B. Baltes (Eds.), *Life-span developmental psychology*. New York: Academic Press.

Carter, H. D. (1940). The development of vocational attitudes. *Journal of Consulting Psychology, 4,* 185–191.

Cook, D. L. (1951). An investigation of three aspects of free-response and choice-type tests at the college level. *Dissertation Abstracts, 15,* 1351.

Cook, D. L. (1958). The use of free response data in writing choice-type items. *Journal of Experimental Education, 27,* 125–133.

Crites, J. O. (1958, March). *Vocational maturity and vocational adjustment.* Paper presented at the meeting of the American Personnel and Guidance Association, St. Louis.

Crites, J. O. (1961). A model for the measurement of vocational maturity. *Journal of Counseling Psychology, 8,* 255–259.

Crites, J. O. (1964). Proposals for a new criterion measure and research design. In H. Borow (Ed.), *Man in a world at work.* Boston: Houghton Mifflin.

Crites, J. O. (1965). Measurement of vocational maturity in adolescence: I. Attitude Test of the Vocational Development Inventory. *Psychological Monographs, 79,* (2 Whole No. 595).

Crites, J. O. (1969). *Vocational psychology.* New York: McGraw-Hill.

Crites, J. O. (1973). Career decision processes. In E. L. Herr (Ed.), NVGA *decennial volume.* Boston: Houghton Mifflin.

Crites, J. O. (1974a). Methodological issues in the measurement of career maturity. *Measurement and evaluation in guidance, 6,* 200–209.

Crites, J. O. (1974b). The Career Maturity Inventory. In D. E. Super (Ed.), *Measuring vocational maturity in counseling and evaluation.* Washington, D.C.

Crites, J. O. (1978). *Theory and research handbook for the career Maturity Inventory* (2nd ed.). Monterey, CA: CTB/McGraw-Hill.

Crites, J. O., Wallbrown, F. H., & Blaha, J. (1985). The Career Maturity Inventory: Myths and realities-a rejoinder to Westbrook, Cutts, Madison, And Arcia (1980). *Journal of Vocational Behavior, 26,* 221–238.

Dysinger, W. S. (1950). Maturation and vocational guidance. *Occupations, 29,* 198–201.

Ginzberg, E., Ginsburg, S. W., Axelrad, S., & Herma, J. L. (1951). *Occupational choice.* New York: Columbia University Press.

Hahn, M. K., & McLean, M. S. (1955). *Counseling psychology.* New York: McGraw-Hill.

Henchley, C. L. (1981). Personal communication.

Herr, E. L., & Cramer, S. H. (1972). *Vocational guidance and career development in the schools: Towards a systems approach.* Boston: Houghton Mifflin.

Holden, G. S. (1961). Scholastic aptitude and the relative persistence of vocational choice. *Personnel and Guidance Journal, 40,* 36–41.

Holland, J. L. (1985). *Making vocational choices: A theory of vocational personalities and work environments.* Englewood Cliffs, NJ: Prentice-Hall.

Kessen, W. (1960). Research design in the study of developmental problems. In P. H. Mussen (Ed.), *Handbook of research methods in child development* (pp. 36–70). New York: Wiley.

Lofquist, L. H., & Dawis, R. V. (1969). *Adjustment to work.* New York: Appleton-Century-Crofts.

Meade, C. J. (1974). *A comparison of the cross-sectional and the longitudinal data on the Career Maturity Inventory Attitude Scale.* Unpublished manuscript.

Rathburn, C. (1973). *Career Maturity Inventory-Attitude Scale: Analyses of longitudinal data.* Unpublished manuscript.

Roe, A. (1956). *The psychology of occupations.* New York: Wiley.

Schaie, K. W. (1965). A general model for the study of developmental problems. *Psychological Bulletin, 64,* 92–107.

Schaie, K. W. (1970). A reinterpretation of age related changes in cognitive structure and functioning. In L. R. Goulet & P. B. Baltes (Eds.), *Life-span developmental psychology.* New York: Academic Press.

Spiker, C. C. (1966). The concept of development: Relevant and irrelevant issues. *Monographs of the Society for Research in Child Development, 41,* 40–54.

Super, D. E. (1942). *The dynamics of vocational adjustment.* New York: Harper.

Super, D. E. (1953). A theory of vocational development. *American Psychologist, 8,* 185–190.

Super, D. E. (1955). The dimensions and measurement of vocational maturity. *Teachers College Record, 57,* 151–163.

Super, D. E. (1957). *Psychology of careers.* New York: Harper.

Super, D. E., Crites, J. O., Hummel, R. C., Moser, H. P., Overstreet, P. L., & Warnath, C. F. (1957). *Vocational development: A framework for research.* New York: Teachers College Bureau of Publications.

Super, D. E., & Crites, J. O. (1962). *Appraising vocational fitness* (rev. ed.). New York: Harper & Row.

Super, D. W., & Overstreet, P. L. (1960). *The vocational maturity of ninth grade boys.* New York: Teachers College Bureau of Publications.

Vernon, P. E. (1950). *The structure of human abilities.* London: Methuen.

Wallbrown, F. H., Silling, S. M., & Crites, J. O. (1986). Testing Crites' model of career maturity: A hierarchical strategy. *Journal of Vocational Behavior, 28,* 183–190.

Westbrook, B. W. (1976a). Interrelationship of career choice competencies and career and career choice attitudes of ninth-grade pupils: Testing hypotheses derived from Crites' model of career maturity. *Journal of Vocational Behavior, 8,* 1–12.

Westbrook, B. W. (1976b). The relationship between vocational maturity and appropriateness of vocational choices of ninth-grade pupils. *Measurement and Evaluation in Guidance, 9,* 75–80.

Westbrook, B. W., Cutts, C. C., Madison, S. S., & Arcia, M. A. (1980). The validity of the Crites model of career maturity. *Journal of Vocational Behavior, 16,* 249–281.

Wherry, R. J., Sr. (1984). *Contributions to correlational analysis.* Orlando, FL: Academic Press.

Williamson, E. G. (1939). *How to counsel students.* New York: McGraw-Hill.

III WORK EXPERIENCE AND ADOLESCENT VOCATIONAL DEVELOPMENT

7

Adolescents and Work: A Longitudinal Perspective on Gender and Cultural Variability

Emmy E. Werner
University of California, Davis

INTRODUCTION

Cross-cultural research on the development of orientation toward work is still in its infancy and falls roughly into two categories: a small, but growing body of literature on the issue of child labor and its relationship to economic development in the Third World, and research on the labor market experiences of minority youth in industrialized countries, such as the United States.

In both categories, researchers have focused primarily on socioeconomic analyses, and secondarily on political issues, but the impact of work experience on psychological development has yet been only superficially addressed. Also, definitions of what constitutes "work," "labor," "child," or "youth" vary from setting to setting, depending on whether one deals with preindustrial, traditional societies, societies in transition to a market economy, or societies like the United States that are industrialized and require extensive schooling before entrance into the labor market.

As yet, cross-cultural research has not systematically attempted to place the work experience of young people within the context of anthropological theory, such as Erikson's perspectives on the development of ego and work identity (1959). Most of the cross-cultural studies cited in the annotated bibliography by C. Moore, published in *Child Development and International Development: Research–Policy Interfaces* (Wagner, 1983) are descriptive, based on cross-cultural samples from a variety of Third World settings, and focus on the work experience of young males, neglecting the role of females in economic development (Bosenrup, 1970).

Even in industrialized societies, such as the United States, longitudinal studies that examine the major variables that contribute to the occupational socialization of adolescents are rare, and draw on predominantly Caucasian samples from urban areas in California, such as Oakland (Elder, 1974) or Orange County (Steinberg, Greenberger, Garduque, Ruggiero, & Vaux, 1982; Steinberg, Greenberger, Vaux, & Ruggiero, 1981). Rarer still are prospective studies that look at the impact of work experience on adolescent development (Frantz, 1980; Steinberg et al., 1982).

The Kauai Longitudinal Study, which followed a cohort of 518 Oriental and Polynesian youth born in 1955 on a rural Hawaiian island from birth to young adulthood, provides us with a unique opportunity to (a) consider gender and cultural variability in adolescents' work status, occupational aspirations and occupational reward values, and (b) to examine childhood antecedents and correlates of adolescents' occupational socialization.

THE SETTING: KAUAI AND ITS PEOPLE

The youth whose lives we studied from the prenatal period to the threshold of adulthood represent the cohort of 1955 births on Kauai, an island at the northwest end of the Hawaiian chain. The 44,000 people who live on the "Garden Island" are for the most part descendents of immigrants from Southeast Asia who came to work for the sugar and pineapple plantations. Many intermarried with the local Hawaiians. Today, the three largest ethnic groups on Kauai (which account for three-fourths of all inhabitants) are the Japanese, the Pilipino, and the part- and full-Hawaiians.

The Japanese began to arrive on Kauai in large numbers in the 1890s and moved quickly from plantation labor to supervisory, business, and professional positions. Today they are predominant in the middle class on the island.

Beginning in 1907, large numbers of Pilipino men were brought in as additional sources of plantation labor, a process repeated in 1946 when they served to ease the wartime labor shortage. Relative to their length of stay on the island, the Pilipino have shown a slower rate of upward mobility than the Japanese, and are found today predominantly in the lower and lower-middle classes.

A person of any Hawaiian ancestry, no matter how slight the admixture of native blood, if it is recognized and known, is designated as part-Hawaiian in the islands. Most part- and full-Hawaiians have remained at the bottom of the socioeconomic ladder on Kauai and are, like the Native Americans, "strangers in their own land" (McNassor & Hongo, 1972).

When our study began, Hawaii was still a territory, but in 1959 the islands became the 50th state of the Union. Statehood brought rapid economic changes to Kauai. Whereas the economy had once been based almost entirely on sugar and pineapple production, the 1960s and 1970s brought a rapid expansion of the tourist industry.

Sugar continues to be one of Kauai's major enterprises, but increasing consideration is given to diversified agriculture. With increased mechanization, urbanization, and new local and export markets, the job opportunities for Kauai's youth are rapidly shifting. Other economic changes have been brought about by an increase in the government work force and in retail trade and construction. Major scientific and military installations have developed on the west side of the island that provide important contributions to space explorations and general strategic defense.

METHOD

Study Population

Our study population represents a kaleidoscope of the different ethnic groups on the island: Japanese (34%), part- and full-Hawaiians (24%), Pilipino (18%), ethnic mixtures other than Hawaiian (14%), Portuguese from the Azores (6%), Anglo-Caucasians (3%), and a few Chinese, Koreans, and Puerto Ricans. About half of the youth (55%) grew up in families where the fathers were semi- or unskilled laborers and where the mothers had only 8 years or less of formal schooling.

Procedures

Our study began with an evaluation of the cumulative effects of preperinatal stress and the quality of the caregiving environment on the physical, cognitive, and social development of the 1955 birth cohort in the postpartum period and at age 1 year. It continued with follow-ups at 2 and 10 years and in late adolescence (at 17–18 years). For two subsamples (the teenage mothers and the offspring of psychotic parents) we have additional follow-up data at age 25. A follow-up in adulthood is now completed.

Throughout the study, attrition rates have remained relatively low. Ninety-six percent of the birth cohort participated in the 2-year follow-up, 88% in the 18-year follow-up, and 72% in the 30-year follow-up.

The attrition rate at age 18 is identical to rates reported by Elder (1974) in a follow-up study of *The Children of the Great Depression*, in Oakland, California, and compares favorably with rates reported by Steinberg et al. (1982) in their short-term longitudinal study of the impact of work experience on adolescent development in Orange County, California.

Our periodic assessments included a variety of measures of the constitutional and behavioral characteristics of the children, their families, and the larger social context in which they grew up. A detailed account of the methodology and the complete data base of the study can be found in *Kauai's Children Come of Age* (Werner & Smith, 1977) and in *Vulnerable, but Invincible: A Longitudinal Study of Resilient Children and Youth* (Werner & Smith, 1982).

Characteristics of the Home Environment

Independent assessments of the quality of the home environment were made at birth and at ages 2, 10, and 18. Included in the present analysis are the educational level of both parents (based on years of completed schooling), the mother's employment (before and after her child entered school), as well as ratings of the socioeconomic status and of the quality of educational stimulation and emotional support provided by the family at age 10. These ratings were based on interviews and observations during home visits, and ranged on a 5-point scale from 1, "very favorable," to 5, "very unfavorable." They were made by psychologists who had no knowledge of the children's status.

Socioeconomic status ratings are based on the father's occupation, income level, steadiness of employment, and condition of housing. The rating is based primarily on father's occupation categorized in one of five groups: (1) professional; (2) semiprofessional, proprietorial and managerial; (3) skilled trade and technical; (4) semiskilled; and (5) unskilled or day laborer.

The rating of educational stimulation took into account opportunities provided in the home for enlarging the child's vocabulary, intellectual interests and activities of the family, values placed by the parents on education, work habits emphasized in the home, learning facilities provided by the parents, availability of books and periodicals, and opportunities for exploration in the community at large (use of library and recreational facilities).

The rating of emotional support took into account the interpersonal relations between parent and child, opportunities available for satisfactory identification, and methods of reward and punishment used in disciplining the child. The intercorrelations between the environmental ratings at age 10 ranged from .37 (SES/emotional support) to .57 (SES/educational stimulation).

In the interview conducted with the youth at age 18 were a number of questions that dealt with the family. For the purpose of this analysis, we selected the youth's responses to the questions that dealt with mother's and father's goals for their offspring; with the degree of structure provided by the family in adolescence, including the subject of rules and regulations (i.e., chores, homework); with the youth's view of the achievement demands made by each parent; and with their evaluation of the degree to which each parent had influenced them with regard to their educational and occupational aspirations.

Characteristics of the Youth

Among measures of scholastic aptitude and achievement included in the present analysis are IQ scores from the Primary Mental Abilities (PMA) test (Thurstone & Thurstone, 1954), grade 5; percentile scores from the Cooperative School and College Ability test (SCAT, 1966), grades 8–10; and from the Sequential Test of Educational Progress (STEP, 1966), grades 5, 8–10, and 12. Among personality measures included in the analysis are scores from the California Psychological Inventory (CPI) (Gough, 1969) and the Nowicki Locus of Control Scale (Nowicki, 1971), grade 12.

The 18 subscales of the CPI cluster in four classes: (1) measures of poise, ascendency, self-assurance, and interpersonal adequacy; (2) measures of socialization, maturity, responsibility, and interpersonal structuring of values; (3) measures of achievement potential and intellectual efficiency, and (4) measures of intellectual and interest modes.

The Nowicki Locus of Control Scale measures the degree to which a person believes that a behavioral event is contingent upon his or her own actions. *Externals* tend to believe that events happen to them as a result of fate, luck, or other factors beyond their control. *Internals* tend to believe that their own actions determine the positive or negative reinforcement they receive.

In addition, we have the youths' own evaluations of their strong points from their 18 year interviews. These were classified into three major categories (1) achievement, assertiveness, hard work, perseverance; (2) special talents (athletic ability, artistic ability, dramatic, or musical talents); and (3) social skills (good nature or good looks, even temper, loyalty, patience).

We also had access to the records of police and family court and noted any delinquent acts committed by the members of the 1955 cohort between ages 10 and 18, such as first- and second-degree larceny; first- and second-degree burglary; car theft; malicious injury; assault and battery; possession, sale, and abuse of hard drugs; forgery and/or passing of forged checks.

Adolescent Work Status and Aspirations

Information on the nature of employment and on educational and vocational plans was obtained from 518 youth (260 F, 258 M) in grade 12. Responses came from a biographical questionnaire and/or a semistructured interview.

Adolescent work status was classified as a dichotomous variable that differentiated between youth who held some regular paid employment (outside of their own family) during high school and those who did not.

Educational aspirations were coded along a 6-point scale, ranging from high school graduation to completion of graduate or professional school training. *Occupational aspirations* were coded according to the U.S. Census Occupational

Classification System. It was also noted whether the youth planned to work in an occupation that would place him or her at the same (or lower) occupational level than the father or at a level above that of the father's present occupation.

A semistructured interview, conducted with a subsample of 168 12th graders (85 F, 83M), matched by SES and ethnicity, yielded information on a number of additional variables that are included in this analysis:

Definition of vocational plans was coded along a 5-point scale, ranging from a definite plan to enter a specific occupation to undecided.

Information on occupational reward values came from responses to two questions: *Features of job considered important* were classified as either predominantly extrinsic (i.e., hours worked, good income, little stress or tension, job security) or predominantly intrinsic (i.e., freedom from supervision; freedom to develop own ideas, chance to express one's self; interesting work).

Career or job success was classified as a dichotomous variable which differentiated between youth who considered it an important life goal, and youth who preferred other life goals instead, such as close, intimate relationships with friends, or a happy, successful marriage.

For the young women who participated in the 18 year interview, additional information was available on whether they planned to combine work and marriage, on the time of work, marriage, and parenthood, and on whether they aspired toward a conventional job (such as clerical work, retail selling, nursing) or toward nontraditional occupations for women (such as the law, medicine, or service with the armed forces or the police).

Plan of Analysis

We first examined the frequencies, by sex and ethnic group, on each of the variables that denote adolescents' work status, occupational aspirations and occupational reward values. The analysis of sex differences is based on all the available responses from the young men and women in the 1955 cohort. The analysis of the ethnic differences was restricted to the youth from the three major ethnic groups on the island: the Japanese, the Pilipino, and the part- and full-Hawaiians (who account for three-fourths of all the respondents).

We then examined family and personal characteristics in childhood and adolescence that significantly differentiated between high school seniors who varied in work status, occupational aspirations, and occupational reward values. Analyses by Chi-square, *t*-tests, and ANOVA, where appropriate, were done separately for males and females.

In the final and predictive phase of the study, we used stepwise discriminant function analyses to discover combinations of family and personal attributes (including work status) that maximally differentiated across time (from early childhood to adolescence) among youths who differed in their occupational aspirations and occupational reward values by age 18. These analyses are based on the response of the 168 youths who participated in the semistructured interview at age 18, and were done separately for each sex.

RESULTS

Adolescents' Work Status, Occupational Aspirations and Occupational Reward Values

TABLE 7.1
Dimensions of Adolescents' Work Orientation at Age 18, by Gender
(1955 Birth Cohort, Kauai)

Variables	Males (N:258) %	Females (N:260) %	p
*Has had regular paid employment	60.9	50.7	<.10
Main reason for working			
To make money	73.1	65.1	
To gain experience	20.3	32.1	<.05
*Plans for future schooling			
High school graduation or less	15.0	10.1	
Technical training, incl. jr. college	38.5	43.8	
Four-year college and/or grad. school	46.6	37.1	<.10
	(N:85) %	(N:83) %	
**Definitiveness of vocational plans			
Definite plans for specific occupation	45.3	49.3	
Considers alternative option	40.0	26.0	
No clearcut vocational plans	14.7	24.7	
**Occupation S wants to go into is			
Same level as father's occupation or below	75.5	62.1	
Above level of father's occupation	24.5	37.9	
**Features of job considered important are			
Mainly extrinsic	46.2	50.0	
Mainly intrinsic	53.8	50.0	
**Importance of career or job success as life goal			
Most important	56.6	25.9	<.0001
**For F Only			
Plans to combine employment and marriage		80.5	
Plans to work after children are born		66.0	
Plans to go into nontraditional occupation		16.3	

*Source: Questionnaires and interviews combined
**Source: Interviews only

TABLE 7.2
Dimensions of Adolescents' Work Orientation at Age 18 by Ethnic Groups
(1955 Birth Cohort, Kauai)

Variables	Japanese (N:184) %	Pilipino (N:92) %	Part-Hawaiian (N:104) %	p
Has had regular paid employment	40.0	52.0	70.0	<.05
Main reason for working				
To make money	75.8	65.8	51.7	
To gain experience, out of interest	18.2	23.7	39.7	
Plans for future schooling				
High school graduation or less	7.1	13.0	27.9	
Technical training, incl. junior college	29.0	42.4	51.9	
Four-year college and/or graduate school	63.0	44.6	20.2	<.0001
Definitiveness of vocational plans				
Definite plans for specific occupation	44.0	47.1	44.7	
Considers alternative options	52.0	29.4	23.4	
No clearcut vocational plans	4.0	23.5	31.9	<.05
Occupation S wants to go into is				
Same level as father's occupation or below	66.6	62.5	62.5	
Above level of father's occupation	33.3	37.5	37.5	
Features of job considered important are				
Mainly extrinsic	52.8	45.7	40.0	
Mainly intrinsic	47.2	54.3	60.0	
Importance of career or job success as life goal				
Most important	43.0	54.0	36.5	<.05

Adolescent Work Status

Some 55% of high school seniors on Kauai were holding some regular part-time job when they responded to the biographical questionnaire, a figure comparable to the results of recent surveys on the U.S. mainland (Lewin-Epstein, 1981; Lewis, Gardner, & Seitz, 1983).

The jobs held by the adolescents on Kauai were fairly sex-typed. Adolescent males were working in the following kinds of jobs: manual labor in commercial or industrial settings, such as garages and filling stations (46%); plantation labor (26%); tourist-related jobs, such as busboys and tourist guides (9%); yard work (9%); clerical work (5%); and recreation aides (1%). The most common jobs for adolescent females were in food service in the island's hotels and restaurants (44%) and in retail sales (26%); followed by clerical work (13%); child care (8%); cleaning (8%); plantation labor (5%); and employment as recreation aide (4%) or health aide (1%).

As can be seen in Table 7.1, a slightly higher proportion ($p>.10$) of males (61%) than females (51%) were employed by nonfamily members—a trend also reported by Greenberger and Steinberg (1981) among 10th and 11th graders in Orange County, California.

There was also a significant difference between the sexes in their stated reasons for working while in high school. A higher proportion of adolescent males worked "to make money"; a higher proportion of adolescent females worked "to gain experience" or "out of interest" ($p<.05$).

As can be seen in Table 7.2, there were significant differences among the youth from the three major ethnic groups in their participation in the adolescent work force ($p<.05$). Hawaiians and part-Hawaiians had the highest rates of employment while in high school (70%), Japanese had the lowest (40%), with the Pilipino youth close to average (52%). Among the Pilipino and Hawaiians there were no social class differences between adolescent workers and non-workers. Among the Japanese, however, fewer upper-middle- than lower-middle-class youth held part-time jobs while in high school.

Educational Aspirations

Ninety-seven percent of the cohort of 18-year-olds on Kauai were graduated from high school. This is a remarkably low rate of "educational wastage" and a tribute to the efforts of the public school system to reach potential dropouts through work motivation classes, special classes for pregnant teenagers, off-campus classrooms, and outreach counselors. It also is a tribute to the steadfast belief of the parents and youth in the value of education. Few of the immigrant parents, with the exception of the Japanese, had themselves been high school graduates.

Nearly, one-fifth (19%) of the high school seniors planned to pursue some technical, vocational, or business training beyond high school, and another fifth (21%) were about to enroll in the local community college. Nearly a third (29%) of the high school graduates planned to attend a 4-year college, and 13% hoped to attend graduate school. A slightly higher proportion of males (47%) than females (37%) planned to attend a 4-year college and/or graduate school ($p<.10$).

There were highly significant differences among youth from the three ethnic groups in their levels of educational aspirations ($p<.0001$). Nearly two-thirds of the Japanese and almost one-half of the Pilipino high school seniors planned to go to a 4-year college and/or graduate school. In contrast, only one out of every five among the part- and full-Hawaiian youth planned to attend a 4-year college.

Occupational Aspirations

There were also some striking differences between the occupational levels of fathers and the occupational aspirations of their offspring at age 18, reflecting a strong desire for occupational mobility for a significant proportion of the youth.

Only 2% of the parents' generation held professional jobs. In contrast, 12% of their offspring planned to go into professions, such as law, dentistry, medicine, and teaching.

Only 7% of the parents held proprietory or managerial jobs. In contrast, 38% of the youth planned to go into owner-operated businesses, and an additional 4% aimed for managerial jobs in business.

Thirty-five percent of the fathers were employed in skilled trades or technical jobs. In contrast, only 5% of their offspring planned to go into skilled trades, such as carpenter, mechanic, plumber. Ten percent of the youth, mostly girls, aimed for clerical and secretarial jobs; 15% of the boys planned to join the police or military service.

Forty-two percent of the fathers worked in semiskilled and 14% in unskilled and day labor jobs in the plantations, or in the tourist industry. In contrast, only 14% of the youth chose plantation work, and only 3% work in the tourist industry.

In all three ethnic groups, more than a third of the youth aspired to a job above the occupational level of the father. In each group, a higher proportion of females than males expressed a desire for upward mobility in their vocational plans.

Occupational Reward Values

Both male and female youth on Kauai were about evenly divided between those who would choose a job because of predominantly extrinsic features (such as earnings, working hours, security) and predominantly intrinsic features (such as freedom to develop one's own ideas and freedom from supervision). But a significantly higher proportion of adolescent males (57%) than adolescent females (26%) considered success in a career or job as an important life goal ($p<.0001$).

Among the three ethnic groups, a significantly lower proportion of Hawaiian than Pilipino youth considered a career or job success an important life goal ($p<.05$). A higher proportion of Hawaiian than Japanese youth preferred intrinsic over extrinsic reward values in a future job, and had worked during high school "out of interest" or "to gain experience" rather than "to make money."

Women's Commitment to Work and Family

About two-thirds of the 18-year-old women interviewed planned to work first and marry later. Only one-fifth was solely interested in marriage and not in work outside of the home. The overwhelming majority of young women planned to combine work, marriage, and motherhood, possibly a reflection of the spirit of women's liberation, but also a necessity on an island where the cost of living is high.

Most of the young women on Kauai still aspired toward traditional "female" occupations, such as clerical work, retail selling, nursing, tourist entertainment, or teaching of young children. Only a small proportion (16%) planned to enter "nontraditional" jobs for women, such as ranching, police work, or service with the armed forces.

Antecedents and Correlates of Adolescent Work Status, Occupational Aspirations, and Occupational Reward Values

Adolescent Work Status.   There were no significant social class differences between the females on Kauai who held some paid employment while they attended high school and those who were not employed. Among the males, however, a significantly higher proportion ($p<.05$) of lower-class (69%) and middle-class (58%) youth were in the adolescent work force than among youth from the upper classes (29%). The educational level of the parents and the educational stimulation provided by the family during childhood was also significantly lower for males who worked during adolescence than for those who did not. (See Table 7.3)

Among both sexes, a significantly higher proportion of adolescent workers than nonworkers had received little emotional support by their families during childhood, had been considered "difficult to manage" by parents at age 10, and committed delinquent acts during adolescence (35.8% vs. 23.3% among M; 21.6% vs. 13.3% among F). (See Table 7.4)

By grade 12, the mean scores on the CPI subscales, Responsibility, Socialization, and Achievement via Independence were significantly lower for young men and women who held a job while attending high school than for those who did not. By grade 12, there also were significant differences between males and females who held a job, and their same-sex peers who did not, on the verbal, quantitative, and total scores of the SCAT, and on the reading, writing, and math sections of the STEP. Young men and women who held jobs had consistently lower mean scores on these scholastic aptitude and achievement tests than did their adolescent peers who were not in the labor force. This difference between workers and nonworkers was significant among youth in all major ethnic groups.

By age 18 a significantly lower proportion of adolescent workers than nonworkers planned to attend a 4-year college and/or graduate school. This was true for both sexes and all ethnic groups.

Definitiveness of Vocational Plans

Family characteristics found more frequently among adolescent males with definite vocational plans at age 18 were: a mother who was employed outside of the home when her son was preschool age, and a household where there was structure and rules that applied to chores and homework. Among males with definite

TABLE 7.3
Antecedents and Correlates of Employment During Adolescence: Males
(1955 Birth Cohort, Kauai)

Variables	M Who Had Some Paid Employment (N:134)		M Who Had No Paid Employment (N:86)		p
	X	SD	X	SD	
Father's education	9.5	3.1	10.5	3.0	<.05
(grades completed)					
Mother's education	10.4	2.8	11.3	2.3	<.01
(grades completed)	%		%		
Child difficult to manage (age 10)	15.8		4.7		<.05
Emotional support in home (2-10)					
(Very) High	19.4		34.9		
Adequate	38.8		39.5		<.01
(Very) Low	41.8		25.6		
Educational stimulation in home (2-10)					
(Very) High	9.7		24.4		
Adequate	35.1		36.0		<.01
(Very) Low	55.2		39.5		
	X	SD	X	SD	
PMA reasoning factor (grade 5)	103.0	15.9	106.8	18.7	<.10
SCAT-Midpercentile rank (grade 12)					
Verbal	32.2	23.5	41.4	25.3	<.05
Quantitative	39.4	28.8	51.4	32.7	<.05
Total	34.5	25.7	45.3	29.8	<.05
STEP-Midpercentile rank (grade 12)					
Reading	28.6	24.4	41.9	25.4	<.01
Writing	30.9	24.3	38.0	24.5	<.05
Math	43.0	24.9	53.8	29.0	<.10
CPI subscales (grade 12)					
Responsibility	20.6	4.0	22.1	4.9	<.10
Socialization	29.9	6.0	32.1	6.5	<.05
Self-control	20.2	5.4	22.4	6.5	<.05
Achievement via conformance	18.4	4.2	20.0	4.3	<.05
	%		%		
Plans for future schooling					
High school graduation or less	24.0		7.0		
Technical training,	44.0		31.4		
including jr. college					
Four-year college and/or grad. school	32.0		61.6		<.0001

vocational plans, there was a significantly higher proportion for whom it had been very important to do well in school than among males who had not yet made any career plans by age 18. (See Table 7.5)

Most of the males on Kauai who planned to enter a specific occupation by age 18 came from families that offered relatively little educational stimulation during childhood, and their mean scores on achievement tests (STEP) in grade 5 and on tests of scholastic aptitude (SCAT) in grade 12 were significantly lower than those of males who were not yet committed to a specific job. By grade 12, they also scored lower on the CPI scale, Capacity for Status, suggesting that they may have lacked some of the personal qualities that lead to status and social mobility, qualities that enabled their peers to entertain a "vocational moratorium" before making a commitment to a career.

In contrast to the males, adolescent females with definite vocational plans by age 18 did not differ from females without such plans in family background characteristics. But they had significantly higher PMA and (nonverbal) reasoning scores in grade 5, had higher mean scores on reading tests in grades 8 and 10, and scored higher on the CPI scales, Socialization and Femininity, in grade 12 than women without definitive vocational plans. (See Table 7.5)

Occupational Mobility

A high proportion of the young men and women who aimed toward a career that would put them above the occupational level of their father came from families in which the breadwinner had been a semi- or unskilled laborer on the sugar planta- tions. Such upwardly mobile males and females had significantly higher mean scores on the CPI scale, Self-acceptance, than same-sex peers who wanted jobs comparable to or below the occupational level of their parents. (See Table 7.6.)

Among the males, the upwardly mobile group contained a high proportion of young men whose mothers expected them to go to college, and who valued among their strong points assertiveness, hard work, and perseverance. Upwardly

TABLE 7.4
Antecedents and Correlates of Employment During Adolescence: Females

Variables	F Who Had Some Paid Employment (N:115)		F Who Had No Paid Employment (N:112)		p
	%		%		
Child difficult to manage (age 10)	14.8		1.8		<.001
Emotional support in home (2-10)					
(Very) High	23.5		25.0		
Adequate	31.3		47.3		
(Very) Low	45.2		27.7		<.01
Foreign language spoken in home	33.9		54.5		<.01
	X	SD	X	SD	
PMA IQ (grade 5)	103.5	12.1	107.3	11.3	<.05
PMA reasoning factor	105.9	16.4	111.0	15.5	<.05
SCAT-Midpercentile rank (grade 12)					
Verbal	31.1	24.4	46.4	28.9	<.001
Quantitative	37.4	30.5	51.4	30.3	<.01
Total	34.7	27.1	48.5	30.9	<.01
STEP-Midpercentile rank (grade 12)					
Reading	41.1	26.4	53.3	28.7	<.01
Writing	42.8	27.1	57.7	28.9	<.01
Math	36.3	24.7	45.6	26.7	<.01
CPI subscales (grade 12)					
Responsibility	22.3	5.9	24.9	5.4	<.01
Socialization	31.7	6.6	36.1	6.2	<.001
Achievement via conformance	19.0	5.0	21.2	5.2	<.01
Achievement via independence	12.9	4.1	14.3	3.9	<.05
	%		%		
Plans for future schooling					
High school graduation or less	25.5		15.9		
Technical training, including jr. college	53.6		34.5		
Four-year college and/or grad. school	20.9		49.6		<.0001

TABLE 7.5
Antecedents and Correlates: Definitiveness of Vocational Plans

| | Males | | |
Variables	M with Definite Vocational Plans or Options (N:64)	M Without Definite Vocational Plans (N:11)	p
	%	%	
Mother employed when M was preschool age	33.9	--	<.10
Mother employed before M entered school	52.5	20.0	<.10
Parents often read books to M before he entered	38.1	90.9	<.01
Educational stimulation in home (2-10)			
(Very) High	4.7	22.3	
Adequate	32.8	27.3	<.01
(Very) Low	62.5	45.5	<.01
Emotional support in home (2-10)			
(Very) High	12.5	36.4	
Adequate	31.3	36.4	<.01
(Very) Low	56.3	27.3	
Importance of rule in household (re chores, homework)	53.6	11.1	<.05
Importance to M of doing well in school			
Very important	36.4	9.1	
Important	30.3	54.5	<.01
Doesn't care	33.3	36.4	

	X	SD	X	SD	
STEP-Midpercentile rank (grade 5)					
Reading	35.1	27.1	64.3	19.4	<.01
Writing	48.2	25.9	68.0	23.0	<.01
Math	43.8	29.8	73.3	19.7	<.01
SCAT-Midpercentile rank (grade 12)					
Verbal	31.8	24.4	53.9	26.4	<.05
Quantitative	36.3	30.1	60.7	25.0	<.05
Total	32.4	26.6	58.1	25.3	<.05
CPI subscale (grade 12)					
Capacity for status	13.2	3.7	16.4	2.4	<.01

| | Females | | |
Variables	F with Definite Vocational Plans or Options (N:55)	F Without Definite Vocational Plans (N:17)	p

	X	SD	X	SD	
PMA IQ (grade 5)	102.1	10.9	95.9	8.8	<.05
PMA reasoning factor	104.6	14.7	96.4	14.2	<.01
STEP-Midpercentile rank (grades 8-10)					
Reading	42.1	26.2	24.7	19.0	<.05
CPI subscales (grade 12)					
Socialization	31.3	6.2	26.5	7.0	<.05
Femininity	23.8	4.2	21.4	2.7	<.05

172

TABLE 7.6
Antecedents and Correlates: Occupational Mobility

Males

Variables	M Who Are Upwardly Mobile (N:13)	M Who Are Not Upwardly Mobile (N:40)	p
	%	%	
Father's occupational level			
Professional/Managerial	0.0	22.5	
Skilled trade/technical	30.8	65.0	
Semi- or unskilled laborer	69.2	12.5	<.001
Mother's achievement demands for M			
High school graduation or less	15.4	13.9	
Technical training beyond high school	23.1	44.4	
College or graduate school	53.8	16.7	
Leaves it up to M	7.9	25.0	<.05
M's evaluation of his strong points:			
Assertiveness, hard work, perseverance	41.7	5.9	
Special talents	8.3	20.6	
Social skills	50.0	73.5	
	X SD	X SD	
CPI subscales (grade 12)			
Self-acceptance	20.8 3.7	16.9 3.7	<.01
Tolerance	10.8 3.4	14.2 4.8	<.05

Females

Variables	F Who Are Upwardly Mobile (N:25)	F Who Are Not Upwardly Mobile (N:41)	p
	%	%	
Father's occupational level			
Professional/managerial	0.0	4.9	
Skilled trade/technical	52.0	75.6	
Semi- or unskilled laborer	48.0	19.5	<.05
Mother was employed when daughter was preschool age	54.2	22.5	<.05
F considers her mother's influence to be			
Strong	26.1	19.4	
Moderate	56.5	33.3	
Weak	17.4	47.2	<.10
Educational stimulation in home (2-10)			
(Very) High	12.0	2.4	
Adequate	12.0	34.1	
(Very) Low	76.0	63.4	<.10
Importance for F to do well in school			
High	60.0	22.0	
Moderate	28.0	53.7	
Low	12.0	24.3	<.01
Career success is important life goal for F	48.0	17.1	<.01
	X SD	X SD	
CPI subscales (grade 12)			
Dominance	21.9 6.1	18.6 5.3	<.05
Capacity for status	13.3 3.3	11.5 3.0	<.05
self-acceptance	19.4 3.5	17.7 2.9	<.05
Achievement via conformance	19.8 4.9	15.4 4.8	<.10
Achievement via independence	11.7 4.6	9.8 2.9	<.10
Locus of Control			
Internal-External	14.3 4.8	18.1 4.7	<.10

mobile males had also significantly lower mean scores on the CPI scale, Tolerance, than less mobile men, reflecting a less permissive and less easy-going attitude than their peers. They did not tolerate incompetence and did not suffer fools gladly.

Among the females, the upwardly mobile group contained a high proportion of young women with mothers who had been employed when their daughters were of preschool age, and who had exerted a strong influence on them. The majority of the upwardly mobile women had considered it important to do well in school, and a career or job success was an important life goal for them. They had more "internal" scores on the locus of control scale than their same-sex peers who were not upwardly mobile, and scored also significantly higher than less mobile women on the CPI scales, Dominance, Capacity for Status, and Achievement via Independence.

Occupational Reward Values

Adolescent males who preferred intrinsic reward values in a job had higher mean scores on the PMA IQ and the (nonverbal) reasoning factor in grade 5 than their same-sex peers who preferred extrinsic occupational reward values. By grade 12, they also scored higher on the CPI subscales, Sense of Well-being, Socialization, Achievement via Conformance, Intellectual Efficiency, Flexibility, and Femininity. They appeared to be in good mental health, were adaptable and socially mature, effectively utilized the abilities they had, and were more nurturant, sensitive, and emotionally expressive than adolescent males who preferred extrinsic reward values. (See Table 7.7)

In contrast to the adolescent males, adolescent females showed no differences in ability and personality characteristics between those who preferred intrinsic over extrinsic occupational rewards. But a significantly higher proportion of adolescent females who preferred intrinsic over extrinsic reward values had grown up in homes with strong emotional support during early and middle childhood and had considered it very important to do well in school. A significantly higher proportion of females who favored intrinsic over extrinsic reward values had also held regular paid jobs during adolescence.

Career or Job Success as Important Life Goal

Adolescent males who valued a career or success in a job as an important life goal tended to come more often from families where the mother worked before their sons were 2-years-old than did males who preferred other life goals (i.e., close relationship with friends, happy marriage). (See Table 7.8)

In grade 5, these career-oriented males had already significantly higher mean scores on the PMA IQ and (nonverbal) reasoning tests than peers who considered noncareer goals more important. In grade 12 they scored higher on the CPI

TABLE 7.7
Antecedents and Correlates: Choice of Job Features

Males					
Variables	M Considers Mostly Intrinisc Features of Job Important (N:30)		M Considers Mostly Extrinsic Features of Job Important (N:24)		p
	X	SD	X	SD	
PMA IQ (grade 5)	103.7	11.1	96.0	7.5	<.01
PMA reasoning factor	107.7	15.9	96.3	13.0	<.01
CPI subscales (grade 12)					
Sense of well-being	27.6	5.8	22.5	5.9	<.01
Socialization	32.2	7.1	28.2	5.8	<.05
Achievement via conformance	20.8	4.3	17.5	2.8	<.01
Intellectual efficiency	29.1	6.3	24.2	4.4	<.01
Flexibility	10.2	4.3	7.8	3.0	<.05
Femininity	16.0	2.8	18.1	3.5	<.05

Females					
Variables	F Considers Mostly Intrinsic Features of Job Important (N:26)		F Considers Mostly Extrinsic Features of Job Important (N:26)		p
Emotional support in home (2-10)					
(Very) High	30.8		4.0		
Adequate	3.8		28.0		<.01
(Very) Low	65.4		68.0		
F considers her mother's influence to be					
Strong	39.1		12.0		
Moderate	26.1		32.0		
Weak	34.8		56.0		<.10
Importance for F to do well in school					
High	53.8		23.1		
Moderate	30.8		65.4		
Low	15.4		11.5		<.05
F had paid employment during adolescence	96.0		76.9		<.05
	X	SD	X	SD	
STEP-Midpercentile rank (grades 8-10): Reading	49.3	23.1	28.3	23.8	<.01

subscales, Sociability, Social Presence, Responsibility, and Socialization, reflecting an outgoing, poised, conscientious and socially mature approach to life.

Women who considered the pursuit of a career or job success an important life goal at age 18 had grown up in families that provided more educational stimulation than the families of women who valued other life goals more. Among women who valued job success was a high proportion whose parents, especially their fathers, had exerted a strong influence on them.

TABLE 7.8
Antecedents and Correlates: Job Success as Life Goal

Males

Variables	M For Whom Career Or Job Success is Most Important Life Goal (N:47)		F For Whom Career Or Job Success is Not Most Important Life Goal (N:36)		p
	%		%		
Mother employed before M was 2-years-old	37.0		17.1		<.10
	X	SD	X	SD	
PMA IQ (grade 5)	102.8	10.8	97.3	10.9	<.05
PMA reasoning factor	105.7	14.8	97.3	15.6	<.05
CPI subscales (grade 12)					
Sociability	20.9	4.3	18.5	4.7	<.05
Social presence	31.8	4.1	29.2	5.1	<.05
Responsibility	21.7	4.7	19.5	4.1	<.05
Socialization	31.4	6.8	28.0	5.5	<.05
Definitiveness of vocational plans at age 18:	%		%		
Definite vocational plans	58.1		28.1		<.05
Considers alternative options	27.9		56.3		
No definitive vocational plans	14.00		15.6		

Females

Variables	F For Whom Career or Job Success is Most Important Life Goal (N:22)	F For Whom Career or Job Success is Not Most Important Life Goal (N:65)	p
Educational stimulation in home (2-10)	%	%	
(Very) High	27.3	16.01	
Adequate	36.4	19.4	
(Very) Low	36.4	64.5	<.10
F considers her father's influence to be			
Strong	23.8	14.8	
Moderate	57.1	31.5	
Weak	19.0	53.7	<.05
F considers her mother's influence to be			
Strong	23.8	20.4	
Moderate	57.1	33.3	
Weak	19.0	46.3	<.10
Importance of rules in household (during adolescence)			
Importance for F to do well in school			
High	63.6	27.0	
Moderate	31.8	49.2	<.01
Low	4.5	23.8	
F's intrinsic satisfaction with her own educational achievement			
Doing very well	57.1	29.6	
Adequate	28.6	38.9	
Not doing well	14.3	31.5	<.10
F has had paid employment during adolescence	68.2	90.3	<.05

176

Women who considered job success an important life goal came also more frequently from families who provided rules for them in adolescence, especially with regard to the completion of chores. A significantly higher proportion of these women considered it very important to do well in school, and they were more satisfied with their educational achievement than were women who pursued other life goals. A smaller proportion of women who valued a career or job success had held jobs in high school than among women who valued other life goals more.

The majority of women who planned to combine a career and family life at age 18 tended to be already high achievers (on tests of educational progress) at age 10. By the time they reached grade 12, they were more internal in their locus of control than women who did not plan to combine a career and marriage ($p<.01$), reflecting a strong belief in the control of their own fate. (See Table 7.9)

Significant Discriminators of Adolescent's Occupational Aspirations and Occupational Reward Values

We now take a look at the relationship *across time* between family characteristics and personal attributes in childhood and adolescence that significantly discriminated between youth who differed in their occupational aspirations and reward values at age 18.

The 15 perdictors entered in forward stepwise discriminant function analyses consisted of six family characteristics and nine personal attributes. One variable was either added to or removed from the equation until optimum discriminant functions were achieved. The variable added was the one that, when partialed on the previously entered variables, had the highest multiple correlations with the dependent variables, i.e., definitiveness of vocational plans, occupational mobility, preference for extrinsic vs. intrinsic occupational reward values, and job success as a life goal.

The effectiveness of the discriminant functions was tested by computing the rates of correct classifications on the four dependent variables, separately for each sex. The standardized discriminant function coefficients for the adolescent males and females are presented in Table 7.10. Each standardized discriminant function coefficient represents the relative contribution of its associated variable to the discriminant function.

Definitiveness of Vocational Plans

Six of the 15 variables entered in the stepwise analysis separated males who had definite vocational plans at age 18 from those who did not. Seven of the variables differentiated the females who had definite vocational plans at age 18 from those

TABLE 7.9
Committment to Work and Family Females
(1955 Birth Cohort, Kauai)

Variables	F Who Plan to Combine Both Work and Family (N:58)		F Who do Not Plan to Combine Both Work and Family (N:14)		p
F considers her mother's influence to be	%		%		
Strong	27.8		--		
Moderate	40.7		53.8		<.10
Weak	31.5		46.2		
Importance of rules in household (re chores)	70.4		41.7		<.10
F's intrinsic satisfaction with her educational achievement					
Doing very well	39.7		28.6		
Adequate	39.7		21.4		
Not doing well	20.7		50.0		<.10
	X	SD	X	SD	
STEP-Midpercentile rank (grade 5)					
Reading	50.0	26.5	31.1	15.8	<.05
Writing	56.5	27.2	35.0	23.3	<.05
Locus of Control (grade 12)	14.2	3.8	17.7	5.4	<.05

Timing: Marriage/Parenthood/Employment

Variables	F Who Plan to Work Until Marriage or Children are Born (N:15)	F Who Plan to Return to Work After Child Enters School (N:28)	F Who Plan to Work Regardless of Age of Children (N:21)	p
	%	%	%	
Rules in household during adolescence				
Important	100.0	61.5	55.0	<.05
Subject matter of rules, chores, homework	83.3	19.2	45.0	<.01

Traditional vs. Unconventional Job Choices

Variables	F Who Chose Unconventional Jobs/Careers (N:13)		F Who Chose Traditional Jobs/Careers (N:67)		p
	X	SD	X	SD	
CPI subscales					
Communality	19.2	7.0	23.1	3.4	<.01
Femininity	19.9	4.3	23.9	3.9	<.01

TABLE 7.10
Significant Discriminators on Four Dimensions of Adolescent Work Orientation,
by Gender (1955 Birth Cohort: Kauai)

Variables	Standardized Discriminant Function Coefficient for Males (N:83)	Variables	Standardized Discriminant Function Coefficient for Females (N:85)
Definitive of Vocational Plans			
Father's education	+.85	Father's education	-1.07
Emotional support in home (2-10)	+.54	Emotional support (2-10)	+.52
Mother employed before M entered school	+.43	Mother's influence on F	+.41
Foreign language spoken in home	+.55	F has had paid employment in adolescence	+1.09
STEP reading (grade 5)	-.36	CIP Subscales:	
CPI Subscale:		Socialization	+.57
Achievement via independence	-.79	Achievement via independence	-.38
		Locus of control	-.53
Occupational Motility			
Mother's influence on M	+.65	Mother employed before M entered school	+.63
Educational stimulation in home (2-10)	+.53	Emotional support in home (2-10)	-.47
STEP reading (grade 5)	+1.04		
M has had paid employment in adolescence	+.92	CPI Subscale: Socialization	+.59
Locus of control	+.57		
Preference: Extrinsic-Intrinsic Features of Job			
Mother employed before M entered school	-.50	Mother employed before F entered school	-.68
Foreign language spoken in home	+.97	Foreign language spoken in home	+1.38
Emotional support in home (2-10)	+.49	Emotional support in home (2-10)	-.76
CPI Subscales:		Mother's influence on F	+1.14
Responsibility	+.56	CPI Subscales:	
Intellectual efficiency	-.62	Responsibility	+1.45
Achievement via conformance	-1.04	Intellectual efficiency	-.98
Locus on control	+.46	Achievement via independence	-.89
		Socialization	+1.11
		F has had paid employment in adolescence	-.74
Career of Job Success as Important Life Goal			
Father's education	-.64	Emotional support in home (2-10)	+.54
Mother employed before M entered school		CPI Subscales:	
Foreign language spoken at home	+.59	Responsibility	-.85
CPI Subscales:		Achievement via independence	+.72
Responsibility	+1.38		
Achievement via conformance	-.84		
Locus of control	+.48	Locus of control	+.54

who did not. For both sexes, the separation between the two groups was significant ($p<.02$); 80% of the males and 80% of the females with definite vocational plans were correctly classified.

Among the variables that appeared in the discriminant functions for both sexes were: father's education; emotional support provided by the family in childhood; and the CPI scale, Achievement via Independence. Additional variables that discriminated between the males were: mother's employment before son entered school, a foreign language spoken at home, and STEP reading score in grade 5. Additional variables that discriminate between the females were: S's rating of mother's influence on her; the CPI scale, Socialization; the Locus of Control score; and work status in adolescence.

Occupational Mobility

Five of the 15 variables entered in the stepwise analysis discriminated between males whose occupational aspirations put them above the occupational level of their fathers and those who planned to enter jobs at the same occupational level as their fathers. Three of the 15 variables discriminated between females who were upwardly mobile (according to their vocational plans) and those who were not. The separation between the two groups was highly significant for the males ($p<.05$), but *not* for the females: 85% of the upwardly mobile males, but only 60% of the upwardly mobile females were correctly classified.

Variables that significantly discriminated between males who aspired toward occupations that would place them above the level of their fathers and those who did not included: the educational stimulation provided by the family in childhood; S's ratings of the mother's influence on him; STEP reading score in grade 5, locus of control score in grade 12, and work status in adolescence.

Variables that differentiated between females who aspired toward occupations that would place them above the level of their fathers' and those who did not included: emotional support provided by the family in childhood; mother's employment before daughter entered school; and the CPI scale, Socialization.

Preference for Extrinsic vs. Intrinsic Occupational
Reward Values

Seven of the 15 variables entered in the stepwise analysis separated males who preferred mostly extrinsic features in a job from those who preferred mostly intrinsic features. Nine of the 15 variables differentiated between females who preferred extrinsic occupational reward values and females who preferred intrinsic ones. For both sexes, the separation between the two groups was significant ($p<.01$), correctly classifying 79% of the males and 77% of the females with extrinsic preferences.

Among the variables that appeared in the discriminant functions for *both* sexes were: mother's employment before child entered school; emotional support provided by the family in childhood; a foreign language spoken at home; and the CPI scales, Responsibility and Intellectual Efficiency.

Additional variables that discriminated between the males were the CPI scale, Achievement via Conformance, and the Locus of Control Scale score. Additional variables that discriminated between the females were the CPI scales, Socialization and Achievement via Independence, and work status in adolescence.

Job Success as Important Life Goal

Six of the 15 variables entered in the stepwise analysis separated males who considered job success an important life goal from those who did not. Four of the 15 variables differentiated between females who considered a career and job success an important life goal and those who did not. For males the separation between the two groups was significant on the $p<.01$ level, for females on the $p<.06$ level. The discriminant functions correctly classified 64% of the males and 65% of the females.

Among the variables that appeared in the discriminant functions for *both* sexes were: the CPI Scales of Responsibility and Achievement via Independence, and the Locus of Control Score. Additional variables that discriminated between the males were: father's education, mother's employment before son entered school, and a foreign language spoken at home. An additional variable that discriminated between the females was the emotional support provided by the family in childhood.

DISCUSSION

Our longitudinal data come from a rather unique setting—a small rural Hawaiian island—and from a population of Oriental and Polynesian youth. Yet they complement and extend a number of findings from studies of the urban youth market on the U.S. mainland, notably those by Greenberger and Steinberg (1981) and Steinberg et al. (1982) in Orange Country, California, and by Osterman (this volume) in Boston, Massachusetts. We find both "good news and bad news" associated with the employment experiences of adolescents, but also noteworthy gender and cultural differences in the relationship between work, adolescents' education and occupational aspirations and reward values.

For both sexes, employment in adolescence meant generally unskilled and casual work in what economists characterize as "secondary jobs" that are found through personal contacts, either relatives or peer friends (see Osterman, this volume).

For both sexes, employment in adolescence was associated with lowered educational achievement and lowered educational aspirations by grade 12. Among boys, a smaller proportion of the workers than the nonworkers aspired toward a job that would place them above the occupational level of their fathers; among girls, a smaller proportion of the workers considered job success an important life goal than did their nonworking peers.

Our longitudinal data also show that there were more boys and girls with little emotional support and with fewer opportunities for satisfactory identification with a parental model among youth who held paid jobs during adolescence than among those who did not. A significant proportion of adolescent workers had been considered "difficult to manage" by their parents at age 10. In adolescence, these working youth tended to score lower on measures of responsibility, socialization, and social maturity than did their nonworking peers.

We also found, as did Ruggiero, Greenberger, and Steinberg (1982) in California, that employed teenagers were more likely to commit delinquent acts than same-sex peers who were not in the work force in adolescence.

Our data suggest that the occupational deviance, cynicism, and lack of social responsibility noted by others in *both* cross-sectional and short-term longitudinal studies of adolescent workers (Ruggiero et al., 1982; Steinberg et al., 1982) may be attributable, in part, to a selection process that was already operating *before* the youth joined the work force.

Employment status in adolescence was generally less predictive of the occupational aspirations and occupational reward values held by the youth at age 18 than personality characteristics, such as their locus of control, their achievement orientation, and their sense of responsibility. Family background characteristics, such as parental education, the emotional support provided by the parents during childhood, and the mother's employment status before their offspring entered school, were also more discriminating than actual work experience during adolescence.

Gender Variability

On Kauai, the majority of adolescent women tended to work at and choose traditionally sex-typed jobs, and anticipated combining work, marriage, and parenthood in adulthood. Fewer women than men anticipated going to a four year college or professional school, and a lower proportion of females than males considered a career or job success their most important life goal. Yet for the girls, but not for the boys, paid employment in adolescence was the one variable that discriminated most between those with definite vocational plans for a specific occupation at age 18.

The "occupational moratorium" that has been recognized by Osterman in his studies of urban male youth as a period in which adventure-seeking and peer-group activities are more important than commitment to work may not as readily apply to young women of the same generation. In contrast to the males interviewed by Osterman in Boston (see this volume) and in contrast to their male peers on Kauai, the females in this (1955) birth cohort made an earlier commitment to the adult responsibilities of a steady job, marriage, and parenthood (as we noted in our follow-up studies at 25 and 30).

On Kauai, a higher proportion of adolescent women than men planned to enter an occupation that was above the level of that of their fathers. Among these women, more than half had mothers who had held outside employment when their daughters were still preschoolers, and they reported that these working mothers had been a strong influence on them. Mothers who worked outside of the home when their daughters were small children were also considered strong role models by those adolescent women who valued intrinsic features in their job and who themselves had a commitment to *both* work and family.

The influence of the mother as an important role model in the occupational socialization of young women has also been noted in a number of other studies on the U.S. mainland among Caucasians (Smith, 1980), as well as ethnic minority youth, such as blacks (Dillard & Campbell, 1981), Hispanics (Gandara, 1982), and Pacific-Asians (Machida-Fricker & Werner, 1976).

On Kauai, mothers who were gainfully employed while their children were still preschoolers also made a significant impact on the occupational aspirations and occupational reward values of their sons, i.e., their vocational plans, their preference for extrinsic vs. intrinsic features of the job, and the importance of career or job success as a life goal at age 18 (see Table 7.10).

Since this cohort was born, the proportion of women in the labor market has doubled, and the fastest growing section among working women are those with preschool children. Today, more than half of all preschool children in the United States have mothers in the work force. We have strong reasons to suspect from our data that this unplanned social experiment will make a significant impact on the attitudes of the next generation toward work and its reward values that may differ for men and women.

Cultural Variability

Future studies of the occupational socialization of youth need also to pay more attention to the various ethnic groups that are represented in the adolescent work force. In some states of the Union, notably Hawaii and California, members of ethnic minorities will soon outnumber Caucasians in the high school population. Sowell (1981) reminds us that research on ethnic minorities needs to take into account the educational level of the immigrants or sojourners, their length of stay in this country, and their fertility level. All of these variables will affect their economic status and, in turn, the occupational aspirations of their offspring.

This is quite apparent when we contrast the educational and occupational aspirations of the Japanese, Pilipino, and Hawaiian youth on Kauai: The Japanese youth descend from immigrants who were a highly selected sample of their homeland's population. Their selectivity was not in financial terms, but in terms of human potential. They were an educated people who valued reading. Today, the Japanese youth, as a group, have the highest educational aspirations and the lowest proportion of adolescents in the work force on Kauai. Coming from predominantly middle-class and small families (Mean N of children: 3), they appear to value the pursuit of life goals that maintain their status in an achievement-oriented society, but without losing their concern and sense of obligation to family relationships (DeVos, 1973; Werner & Smith, 1977).

The Pilipino youth descend from sojourners and immigrants who were less educated than the Japanese and came to Kauai two generations later. As late as 1950, the median level of education of the Pilipino males in Hawaii was only 6 grades. Today, their offspring, while still in the lower and lower-middle classes and with large families (Mean N of children: 5), respond like an upwardly mobile subculture. They tend to identify enough with the mainstream American culture to value striving for status and success (see also Ogbu, 1974, and this volume). Nearly half of the Pilipino youth on Kauai planned to enter a 4-year college and/or graduate school, and more than half considered success in a career or job their most important life goal.

The Hawaiians, in contrast, fit in many ways Ogbu's (1974) definition of a "caste-like minority." Under the impact of successive immigrations, they lost most of their lands and many lives. Today, the part-Hawaiians, through inter-marriage with the immigrants, are among the fastest growing ethnic groups in the island. They tend to have large families (Mean N of children: 6) and prefer a life style that values cooperation, interpersonal relationships, and spontaneity. As a group, Hawaiian youth had the lowest educational aspirations among the 18-year-olds on Kauai, but the highest proportion of adolescent youth in the work-force—nearly double that of the Japanese. Hawaiian youth valued intrinsic features in their job more and success in a job or career less than the other ethnic groups on Kauai. A higher proportion of Hawaiian adolescents had no clearcut occupational plans by age 18.

Our findings, as do those of Osterman (in this volume), point to the need to explore the cultural relativity of the concept of an "occupational moratorium" that was first postulated by Erikson (1959) in his essay on "The Problem of Ego Identity." Erikson surmises that social institutions support the strength and dis-tinctiveness of work identity by offering those who are still learning and experi-menting a *status of the moratorium*, an apprenticeship, characterized by defined duties, sanctioned competitions, and special freedom, yet integrated with the hierarchies of expectable jobs and careers, castes, and classes (p. 145). Osterman (this volume) finds such a stage among working-class youth in metropolitan Boston, but on rural Kauai, such a vocational moratorium appears to apply more for the college-bound middle-class Japanese youth and the upwardly mobile lower-middle-class Pilipino than for the Hawaiians, most of whom are still at the bottom of the socioeconomic ladder.

College intention is strongly associated with the importance of career success as a long-term goal in life among the Japanese on Kauai, and to a lesser extent for the Pilipino, but for most Hawaiians such a moratorium stage is a luxury they cannot afford. For the overwhelming majority of the Hawaiians on Kauai, opportunities in the job market in the future will not be very different from what they have found in their teenage jobs. Hence most Hawaiian youth express more interest in intrinsic features of the job, such as freedom from supervision and the chance "to do your thing," and value success in a career less.

Yet comparative studies of high achievers among Hawaiians have shown that in this group, as in the other ethnic minorities, mothers can be an influential role model for their sons and daughters, motivating them to do well in school and to aspire toward higher education and better jobs (Machida-Fricker & Werner, 1976; McNassor & Hongo, 1972). Among the Hawaiians, as among the Japanese and Pilipino, the mothers of high-achieving adolescents had, as a rule, more education that the fathers, and close, positive relationships with their offspring.

Topics for Future Research

An underlying premise of this chapter has been that a developmental (and intergenerational) perspective can considerably enhance the understanding of the process of occupational socialization. A promising research strategy for future studies in this area is offered by Bronfenbrenner (1979) in *The Ecology of Human Development*.

Bronfenbrenner views the development of an individual within the context of a series of concentric circles, each embedded within the next. Most studies of adolescents' occupational socialization, so far, have dealt with *micro-systems*, i.e., "the relationships between the developing person and environment in an immediate setting containing that person." Greenberger and Steinberg's (1981) study of the workplace as a context for the socialization of youth is such an example, or research that focuses on the dyadic relationship between parents' career behavior and the career development of their adolescent offspring (Dillard & Campbell, 1981); Smith, 1980). Absent, so far, in the studies of microsystems is the consideration of other role models besides parents. Anecdotal evidence from the Kauai Longitudinal Study leads us to believe that, especially among minority youth, older siblings, cousins, and members of the extended family can play an important role in occupational socialization that needs to be further explored. There is also a need for a more careful scrutiny of the role of sib-caretaking as a precursor of future work orientation, especially among adolescent girls (Werner & Smith, 1982; Werner, 1984).

There have been a few studies of *mesosystems*, i.e., "the interrelationships among major settings, containing the person," such as the world of work and the family (Elder, 1974), or work, school, and family (Greenberger, Steinberg, Vaux, & McAuliffe, 1980; Steinberg et al., 1982). One relationship that has not been systematically addressed is the relationship between training and work experience in the Armed Forces and later work in the civilian sector. A significant proportion of the youth on Kauai, especially among the part-Hawaiians and the Pilipino, volunteered for military service to gain specialized vocational skills that they hoped would transfer to civilian life.

Even rarer are studies that examine the *exosystem,* i.e., "the impact of other social structures—both formal and informal—that do not themselves contain the developing person, but impinge upon or encompass the setting in which that person is found." The mass media's depiction of occupational roles for minority youth, the transportation system to and from work, the availability of childcare providers for teenage parents who work—these are all part of the exosystem whose influences are apparent in our interviews with the adolescents on Kauai, but which have not been systematically explored.

Last, but not least, there are a number of important trends in the *macrosystem,* i.e., "the institutional patterns, such as economic, educational, legal, social, and political systems of which the micro-, meso-, and exo-system are the concrete manifestations," that need to be more systematically studied.

Among them are: changes in children's rights and child labor laws; the impact of changing sex roles and affirmative action programs that have given youth a wider access to "non-traditional" vocational training and occupations; and, perhaps most importantly, the consequence of massive influx of women with young children into the labor force and their impact on the occupational socialization of the next generation. It is a research agenda that requires the best conceptual and methodological tools of the disciplines presented in this volume.

REFERENCES

Bosenrup, E. (1970). *Women's role in economic development.* London: Allen and Unwin.

Bronfenbrenner, U. (1979). *The ecology of human development.* Cambridge, MA: Harvard University Press.

DeVos, G. (1973). *Socialization for achievement: Essays on the cultural psychology of the Japanese.* Berkeley: University of California Press.

Dillard, J. M., & Campbell, N. (1981). Influence of Puerto Rican, Black and Anglo parents' career behavior on their adolescent children. *Vocational Guidance Quarterly, 30*(2), 139–148.

Elder, G. H., Jr. (1974). *Children of the Great Depression.* Chicago: University of Chicago Press.

Erikson, E. H. (1959). The problem of ego identity. *Psychological Issues,* Monograph 1, 101–164.

Frantz, R. S. (1980). The effects of early labor market experience upon internal-external locus of control among young male workers. *Journal of Youth and Adolescence, 9*(3), 203–210.

Gandara, P. (1982). Passing through the eye of the needle: High achieving Chicanas. *Hispanic Journal of Behavior Sciences, 4*(2), 167–180.

Gough, H. (1969). *California Psychological Inventory Manual* (rev. ed.). Palo Alto: Consulting Psychologists Press.

Greenberger, E., & Steinberg, L. D. (1981). The workplace as a context for the socialization of youth. *Journal of Youth and Adolescence, 10,* 185–210.

Greenberger, E., Steinberg, L., Vaux, A., & McAuliffe, S. (1980). Adolescents who work: Effects of part-time employment on family and peer relations. *Journal of Youth and Adolescence, 9*, 189–202.

Lewin-Epstein, N. (1981). *Youth employment during high school*. Washington, D.C.: National Center for Education Statistics.

Lewis, N. V., Gardner, J. A., & Seitz, P. (1983). *High school work experience and its effects*. Columbus OH: National Center for Research in Vocational Education, Ohio State University.

Machida-Fricker, S. K., & Werner, E. E. (1976). Achievement orientation of adolescent women of Hawaiian-, Japanese- and Pilipino-American descent. *JSAS Catalog of Selected Documents in Psychology, 6*(3), 69.

McNassor, D., & Hongo, R. (1972). *Strangers in their own land: Self-desparagement in ethnic Hawaiian youth on the island of Hawaii*. Mimeographed. Claremont, CA: Claremont College Department of Education.

Moore, C. (1983). Child labor and national development: An annotated bibliography. In D. A. Wagner (Ed.), *Child development and international development: Research-policy interfaces* (pp. 87–106). San Francisco: Jossey-Bass.

Nowicki, S. (1971). Correlates of locus of control in a secondary school population. *Developmental Psychology, 4*, 477–478.

Ogbu, J. U. (1974). *The next generation: An ethnography of education in an urban neighborhood*. New York: Academic Press.

Ruggiero, M., Greenberger, E., & Steinberg, L. D. (1982). Occupational deviance among adolescent workers. *Youth and Society, 13*, 423–448.

SCAT (Cooperative School and College Ability Tests). (1966). *Cooperative tests and services*. Princeton, NJ: Educational Testing Service.

Smith, E. R. (1980). Desiring and expecting to work among high school girls: Some determinants and consequences. *Journal of Vocational Behavior, 17*(2), 218–230.

Sowell, T. (1981). *Ethnic America: A history*. New York: Basic Books.

Steinberg, L. D., Greenberger, E., Vaux, A., & Ruggiero, M. (1981). Early work experience: Effects on adolescent occupational socialization. *Youth and Society, 12*, 403–422.

Steinberg, L. D., Greenberger, E., Garduque, L., Ruggiero, M., & Vaux, A. (1982). Effects of working on adolescent development. *Developmental Psychology, 18*(3), 385–395.

STEP (Sequential Tests and Educational Progress). (1966). Cooperative tests and services. Princeton, NJ: Educational Testing Service.

Thurstone, L., & Thurstone, T. G. (1954). *SRA primary mental abilities: Examiner's manual*. Chicago: Science Research Associates.

Wagner, D. (Ed.). (1983). *Child development and international development: Research-policy interfaces*. San Francisco: Jossey-Bass.

Werner, E. E. (1984). *Child care: Kith, kin and hired hands*. Baltimore: University Park Press.

Werner, E. E., & Smith, R. S. (1977). *Kauai's children come of age*. Honolulu: University of Hawaii Press.

Werner, E. E., & Smith, R. S. (1982). *Vulnerable, but invincible: A longitudinal study of resilient children and youth*. New York: McGraw-Hill.

8

Characteristics of High School Students' Paid Jobs, and Employment Experience After Graduation

David Stern
University of California, Berkeley

Yoshi-fumi Nakata
Doshisha University, Kyoto, Japan

This chapter describes the prevalence of certain qualitative characteristics of teenage jobs, measured by a survey of young workers in 1979. Qualitative aspects of paid jobs held by teenagers received very little systematic attention in the past. Recently, however, a series of pioneering studies by Greenberger, Steinberg, and associates have led them to conclude that the poor quality of many contemporary teenage jobs threatens to make the young workers "economically rich, but . . . psychologically poor" (Greenberger & Steinberg, 1986, p. 238). Using longitudinal data on teenagers initially interviewed in 1979, we examine the consequences of qualitative differences in their 1979 jobs.

The data analyzed here, from the National Longitudinal Survey of Youth labor market experience, show that there are indeed differences among jobs in quality and quantity of social contacts, opportunities for using and developing valuable skills, and the job's potential intrinsic interest to a teenager. In addition to summarizing the prevalence of these job characteristics by gender and race of the person reporting them, we compare teenagers' and adults' characterizations of their jobs. Finally, we analyze connections between teenagers' 1979 job characteristics and their subsequent experience in the labor market. Among a subsample who were interviewed before graduating from high school in 1979 and then again in 1980, 1981, and 1982, we find some associations between qualitative aspects of jobs held during high school and labor market success during the subsequent three years. Of the qualitative dimensions measured here, skill use and development is most strongly associated with subsequent success in the labor market.

189

BACKGROUND

In the 1970s many observers of American high schools argued for providing more work experience and other kinds of experiential education (Conrad & Hedin, 1977; National Commission on the Reform of Secondary Education, 1973; National Panel on High School and Adolescent Education, 1976; President's Science Advisory Committee, 1973). One fundamental concern was that separation of adolescents from adult work, and emergence of a "youth culture," impaired the development of teenagers into productive adults. This is still a concern (see Centre for Educational Research and Innovation, 1983; Coleman & Husen, 1985).

Recent advocates of work experience for teenagers have contended that paid employment no longer exposes them to such risk of bodily harm or economic exploitation as it did in the past, before the enactment of laws regulating child labor and requiring attendance in school. Advocates have offered various proposals for making work experience more available to young people, including a reduced minimum wage for teenagers, a lower legal age for leaving school, and more awarding of academic credit for students' outside employment.

In the 1970s, this last idea caught on. For instance, a national survey of high schools in 1977 found 64.5% of the schools gave academic credit for off-campus work experience or occupational training (Abramowitz & Tenenbaum, 1978). A 1978 survey of high school juniors and seniors in the San Francisco Bay region found that 26% had received credit for work experience (Stern, 1980). Work experience also was an important element of programs designed in the 1970s to help alleviate youth unemployment. The 1977 Youth Employment and Demonstration Projects Act created several such programs. The intent was to improve the employment prospects of low-income youths who lacked work experience, and who tend to have relatively high rates of unemployment even when the overall unemployment rate is low. Since this group also contains a relatively high proportion of school dropouts and low achievers, the new programs often attempted to encourage high school completion by having schools award credit for time spent working in outside jobs, or even providing paid jobs as an incentive for students to finish school (Hahn, 1979).

The presumption that paid work experience produces positive consequences for teenagers has been fortified by statistical evidence that new high school graduates earn more money and experience less unemployment if they spent more time working in paid jobs while they were still students in high school (D'Amico & Baker, 1984; Meyer & Wise, 1982). A growing proportion of high school students have been taking paid jobs, whether this is good for them or not: The rise in labor force participation among high school students from 1950 to 1980 has been documented by Greenberger and Steinberg (1986). Michael and Tuma (1984) show the prevalence of paid work in 1979 among teenagers as young as 14, and Lewin-Epstein (1981) gives details for high school sophomores

190

and seniors in 1980. Most American teenagers now have some kind of paid work experience while they are still in high school, and most of the work is in jobs that are *not* sponsored by schools or other public agencies.

Despite the growing popularity of work experience for teenagers, and contrary to the arguments of its advocates, Greenberger and Steinberg (1986) contend that "involvement in a job may not advance the transition to adulthood so much as prolong youngsters' attachment to the peer culture" (p. 7). They document the declining proportion of teenagers employed in traditional craft, factory, and farm work, and the rising proportion employed in new service and sales jobs. Approximately half of all employed teenagers now are either store clerks or food service workers. According to Greenberger and Steinberg, the new teenage jobs provide less opportunity to learn valuable skills or knowledge, and also less often bring teenagers "into contact with adults who have a stake in preparing them for adulthood" (p. 50). In addition, Greenberger and Steinberg contend that working teenagers now contribute less of their income to their families than was true in the past. Indeed, acquiring the money to buy luxuries for themselves is the teenagers' main expressed motive for working. This, according to Greenberger and Steinberg, is not conducive to positive development.

In their own 1978–79 study of high school sophomores and juniors in suburban Orange County, California, the Greenberger-Steinberg group found cause for concern about the developmental consequences of teenage work. Although working does give young people responsibility for managing money, and there is more opportunity to be helpful to other people at work than at school, the researchers found about one-fifth of the working students said they did not meet their obligations at work, and an equal number said they felt no interdependence with other workers. Fewer than 5% said they ever went beyond the call of duty in their performance at work. The findings on contact with adults were also mixed—about one-third of the working students developed friendly relationships with adults at work, but fewer than 10% would definitely discuss personal problems with adult coworkers or supervisors (Greenberger & Steinberg, 1981).

Other findings from the Orange County sample are more disturbing. About 41% of the young workers had committed an act of theft on the job, and 45% had committed a deviant act other than theft, such as calling in sick when not, or being intoxicated or high on drugs while at work. More than 60% had committed either theft or something else improper (Ruggiero, Greenberger, & Steinberg, 1982). Furthermore, a cynical view of work as intrinsically unrewarding, pointless, and meaningless was more prevalent among working students than among their nonworking classmates, and those who worked more hours a week were more cynical about work. Working long hours in out-of-school jobs also appears to depress grades in school (Steinberg, Greenberger, Garduque, & McAuliffe, 1982).

The Greenberger-Steinberg sample consisted of middle-class, suburban teenagers who held "naturally occurring," unsubsidized jobs. As mentioned above, there have also been a number of public programs to provide work experience for low-income, unemployed teenagers. Dement (1982) gives a good description of these programs. Some provide summer jobs, some offer year-round employment for teenagers who are not in school, and other programs have created part-time work for high school students. Most of this work is "synthetic": It is organized to provide experience for young people and would not otherwise exist. Evaluations of these programs have found disappointing results (Burtless, 1984; Dement, 1982; Manpower Demonstration Research Corporation, 1980; Taggart, 1981). Since only low-income, unemployed youth are eligible for these programs, it is possible that a stigma attaches to them. There may actually be a negative credentialling effect, if would-be employers assume that participants in these programs are *ipso facto* undesirable as employees. If the stigmatizing effect is strong enough, a program might fail to improve participants' employability even though it taught them a great deal. No one really knows whether the disappointing results of compensatory work experience programs are due to an image problem or to poor quality of the work experience itself. Only one published study has analyzed actual data on the quality of work experience in any of the various public programs (Ball, Gerould, & Burstein, 1980), but that study did not follow participants over time to find out whether variations in program quality made any difference later.

To summarize: The presumption that work experience is necessarily good for teenagers has been called into question by the findings that (1) work experience programs for low-income, unemployed teenagers have not been effective in improving their success in the job market; and (2) among teenagers in general, those who work during high school do have more success in the labor market subsequently, but the jobs they have as students often do not demand much responsibility or teach any important skills, and may even promote cynicism and unethical behavior at work. These findings raise questions about the quality of teenagers' work experience. Would subsidized work experience programs be more effective if they offered better quality work? Among the naturally occurring, unsubsidized jobs available to teenagers, are some jobs demonstrably better than others? Is it possible to identify some characteristics of teenage jobs that are associated with later economic, social, and psychological outcomes? The following sections present some new evidence pertaining to these questions, focusing in particular on characteristics of naturally occurring teenage jobs and their relation to subsequent economic outcomes.

DATA AND FINDINGS

The best data for measuring the influence of characteristics of jobs held by high school students come from the National Longitudinal Survey (NLS) of Youth Labor Market Experience. This survey interviewed a nationally representative sample of 12,686 youth age 14 to 22 in 1979. The panel has been interviewed again in each subsequent year (Center for Human Resource Research, 1983). For our analysis we selected seniors in high school at the time of the 1979 interview who were also interviewed again in 1980, 1981, and 1982. Our purpose is to determine whether and how various attributes of students' jobs are related to their early success in the labor market after they graduate.

We restricted our analysis to seniors for several reasons. Seniors are more likely than younger students to be employed (Michael & Tuma, 1984), and the jobs they hold are much less likely to be unstructured, informal arrangements like baby sitting (Lewin-Epstein, 1981, pp. 104–106). Finally, since the national economy was so volatile in the 1980–85 period, it is best to analyze each age cohort separately, and the 1979 seniors are the first cohort of seniors in the NLS survey.

The NLS data are better for our purposes than other available longitudinal surveys because they include more information about qualitative dimensions of students' jobs. We examined the 1979 data on students' current jobs, i.e., jobs held during the week prior to the 1979 interview. Analysis of this information therefore implies restricting the sample to those seniors who were currently employed in 1979.

We also imposed one other major restriction on the sample by including only seniors who graduated from high school but did *not* go directly to postsecondary school or college. Even though many college students also work, their capabilities and objectives in the labor market are different from those of their age peers who do not attend school (see Meyer & Wise, 1982). Therefore, we excluded anyone who was enrolled in school after September 1, 1980.

Table 8.1 shows how these restrictions affected the size and composition of our sample. We started with 1091 individuals who were high school seniors in 1979 and remained in the survey through 1982. Of this total, 702 were not attending school after September 1, 1980 and 356 of these 702 provided complete data on jobs they had held during the week before this interview in 1979. Of the total 1091, there were 558 who had provided complete data on their current jobs in 1979, but only 356 of these were not in school in 1980–81. Variables in Table 8.1 are defined as follows:

- *Fraction of time unemployed* is the number of weeks unemployed divided by number of weeks in the labor force. Weeks in the labor force is the sum of weeks unemployed and weeks employed. Data for each calendar year were compiled from employment histories recorded in the following year.
- *Hourly wage* is total income from wages, salaries, and self-employment, divided by total number of hours worked during the year.
- *Age* is at the time of the 1979 interview. Most interviews took place in the spring.

TABLE 8.1

Characteristics of 1979 Seniors, Unweighted Data (Standard Deviation in Parentheses)

	(1) Whole Sample	(2) Not in School in 1980-1981	(3) Holding Jobs at 1979 Interview	(4) Not in School 1980-1981 and Holding Jobs at 1979 Interview
Sample size	1091	702	558	356
Mean fraction of time unemployed in 1980	0.162 (0.289)	0.183 (0.307)	0.115 (0.245)	0.129 (0.261)
Mean fraction of time unemployed in 1981	0.145 (0.273)	0.158 (0.289)	0.117 (0.249)	0.136 (0.269)
Mean hourly wage 1980	3.070 (3.103)	3.040 (3.251)	3.390 (2.903)	3.360 (2.848)
Mean hourly wage 1981	3.531 (3.075)	3.508 (3.022)	3.856 (2.957)	4.002 (3.116)
Proportion not in school in 1980-1981	0.643 (0.479)	1 (0)	0.638 (0.481)	1 (0)
Mean age in 1979	17.565 (0.721)	17.662 (0.753)	17.545 (0.668)	17.624 (0.707)
Proportion with no man in household at age 14	0.160 (0.367)	0.175 (0.380)	0.136 (0.343)	0.154 (0.362)
Mean years schooling of parent with more schooling	12.038 (3.254)	11.264 (3.008)	12.284 (3.103)	11.613 (2.764)
Mean hours per week worked for pay in 1978-79	10.519 (10.574)	11.133 (11.138)	15.652 (10.076)	16.565 (10.321)
Proportion expecting to be in school 5 years after 1979 interview	0.311 (0.463)	0.222 (0.416)	0.278 (0.448)	0.190 (0.393)
Proportion Black or Hispanic	0.426 (0.495)	0.440 (0.497)	0.330 (0.471)	0.343 (0.475)
Proportion male	0.486 (0.500)	0.5 (0.500)	0.507 (0.500)	0.537 (0.499)
Proportion living outside metropolitan area, 1979	0.320 (0.467)	0.36 (0.480)	0.307 (0.462)	0.338 (0.474)
Mean unemployment rate in local area, 1979	6.166 (2.150)	6.225 (2.157)	6.101 (2.200)	6.119 (2.157)
Mean fraction of disadvantaged students in high school, 1979 (school survey)	0.236 (0.232)	0.261 (0.239)	0.198 (0.213)	0.227 (0.223)
Mean drop-out rate in high school, 1979 (school survey)	0.144 (0.175)	0.158 (0.185)	0.132 (0.151)	0.150 (0.167)
Mean fraction White in high school, 1979 (school survey)	0.705 (0.306)	0.700 (0.306)	0.753 (0.280)	0.746 (0.290)

- *No man in household* means no father, stepfather, or other adult male was present when the respondent was 14 years old, as reported in 1979.
- *Years schooling of parent with more schooling* is the level completed by the mother or father (or the adult female or male in the household) when respondent was 14, whichever is greater.
- *Hours per week worked for pay in 1978–79* is total hours worked between January 1, 1978 and the 1979 interview, divided by the number of weeks for which employment status was accounted for during that period. This is based on the employment history recorded in the 1979 interview.

The remaining variables are self-explanatory. The last three were obtained from a survey of the high schools in which students in the sample were enrolled in 1979.

The 1979 seniors who did not attend postsecondary school in 1980–81 came from less advantageous family backgrounds and had less labor market success in 1980 and 1981 than the sample as a whole. Just the reverse is true for 1979 seniors who held jobs during the week before the first interview. These two selection effects therefore offset each other when we restrict our sample to 1979 seniors who were both employed at the time of the interview and not in school in 1980–81. In other words, most of the values in the first and fourth columns of Table 8.1 lie between the values in columns two and three.

Qualitative characteristics of 1979 seniors' current jobs are displayed in Tables 8.2 through 8.23, which appear in the Appendix to this chapter showing unweighted numbers of individuals, and proportions of column totals in parentheses. The sample in these tables consists of seniors who were employed during the week before the 1979 interview and did not attend school after September 1, 1980. All but three of the job-quality variables are based on reports by respondents about their own jobs in 1979. These reports were elicited by questions that have been used in previous surveys of working conditions (Quinn & Shepard, 1974; Quinn & Staines, 1979). The other three variables are ratings of the occupation in which the student's 1979 job was classified, using the *Dictionary of Occupational Titles* (U.S. Employment Service, 1977).

Because some of these job-quality measures appear to overlap, we combine them into groups. There are many ways to do such grouping. Here we report results from grouping variables based on five prior theoretical dimensions:

- *Rights and compensation* (Tables 8.2–8.6). These variables indicate whether the job is part of an established organization or trade where workers have better job security, pay, fringe benefits, and prospects for promotion. (See Doeringer & Piore, 1971.) Tables 8.2–8.6 show that boys reported these attributes more often than girls.
- *Motivation potential* (Tables 8.7–8.12). These variables reflect whether the job is felt to be worth doing well, and whether it provides clear feedback on

how well the worker is actually doing. The six indicators here are among the characteristics that can make a job "generally motivating," according to some organizational psychologists (Hackman & Lawler, 1971; Hackman & Oldham, 1976; Katzell & Yankelovich, 1975, pp. 184–185). Students who give their jobs high ratings on this dimension are apparently getting some support to believe that work can be intrinsically interesting. Tables 8.7–8.12 reveal no pronounced association between these variables and sex or race. But Table 8.27 (see p. 201) shows that motivation potential appears to be higher in jobs held by seniors who are older and whose parents have more education.

- *Skill use and development* (Tables 8.13–8.16). This dimension includes a self-reported judgment of the job's value for developing new skills, and the three ratings of complexity of the occupation in which the job was classified, according to the *Dictionary of Occupational Titles* (DOT). Examples of occupations held by members of this sample in 1979, in ascending order of complexity (using all three DOT ratings), are: busboy, waiter, food counter and fountain worker, stock handler, sales clerk, billing clerk, cashier, cook, and auto mechanic. Tables 8.14–8.16 clearly show, and Table 8.27 confirms, that occupations performed by females were rated as more complex.
- *Physical comfort* (Tables 8.17–8.19). These are straightforward measures of physical amenity. Evidently boys' jobs more often expose them to dangerous or unhealthy conditions. (Absence of these conditions implies a higher value of the "physical comfort" index.)
- *Social contact* (Tables 8.16 and 8.20–8.23). These variables indicate the amount of contact on the job, and positive feelings about that contact, with other people in general and co-workers and supervisors in particular. Tables 8.20–8.23 show black and Hispanic seniors have less of these and Table 8.24 shows students with more highly educated parents have more.

We constructed a numerical index for each of these five dimensions, by computing a weighted average of the constituent variables for which valid data were available. Weights were chosen so that each separate constituent variable contributed approximately the same amount of variance to the index. For instance, the five variables measuring "rights and compensation" each contributed approximately one-fifth of the total variance of that index. Means (and standard deviations) of the five indices are:

	All seniors holding jobs at 1979 interview (n = 558)	Seniors holding jobs at 1979 interview and not in school 1980–81 (n = 356)
Rights and compensation	2.02 (0.71)	2.09 (0.72)
Motivation potential	2.67 (0.57)	2.69 (0.57)

Skill use and development	1.73 (0.62)	1.72 (0.62)
Physical comfort	3.31 (0.57)	3.27 (0.57)
Social contact	2.77 (0.54)	2.74 (0.55)

To determine whether these five indices are sufficiently distinct from each other to be useful as separate measures, we regressed each on the other four. The proportion of variance *not* explained ranged from 72% for the index of "motivation potential" up to 97% for the index of "physical comfort." The five indices therefore do appear to be sufficiently distinct.

We also computed the correlation of each index with the Duncan prestige score for the occupation in which the student's 1979 job was classified. "Motivation potential" and "rights and compensation" both had correlations less than 0.1 in absolute value with the Duncan index; the latter was actually negative. "Physical comfort" and "social contact" both had positive correlations of 0.28 with Duncan score. "Skill use and development" had the highest correlation, 0.56. Three of the four components of the skill index are, like the Duncan index, based on occupational classification; this accounts for the high correlation. As a group, though, these five indices cannot be considered mere proxies for occupational prestige. Table 8.24, which shows means of the quality indices for students' jobs in different occupational categories, reveals a pattern similar to the correlations with the Duncan index.

Comparison of Teenagers' and Adults' Jobs.   The actual distribution of 1979 seniors' jobs among different occupations is shown in Table 8.25, along with the occupational distribution for the whole U.S. labor force in 1979. The high school students are overrepresented in sales and clerical, as well as in low-skilled labor, service, and farm jobs. Their average hourly wage was less than half that of the labor force as a whole.

Qualitative comparison between the job held by 1979 NLS seniors and the entire labor force is in Table 8.26. Some of the 1979 NLS questions about qualitative characteristics of jobs were also asked in the 1977 Quality of Em-

TABLE 8.24
Mean Values of Job Quality Indexes for Current Job of 1979 Seniors, by Occupation

Occupation	Rights and Compensation	Motivation Potential	Skill Use and Development	Physical Comfort	Social Contact
Professional or managerial	2.20	2.84	2.42	3.50	3.15
Sales or clerical	1.89	2.61	2.25	3.49	2.91
Craft	2.21	2.86	2.35	2.98	2.64
Operative	2.15	2.66	1.66	2.98	2.73
Laborer, service, or farm	1.99	2.59	1.38	3.20	2.62

TABLE 8.25
Wages and Occupational Distribution for 1979
Seniors and U.S. Labor Force

	1979 High School Seniors	1979 U.S. Labor Force[a]
Mean Wage Rate in 1979	$2.98	$6.16
Occupational distribution	100.0%	100.0%
1. Professional or managerial	3.7%	26.4%
2. Sales or clerical	30.0%	24.5%
3. Crafts	5.3%	13.3%
4. Operatives	9.6%	15.0%
5. Laborors, service, or farm	51.4%	20.8%

[a]*Statistical Abstract of the United States, 1980* (U.S. Department of Commerce, Bureau of the Census), Tables 696, 699.

ployment Survey, which polled a national sample of 1515 employed persons age 16 or older (Quinn & Staines, 1979). Tables 8.26 shows 1979 seniors, compared to the workforce as a whole, were relatively unlikely to receive fringe benefits, do a number of different things on the job, see the job as very significant, exercise independence, or develop close friendships on the job. On the other hand, the high school students more often said the physical surroundings at work were pleasant, the chances for promotion were good, and, somewhat surprisingly, that they produced a complete product or service. This last difference may reflect adults' greater awareness of the larger context for their individual jobs.

Table 8.27 summarizes how the five job quality indices are associated with characteristics of the 1979 seniors themselves. Boys do more physically harrowing work, and are more likely to be awarded the rights and compensation of full-fledged workers, but their jobs are less complex and skill-enhancing. Black and Hispanic students are more often restricted to jobs where they have less contact with other people. Seniors with highly educated parents more often get the jobs with a lot of social contact. They also more frequently report that they know and care whether they are performing well in their jobs. Students who are older also report more motivation potential in their jobs, as well as more rights and compensation. These associations are consistent with well-known patterns of employment by race, sex, and socioeconomic status. We may therefore feel some confidence that the data are valid. At the same time the low values of R^2 in Table 8.27 mean that these five job quality indices are not just surrogates for students' socioeconomic characteristics.

Predicting Early Success in the Labor Market.   Tables 8.28 and 8.29 show regression coefficients for hypothetical predictors of wages and unemployment rates among 1979 seniors who graduated, entered the labor force, and did not attend postsecondary school. Regressions were run with and without 1979 job quality indexes included among the predictors. The full set of five indexes contributed significantly ($F(5, 142) = 2.38$) to reducing unexplained variance in

TABLE 8.26

Reported Characteristics of Current Jobs, 1979 Seniors and 1977 Quality of Employment Survey: Percent Affirmative Responses

	1979 Seniors Survey	1979 Quality of Employment Survey
Rights and Compensation		
Does your employer make medical, surgical, or hospital insurance that covers injuries or illness of the job available to you?	29.2	78.1
Does your employer make paid vacation available to you?	34.5	80.8
Thinking of your present job, would you say the pay is good?	67.4[a]	65.2[a]
Thinking of your present job, would you say the job security is good?	75.0[a]	75.3[a]
Thinking of your present job, would you say the chances for promotion are good?	61.2[a]	42.0[a]
Motivation Potential		
Do you have to do a number of different things on your job?	59.0[b]	86.1[c]
On your job, do you produce a whole product or perform a complete service?	87.0[b]	66.8[c]
Does your job give you the feeling that the job itself is very significant or important in the broader scheme of things?	67.3[b]	84.4[c]
Does your job give you the feeling that you know whether or not you are performing your job well or poorly?	91.5[b]	93.1[c]
Thinking of your present job, would you say you are given a chance to do the things you do best?	71.0[a]	64.1[a]
Does your job require independent thought or action?	68.6[b]	82.3[c]
Skill Use and Development		
Thinking of your present job, would you say the skills you are learning would be valuable in getting a better job?	65.1[a]	N.A.
Complexity of relations with things (DOT categories) -- driving, operating, controlling, precision working, setting up --	26.4	N.A.

(continued....)

(Table 8.26 continued)

	1979 Seniors	1979 Quality of Employment Survey
Skill Use and Development		
Complexity of relations with data (DOT categories) -- analyzing, coordinating, synthesizing --	8.0	N.A.
Complexity of relations with people (DOT categories) -- persuading, diverting, supervising, instructing --	8.6	N.A.
Physical Comfort		
Thinking of your present job, would you say the physical surroundings are pleasant?	88.7[a]	71.7[a]
Thinking of your present job, would you say the job is dangerous?	20.1[a]	N.A.
Thinking of your present job, would you say you are exposed to unhealthy conditions?	13.3[a]	N.A.
Social Contact		
Thinking of your present job, would you say your job gives you a lot of opportunity to deal with other people?	62.3[d]	N.A.
Can you develop close friendships in your job?	52.8[e]	85.0[c]
Thinking of your present job, would you say your coworkers are friendly?	95.1[a]	92.1[a]
Thinking of your present job, would you say your supervisor is competent in doing the job?	93.8[a]	81.1[a]
Complexity of relations with people (DOT categories) -- pursuading, diverting, supervising, instructing --	8.6	N.A.

[a]Those who said, "somewhat true" or "very true."
[b]Those who said, "a moderate amount," "quite a lot," or "a maximum amount."
[c]Those who said, "agree" or "strongly agree."
[d]Those who said, "quite a lot" or "a maximum amount."
[e]Those who said, "quite a lot" or "a maximum amount."

TABLE 8.27
Regressions for Quality Dimensions of 1979 Job
(Coefficients and Standard Errors)

	Dimensions of 1979 Job Quality				
	Rights and Compensation	Motivation Potential	Skill Use and Development	Physical Comfort	Social Contact
Male	0.234** (0.062)	0.057 (0.051)	-0.141** (0.054)	-0.189** (0.051)	-0.043 (0.038)
Black or Hispanic	0.023 (0.071)	-0.029 (0.058)	-0.057 (0.061)	-0.013 (0.059)	-0.152** (0.044)
Parent years Schooling	-0.007 (0.011)	0.022** (0.009)	0.005 (0.009)	0.007 (0.009)	0.027** (0-007)
No man in house, age 14	-0.080 (0.091)	0.050 (0.074)	0.091 (0.078)	0.056 (0.075)	0.009 (0.056)
Living outside metropolitan area, 1979	0.000 (0.069)	0.076 (0.055)	-0.030 (0.059)	-0.040 (0.056)	0.013 (0.042)
Age	0.091* (0.049)	0.088** (0.040)	-0.037 (0.042)	0.025 (0.040)	0.046 (0.030)
Intercept	1.850** (0.177)	2.235** (0.143)	1.834** (0.152)	3.283** (0.145)	2.498** (0.108)
R^2	0.044	0.035	0.024	0.030	0.078
n	512	512	512	512	512

$*p \leq 0.1$
$**p \leq 0.05$

unemployment but not in wages ($F = 1.75$). However, the single dimension of skill use and development is significantly associated with both outcomes. Students whose 1979 jobs engaged them in more complex dealings with people, things, or data, or who said they were learning skills that would be valuable in getting a better job, were likely to earn money at a higher hourly rate in 1980–82. They were also likely to experience less unemployment.

Tables 8.28 and 8.29 also show that students who spent more time working for pay in 1978 and 1979 (prior to the interview in spring, 1979) had significantly higher hourly earnings and less unemployment in 1980–82. This replicates findings of D'Amico and Baker (1984) with the NLS data. It also replicates the finding of Meyer and Wise (1982), who used data from the National Longitudinal Study of the High School Class of 1972.

Among the predictors other than high school work variables in Tables 8.28 and 8.29, parent's educational attainment is significantly associated with higher hourly earnings after graduation. Males are likely to earn higher hourly pay, but also to experience more unemployment.

Restricting the sample can cause selection bias (Heckman, 1979; Maddala, 1983). Would the inferences we draw from data on high school graduates who do not go to college also be valid for college-goers if they were not in college? The answer is no, if the probability of college attendance is correlated with unmeasured influences on (potential) labor market outcomes. However, if that

TABLE 8.28
Regression Coefficients for Hypothetical Predictors of
Average Wage Rate, 1980-82
(Standard Errors in Parentheses)

	Without Job Quality	With Job Quality
No man in house, age 14	0.052041 (0.487150)	0.012641 (0.485035)
Parent years schooling	0.147228** (0.066913)	0.140112** (0.068110)
Average hours/week paid job 1978-1979	0.038248** (0.015903)	0.049232** (0.016533)
Black or Hispanic	-0.090609 (0.0383389)	0.027079 (0.382712)
Male	0.545926 (0.333580)	0.809222** (0.344695)
1979 Job Quality		
Rights and compensation	--	-0.346461 (0.274942)
Motivation potential	--	-0.398426 (0.341989)
Skill use and development	--	0.641009** (0.303867)
Physical comfort	--	0.382595 (0.318539)
Social contact	--	0.291757 (0.431208
Selection term	0.114010 (0.878094)	0.318717 (0.382031)
Intercept	1.384057 (0.914232)	-0.350433 (1.485035)
n	154	154
R^2	0.1013	0.1534

*$p \leq .05$
**$p \leq .01$

correlation can be estimated, the resulting bias can be corrected (see Meyer & Wise, 1982). For this purpose we use a linear procedure devised by Olsen (1980). The probability of not attending college was estimated for all 1979 seniors who were employed in the week before the 1979 interview. Generalized least-squares (GLS) estimation was used. The predicted probability, minus one, was entered as a selection term in the regressions reported in Table 8.28 and 8.29. The coefficient on the selection term was not significant and presence of the selection term scarcely changed the coefficients on other predictors. We conclude that selection bias is not a serious problem here.

Summary of Findings. Teenagers' jobs do vary in quality (e.g., see Tables 8.7, 8.13, 8.14, 8.21), even though they are concentrated in services, sales, and

TABLE 8.29
Regression Coefficients for Hypothetical Predictors of
Proportion of Time Unemployed, (1980-82)
(Standard Errors in Parentheses)

	Without Job Quality	With Job Quality
No man in house, age 14	0.026233 (0.045870)	0.013883 (0.045185)
Parent years schooling	-0.003539 (0.006301)	-0.001372 (0.006345)
Average hours/week paid job 1978-1979	-0.003484** (0.001497)	-0.002862** (0.001540)
Black or Hispanic	0.030092 (0.036100)	0.028229 (0.035653)
Male	0.069338** (0.031410)	0.066934** (0.032111)
1979 job quality		
Rights and compensation	--	-0.056506** (0.025613)
Motivation potential	--	0.044149 (0.031859)
Skill use and development	--	-0.065788** (0.028308)
Physical comfort	--	0.014139 (0.029674)
Social contact	--	0.005529 (0.040170)
Selection term	0.034548 (0.035601)	0.023049 (0.035589)
Intercept	0.207998** (0.086084)	0.221797 (0.149805)
n	154	154
R^2	0.0773	0.1492

*$p \leq .05$
**$p \leq .01$

labor (Table 8.25). Compared to adults' jobs, teenagers' jobs on average provide fewer fringe benefits, require less independence, give the employee a smaller number of different things to do, and offer less opportunity to make close friendships (Table 8.26). Among five indices we created to reflect different qualitative aspects of teenagers' jobs, skill use and development is most clearly associated with labor market outcomes in the first three years subsequent to high school graduation. Recent graduates whose senior-year jobs gave them more opportunity to exercise and improve their skills in dealing with people, things, or data were able to earn more pay per hour worked, and spent less of their time looking for work. Less unemployment and higher hourly earnings also were obtained by new graduates who spent a larger number of hours per week in paid employment during their junior and senior years (Tables 8.28 and 8.29).

DISCUSSION

The presumption that paid work experience during high school has positive consequences is supported here by the finding, consistent with earlier studies, that the amount of time spent in paid jobs during high school is positively associated with labor market success in the first 3 years after graduation. At the same time, the idea that qualitative differences among teenagers' jobs are also consequential is supported by our finding of greater initial success in the labor market among recent graduates whose high school jobs gave them more chance to use and develop skills. Therefore, with regard to economic outcomes alone, there is reason to consider quality as well as quantity of paid work experience in deciding what is likely to be good for teenagers.

It is possible that data on noneconomic consequences—the kinds of psychosocial outcomes emphasized by Greenberger and Steinberg (1986)—would reveal a stronger connection with qualitative aspects of students' jobs other than skill use and development. In particular, aspects such as whether the work itself seems important "in the broader scheme of things" (see Table 8.9) might correlate highly with success in the psychosocial task of identity formation. This and other indicators of what we call the "motivation potential" of jobs do not correlate with economic outcomes assessed by the NLS, and we are unaware of any other existing data that would make it possible to test for association between qualitative aspects of students' paid jobs and their psychosocial development. Collecting such data would shed new light on the relations between work experience and adolescent development.

Two Interpretations. Our main new finding from the NLS data—that skill use and development in paid jobs during high school is associated with success in the labor market after graduation—could result from two different processes: a learning process and a screening process. The learning process consists of students acquiring new skills through their experience at work, and these skills being rewarded by employers in subsequent years. The screening process consists of students who already show greater talent being selected for more demanding jobs even while they are in high school, and subsequent employers simply following suit. Both processes may operate together, but to the extent that one or the other can be said to explain our finding, the practical implications are different, as we will explain.

A Human Capital Interpretation. The learning-process interpretation of our finding is an application of standard "human capital" theory: Work experience begets skills, which employers subsequently recognize and reward (Becker, 1975; Mincer, 1979). Following Becker, it has become conventional to speak of specific and general skills; the former valuable only in one or a few workplaces, the latter of more ubiquitous value. Assuming that most high school students are not fully trained before they start their jobs, they must acquire some mix of specific and general skills while they are employed. The more demanding the job, the more they have to learn. The more they learn, the greater their value to subsequent employers, and the more success they will have in the labor market after they graduate.

For teenagers, the process of learning on the job not only imparts a mix of specific and relatively general skills related to that job, but also contributes to development of some very general capacity for learning in the context of work. Since teenagers cannot have had a long work history, their very capacity for learning on the job must develop with experience. They must become more adept at sizing up new assignments, seeing the sequence of steps or set of operations required, realizing what they do and do not know how to do, figuring out what additional information or resources are necessary, finding the information or resources they need or else coping with the lack of them, thinking of alternatives, recognizing opportunities, keeping in mind what the purpose of the assignment is, and so on. These are very general skills (cf. Schultz, 1975). It seems likely that jobs that are more complex will also, as a by-product, develop more of this capacity for learning in the context of work. Therefore, ''skill use and development'' in teenagers' jobs also stands for opportunity to develop the capacity for learning on the job, and students who experience more of it in high school do better in the labor market after they graduate. This interpretation is supported by the work of Kohn and Schooler (1978), who found that men with more complex jobs develop greater intellectual flexibility.

The capacity for learning on the job has been a prominent concept in policy discussions about high schools and future skill demands in the labor market. For instance, the National Academy of Sciences Panel on Secondary School Education for the Changing Workplace (1984), chaired by Richard Heckert of Dupont, and with a majority of members representing large American corporations, wrote:

> The major asset required by employers of high school graduates . . . is the ability to learn and to adapt to change in the workplace. The continual evolution of work functions will require that workers master new knowledge and new skills throughout their working lives. The ability to learn will be the essential hallmark of the successful employee. (p. xi)

Why the Importance of Workers' Capacity to Learn is Perceived to be Growing. There are several reasons why many observers of the changing American economy have concluded that work in the future is going to require more capacity for learning on the part of workers. First, technological change and shifting markets are adding more novelty to existing jobs, speeding the process of job destruction and creation, and altering the kinds of goods and services produced. Possible changes in the product mix have been described by Robert Reich

(1983), who argues that the United States and other industrialized countries will be able to thrive in the world economy only if they move away from standardized, high-volume manufacturing toward specialized, low-volume production, requiring "flexible systems" Flexible-system production depends critically on employees' skills, especially their capacity for learning on the job. According to Reich,

> . . . much of the training of necessity occurs on the job, both because the precise skills to be learned cannot be anticipated . . . and because individuals' skills are typically integrated into a group whose collective capacity becomes something more than the simple sum of its members' skills. (p. 135)

A second reason why workers' capacity for learning is believed to be growing in importance is that, as production becomes more highly automated, learning may become a more integral part of work. This kind of production has been analyzed in depth by Larry Hirschhorn (1984). He describes the historical development of cybernetic technology, which uses low-energy sensors and electronics to control high-energy physical processes. This technology has been applied to continuous-process manufacture of various commodities including petroleum products and other chemicals, metal machining, nuclear power, cement, and food. Continuous-process production is automated in the sense that human hands do not manipulate materials. Unlike assembly lines, these productive processes do not require people to perform repetitive physical tasks at high speed. But they do require human senses and intelligence to pay attention and intervene when things go wrong—as they do, and in unanticipated ways. When such failures occur, people have to learn. Since failure is sometimes dangerous (as when nuclear power plans overheat or chemical plants leak poisons) and always costly, workers have to learn fast. But these technologies also require people to keep learning even when systems do not actually break down. Operators have to keep tuning the system to keep it operating efficiently, since running a plant at less than capacity is costly. Unlike the assembly line, however, what constrains the pace of continuous-process production is not how fast workers move, but how fast they learn. Learning becomes an integral part of the work itself.

A third reason why the capacity for learning at work may become more important is that increasing numbers of employers are finding it worthwhile to increase employees' involvement in decision-making, even in the absence of major changes in technology or product mix. An example is the huge automobile plant in Fremont, California. Closed by General Motors in 1982, it was reopened in 1984 by New United Motor Manufacturing, Inc. (NUMMI), a joint venture of General Motors and Toyota. Workers continue to be represented by the United Auto Workers, but relations between labor and management are structured to be more cooperative and less adversarial than before. Eighty percent of the plant's 2400 employees are covered by a single job description, with three additional classifications covering skilled trades. This contrasts with more than 100 classifications in some General Motors plants. The simpler classification system allows assembly line workers to operate in small groups that divide up the task as they see fit. Selection and orientation of workers emphasizes group participation in problem solving. Workers have been involved in designing their own production areas. The whole organization is less hierarchical, with fewer inspectors and fewer layers of supervision. According to the plant manager, "A lot of things that might be done by American companies at the managerial level are done here at the team level." Teams are responsible for continued adaptation and improvement, which require continued learning by workers.

Employee involvement is also one of the reasons for recent reductions in the average size of U.S. manufacturing plants. Based on research by Roger Schmenner, *Business Week* (October 22, 1984, p. 156) reported the average plant built before 1970 and still operating in 1979 employed 644 people, compared to 241 people in the average plant opened between 1970 and 1979. *Business Week* estimates the average plant opening in the 1980s will employ 210 people. Smaller factories enable hourly employees to become "part of the flow of ideas," have "an impact on day-to-day operations," and feel "a sense of ownership." Continued learning is required.

In one form or another, employee involvement appears to be spreading, not only in manufacturing, but also in finance, trade, government, and other parts of the service sector. The New York Stock Exchange (1982) surveyed a sample of U.S. corporations employing at least one hundred people, and estimated that 54% of employees in this group of companies were in firms that had adopted some kind of program to encourage more sharing of responsibility—for instance, through quality circles, job rotation, or participatory goal-setting. These programs require employees who are able and willing to keep learning on the job.

Although many observers foresee increasing demand for general problem-solving abilities among U.S. workers, we should note that this conclusion is not unanimous. For a dissenting view, see Levin and Rumberger (1983, 1984).

Implications of the Human Capital Interpretation.   If increased capacity for learning on the job results from high school students' experience in jobs that provide more opportunity for skill use and development, and if this capacity is becoming more important in the labor market, then logically it would be beneficial if more skill use and development could somehow be built into teenagers' work experience. Whether this could best be done by enriching jobs offered by employers or by creating new kinds of synthetic jobs or service opportunities is beyond the scope of this paper. However, in principle the practical implication is clear: Just as schools should try to develop general skills for learning and problem solving, work experience should build capacity for learning by requiring young workers to perform complex new tasks.

A Screening Interpretation.   It is possible that the general capacity for learning in the context of work is merely a manifestation of general intelligence, and that it is determined, if not genetically, then by early experiences in family and school, not by experience in paid jobs during adolescence. According to this interpretation, learning the kinds of things one has to do at work does not contribute anything further to the development of capacity for learning. To the contrary, teenagers who already have greater capacity for learning will be recognized by employers on the basis of job interviews or personal recommendations. These youngsters will be selected for the more complex jobs, which require more learning. If employers' experience confirms that smart kids do a better job than others, then the selection process is rational for them. By continuing to hire such students for the more complex, high-status jobs (recall that skill use and development is positively correlated with the status of teenagers' jobs in the occupational hierarchy), students' employers signal to subsequent employers that these are desirable employees. Early work experience may not develop the general capacity for learning, but it identifies youngsters who already have that capacity. Therefore, students whose high school jobs provide more opportunity for using and developing skills will do better in the labor market after graduation. This interpretation of work experience as screening parallels the theory of schooling-as-screening developed by Spence (1973) and Arrow (1973).

Different implications follow from this than from the human capital interpretation. If general capacity for learning at work is not developed on the job, there is simply no point in trying to provide work experience that will develop teenagers' capacity for learning. Doing so might conceivably even interfere with the efficient operation of the market, which is continually selecting certain people for more complex work, and thereby certifying them as promising candidates for future advancement.

CONCLUSION

We have discovered considerable variation in qualitative aspects of jobs held by students while they are in high school. One qualitative dimension in particular— the degree to which the student's job provides opportunity to use and develop valuable skills—is positively associated with success in the job market during the first three years after graduating from high school. This could result from a screening process, in which employers recognize the more able students, and certify their ability to later employers by giving the more able students more complex work to do. Alternatively, the association between skill use and development on the high school job and subsequent success in the labor market could result from differential amounts of learning on the high school job. Among other skills, students with more complex jobs may develop a greater capacity for learning in the context of work, a capacity that is said to be increasingly important in the changing national economy. These two interpretations have very different implications for policy. If more complex jobs enable teenagers to *develop* capacity for learning at work, then it would be beneficial to create more complex jobs for additional teenagers. If more complex jobs merely *demonstrate* a capacity the teenage workers already possess, then there is no point in trying to create more complex jobs for other teenagers.

Whichever of these interpretations is deemed more plausible, the finding that more use and development of skills in students' jobs pays off for those students after they graduate does provide some partial reassurance for those concerned about the discoveries of Greenberger, Steinberg, and associates. Not all teenage jobs are equally bad. Furthermore, the labor market apparently gives students at least one useful signal: To the extent that high school students have any choice about the jobs they take, they are likely to be better off economically after graduation if they choose jobs where they can use and develop their skills while in high school.[1]

REFERENCES

Abramowitz, S., & Tenenbaum, E. (1978). *High school '77, a survey of public secondary school principals.* Washington, DC: National Institute of Education.

Arrow, K. J. (1973). Higher education as a filter. *Journal of Public Economics, 2,* 193–216.

Ball, J., Gerould, D. M., & Burstein, P. (1980). *The quality of work in the youth entitlement demonstration.* New York: Manpower Demonstration Research Corp.

Becker, G. S. (1975). *Human capital* (2nd ed.). Chicago, IL: University of Chicago Press.

Bullock, R. J. (1984). Gainsharing—a successful track record. *World of Work Report, 9*(8), 3–4.

Burtless, G. (1984). Manpower policies for the disadvantaged: What works? *Brookings Review, 3*(1), 18–22.

Business Week (Oct. 22, 1984). Small is beautiful now in manufacturing. Pp. 152–156.

Center for Human Resource Research (1983). *NLS Handbook.* Columbus, OH: Ohio State University.

Centre for Educational Research and Innovation (1983). *Education and work: The views of the young.* Paris: Organisation for Economic Cooperation and Development.

Coleman, J. S., & Husen, T. (1985). *Becoming adult in a changing society.* Paris: Organisation for Economic Cooperation and Development.

Conrad D., & Hedin, D. (1977). Learning and earning citizenship through participation: In J. P. Shaver (Ed.), *Building rationales for citizenship education* (pp. 48–73). National Council for the Social Studies, Bulletin 52. 48–73.

D'Amico, R., & Baker, P. (1984). The nature and consequences of high school employment: In *Pathways to the future* (Vol. IV). Columbus, OH: Center for Human Resource Research, Ohio State University.

---

[1]If students already know this, and if employers have responded to excess supply of applicants to skill-enhancing jobs by reducing current wages in those jobs, then students would have to forego some current earnings in order to earn more money later. We have not tried to test whether such a pattern does in fact exist.

Dement, E. F. (1982). *Results-oriented work experience programming*. Salt Lake City, UT: Olympus Publishing.

Doeringer, P. B., & Piore, M. J. (1971). *Internal labor markets and manpower analysis*. Lexington, MA: D. C. Heath.

Greenberger, E., & Steinberg, L. D. (1981). The workplace as a context for the socialization of youth. *Journal of Youth and Adolescence, 10*, 185–210.

Greenberger, E., & Steinberg, L. D. (1986). *When teenagers work*. New York: Basic Books.

Hackman, J. R., & Lawler, E. E. (1971). Employee reactions to job characteristics. *Journal of Applied Psychology (Monograph), 55*, 259–286.

Hackman, J. R., & Oldham, G. R. (1976). Motivation through the design of work: Test of a theory. *Organizational Behavior and Human Performance, 16*, 250–279.

Hahn, A. B. (1979). Taking stock of YEDPA—the federal youth employment initiatives, (Part I). *Youth & Society, 2*, 237–261.

Heckman, J. J. (1979). Sample selection bias as a specification error. *Econometrica, 47*(1), 153–161.

Hirschhorn, L. (1984). *Beyond mechanization*. Cambridge, MA: MIT Press.

Katzell, R., & Yankelovich, D. (1975). *Work, productivity, and job satisfaction*. New York: Harcourt Brace Jovanovich.

Kohn, M. L., & Schooler, C. (1978). The reciprocal effects of the substantive complexity of work and intellectual flexibility: A longitudinal assessment. *American Journal of Sociology, 84*(1), 24–52.

Levin, H. M., & Rumberger, R. W. (1983). *The educational implications of high technology*. Stanford, CA: Institute for Research on Educational Finance and Governance, Stanford University, Project Report No. 83-A4.

Levin, H. M., & Rumberger, R. W. (1984). *Forecasting the impact of new technologies on the future job market*. Stanford, CA: Institute for Research on Educational Finance and Governance, Stanford University, Project Report No. 84-A4.

Lewin-Epstein, N. (1981). *Youth employment during high school*. Washington, D.C.: National Center for Education Statistics.

Maddala, G. S. (1983). *Limited-dependent and qualitative variables in econometrics*. Cambridge, England: Cambridge University Press.

Manpower Demonstration Research Corporation Summary and Findings of the National Supported Work Demonstration (1980). Cambridge, MA: Ballinger.

Meyer, R. H., & Wise, D. A. (1982). High school preparation and early labor force experience. In R. B. Freeman & D. A. Wise (Eds.), *The youth labor market problem*. Chicago, IL: University of Chicago Press.

Michael, R. T., & Tuma, N. D. (1984). Youth employment: Does life begin at 16? *Journal of Labor Economics, 2*(4), 464–476.

Mincer, J. (1979). Human capital and earnings. In D. M. Windham (Ed.), *Economic dimensions of education*. Washington, DC: National Academy of Education.

National Academy of Sciences, Panel on Secondary School Education for the Changing Workplace (1984). *High school and the changing workplace, the employers' view*. Washington, DC: National Academy Press.

National Commission on the Reform of Secondary Education (1973). *The reform of secondary education*. New York: McGraw-Hill.

National Panel on High School and Adolescent Education (1976). *The education of adolescents*. Washington, DC: U.S. Government Printing Office.

New York Stock Exchange Office of Economic Research (1982). *People and productivity*. New York.

Olsen, R. J. (1980). A least squares correction for selectivity bias. *Econometrica, 48*(7), 1815–1820.

President's Science Advisory Committee (1973). *Youth: Transition to adulthood.* Washington, DC: U.S. Government Printing Office.

Quinn, R. P., & Shepard, L. J. (1974). *The 1972–73 quality of employment survey.* Ann Arbor, MI: Survey Research Center, University of Michigan.

Quinn, R. P., & Staines, G. L. (1979). *The 1977 quality of employment survey.* Ann Arbor, MI: Institute for Social Research, University of Michigan.

Reich, R. B. (1983). *The next American frontier.* New York: Times Books.

Rist, R. C. (1982). Playing on the margin. *Social Science and Modern Society, 19,* 15–18.

Ruggiero, M., Greenberger, E., & Steinberg, L. D. (1982). Occupational deviance among adolescent workers. *Youth and Society, 13,* 423–448.

Schultz, T. W. (1975). The value of the ability to deal with disequilibria. *Journal of Economic Literature, 13,* 827–846.

Spence, M. (1973). Job market signaling. *Quarterly Journal of Economics, 87,* 355–374.

Steinberg, L. D. (1982). Jumping off the work experience bandwagon. *Journal of Youth and Adolescence, 11,* 183–206.

Steinberg, L. D., Greenberger, E., Garduque, L., & McAuliff, S. (1982). High school students in the labor force: Some costs and benefits to schooling and learning. *Educational Evaluation and Policy Analysis, 4,* 363–372.

Stern, D. (1980). *What is an option? A study of alternatives to the usual high school curriculum.* Summary report to the National Institute of Education (Contract No. 400-77-77). Berkeley, CA: University of California, School of Education.

Taggart, R. (1981). *A fisherman's guide, an assessment of training and remediation strategies.* Kalamazoo, MI: Upjohn Institute.

U.S. Employment Service (1977). *Dictionary of occupational titles.* Washington, DC: U.S. Government Printing Office.

APPENDIX

Tables 8.2 through 8.23 are displayed here. These tables reproduce responses from the NLS sample of high school seniors in 1979 who held paid jobs at the time of the interview and who were not attending school in 1980. Individual tables may be of interest because these data have not been published before. Responses from this sample provide a standard of comparison for subsequent studies.

TABLE 8.2

Does your Employer Make Medical, Surgical, or Hospital Insurance that Covers Injuries or Major
Illnesses Off the Job Available to you?

| | Female | | | Male | | | Male and Female |
	White	Hispanic or Black	Total	White	Hispanic or Black	Total	Total
Yes	23 (0.205)	10 (0.185)	34 (0.204)	45 (0.354)	26 (0.400)	71 (0.368)	105 (0.292)
No	89 (0.795)	44 (0.815)	133 (0.796)	82 (0.646)	39 (0.600)	122 (0.632)	255 (0.708)
Total	112	54	167	127	65	193	360

TABLE 8.3
Does your Employer Make Paid Vacation Available to you?

| | Female | | | Male | | | | Male and Female Total |
	White	Hispanic or Black	Total	White	Hispanic or Black	Total		
Yes	33 (0.292)	19 (0.352)	53 (0.315)	47 (0.376)	23 (0.365)	70 (0.370)		123 (0.345)
No	80 (0.708)	35 (0.648)	115 (0.685)	78 (0.624)	40 (0.635)	119 (0.630)		234 (0.655)
Total	113	54	168	125	63	189		357

TABLE 8.4

Thinking of your Present Job, Would you Say the Pay is Good?

	Female			Male			Male and Female Total
	White	Hispanic or Black	Total	White	Hispanic or Black	Total	
Not at all true	11 (0.097)	11 (0.200)	22 (0.130)	6 (0.046)	9 (0.130)	15 (0.075)	37 (0.100)
Not too true	23 (0.204)	15 (0.273)	38 (0.225)	28 (0.215)	16 (0.232)	45 (0.225)	83 (0.225)
Somewhat true	67 (0.593)	19 (0.345)	86 (0.509)	72 (0.554)	27 (0.391)	99 (0.445)	185 (0.501)
Very true	12 (0.106)	10 (0.182)	23 (0.136)	24 (0.185)	17 (0.246)	41 (0.205)	64 (0.173)
Total	113	55	169	130	69	200	369

TABLE 8.5
Thinking of your Present Job, Would you Say the Job Security is Good?

	Female			Male			Male and Female Total
	White	Hispanic or Black	Total	White	Hispanic or Black	Total	
Not at all true	10 (0.089)	6 (0.109)	16 (0.095)	11 (0.085)	8 (0.116)	19 (0.095)	35 (0.095)
Not too true	17 (0.152)	10 (0.182)	27 (0.161)	21 (0.162)	9 (0.130)	30 (0.150)	57 (0.155)
Somewhat true	55 (0.491)	22 (0.400)	77 (0.458)	61 (0.469)	29 (0.420)	91 (0.455)	168 (0.457)
Very true	30 (0.268)	17 (0.309)	48 (0.286)	37 (0.285)	23 (0.333)	60 (0.300)	108 (0.293)
Total	112	55	168	130	69	200	368

TABLE 8.6
Thinking of your Present Job, Would you Say the Chances for Promotion are Good?

	Female			Male			Male and Female Total
	White	Hispanic or Black	Total	White	Hispanic or Black	Total	
Not at all true	29 (0.259)	15 (0.278)	44 (0.263)	19 (0.148)	8 (0.119)	27 (0.138)	71 (0.196)
Not too true	27 (0.241)	9 (0.167)	36 (0.216)	23 (0.180)	10 (0.149)	34 (0.173)	70 (0.193)
Somewhat true	31 (0.277)	17 (0.315)	49 (0.293)	48 (0.375)	22 (0.328)	70 (0.357)	119 (0.328)
Very true	25 (0.223)	13 (0.241)	38 (0.228)	38 (0.297)	27 (0.403)	65 (0.332)	103 (0.284)
Total	112	54	167	128	67	196	363

TABLE 8.7

How Much Opportunity Does this Job Give you to do a Number of Different Things?

| | Female | | | Male | | | Male and Female |
	White	Hispanic or Black	Total	White	Hispanic or Black	Total	Total
A minimum amount	23 (0.198)	8 (0.145)	31 (0.180)	19 (0.140)	23 (0.329)	43 (0.208)	74 (0.195)
Not too much	25 (0.216)	18 (0.327)	43 (0.250)	26 (0.191)	12 (0.171)	38 (0.184)	81 (0.214)
A moderate amount	29 (0.250)	11 (0.200)	40 (0.233)	38 (0.279)	18 (0.257)	56 (0.271)	96 (0.253)
Quite a lot	29 (0.250)	14 (0.255)	44 (0.256)	33 (0.243)	13 (0.186)	46 (0.222)	90 (0.237)
A maximum amount	10 (0.086)	4 (0.073)	14 (0.081)	20 (0.147)	4 (0.057)	24 (0.116)	38 (0.100)
Total	116	55	172	136	70	207	379

217

TABLE 8.8

How Much Opportunity Does this Job Give you to do a Job from Beginning to End (That is, the Chance to do the Whole Job)?

	Female			Male			Male and Female Total
	White	Hispanic or Black	Total	White	Hispanic or Black	Total	
A minimum amount	10 (0.086)	6 (0.109)	16 (0.093)	7 (0.052)	9 (0.129)	16 (0.078)	32 (0.085)
Not too much	4 (0.034)	4 (0.073)	9 (0.052)	3 (0.022)	5 (0.071)	9 (0.044)	18 (0.048)
A moderate amount	28 (0.241)	10 (0.182)	38 (0.221)	24 (0.178)	12 (0.171)	36 (0.176)	74 (0.196)
Quite a lot	42 (0.362)	21 (0.382)	63 (0.366)	58 (0.430)	26 (0.371)	84 (0.410)	147 (0.390)
A maximum amount	32 (0.276)	14 (0.255)	46 (0.267)	43 (0.319)	18 (0.257)	61 (0.298)	107 (0.284)
Total	116	55	172	135	70	205	377

TABLE 8.9

How Much Does your Job Give you the Feeling that the Job Itself is Very Significant or Important in the Broader Scheme of Things?

	Female			Male			Male and Female Total
	White	Hispanic or Black	Total	White	Hispanic or Black	Total	
A minimum amount	19 (0.165)	5 (0.091)	24 (0.140)	9 (0.066)	13 (0.188)	22 (0.107)	46 (0.122)
Not too much	25 (0.217)	13 (0.236)	38 (0.222)	27 (0.199)	12 (0.174)	40 (0.195)	78 (0.207)
A moderate amount	26 (0.226)	14 (0.255)	41 (0.240)	37 (0.272)	12 (0.174)	49 (0.239)	90 (0.239)
Quite a lot	32 (0.278)	14 (0.255)	46 (0.269)	48 (0.353)	21 (0.304)	69 (0.337)	115 (0.306)
A maximum amount	13 (0.113)	9 (0.164)	22 (0.129)	15 (0.110)	11 (0.159)	26 (0.127)	48 (0.128)
Total	115	55	171	136	69	205	376

TABLE 8.10

How Much Does Your Job Give You the Feeling that You Know Whether or not You are Performing Your Job well or Poorly?

	Female			Male			Male and Female Total
	White	Hispanic or Black	Total	White	Hispanic or Black	Total	
A minimum amount	3 (0.027)	6 (0.109)	9 (0.053)	3 (0.024)	10 (0.147)	13 (0.066)	22 (0.060)
Not too much	2 (0.018)	3 (0.055)	5 (0.030)	2 (0.016)	1 (0.015)	4 (0.020)	9 (0.025)
A moderate amount	28 (0.248)	13 (0.236)	41 (0.243)	26 (0.205)	7 (0.103)	33 (0.168)	74 (0.203)
Quite a lot	54 (0.478)	21 (0.382)	76 (0.450)	64 (0.504)	36 (0.529)	100 (0.510)	176 (0.482)
A maximum amount	26 (0.230)	12 (0.218)	38 (0.225)	32 (0.252)	14 (0.206)	46 (0.235)	84 (0.230)
Total	113	55	169	127	68	196	365

TABLE 8.11

Thinking of your Present Job, Would you Say you are Given a Chance to do the Things you Do Best?

	Female			Male			Male and Female Total
	White	Hispanic or Black	Total	White	Hispanic or Black	Total	
Not at all true	8 (0.071)	4 (0.073)	12 (0.071)	9 (0.069)	7 (0.101)	16 (0.080)	28 (0.076)
Not too true	22 (0.195)	11 (0.200)	33 (0.195)	35 (0.269)	11 (0.159)	46 (0.230)	79 (0.214)
Somewhat true	58 (0.513)	19 (0.345)	77 (0.456)	59 (0.454)	29 (0.420)	89 (0.445)	166 (0.450)
Very true	25 (0.221)	21 (0.382)	47 (0.278)	27 (0.208)	22 (0.319)	49 (0.245)	96 (0.260)
Total	113	55	169	130	69	200	369

TABLE 8.12
How Much Opportunity Does this Job Give you for Independent Thought or Action?

	Female			Male			Male and Female Total
	White	Hispanic or Black	Total	White	Hispanic or Black	Total	
A minimum amount	8 (0.069)	7 (0.127)	15 (0.087)	18 (0.132)	11 (0.157)	29 (0.140)	44 (0.116)
Not too much	27 (0.233)	15 (0.273)	43 (0.250)	18 (0.132)	13 (0.186)	32 (0.155)	75 (0.198)
A moderate amount	35 (0.302)	16 (0.291)	51 (0.297)	33 (0.243)	15 (0.214)	48 (0.232)	99 (0.261)
Quite a lot	39 (0.336)	14 (0.255)	53 (0.308)	54 (0.397)	18 (0.257)	72 (0.348)	125 (0.330)
A maximum amount	7 (0.060)	3 (0.055)	10 (0.058)	13 (0.096)	13 (0.186)	26 (0.126)	36 (0.095)
Total	116	55	172	136	70	207	379

TABLE 8.13

Thinking of your Present Job, Would you Say the Skills you are Learning Would be Valuable in Getting a Better Job?

	Female			Male			Male and Female Total
	White	Hispanic or Black	Total	White	Hispanic or Black	Total	
Not at all True	11 (0.098)	8 (0.145)	19 (0.113)	17 (0.131)	8 (0.118)	25 (0.126)	44 (0.120)
Not too true	31 (0.277)	10 (0.182)	41 (0.244)	24 (0.185)	19 (0.279)	43 (0.216)	94 (0.229)
Somewhat true	33 (0.295)	17 (0.309)	51 (0.304)	41 (0.315)	17 (0.250)	59 (0.296)	110 (0.300)
Very true	37 (0.330)	20 (0.364)	57 (0.339)	48 (0.369)	24 (0.353)	72 (0.362)	129 (0.351)
Total	112	55	168	130	68	199	367

TABLE 8.14
Complexity of Relations with Data (DOT Categories)

	Female			Male			Male and Female Total
	White	Hispanic or Black	Total	White	Hispanic or Black	Total	
Comparing	29 (0.246)	18 (0.327)	47 (0.270)	69 (0.486)	42 (0.600)	112 (0.526)	159 (0.411)
Copying	4 (0.034)	5 (0.091)	9 (0.052)	2 (0.014)	2 (0.029)	4 (0.019)	13 (0.034)
Computing	42 (0.356)	12 (0.218)	54 (0.310)	24 (0.169)	8 (0.114)	32 (0.150)	86 (0.222)
Compiling	34 (0.288)	19 (0.345)	54 (0.305)	32 (0.225)	13 (0.186)	45 (0.211)	98 (0.253)
Analyzing	5 (0.042)	1 (0.018)	7 (0.040)	9 (0.063)	3 (0.043)	12 (0.056)	19 (0.049)
Coordinating	4 (0.034)	0 (0.0)	4 (0.023)	5 (0.035)	2 (0.029)	7 (0.033)	11 (0.028)
Synthesizing	0 (0.0)	0 (0.0)	0 (0.0)	1 (0.007)	0 (0.0)	1 (0.005)	1 (0.003)
Total	118	55	174	142	70	213	387

TABLE 8.15
Complexity of Relations with Things (DOT Categories)

	Female			Male			Male and Female Total
	White	Hispanic or Black	Total	White	Hispanic or Black	Total	
Handling	76 (0.644)	37 (0.673)	114 (0.655)	85 (0.599)	46 (0.657)	132 (0.620)	246 (0.636)
Feeding, Offbearing	0	0	0	1 (0.007)	1 (0.014)	2 (0.009)	2 (0.005)
Tending	0	0	0	1 (0.007)	3 (0.043)	4 (0.019)	4 (0.010)
Manipulating	9 (0.076)	1 (0.018)	10 (0.057)	17 (0.120)	6 (0.866)	23 (0.108)	33 (0.085)
Driving, operating	2 (0.017)	0	2 (0.011)	9 (0.063)	4 (0.057)	13 (0.061)	15 (0.039)
Operating, controlling	25 (0.212)	16 (0.291)	41 (0.236)	7 (0.049)	2 (0.029)	9 (0.042)	50 (0.129)
Prcision working	6 (0.051)	1 (0.018)	7 (0.040)	19 (0.134)	8 (0.114)	27 (0.127)	34 (0.088)
Setting up	0	0	0	3 (0.021)	0	3 (0.014)	3 (0.008)
Total	118	55	174	142	70	213	387

TABLE 8.16
Complexity of Relations with People (DOT Categories)

	Female			Male			Male and Female Total
	White	Hispanic or Black	Total	White	Hispanic or Black	Total	
Taking Instructions, helping	26 (0.220)	17 (0.309)	44 (0.253)	73 (0.514)	36 (0.514)	110 (0.516)	154 (0.398)
Serving	43 (0.364)	16 (0.291)	58 (0.333)	16 (0.113)	13 (0.186)	29 (0.136)	87 (0.225)
Speaking, signaling	34 (0.288)	18 (0.327)	52 (0.299)	43 (0.303)	18 (0.257)	61 (0.286)	113 (0.292)
Persuading	9 (0.076)	5 (0.091)	14 (0.080)	6 (0.042)	3 (0.043)	9 (0.042)	23 (0.059)
Diverting	0	0	0	1 (0.007)	0	1 (0.005)	1 (0.003)
Supervising	4 (0.034)	0	4 (0.023)	2 (0.014)	0	2 (0.009)	6 (0.016)
Instructing	2 (0.017)	0	2 (0.011)	1 (0.007)	0	1 (0.005)	3 (0.008)
Total	118	55	174	142	70	213	387

TABLE 8.17

Thinking of your Present Job, Would you Say the Physical Surroundings are Pleasant?

	Female			Male			Male and Female Total
	White	Hispanic or Black	Total	White	Hispanic or Black	Total	
Not at all true	6 (0.053)	3 (0.055)	9 (0.053)	7 (0.054)	2 (0.029)	9 (0.051)	18 (0.052)
Not too true	16 (0.142)	5 (0.091)	21 (0.124)	15 (0.115)	8 (0.116)	0 (0.0)	21 (0.061)
Somewhat true	47 (0.416)	25 (0.455)	72 (0.426)	55 (0.423)	34 (0.493)	90 (0.508)	162 (0.468)
Very true	44 (0.389)	22 (0.400)	67 (0.396)	53 (0.408)	25 (0.362)	78 (0.441)	145 (0.419)
Total	113	55	169	130	69	177	346

TABLE 8.18
Thinking of Your Present Job, Would You Say the Job is Dangerous?

	Female			Male			Male and Female Total
	White	Hispanic or Black	Total	White	Hispanic or Black	Total	
Not at all true	60 (0.531)	37 (0.673)	97 (0.574)	48 (0.369)	30 (0.435)	78 (0.390)	175 (0.474)
Not too true	32 (0.283)	14 (0.255)	47 (0.278)	44 (0.338)	28 (0.406)	73 (0.365)	120 (0.325)
Somewhat true	20 (0.177)	3 (0.055)	23 (0.136)	30 (0.231)	6 (0.087)	36 (0.180)	59 (0.160)
Very true	1 (0.009)	1 (0.018)	2 (0.011)	8 (0.062)	5 (0.072)	13 (0.065)	15 (0.041)
Total	113	55	169	130	69	200	369

TABLE 8.19

Thinking of Your Present Job, Would You Say You are Exposed to Unhealthy Conditions?

	Female			Male			Male and Female Total
	White	Hispanic or Black	Total	White	Hispanic or Black	Total	
Not at all true	77 (0.681)	40 (0.727)	118 (0.698)	75 (0.577)	35 (0.507)	110 (0.550)	228 (0.618)
Not too true	24 (0.212)	6 (0.109)	30 (0.178)	37 (0.285)	24 (0.348)	62 (0.310)	92 (0.249)
Somewhat true	9 (0.080)	4 (0.073)	13 (0.077)	16 (0.123)	5 (0.072)	21 (0.105)	34 (0.092)
Very true	3 (0.027)	5 (0.091)	8 (0.047)	2 (0.015)	5 (0.072)	7 (0.035)	15 (0.041)
Total	113	55	169	130	69	200	369

TABLE 8.20

How Much Opportunity Does this Job Give You to Deal with Other People?

| | Female | | | Male | | | Male and Female |
	White	Hispanic or Black	Total	White	Hispanic or Black	Total	Total
A minimum amount	9 (0.078)	6 (0.109)	15 (0.087)	7 (0.051)	18 (0.257)	25 (0.121)	40 (0.106)
Not too much	11 (0.095)	10 (0.182)	21 (0.122)	20 (0.147)	12 (0.171)	33 (0.159)	54 (0.142)
A moderate amount	13 (0.112)	4 (0.073)	17 (0.099)	25 (0.184)	7 (0.100)	32 (0.155)	49 (0.129)
Quite a lot	49 (0.422)	25 (0.455)	74 (0.430)	59 (0.434)	23 (0.329)	82 (0.396)	156 (0.412)
A maximum amount	34 (0.293)	10 (0.182)	45 (0.262)	25 (0.184)	10 (0.143)	35 (0.169)	80 (0.211)
Total	116	55	172	136	70	207	379

TABLE 8.21

How Much Opportunity Does this Job Give You to Develop Close Friendships in Your Job?

	Female			Male			Male and Female Total
	White	Hispanic or Black	Total	White	Hispanic or Black	Total	
A minimum amount	9 (0.078)	3 (0.055)	13 (0.076)	8 (0.059)	9 (0.129)	17 (0.082)	30 (0.079)
Not too much	14 (0.121)	14 (o.255)	28 (0.163)	14 (0.103)	9 (0.129)	24 (0.116)	52 (0.137)
A moderate amount	28 (0.241)	13 (0.236)	41 (0.238)	38 (0.279)	18 (0.257)	56 (0.271)	97 (0.256)
Quite a lot	48 (0.414)	22 (0.400)	70 (0.407)	54 (0.397)	23 (0.329)	77 (0.372)	147 (0.388)
A maximum amount	17 (0.147)	3 (0.055)	20 (0.116)	22 (0.162)	11 (0.157)	33 (0.159)	53 (0.140)
Total	116	55	172	136	70	207	397

TABLE 8.22
Thinking of Your Present Job, Would You Say Your Coworkers are Friendly?

	Female			Male			Male and Female Total
	White	Hispanic or Black	Total	White	Hispanic or Black	Total	
Not at all true	3 (0.027)	3 (0.036)	5 (0.030)	0 (0.0)	2 (0.030)	2 (0.010)	7 (0.019)
Not too true	3 (0.027)	2 (0.036)	5 (0.030)	1 (0.008)	2 (0.030)	4 (0.020)	9 (0.025)
Somewhat true	17 (0.153)	19 (0.345)	36 (0.216)	19 (0.148)	12 (0.180)	31 (0.158)	67 (0.184)
Very true	88 (0.793)	32 (0.582)	121 (0.725)	108 (0.844)	51 (0.761)	159 (0.811)	280 (0.767)
Total	111	55	167	128	67	196	363

TABLE 8.23

Thinking of your Present Job, Would you Say your Supervisor is Competent in Doing the Job?

| | Female | | | Male | | | Male and Female |
	White	Hispanic or Black	Total	White	Hispanic or Black	Total	Total
Not at all true	3 (0.027)	1 (0.018)	4 (0.024)	0 (0.0)	1 (0.015)	2 (0.010)	6 (0.016)
Not too true	3 (0.027)	5 (0.091)	8 (0.048)	2 (0.048)	7 (0.103)	9 (0.045)	17 (0.046)
Somewhat true	33 (.295)	14 (0.255)	47 (0.280)	27 (0.209)	17 (0.250)	44 (0.222)	91 (0.249)
Very ture	73 (0.652)	35 (0.636)	109 (0.649)	100 (0.775)	43 (0.632)	143 (0.722)	252 (0.689)
Total	112	55	168	129	68	198	366

233

9 The Job Market for Adolescents

Paul Osterman
Massachusetts Institute of Technology

For many decades the high unemployment rates of youth have focused public attention upon their problems and upon programs to solve them. Indeed, youth unemployment has been one of the few social policy issues that both conservatives and liberals have agreed to address. Even in Thatcher's Great Britain a major youth employment initiative is currently underway. Yet despite this public attention, and the resulting efforts by economists to study the problem, there is still no generally agreed upon diagnosis. This paper examines some of the various views held by economists and presents my own interpretation.

The first part of the paper reviews some of the key facts. This is important because those facts dispel some of the myths surrounding the issue. Presented next, are some of the major explanations or stories concerning what has gone wrong in the youth labor market. Finally, we move from a discussion of the problems in the youth labor market to a more general discussion of the normal structure of that labor market as it affects most youth.

THE BASIC FACTS

The best way to get a sense of the overall patterns in the youth labor market is to examine the patterns in the aggregate data. Table 9.1 presents unemployment rates for different youth subgroups. These are the most widely used indices and they tell a familiar story. Unemployment rates for young people are above those of adults and show a secular upward trend. Furthermore, the unemployment rates of minorities are well above those of whites and are virtually of crisis proportions.

235

TABLE 9.1
Unemployment Rates

	1957	1964	1978	1982
White males				
16 - 19	11.5%	14.7%	13.5%	21.7%
20 - 24	7.1	7.4	7.6	14.3
Black males				
16 - 19	18.4%	24.3	34.4	44.0
20 - 24	12.7	12.6	20.0	29.2
White females				
16 - 19	9.5	14.9	14.4	19.0
20 - 24	5.1	7.1	8.3	10.9
Black females				
16 - 19	20.2	31.6	38.4	43.8
20 - 24	12.2	18.3	21.3	26.8

Dramatic as these figures are, most analysts consider the unemployment rate to be a poor indicator for the youth labor market because:

1. There are measurement problems: To be unemployed an individual must be reported as actively looking for work. In most cases, data are drawn from surveys in which parents are asked about their children's search, and evidence suggests that the answers are often inaccurate. In addition, many youth work in casual jobs, and search patterns are not as formal or recognizable as is the case for adults.

2. Changes over time in the unemployment rate are difficult to interpret because of the importance of changes in youth labor force participation patterns. The unemployment rate can rise or fall simply because more youth are in or out of the labor force despite the fact that the number of youth jobs (or the percentage of the cohort employed) may move in the opposite direction. This is especially important to consider given the substantial changes in school enrollment rates that have occurred over the past several decades.

To aid in understanding the nature of these background trends, Tables 9.2 and 9.3 present data on school enrollment rates and labor force participation rates. In Table 9.2 we observe that enrollment rates of white men have declined over the last 2 decades, those of white women have shown a modest rise, and the enrollment rates of young blacks of both sexes have increased dramatically. Young people who are in school work less than those out of school; hence, simply on the basis of these enrollment patterns it is reasonable to expect that employment rates would have increased for white men and decreased for the other subgroups[1]

---

[1]While it is true that employment rates of in-school youth are below those of the not enrolled, this disparity has declined in recent years as the employment rate of in-school youth has risen. However, the employment rates of in-school youth continue to be below those of their out-of-school brethren.

TABLE 9.2
School Enrollment Rates of 16- and 24-Year-Olds

	1964	1969	1974	1979
White males	51.1%	56.4%	45.9%	43.9%
Black males	39.4	47.2	49.0	47.1
White females	36.5	39.2	39.2	40.2
Black females	34.2	38.4	41.8	40.2

It is important to understand that the rise of black relative to white school enrollment rates, while encouraging, does not imply achievement of educational equality. Dropout rates remain higher for blacks than whites, and school achievement scores and college attendance lag (Ellwood & Wise, 1983, p. 23).

A second consideration underlying the unemployment patterns is the labor force participation rates of the different groups. Table 9.3 demonstrates that the participation rates of both white men and women have risen in recent years while those of nonwhite men have fallen sharply. The rates of nonwhite women have increased, but not as rapidly as those for white women. The decline in nonwhite male participation rates—a decline far steeper than that predicted by the rise in their school enrollment rates—suggests that the difficulties that this group faces has led to discouragement and withdrawal.

We began by arguing that the unemployment rate is a poor measure of labor market outcomes for young people, and we then examined some of the key factors underlying that rate. It is now appropriate to return and examine alternative outcome measures. Table 9.4 presents what is probably the best measure: the employment-to-population ratios of young people broken down by school enrollment status. Three key facts stand out:

1. For both sexes regardless of enrollment status, the proportion of the white cohort working has remained either stable or has increased. Whatever the youth

TABLE 9.3
Labor Force Participation Rates

	1957	1964	1978	1982
White males				
16 - 19	59.2%	52.7%	65.0%	61.2%
20 - 24	86.7	85.7	87.2	87.1
Black males				
16 - 19	58.8	50.0	45.4	42.8
20 - 24	89.6	89.4	78.0	79.7
White females				
16 - 19	42.1	37.8	56.8	55.1
20 - 24	45.8	48.8	69.3	72.0
Black females				
16 - 19	33.2	31.7	38.2	34.8
20 - 24	46.6	53.6	62.8	60.6

TABLE 9.4
Employment-to-Population Ratios by Enrollment Status
16- to 24-Year-Olds

	1964	1969	1974	1979
Enrolled				
White males	34.1%	41.4%	43.8%	45.4%
Black males	30.1	29.4	26.4	23.4
White females	23.3	34.7	40.4	45.4
Black females	15.4	22.3	18.2	20.6
Not enrolled				
White males	86.7	88.1	85.4	85.7
Black males	80.5	82.4	72.1	69.8
White females	47.3	55.1	60.2	66.0
Black females	48.0	50.7	46.9	43.1

labor market crisis may be, it is not one that has affected young whites with respect to employment opportunities (although wages for young white men—but not women—fell relative to adults).

2. The employment-to-population ratios of young blacks are well below those of whites, and this is true for both sexes.

3. The *relative* position of young blacks has worsened dramatically compared to that of young whites.

To summarize, the youth labor market problem is largely one of low minority employment rates. Despite the baby boom and the resulting influx of large numbers of young white teenagers, the labor market responded well and provided them with jobs. What is going wrong is that for some reason young blacks are simply not sharing in this job growth. From the viewpoint of public policy, this is the issue that must be addressed.

WHY ARE BLACK YOUTH EMPLOYMENT LEVELS SO LOW?

The question confronting us here is not why youth unemployment in general is so high. This question must be examined in the context of a general understanding of the youth labor market and will be addressed in the next section. Rather, at this point we want to understand the source of the large and widening differential between black and white teenagers.

There are two explanations of this widening differential that we can mention briefly but dismiss. The first, advanced by Cogan (1982), is that the movement of blacks from the rural South to the urban North, and the consequent shift in the occupational and industrial mix of jobs, lies behind the deterioration. Whatever the merits of this explanation for the 1945–1970 period—the years for which

Cogan develops his case—that migratory stream was largely played out by 1970. Yet it was precisely in the 1970s that the worst deterioration relative to white teens took place.

A second, more common, explanation is the baby boom. The sharp increase in the numbers of youth in the labor market might be expected to increase their unemployment rates, and the baby boom was sharper for blacks than for whites. However, closer examination discredits this explanation. First, as we have seen, the labor market responded quite well and created enough jobs so that the employment-to-population ratios for whites rose over this period. Second, the sharper baby boom—i.e., the greater relative increase in the supply of black youth—would only make a difference if there were some other factor that differentiated blacks from whites in the eyes of employers. If the two groups were essentially equivalent, then an increase in the supply of one would have symmetrical effects upon the other. Hence we must still search for this other factor.

The key explanations that have been proposed can be grouped into the demand or the supply side of the labor market. One important supply side explanation is a disinterest by black youth in working, arising perhaps from inadequate socialization, unrealistic expectations, or alternative income sources, such as crime. A second supply side explanation is that black youth are simply, on average, not as well prepared for work as white youth and that this—perhaps combined with the minimum wage—limits their employment prospects. On the demand side, the candidates include changes in the nature and location of jobs and discrimination.

The underlying argument behind the disinterest in work explanation is most often the simple one that young people have alternative income opportunities—crime, welfare, and off the books work—that make legitimate minimum wage or near minimum wage jobs unattractive. For this argument to explain the black/white differential, it must be further argued that these alternative income opportunities are more readily available (or more acceptable) to blacks.

Although this is the most common version of the disinterest argument, a spiritually quite different variant has been developed by Piore (1979). His story is based on the dynamics of migration in the context of dual labor market theory. The first generation of black migrants from south to north accepted poor quality secondary Northern jobs because their frame of reference was conditions in the rural South. From this perspective the Northern jobs were not so bad, and in any case many of these migrants expected to return south. However, many remained in the North, and their children found themselves expected to accept the same secondary work. The children's frame of reference was the North. In this context, and with sensitivities heightened by the Civil Rights Movement, the jobs were not acceptable. The consequence was either outright rejection of the work or behavior patterns that rendered them an undesirable labor force. In either case, the nature of the black youth labor force changed, and with this change came a deterioration in employment opportunities.

The disinterest in work argument can be translated by the economist's jargon into a discussion of the reservation wage. The reservation wage is the lowest wage that a person will accept in order to take a job. Because various surveys are available that collect data on the reservation wage (by, for example, posing a series of hypothetical questions), this formulation has the advantage of transforming a vague and emotionally loaded argument into one that is measurable and testable.

The basic approach to testing this hypothesis is to correlate an individual's education, training, and work experience with his or her reservation wage. This statistical relationship can then be compared for blacks and whites to see whether the determinants of the reservation wage differ for the two groups.

Several studies, employing different data sets and different estimating techniques, have taken up this issue, and the findings are that blacks do not have an unreasonably high reservation wage (Holzer, 1982; Osterman, 1983). Put differently, after controlling for those factors that are thought to determine wages, the wage expectations of blacks are not out of line or inconsistent with those of comparable whites. These studies appear to lay this particular line of argument to rest. The caveat to this conclusion is that the research does not test for behavior on the job, so this aspect of Piore's argument may still be viable.

The second supply side argument is the straightforward one that minorities are on average less well prepared for work than are whites. In a textbook version of the competitive labor market, wages would adjust (i.e., minorities would receive lower average wages to compensate for their lower productivity or higher training costs), yet in the actual labor market the minimum wage precludes such adjustment. As a consequence, employment levels are lower for the less qualified group.

The evidence that minorities are, on average, less qualified comes from several sources. Higher dropout rates lead to less educational attainment; according to the Carnegie Foundation, "in 1980, 78% of white 19-year-olds in the United States were high school graduates. However, in the same year 61% of black and 56% of Hispanic 19-year-olds held high school diplomas" (quoted in Sum, 1983, p. 20). Along similar lines, the National Assessment of Educational Progress estimates that while 13% of all 17-year-old youth are functionally illiterate, this percentage rises to 44% for black youth and 56% for Hispanics (Manpower Demonstration Research Corporation, 1983, p. 5).

It is very difficult to know how to evaluate such evidence without a clear view of how the youth labor market works. At one extreme is the meritocratic interpretation, which would assign full weight to these achievement disparities. Set against this is the argument that most youth jobs are unskilled so in many cases educational credentials are a screening device.

It is possible, however, to set upper limits on the importance of these qualifications. When regressions predicting employment outcomes are estimated for blacks and whites, the personal characteristic or human capital variables can explain roughly 50% of the racial gap in employment rates (Osterman, 1980). Hence, even if we assign full meritocratic weight or face validity to qualifications, they are responsible for at most half the racial differential. The intuition is that while the employment rates for both black and white high school drop-outs are lower than those of graduates, at each educational level (or other qualification) whites still do better than blacks. Another way of seeing this is to note that the consensus of the literature on the minimum wage is that even sharp reductions in the minimum of youth would leave enormous black/white differentials in employment rates (Brown, Gilroy, & Kohen, 1982; Osterman, 1984).

Another strategy for gauging the impact of personal background is to examine the importance of a much discussed issue—single parent households and poverty backgrounds. Table 9.5 reproduces data developed by Ellwood and Wise on the distribution and impact of these characteristics for black and white teens. As is apparent, and as has been well highlighted in the literature, black youth are much more likely than white youth to come from poor families and to grow up in single parent households. There is also, particularly for out-of-school youth, a strong

TABLE 9.5
Employment Rates by Family Income and Enrollment Status

Family Type/ Income Level	Persons Enrolled in School		Persons Enrolled in School		All Persons Total	
	White	Black	White	Black	White	Black
Single parent						
Family income						
Below poverty line	.189	.084	.204	.227	.195	.122
100-199% of poverty line	.330	.204	.507	.330	.362	.235
200% of poverty line and over	.381	.318	.687	.392	.439	.324
All incomes	.329	.147	.457	.270	.358	.179
Two parent						
Family income						
Below poverty line	.258	.104	.307	.163	.272	.116
100-199% of poverty line	.355	.177	.631	.456	.401	.230
200% of poverty line and over	.432	.272	.745	.671	.473	.315
All incomes	.405	.189	.668	.418	.443	.228

Tabulations of Survey of Income and Education, 1976. From Ellwood and Wise (1983).

relationship between family background and employment status. Nevertheless these data demonstrate that the employment rate gap between the two groups cannot be explained by this factor. "Even if family structure and income levels for blacks were identical to those of whites, the overall employment rate for black teenagers living at home would rise only from 21% to 27%. The overall rate for whites is 48%. Thus the black-white gap cannot be attributed primarily to family background differences. For out-of-school youth, however, as much as one-half of the gap can be attributed to family structure and family income" (Ellwood & Wise, 1983, p. 52).

The prudent conclusion from this line of argument is that differential qualifications can explain a significant—though not precisely determined—fraction of the black/white employment differential, but that there is much more to the story. A large fraction of the differential must also be related to demand considerations. As noted earlier, the two most important candidates are structural changes in the economy and labor market discrimination.

The structural change argument takes two forms. First, the often noted movement of jobs from the inner city to the suburbs is combined with the fact that black youth remain in the city. This implies that distance and transportation barriers may reduce black relative to white youth employment. Although plausible, this argument runs against the counter claim that because white youth have also moved to the suburbs, the competition for inner city blacks may have—on purely spatial considerations—been reduced. In fact, two studies fail to find any support for the suburbanization argument. Osterman (1980) found no correlation between the decentralization of metropolitan areas' employment and black employment outcomes. Ellwood (1983) uses residential data and demonstrates that the employment outcomes for blacks and whites living in close proximity (and thus facing the same spatial situation) is not different than for blacks and whites in general.

The second structural change argument concerns the new skill mix of downtown jobs. As central city employment shifts increasingly to white collar occupations, inner city residents may be unable to compete for these jobs. There have, to my knowledge, been no studies directly evaluating this line of thought, but several considerations cast doubt on its importance. First, at best this argument applies to young adults, not teenagers. Teenagers find employment in unskilled service and retail occupations, and these remain in large numbers in the inner city. Even for young adults, however, all of the available evidence concerning the hiring practices of firms suggests that for occupations below professional levels, on-the-job training is the key source of skill acquisition. This is as true for white collar as it is for blue collar work (Osterman, 1983). Hence although differential qualifications, as noted earlier, are an important factor, there is no reason to believe that shifts in job content add more weight to this argument.

The final demand side consideration is labor market discrimination. The typical economist's approach to this topic is generally wary. Assigning important weight to discrimination implies that markets fail to work well. In addition, discrimination is difficult to observe and measure. As a result, discrimination is typically left as a residual explanation after all other considerations have been given their maximum weight. This procedure, however, can undervalue the importance of discrimination since other legitimate considerations, e.g., educational credentials, may mask discriminatory intent.

The audit technique of sending matched minorities and whites into the market to observe differential treatment is less commonly employed in the labor market than it is in the housing market. Two small-scale studies (Culp and Dunson, 1986; Wallace, 1975) do find differential treatment, but in each case the sample is too small to permit reasonable generalization. The existence of a very substantial employment differential after all factors—training, family background, education, residential location—have been controlled for remains the most convincing evidence. This logic, taken together with anecdotal experiences of youth and employment counselors, leads me to believe that we must accept discrimination as an important cause of the problems.

It is clear that discrimination should be accorded considerable importance, but we must also acknowledge a paradox. There is very good evidence that, at least for well-educated blacks, discriminatory behavior has receded in the labor market (Freeman, 1980). Why then do we have a growing employment rate gap between young blacks and whites at the same time that other measures of labor markets suggest that the treatment of blacks is becoming more fair? The answer to this question must, I think, be based on the ability of firms to select job applicants in an environment of excess supply (or too few jobs). In effect, firms are creaming along some dimension from the minority population with the effect of creating better average outcomes but also leaving out a large residual group. This process of employer choice needs greater attention.

THE STRUCTURE OF THE YOUTH LABOR MARKET

Although the research presented in the previous section helps clarify the sources of disparate racial outcomes, it is ultimately unsatisfactory. It is difficult to know what to make of the various findings without a context into which to place them. What is needed is a general theory of the youth labor market. The goal of this section is to sketch such a theory.

A central observation guiding this theory must be that labor market patterns change with age and that a broader view of the youth labor market than one limited simply to recent school leavers is necessary. The so-called "school to work transition" has been given too much importance. From my perspective, the youth labor market should encompass the period beginning with early work experience and ending when labor market patterns are observationally equivalent to those of adults. This period may cover a number of years and different stages.

TABLE 9.6
Unemployment Rates of a Cohort Over Time

	Unemployment Rate of 16- to 19-Year-Olds 1976 (U.S. Unemployment Rate = 7.7%)	Unemployment Rate of 16- to 19-Year-Olds 1980 (U.S. Unemployment Rate + 7.1%)
White males	17.3%	11.1%
Black males	37.4	22.3
White females	16.3	8.5
Black females	41.6	21.8

Related to this point is the fact that early unemployment experience does not necessarily presage later difficulty. Table 9.6 provides data on the unemployment rates of the same cohort as they age. As is apparent, regardless of the business cycle, unemployment rates fall with age, and there is no *prima facie* case that early unemployment brings with it later problems. Of course, what is true for a cohort as a whole is not necessarily true for particular individuals or subgroups, and a key question is how much unemployment is too much, i.e., at what point does unemployment cease being normal and become symptomatic of later problems?

The theory I am about to report is based on extensive interviews with young people and with firms in the Boston area. The interviews with youth were drawn from a random sample in two Boston neighborhoods (based on the city census). The interviews with firms were not random but rather were determined by access considerations. More information on the methodology and procedures is provided in Osterman (1980). It should be understood here, however, that the interviews with youth are limited to young men; hence the implications for young women have to be drawn with care.

The Behavior of Youth

In the first several years after leaving school, young people are frequently in what might be termed a moratorium period, a period in which adventure seeking, sex, and peer group activities are all more important than work. Some years later comes a settling down, a stage characterized by a very different set of attitudes about work. This movement from moratorium to settling down is largely responsible for the unemployment patterns described earlier.

Perhaps the best way to understand this process is to describe the work histories of representative youths in the sample who have passed through the entire process.

Jim is 22. He left high school after 10th grade in 1972 and held a series of unskilled jobs. For the first year he was a shipper, a job he got by walking in off the street. He quit and worked in a chemical company for 2 months, a job he got through his wife's uncle. He then worked as general help in a paperbox company where his father works, quit that job after 4 months, got a truck-driving job through an ad in a newspaper, was laid off. For 3 months he worked at odd jobs and then took the first formal job he was offered, a laborer in a shipyard. He found this job through a friend. A year and a half later he quit to go to work as a machine operator for a large electronics firm, a job he got through his father-in-law, who is employed there. He has been working at this job for over a year and plans to stay. He says that when he left high school, all he wanted was jobs "to put money in my pocket," but now he has "a sense of responsibility."

Mark, 23, left school in 1968 after the 12th grade. He wanted to do construction work, although he saw it not as permanent but as something to do until something better came along. A friend who worked in a construction company helped him get a job, and he worked as a laborer for 8 months, until he was laid off. He was unemployed for 6 months and said he mostly loafed. He said that he looked an average of 8 hours a week but could recall only one place where he applied for work. Finally, his girl friend's brother got him a job in the telephone company, and he has been there for the past 7 years.

Mario, 25, was born in Sicily and has lived in East Boston since he was 11. He left school after the 12th grade in 1969. For 9 months he neither worked nor looked for work. His first job, which he held for 2 months until being laid off, was a trucker's helper. He got the job by walking in off the street. He got his next job, as a rigger in a steel mill, the same way, and he remained on it until he was laid off 7 months later. He was unemployed for 2 months, and this time he seriously looked for work, searching 15 hours a week. He finally found a job repairing refrigerators, a job he held for 5 years until he quit to take a similar job in another firm. He found both jobs by walking in off the street. He says that after high school he was "lost" for a year or two but then started looking for a trade.

These three young men are representative of the sample. Their stories capture the importance of families and friendship networks in finding jobs, the progression from casual to more serious work environments, and the general absence of career patterns in the sense of continuity of occupation or skill, all issues I take up later.

It is difficult to give precise definitions of stages that unambiguously categorize a youth's behavior into one stage or the other. Observed behavior is partly a manifestation of a state of mind, and it can be difficult to infer the state of mind from behavior. In addition, the same state of mind can lead to very different behavior. Nonetheless, the notion of stages does seem to capture an important aspect of the problem.

Many youths in the moratorium period explicitly indicate that they are interested only in short-term jobs to get money for traveling, buying a car, or recreation. The point is not that they are not planning for a career—virtually none of the men in the sample consciously chose a line of work. Rather a long-term, stable job is not very important to them. Unemployed moratorium youth largely "hang out": They participate in sports, go to the beach, drink, and travel. Those who are working tend to say that they would be in no hurry to find another job if they found themselves out of work.

The settling-down stage is characterized by the understanding that a steady job is important and desirable. As one youth said, "When I left school I wasn't interested in the kind of work I did. Now I'm getting older and have to look out for myself." A young welder for Amtrak said, "After high school I didn't know what I wanted to do. I just looked for any job. Now I would like to start my own business, probably involving welding. What's changed is that I need the money. When I got out of school, if I had $20 or $30 I was flying." Young people settle down for a variety of reasons. Often it is simply to look out for themselves, to plan for the future. In other instances marriage and children are the precipitating factors. In yet other cases, peer pressures seem to play a role because as friends settle down the pressure builds to follow suit in order to maintain a comparable lifestyle.

Settling-down behavior is characterized by steadier commitment to a job and to the labor force. There is less quitting, and average job tenure increases. When unemployed, young men in the settling-down period search more intensively for a job and show much less tendency to drop out of the labor force.

An obviously important question is what determines the transition from one stage to another in this model. There appear to be three elements to the answer. First, and most fundamentally, what drives the transition is maturity and life circumstances, such as marriage. As people age, their values shift, and when they marry they need to provide steady support to their family. However, while maturation is the most central determinant, it is conditioned by two other considerations, factors that might either accelerate or retard the process. The first is financial constraints. A young person whose earnings are important to his or her family (parents) will settle down more quickly than someone under less pressure. The second factor is the institutional and social environment. A person whose peers are settling down or who is involved in a socially defined path (e.g., a son whose father is holding a job for him in a factory) will likely settle down more quickly than he would otherwise.

These stages have several implications for interpreting labor market outcomes. Unemployment clearly has different meanings for different groups. For many in the moratorium stage, unemployment is the result of the unstable behavior characteristic of this stage. Furthermore, the welfare interpretation of unemployment varies with the stage. Unemployment is a greater hardship for a 24-year-old trying to raise a family than it is for a 17-year-old living at home who would rather be on the beach.

Jobs

The behavioral patterns of young men obviously form only half of the picture of the youth labor market; the other half is the nature of the jobs. In their early years in the labor market, youths generally work in firms that provide unskilled and casual work. These jobs, which some economists characterize as secondary jobs, are typically held in the moratorium period. Settling down frequently occurs in firms offering jobs that involve greater skill, better long-term prospects for advancement, and greater job security. These jobs can be characterized as primary labor market jobs.

Youth typically work in secondary jobs not simply in school or during the summer but also during the first several years after leaving school. In addition, the range of jobs is broader than babysitting, farm labor, and retail sales; and the jobs are more closely linked to the regular economy. For example, unskilled factory jobs fall into the category of first jobs. The jobs held by young people during this period are also held by older workers, particularly older women, and in urban areas by adult blacks and Spanish-speaking people. There is no exclusively youth segment of the labor market.

It is most useful to think of these jobs in terms of primary and secondary jobs, terms that grow out of dual labor market theory (Doeringer & Piore, 1971). Secondary jobs can be defined either descriptively or in the context of a broad theory about the nature and operation of the labor market. In descriptive terms, secondary jobs can best be understood by contrasting them with primary jobs. Piore (1970) has made the distinction in these terms:

> The primary market offers jobs which possess several of the following traits: high wages, good working conditions, employment stability and job security, equity and due process in the administration of work rules, and chances for advancement. The secondary market has jobs which, relative to those in the primary sector, are decidedly less attractive. They tend to involve low wages, poor working conditions, considerable variability in employment, harsh and often arbitrary discipline, little opportunity to advance.

Primary jobs thus tend to have strong internal labor markets and offer opportunities for training and for stable employment. They are the jobs into which most young men settle. By contrast, secondary jobs require few skills and offer few opportunities for skill acquisition. Because workers make few investments in acquiring specific skills in secondary jobs and firms make few investments in workers, there is little incentive on either side to encourage job stability. In a sense, from workers' viewpoints all secondary jobs are alike, as there is little basis for choosing among them.

Secondary Jobs

Many, and probably most, youths spend their initial years after school in secondary jobs. Moratorium youths work in secondary firms because these firms find youth to be a satisfactory source of labor while primary firms do not. The unstable behavior of youths in moratorium makes them a risky investment for firms that put resources into training. Secondary firms do not have this problem since they usually provide little training. Nor are they overly concerned if their employees do not stay very long on the job. These firms are interested primarily in an assured supply of low-wage, unskilled labor, and they prefer to employ individuals or groups who are passive and unlikely, for example, to unionize in the face of unstable employment. Youths fit these requirements well. They are plentiful and thus provide such a satisfactory source of labor that some secondary firms organize their production schedules to recruit them. For example, one candy factory I visited, which employs large numbers of Spanish-speaking adults, also runs a special after-school production shift in order to employ youth. Large retail establishments also organize work shifts to attract youth.

These secondary jobs meet the requirements of young people in the moratorium period. The jobs are casual and unskilled. Little penalty is attached to unstable behavior, since all jobs are similar and none lead to careers. The jobs provide spending money with very little responsibility or long-term commitment.

The interviews suggest that there are three major types of secondary employment: large firms, mom and pop stores, and under the table work. The major examples of large secondary firms are security firms, grocery stores, cleaning companies, and a gum products company. All of these firms are large, employing well over 100 workers each. They all paid the minimum wage or very close to it and hired youths for unskilled jobs. The youths who worked in these jobs reported either that the job required only common sense or that it took 1 week or less to learn the job. These firms also hired more frequently than other firms through walk-ins, applicants who came in and asked for work. This is indicative of the unimportance of stable work behavior to the firms. These firms were known to have casual low-paid jobs: Many unemployed youths indicated that they could always find a job in one of these firms. A high percentage of youths in the sample at one time or another, usually in the first two years after school, worked in these firms, but a considerably smaller fraction of youths older than 20 worked in them. These firms provided standby secondary labor jobs for youths in the community.

Examples of small family operations are bakers, small construction contractors, newsstands, gas stations and auto service operations that provide unskilled and some skilled jobs, and restaurants. These firms are small, located in the neighborhood, and family owned. Like the larger employers, they also provide low-paid casual unskilled work without a future, but their atmosphere is quite different from that of the large secondary employers. Although many of the youths who worked in these jobs characterized the work as boring, there was very little of the bitterness about personal relationships, supervision, and working conditions that occurred repeatedly in the descriptions of large secondary employers. The conditions in the small firms, as might be expected, are much more paternalistic and relaxed. Finally, these jobs are virtually always found through personal contacts. Because the firms are small and family run, the few available jobs go to relatives and friends. Except for the occasional son destined to take over the business, most youths soon leave these moratorium jobs in search of better-paying work with a possibility of advancement.

The third category of jobs, described as "under the table" and "off the books" work, consisted of jobs that are not reported to tax, unemployment insurance, and welfare authorities. Youths who characterized themselves as unemployed often indicated that they received some income from occasional jobs such as painting houses, repairing cars, or construction. Except for the off the books aspect, these jobs are similar in structure to the second category; they are neighborhood based and found almost exclusively through family and friends. However, they are very unstable since they are one-time opportunities. Casual criminal activity, which several youths in the sample hinted at, also falls in this category.

Primary Firms

For young men who are successful, the end of moratorium comes with the acquisition of a job in a primary firm, a firm that is large, stable, and likely to provide long-term jobs, security, and reasonable opportunities for promotion and advancement. These firms are typically large enterprises with well-articulated internal labor markets. Jobs in these firms are generally well-paid, and the firms provide a strong measure of job security since, whether or not the firm is unionized, seniority is respected and layoffs occur in the reverse order of seniority. Most of these firms also have reasonably extensive benefit packages. It is for these reasons that I term finding a job in a primary firm *successful* settling down.

The hiring practices of these primary firms are probably the most important determinant of the structure and operation of the youth labor market. These firms provide the best-paid, most sought-after jobs, and their decisions about whom and when to hire determine the availability of labor to the other kinds of firms and also strongly influence the job-holding and search patterns of youth workers.

These firms generally prefer not to hire young men just out of high school who are engaged in moratorium behavior. Obviously this preference is modified by business conditions, and patterns of settling vary with the business cycle. However, on average, the firms prefer to hire youths who have already had some experience in the labor market.

A person who is hired by a primary firm (and passes a probationary period, if there is one) is likely to stay with the firm for a long time. Because the firm invests in training and because the individual has also invested time and resources, both parties have an incentive to maintain a stable employment relationship. Internal labor markets promote this stability, and the worker moves up through the internal labor market as he acquires more skills and as openings become available. It is expensive and disruptive for a firm to train an individual (either formally or through on-the-job training), promote that person to an important place in the production process, and then have him leave.

Because of the importance of stability, the key issue in understanding the hiring process is how firms judge who will and who will not become a stable worker. This concern is often more important to the firm than prior skills or relevant experience. Essentially, the firms seek to evaluate an individual's maturity. The other important factor is the applicant's ability to learn future jobs, not necessarily the job he is being hired for, since that job is simply the first rung on the bottom of the internal ladder.

These considerations explain why a rather nebulous attribute of job applicants, their attitude, was cited consistently by firms as the most important consideration in the hiring decision. This term seems to encompass several attributes: a neat appearance and respectful manner during the interview, a clear interest in the proferred work, willingness to learn the job, and a general alertness. Virtually every firm interviewed cited *attitude* as the main criterion in hiring.

Because firms have to judge the potential stability of the applicant and his ability to mesh well with the work group, it is not surprising that attitude is such an important criterion. In effect, attitude is a proxy for maturity and is a way of screening out moratorium-stage applicants and those who, for other reasons, are judged unlikely to be stable and reliable. Proper attitude is likely to be related to age, and its importance implies that moratorium-stage workers are less likely to be hired by primary firms. This inference is supported by the findings of other studies of industrial hiring practices (Lester, 1954).

The reluctance of primary firms to hire young workers forces youth into the secondary sector where their natural tendencies toward unstable behavior are reinforced. Thus it is the hiring pattern of primary firms that is the central structural characteristic of the youth labor market rather than, as is frequently argued in the popular literature, the youngsters' lack of entry level skills.

Most of the firms whom I interviewed did not place much emphasis on hiring youths who already knew how to do the job. These firms shared the views of an employer interviewed by Lester: "We would rather hire a young man with no molding experience and train him ourselves, than to hire a man with molding experience from another firm and have to break him of acquired habits and really retrain him" (Lester, 1954).

There are two explanations for this attitude. First, much production has firm-specific technology. Two firms may produce the same product with machinery that looks identical. However, the layout of the machines, the organization of the steps, and myriad details make the process quite different for the workers. Thus the advantage of previous experience is diminished. In addition, firms with internal labor markets generally cannot hire from the outside into skilled jobs. Rather, they hire people for unskilled entry positions and train and promote from within. This greatly reduces the advantage of previous skills.

Because skills are thus not of central importance to most firms, inadequate experience cannot explain the inability of young people to find jobs. Most youths in the sample did not already know how to do their primary jobs. At the same time, firms do not generally consider lack of skills a disadvantage, as the preceding quotation implies; on balance, it probably helps.

Although previous job-related experience is not as important as attitude or trainability, some firms do look for relevant previous experience. A history of stable work in a related firm shows maturity and interest in the field. Thus, previous experience is another proxy for maturity and stability. Relevant work experience in a similar job helps the firm acquire and evaluate references. In addition, some skills are industry-specific general skills. For example, in the machine tool industry, being able to read a blueprint might be an industry-specific general skill. Since firms do not want to teach these skills if they can avoid doing so, larger firms try to shift the costs of this training to the school system and to other firms by giving preference to applicants with some previous work experience and by supporting vocational programs in the public schools.

The interviews demonstrate that most jobs are found through personal contacts. Secondary jobs are much more likely to be found through friends, whereas primary jobs are more frequently found through parents and relatives.

The heavy emphasis on friends in secondary jobs confirms that these jobs tend to be either neighborhood small retail or contracting operations, which are likely to have youths from the same area who know each other, or larger firms such as the security and cleaning companies, which have developed reputations for hiring youths and are hence likely already to employ the youth's friends.

Jobs in primary firms are more often found through relatives, and there are more relatives than friends already on the job. This is to be expected, given that these firms are interested primarily in stability. While friends are likely to be poor sources of referrals in this respect, relatives and parents are likely to be good since they can exercise some control.

More striking is that the sample averages well over one previous acquaintance (friend, relative, or parent) per job. The Boston area is very large, yet these youths do not move in an impersonal labor market. Nor is this simply a neighborhood phenomenon; 67% of the jobs in the sample were outside the neighborhood. Clearly youths enter this large dense labor market through channels already traveled by people they know.

OCCUPATIONAL CHOICE

Sociologists, psychologists, and economists have all written extensively on this topic. In general, the sociological-psychological perspective focuses on the formation of ambitions, goals, and aspirations and pays less attention to how these goals are mediated in the labor market. I shall focus here on economic theories of occupational choice; I am in sympathy with elements of sociological-psychologi-cal approach (the moratorium stage can be viewed as a time to form aspirations), but it is not clear that final outcomes are conditioned as much by aspiration as by labor market structure and process.

The standard economic theory of occupational choice is largely a variant of human capital theory. This set of ideas lies at the heart of much recent research in labor economics, and for this reason I shall attempt to see how well the data from the interviews support or contradict these ideas.

An important limitation of both the human capital approach and my analysis is the bias toward individualistic explanations. If the topic is formulated in terms of the question, "Why did John become a _____?", then the individualistic expla-nation makes sense. However, this may not be the most interesting question. More general questions about social stratification or class reproduction lead to research strategies and answers that focus less on individual decision-making than on social and institutional structure. For example, one might ask why children of working-class families tend to remain in the working class while children of professional families maintain their status. Although I touch on some of these issues, the analysis remains largely at the individual level. This focus is necessitated by the nature of the data and can be justified because individual questions are still interesting and because it seems important to come to grips with human capital theory. However, another concern here is the operation of the labor market as an institution, and thus the analysis does go somewhat beyond purely individualistic considerations.

An economic view of occupational choice more general than human capital theory is simply that, all else constant, people respond to economic incentives in choosing jobs. A large fraction of the youths, in response to the question, "What would you like to be doing in 5 years?", mentioned a job other than their current one. Most wanted higher-level jobs and attributed their desire to better pay and opportunity. Clearly, standard economic incentives appeal to the youths, and given a choice between two jobs, these considerations would weigh heavily.

Even at this simple level the relative importance of economic versus other considerations in determining actual outcomes remains a question. For what fraction of young people does the weighing of net occupational advantages actually determine the outcome, and for what fraction is the process different? This question is typically finessed by an appeal to aggregate flows: It does not matter whether the theory is descriptive of most youths; as long as it is descrip-tive of some, an aggregate supply curve will conform to economic predictions. While this may be satisfactory for forecasters, it is incomplete as social science. It is important to discover which model best describes the experience of most people, not simply the relatively few on the margin.

Human capital theory specializes the general principle of net advantage into a tighter, more constrained theory of rational maximizing behavior. The theory makes strong claims, for example, Becker's assertion that human capital theory can explain why youth change jobs frequently. Even if we accept the loose version of economic occupational choice, it pays to examine the human capital version in more detail.

In general, human capital theory is an effort to model in investment terms the decisions of individuals. Choices about how much and what kind of education to acquire, expenditures on health care, and what kind of jobs to take are put into the maximizing framework of microeconomic theory. The essence of the theory is that these decisions are made in a conscious and rational fashion in which the costs and benefits are carefully weighed.

Most of human capital theory touches only indirectly on occupational choice since the theory focuses primarily on decisions concerning education and training rather than jobs. One of the few efforts to apply the theory to job decisions is Richard Freeman's (1971) *Market for College Trained Manpower*. Freeman concludes that labor supply decisions can be successfully modeled in terms of human capital models of occupational choice. He reaches this conclusion by examining aggregate data on the labor supply to various high-level occupations and by analyzing the results of interviews with college students. By showing that economic considerations play a role in occupational choice, Freeman concludes that the human capital choice model is vindicated for college-educated youth bound for the professions. Nothing I have to say here contradicts this conclusion, but it is important to see how well the model stands up for a considerably different group.

Freeman's model captures the essence of the human capital approach. The individual surveys the range of occupations and forms expectations about the future income streams of these occupations. From these expectations, he or she applies a discount rate and determines the present discounted value of each income stream. The individual also calculates the costs of acquiring the human capital necessary to enter the occupation and arrives at the net present value of each occupation. The individual then maximizes a utility function whose arguments are net present value, unearned income, and the nonpecuniary characteristics of each job. The occupation that maximizes the utility function becomes the occupational choice.

This approach seems to imply complete knowledge, lack of uncertainty, access to financing, and other conditions that are unlikely to pertain. These limitations, however, do not vitiate the model in a fundamental way, since they can be incorporated as additional constraints on the decision-making process. The nonpecuniary considerations play a muted role in the model, but this is justified by the academic division of labor. Although these considerations are important (the surge of applications to journalism school following the Watergate case is an example), the human capital theorist would argue that it is sufficient to show that with all else constant the economic calculus plays a role at the margin. Although this is true in a formal sense, it raises the question of human capital theory's importance relative to other considerations in explaining outcomes.

The determination of outcomes is summarized by Freeman (1971): "Characteristically, it (occupational choice) is an 'all or nothing' decision in which one career is selected from a set of mutually exclusive alternatives." Furthermore, "the worker investing in human capital normally limits himself to a single occupation because of the time it takes to learn skills and because investments are typically made early in order to maximize the period of return." The key assumptions here are that workers have careers, that the careers are in some nontrivial sense selected, and that once selected the careers are followed. How well do the work histories of the youths in the sample match these assumptions?

Several points in the interviews cast doubt on the underlying logic of the human capital model:

1. The sequence of jobs held by youth does not follow career patterns. More often, the jobs are random with respect to skills and occupations.

2. Because most jobs are found through personal contacts, the range and role of careful search and rational choice seems limited.

3. Unemployed youths generally take the first job offered, and they do so even though they have applied for a wide range of jobs with varying characteristics.

4. When asked how they found their jobs, youths rarely described the process in terms of choice or selection.

An analysis of the job holding pattern of youth in the sample shows that very few youths have what is conventionally thought of as a career. There is enormous variety in the jobs actually held, both with respect to the nature of the work and with respect to the kind of firm. The systematic movement between jobs which is characteristic of careers is absent for these young people. Such a pattern could, of course, result from the structure of opportunities. The young people in this sample may have chosen and felt committed to an occupation but were forced to settle for a job in another area. However, the same wide range of firms and skills is found in the jobs that these youths sought. (Youth were asked about all jobs they had looked for as well as those they found.) That is, even when looking for work, they showed little evidence of pursuing a chosen occupation or industry. Thus the notion of an occupational choice seems weakened.

However, the human capital approach can be recast in terms of labor market exploration. If youths lack information on the nature of jobs and the structure of opportunities within particular firms, they may move from job to job until they find the optimum setting. However, the observed nature of the process is contrary to the model. First, most of the first jobs held by the youths in the sample are virtually devoid of learning and advancement opportunities. Nor did this come as a surprise to the youths who sought those jobs. There is considerable knowledge in the community about the nature of firms that provide secondary work, and it seems unlikely that the youths would expect very much from these jobs. The early jobs are not the sort predicted by the learning or search models.

In addition, unemployed youths generally take the first job they are offered. In 78% of the periods of unemployment that ended by finding a job, that job was the first one offered. This finding in my sample has been replicated in other studies. Thus there is little evidence of search for bundles of learning and earning opportunities.

That most jobs, both primary and secondary, are found through personal contacts also weakens the human capital interpretation. This method of job acquisition implies a considerably narrower range of search and choice than is implied by the model. From the viewpoint of the youth, if not from that of an observer concerned with social structure, the jobs are available as a result of accident and chance, not active search and evaluation of alternative jobs. One function served by advanced education is to broaden this range of possibilities, both by bringing to bear credentials that may substitute for personal contacts and by widening the range of personal contacts to include teachers and colleagues in addition to family and friends. However, for the youths in this sample, and possibly for other youths in similar circumstances, the range of contacts is narrow, and jobs are found more by accident than by design.

The youths themselves accurately perceive the nature of the process. When they were asked, "How did you become a _____?", their answers overwhelmingly stressed chance, not design. Thirty percent of the youths said they "lucked into their job," and another 40% attributed their occupation to a contact. Only 8% indicated they had a previous interest in the field or examined jobs and selected one. The remaining 22% mentioned school, the typical answer being a shop course. Thus, only 30% of the sample (the group who planned plus the school group) seem to fit the human capital model.

What scope is there for the role of choice? The evidence suggests that choice occurs with respect to broad occupational categories. This evidence derives from responses to questions about the jobs that the youths would refuse. Some youths, for example, said they would refuse indoor work; others rejected outdoor labor. Some youths made a distinction between working in a factory and other jobs. Some youths distinguished between jobs "with a future" as opposed to casual labor. These seem to be the categories among which choices are made. However, within these categories, for example, "indoor nonfactory work with a future," there is enormous variety with respect to occupation, firm, and pay levels. The job that a youth gets from among the great variety is more a function of labor market structure than of individual decision making.

SUMMARY

For many youths, the process of entry and adjustment to the labor market is lengthy and involves distinct periods. The behavior of the youths changes over time, moving from a period of casual attachment to an increasing commitment to work and to stable behavior. At the same time the youths hold jobs in firms with quite different characteristics. Secondary firms provide the unskilled casual jobs characteristic of the moratorium stage, while primary firms seek to hire older youth who are prepared to settle down.

This pattern is not invariant over the business cycle because a strong economy leads some primary firms to hire workers they would normally avoid. However, the essential structure does not change. Finally, the youth in this labor market do not appear to have careers or to choose occupations in the manner predicted by conventional economic models. Although choice and economic considerations are not unimportant, the structure of the labor market, access to contacts, and chance play central roles.

REFERENCES

Brown, C., Gilroy, C., & Kohen, A. (1982, June). The effect of the minimum wage on employment and unemployment. *Journal of Economic Literature, Vol. XX*, 487–528.

Cogan, P. (1982, September). The decline in black teenage employment: 1950–70. *American Economic Review, 72*, 621–638.

Culp, J., & Dunson, B. (1986). Brothers of a different color; A preliminary look at employer treatment of White and Black youth. In R. Freeman & H. Holzer (Eds.), *The Black youth employment crisis* (pp. 233–260). Chicago: University of Chicago Press.

Doeringer, P. B., & Piore, M. J. (1971). *Internal labor markets and manpower analysis.* Lexington, MA: D. C. Heath.

Ellwood, D. T. (1983, August). *The spatial mismatch hypothesis: Are there teenage jobs missing in the ghetto?* Cambridge, MA: National Bureau of Economic Research. (mimeo)

Ellwood, D. T., & Wise, D. A. (1983, January). *Youth employment in the seventies: The changing circumstances of young adults.* Cambridge, MA: National Bureau of Economic Research.

Freeman, R. B. (1971). *The market for college trained manpower.* Cambridge, MA: Harvard University Press.

Freeman, R. B. (1980). Black economic progress since 1964: Who has gained and why? In S. Rosen (Ed.), *Low income labor markets.* Chicago: University of Chicago Press.

Holzer, H. J. (1982, November). *Black youth nonemployment: Duration and job search behavior.* Cambridge, MA: National Bureau of Economic Research. (mimeo)

Lester, R. (1954). *Hiring practices and labor competition.* Princeton, NJ: Industrial Relations Section, Princeton University.

Manpower Demonstration Research Corporation (1983, December). *Serving disadvantaged school dropouts: A symposium.* New York.

Osterman, P. (1980). *Getting started: The youth labor market.* Cambridge, MA: MIT Press.

Osterman, P. (1983). The mismatch hypothesis and internal labor markets: A study of white collar employment. *Proceedings of the Industrial Relations Research Association,* Madison, WI.

Osterman, P. (1984, June 27). *Testimony before the Joint Economic Committee on Proposals for a Differential Minimum Wage.*

Piore, M. J. (1970). Jobs and training. In S. H. Beer (Ed.), *The state and the poor.* Cambridge, MA: Winthrop.

Piore, M. J. (1979). *Birds of passage: Long distance migrants in industrial society.* Cambridge, England: Cambridge University Press.

Sum, A. (1983, December). *Educational attainment, academic ability, and the employability and earnings of young persons.* Northeastern University. (mimeo)

Wallace, P. (1975). *Pathways into work.* Lexington, MA: D. C. Heath.

IV SOCIAL CHANGE AND VOCATIONAL DEVELOPMENT

10

Adolescent Personality and Women's Work Patterns

Ravenna Helson
Teresa Elliott
Janet Leigh
University of California, Berkeley

How adolescent personality is related to the work lives of adults is a question that must be answered by looking at people who were young in the past. This chapter focuses on relationships between personality characteristics of some 100 students at a private women's college in 1958 and 1960 and the amount, span, and status level of their participation in the labor force by age 43. Of course, women who are middle-aged now had, as late adolescents, expectations that were very different from those of college women today. Furthermore, their personalities and prospects were construed differently by social scientists.

It seemed to us that it would be an interesting use of longitudinal data to test ideas about late adolescent personality and the vocational lives of women as they were formulated in the 1960s, when our sample of women were entering the adult world. We bring together (or at least consider adjacently) two conceptual frameworks: that of Zytowski and other researchers from the field of vocational psychology and that of Erikson, Marcia, and others from the field of personality development. On the basis of these frameworks we have selected variables and make hypotheses to predict work patterns of the women at age 43. Having presented the findings, we will discuss strengths and weaknesses of the theories and the relevance of the study for women's career development today.

Two other contributions of this chapter may be mentioned. The first is that the adolescent expectations of our longitudinal sample are placed in the historical context of several decades of expectations of women who came before and after them at the same institution. Second, we offer a measure of status level of work that we believe has advantages over assessment of work in terms of the proportion of men in the field or commonly used measures of socioeconomic status.

To begin, we consider three ideas about female adolescents or women's personality and work patterns that were current in the 1960s and early 1970s: (1) participation in paid work was behavior that deviated from women's normative role as homemaker, (2) amount and nature of participation in work was unpredictable from women's own interests and personality, and (3) female adolescent identity was typically unformed but showed several variations with different implications for vocational participation. The treatment of these ideas will be brief and tailored for purposes of the study. An excellent recent presentation of the field of women's vocational development is that of Betz and Fitzgerald (1987). A treatment of adolescent identity patterns and their sequelae in women which is more theoretically elaborated, psychodynamic, and case-oriented than ours is that of Josselson (1987).

Conceptualization and Measurement of Women's Participation in Work as "Deviant"

In an influential model of women's participation in the labor force, Zytowski (1969) offered as central postulates that the modal life role of women is that of homemaker; and, on the grounds that homemaking and vocational participation are, to a large extent, mutually exclusive, that vocational participation constitutes a departure from this role. The degree of departure, he said, may be measured in two ways: the extent to which work displaces or interferes with the role of homemaker as assessed in the timing and span of work-involvement; and what he called the "degree of participation," or nontraditionality, which he, like Rossi (1965), defined in terms of the proportion of males in the occupation.

In 1969, Zytowski's model summed up several of the main lines of research in the new field of women's career development. One of the first questions that had been asked about women and work was how young women with an orientation toward a career differed in personality from those with the conventional orientation toward homemaking (Hoyt & Kennedy, 1958). In other words, in what ways were career-oriented women "deviant"? As women increasingly combined work and homemaking, there was discussion of the best strategy of timing. Matthews (1960) and her mentor, Tiedeman (1959), thought the intellectual productivity of normal women who had not been wounded by trauma would be "released" only after their fulfillment as wives and mothers.

The feminist movement began with a book on the plight of the homemaker (Friedan, 1963). As the sexual division of labor and its power implications became a major theme (Bird, 1968), Rossi's reformulation (1965) of the homemaker-careerist dichotomy stimulated a large body of research. The new question was how women who chose fields of work in which women traditionally predominated, such as elementary teaching, home economics, and nursing, differed from those who choose pioneer or non-traditional fields in which men were predominant, such as law or engineering, Though some early studies (Brown, 1956; Vetter & Lewis, 1964) portrayed women with a career orientation as less feminine and more constricted or maladjusted than those with a homemaking orientation, Rand (1968), Bachtold and Werner (1970), and other later researchers found career-oriented women, especially the nontraditional careerists, to have desirable "masculine" characteristics such as confidence, independence, and intellectual interests.

It was increasingly recognized that a single distinction, such as traditional-nontraditional, was insufficient to describe women's vocational participation (Osipow, 1973). Super (1957) had attempted to classify women's patterning of family and career, and Zytowski (1969) did something similar in his proposal that measures of timing and span be combined with the measure of traditionality. Work of this sort continues, the number and nature of categories that are most useful varying with cohort and sample. Ellen Betz (1984), following up a large number of women graduates of the class of 1968 at the University of Minnesota, reported that high commitment to a pioneer or nontraditional occupation was no longer "unusual" (as it had been classified by Zytowski in 1969). This fact suggests that the assessment of women's work in terms of its deviance from the norm may be of decreasing value.

Instead of the traditional-pioneer distinction, this study uses ratings of the *status level* of work. The most widely-used measure of occupational status, the Duncan socioeconomic index (Hauser & Featherman, 1977), is based on the average education and salary of people in a given occupation. An artist or dancer has a lower score than an elementary teacher, and no distinction is made among individuals who have achieved more or less permanence or recognition in their work. Finding the Duncan index insensitive to important differences in our sample, we devised a rating scale that is anchored in terms of occupations that many college-educated women choose. It is intended to measure level of responsibility, skill, autonomy, and opportunity for self-expression. We expect it to reflect strong career-orientation (next section).

This study measures timing of work and amount of work-involvement to assess what Zytowski conceptualized as departure from the norm of homemaker—though they need not be thought of in this way. In addition we measure work in terms of the status that it affords.

The Unpredictability of Women's Work Patterns

"Since the achievement of women is so largely determined by extraneous circumstances and is in any case so difficult to estimate, my investigation of the causes of success and failure in gifted subjects has been confined to the male group," wrote Terman (1947; see 1970, p. 39). In his well-known longitudinal study of the gifted, who were 21 years old in about 1930, the female subjects "married after their schooling was over and fell into the domestic role," or, if they did not marry, took "whatever kind of respectable employment was at hand" (Terman, 1947/1970, p. 39). It was easy enough to predict that *if* women worked in the labor force they would be elementary teachers, librarians, or secretaries, but little relation was found between field of work or level of achievement and the individual personality.

Clausen (1986) reports that in the Berkeley longitudinal sample whose members were 21-years-old in the mid-1940s, self-direction or planfulness in adolescence predicted the occupational attainment of men but not of women, though about half of the women were working.

Women's work lives continued to be strongly associated with marital status, motherhood, husband's income, and the sexual division of labor. Did this mean that all women wanted to be homemakers, or that women's individual inclinations were irrelevant? One consideration is that of direction of influence. The finding of many investigators that career women tended to remain single or childless could be interpreted to mean that no one asked them to marry or that they lacked sexual interest or were unable to have children. On the other hand, some of them surely made *choices* about marriage and children in order to maximize their career effort (Harmon, 1970; Perrucci, 1970). Some other women presumably made *choices* that maximized the homemaker role. So "planful" women with different aspirations could have made decisions and begun ways of life that then importantly influenced their subsequent participation in work (Stewart, 1980). In the 1960s the decision to divorce, which was related to personality characteristics of both partners, became increasingly frequent, and it had strong implications for work (Cherlin, 1981). Thus, an association between family status and work does not eliminate the contribution of personality characteristics.

A second consideration in understanding the degree of predictability of women's work patterns is that *strong* vocational commitment seems to be related to personality more than to environmental factors, though for the majority of adolescents, male as well as female, vocational commitment is not strong and is influenced by both personality and environment (Farmer, 1985). For most college women, the combination of personality and environmental factors has made husbands the primary consideration and work secondary, contingent on a variety of influences (Angrist & Almquist, 1975).

In this study we expect to find that college-age personality predicts decisions, such as going to graduate school or getting a divorce, that influence timing and amount of participation in the labor force. However, we expect status level of work—assumed to reflect ability and vocational commitment—to be even more predictable from college-age personality.

The Female Adolescent and Her Occupational Identity

Erikson (1959, 1963) described the major task of adolescence as that of forming an identity. It was primarily the inability to settle on an occupational identity, he thought, that was disturbing to young people. He contrasted the successful achievement of identity with identity diffusion, a state in which the self is poorly differentiated, intimacy is threatening, and the individual is unable to concentrate or sinks into task-irrelevant activity. In Erikson's conceptualization, success in achieving an identity is aided by a relatively dependable store of trust (or confidence), autonomy, initiative, and industry—resources developed in preadolescent epigenetic stages of development.

The concept of crises in adolescent identity was very popular in the 1960s and early 1970s, perhaps because of the war in Vietnam and more generally because this was a period when rigid cultural values were giving way to change. Working within an Eriksonian framework, Marcia (1966) developed an interview that reliably classified college men into four identity statuses: The *identity achieved* were those who had committed themselves in the areas of vocation and ideology after a period of active searching or "crisis"; the *moratorium* group consisted of those who were exploring but had not committed themselves; the *foreclosed* had made a commitment that was parentally derived, without a period of exploration; and the *diffuse* had made no commitment and were not actively searching.

There has been disagreement about the applicability to women of Erikson's theory in general (Franz & White, 1985; Williams, 1977) and of the Marcia categories in particular (Marcia, 1980). In the research of the late 1960s and early 1970s, some investigators found that college women lacked clear enough ideas about their place in the occupational world for this topic to be useful in assigning them an identity status. Questions about premarital intercourse or lifestyle orientation were sometimes added as topics of greater interest and relevance (Schenkel & Marcia, 1972). Some investigators suggested additional statuses on the basis of their studies of women (Donovan, 1975). Some argued that identity development in the female was more subtle, more interwoven with the development of intimacy, and extended over a longer period of time than was the case for males (Josselson, Greenberger, & McConochie, 1977). However, studies increasingly found that occupational issues engaged women as much as men (Kacerguis & Adams, 1980).

Although the literature does not speak with one voice (Bourne, 1978; Marcia, 1980; Waterman, 1982), two main contrasts in personality characteristics have been associated with identity status. The first contrast suggests the dimensions of overcontrol-undercontrol, closed-open, or conservative-liberal. In studies of both males and females, the foreclosed, whose identity has been taken over from parents without having been questioned or challenged, are found to avoid anxiety through repression, to have stereotypical relationships and conventional attitudes, and to be relatively uninterested in intellectual and artistic activity. Both adolescents who have achieved an individual identity after a period of exploration and those who are unsettled, searching for an identity (the moratorium group) are opposite to foreclosed adolescents in many of the above respects. However, the moratorium group is distinctively volatile and anxious.

The second contrast is between individuals high and low in ego-strength and stability. In these respects, young men with an achieved or moratorium status have tended to be higher than the foreclosed or diffuse, but several studies of young women have shown the foreclosed and achieved to demonstrate more ego-strength than those in the moratorium and diffuse categories. One reason given to explain this difference is that foreclosed women appeared strong because they were given more support by the culture than women who explored alternatives to the traditional role (Marcia, 1980). It seemed possible that foreclosed women were able to become more self-defined as their family responsibilities lessened and they took a larger part in the world outside the family (O'Connell, 1976). It was a familiar opinion in the 1960s that the female adolescent should be "foreclosed" in the sense of acceptance of the role of wife and mother but with a tentativeness that would be conducive to a compatible marriage, the young woman choosing a man to whose mold she would adapt herself (Erikson, 1964). See also the research evidence of Douvan and Adelson (1966).

Since the formation of identity in women is considered to continue well into adulthood, Marcia (1980) suggested beginning with middle-aged women and working backwards. This has seemed an appropriate approach for the present study. As there is no measure of the paradigmatic identity statuses in our college data, we have also followed his advice to use these identity concepts flexibly, as they proved useful. We shall not try to separate the diffuse, the smallest category, from moratorium women. We shall hypothesize that women who entered the labor force early will tend to have been those with college-age characteristics generally associated with the achievement and moratorium identity status, and that those who entered late or not at all will tend to have been foreclosed on a homemaker identity, though some late entrants may be expected to have had moratorium (or diffuse) characteristics. Among women who have worked longest, we identify those who achieved a successful identity in paid work by age 43, and among women who have worked least, we identify those who are successful and happy as homemakers. We expect women with a successful identity of either kind, in comparison with those less successful, to have had, as late adolescents, more ego-strength and the other resources of personality conducive to consolidation of identity—trust, autonomy, initiative, and industry. We compare the groups also on personality traits associated with mature cognitive development, another factor thought to affect the achievement of identity (Marcia, 1980; Waterman, 1982). In these analyses, we are interested in the implications for women's participation in work.

Overview of the Study

The several topics that we have discussed are interrelated. Social scientists began to study women's work patterns about 1960 because these patterns were changing, and the situation was unclear to them as to young women themselves. Even the traditional pattern had to be reflected upon and defined. The "foreclosed" adolescent of Erikson and Marcia would, if female, grow into the normative homemaker conceptualized by Zytowski. The assumption that women's work patterns were unpredictable fit the conception of the well-adjusted young woman as waiting to be molded by her husband. Young women who wanted to become self-defined through work were "pioneers" likely to suffer conflict and anxiety.

Though recognizing the interrelatedness of these topics, we treat them separately. Each raises special questions, and as we analyze the data in different contexts, a little redundancy increases confidence that the patterns that emerge are genuine.

In the following section, retrospective cross-sectional data from 700 alumnae of a West Coast women's college show how expectations of college women about their participation in the labor force have changed over 60 years. These data provide context for longitudinal data of the classes of 1958 and 1960 from the same college.

The methods section presents measures of personality, attitudes, and work patterns in the longitudinal study. The measure of status level in work, which we believe has virtues possessed by neither the Duncan index nor the traditional-pioneer distinction for description of women's occupational status, is described in some detail.

The results section begins with correlations of the work patterns of about 100 women at age 43 with demographic variables and college-age personality characteristics. We will see whether correlates of participation in work support Zytowski's model of women's career development: for example, whether low participation in work is associated not only with marriage and children but also with college-age personality measures of normative regulation of behavior and femininity. A series of regression analyses addresses the question of the predictability of amount, timing, and status level of work from demographic and personality measures. We expect that college-age personality will be a significant predictor in all analyses of work variables, but that amount and timing of work will be more affected than status level by demographic (role) variables. We expect status level to be correlated with measures of career-orientation. It should also be correlated with confidence, independence, initiative, and intellectual interest, because these characteristics are associated with career or pioneer orientation (Fitzgerald & Betz, 1983)

The last two sections of results examine hypotheses derived from research on adolescent identity status: that time of entry into the labor force is correlated with college-age characteristics associated with moratorium vs. foreclosed identity, and that successful identity at age 43 is associated with college-age personality resources conducive to building an identity.

In the discussion we review the findings and consider the relevance of the experiences of the classes of 1958 and 1960 for subsequent cohorts of women.

EXPECTATIONS OF COLLEGE WOMEN ABOUT WORK
OVER SIXTY YEARS

In 1983, the alumnae journal of a prominent West Coast women's college published a questionnaire designed as a supplement to a longitudinal study of the classes of 1958 and 1960. The questionnaire was returned by 700 alumnae between the ages of 26 and "over 80." Although the returns cannot be presented as unbiased, results generally conform with what is known to have happened in the lives of college-educated women over the last 60 years.

One set of questions concerned the expectations about various aspects of life that the women and their classmates held when they were in college. Figure 10.1 shows that at two periods there were clear answers to the question, "after college, how long did you expect to work?" Until World War II, women expected to work until they married, as the Terman sample had (Terman, 1947/1970). After the mid-1960s, women expected to work "always." Only during the 1950s was the idea of working until one had children a common expectation. (Some possible answers on the questionnaire, such as "I planned to work until I had children and then again after they were older," received so few checks that they are not included on the graph). From the mid-30s to the mid-60s many women said "my ideas about work were unclear." This was an era during which women were drawn in or out of the labor force by the Depression, World War II, the Baby Boom, the expanding economy of the 1950s, the rising divorce rate, and the pill.

During the period when the longitudinal sample was in college (1956–1960), there was little consensus. The most common idea was to work until one became a mother, but lack of clarity about the place of work in one's life was about equally common, and the idea of working "always" was on the rise.

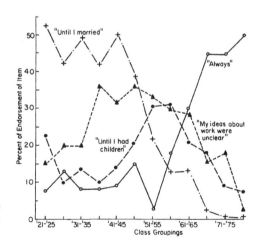

FIG. 10.1. After college, how long did you think that you would work?

266

ADOLESCENT ANTECEDENTS OF WOMEN'S WORK PATTERNS: THE CLASSES OF 1958 AND 1960

Method

Participants and Overall Design of the Longitudinal Study

In 1958 and again in 1960, a representative two-thirds of the senior class (N = 141) at a women's college on the West Coast participated in a study of personality characteristics and plans for the future among college women (Helson, 1967). A follow-up about 5 years later included husbands. In 1981 the women who had participated previously were contacted again. They were then between 42- and 45-years-of-age. There is information sufficient to code work variables for about 75% of the original group.

Measures in the Senior Class Study

Questionnaire Material. A questionnaire included sections devoted to college life and to marriage and vocational plans. Measures coded from the questionnaire include intention to attend graduate school (3-point scale), which is used as an index of career ambition; activities, such as dating and artistic pursuits, used to assess conventionality and intellectuality of interests; and amount of change the senior had experienced over the college years, used as a measure of openness to the new and different.

Inventories. The seniors filled out the California Psychological Inventory (CPI)(Gough, 1957/1987) and a special test form that permitted scoring of the Minnesota Multiphasic Personality Inventory (MMPI)(Hathaway & McKinley, 1943), various research scales developed at the Institute of Personality Assessment and Research (IPAR), and also scales developed at Vassar College as a part of a study of women's personality development during the college years (Webster, Sanford, & Freedman, 1957). The CPI provides a picture of overall functioning in an interpersonal context. There are 20 scales and 3 vector scores that assess its major themes of social poise and assertiveness, normative regulation of behavior, and dispositions to seek achievement and personal competence. There are also various special scales. Among these are Baucom's (1980) measures of masculinity and femininity, which are favorable unipolar scales emphasizing initiative as masculine and socialized sensitivity as feminine. The standard CPI has a bipolar femininity-masculinity scale, but for the purposes of this article, the unipolar scales are easier to interpret and more relevant to hypotheses.

Scales of Special Relevance. To assess concepts of special relevance to the hypotheses, the scales listed below are most important:

conventional rule-upholding: socialization (CPI), social integration (Vassar);

impulse-control: self-control (CPI), impulse-expression (Vassar);

sex-role traditionality: femininity (Baucom, 1980);

career ambition: achievement via independence (CPI);

status seeking and potential: capacity for status (CPI);

control of anxiety: repression and suppression (Vassar), anxiety (Leventhal, 1966), anxiety (Welsh, 1956);

ego-strength and stability: ego-strength (Barron, 1953), K (MMPI), level of effective functioning (CPI), soundness (Barron, 1954);

trust (confidence and comfort in relations with oneself and others): sense of well-being (CPI);

autonomy: independence (CPI);

initiative: dominance (CPI), masculinity (Baucom, 1980);

industry: work orientation (Gough, 1985), intellectual efficiency (CPI), achievement via conformance (CPI);

mature intellectual skills: psychological mindedness (sensitive and shrewd interpersonal perceptiveness) (CPI), achievement via independence (CPI).

Measures in the Age-27 Study

In this report, use is made of two measures from inventories filled out by husbands: the economic value scale from the Study of Values (Allport, Vernon, & Lindzey, 1960), and the autonomy scale of the Adjective Check List (Gough & Heilbrun, 1980).

Measures in the Age-43 Study

Questionnaire Material.   Each woman described the major events of her life since college, year by year, on a chronology chart. Other sections of questionnaire material treated work, marriage, and other topics. Measures of work are described separately below. Answers to seven objective questions about marriage were summed as a marital satisfaction index. The women rated each item on a 5-point scale. The items were taken from Campbell (1980) and concerned how well the woman understood her partner, how well the partner understood her, how much she enjoyed the partner's company, and so forth.

Work Variables.   The work section of the questionnaire included space for a work history with information about dates of work, whether it was paid or unpaid, what percent of a work week it occupied, and its nature. This and the chronology chart were the basis for coding the work variables described below. Other parts of the work section inquired into reasons for the women's choice of her current work, conflicts between work and other aspects of life, and work satisfaction and dissatisfactions.

The *total participation* score represents the amount of time a woman had participated in the work force since graduation from college. A 0-6 scale was used for each year since graduation from college, where 0 meant no time spent in paid work, 3 meant 41–60% of a 40-hour-week, and 6 meant more than 40 hours per week. Each year was assigned a rating based on the highest level of participation for at least half of the year, and the ratings were summed to produce a total score.

A year of entry variable is important in this chapter only as the major contributor to a nine-point rating scale, *time since entry*. Year of entry refers to the year when the woman entered the work force (at no less than 41% time) after which there was no prolonged exit. A prolonged exit was defined as three or more years of no more than minor work participation. Women with prolonged exits who had not resumed work at more than 40% time for at least 3 years do not have year-of-entry scores. *Time since entry* includes these women, assigning them the lowest rating.

The 7-point scale for assessing *status level* of work at age 43 is anchored at the low end by jobs that require (in our sample) a minimum of skill, independence, opportunity for self-expression, responsibility for other adults, or prestige; and at the high end by work that requires talent and training, considerable autonomy and opportunity for expression, and either responsibility for other adults and/or recognition by informed others over a wide area.

The coding instructions usually make the typical level of an occupation clear within a point or two. Evidence of erratic or doubtful performance is used to weight the placement downward, and evidence of achievement or responsibility weights the judgment upward. Thus, an elementary school teacher or service librarian would be given a rating of 2, but if she had lost jobs repeatedly through conflicts with coworkers her rating would be 1, and if she had obtained specialized training her rating would be higher. A nurse or social worker would be placed at 3 unless she had advanced training or took on managerial functions. These examples make clear that traditional women's work at age 43 is rated below average in status level unless the woman has attained a position of responsibility, leadership, or specialization.

Category 4 consists primarily of women who have jobs that involve moderate talent, responsibility, and autonomy (minor administrative positions) or more self-expression and autonomy but with only moderate evidence of stability or recognition (artist, free-lance photographer, fund-raiser). Evidence of sustained success would move women in the latter category to a higher rating.

Business executives or professional women with graduate degrees (taken as evidence of talent and training) would not be rated below 5, but if they showed clear signs of autonomy, responsibility, or recognition, they would be rated 6. Only a few women with national reputations in their field of work were given a rating of 7. A very few women without any status in the world of work were not given a rating.

Ratings of status level at age 43 by the first two raters showed a correlation of .96. A third rater was recruited who had not participated in discussion of the development of the code. Her ratings of 55 cases correlated .93 and .94 with those of the first two raters.[1] Raters had access to the work sections, the chronology charts, and to any enclosures about work that the women might have sent with their materials.

Results

Correlations of Work Variables with Demographic Indices and College Personality

Table 10.1 shows strong support for the familiar idea that women's involvement in work is negatively related to their responsibilities as wives and mothers. Remaining single, marrying late, having few or no children, and divorcing early (discussed in a later section) are related positively to amount of participation and early entry into the work force. Variables that combine several of these aspects of the life history, such as years of marriage, are especially powerful.

Note that status level in work has no significant correlations with wife-mother roles, a somewhat surprising fact that will receive further attention.

Amount of postgraduate education is significantly correlated with all work variables. However, a number of factors sometimes found to affect women's employment, such as age of youngest child or geographical mobility, show no significant relationship in this study.

Table 10.2 shows college-age personality characteristics (CPI) that are correlated with work variables. Total participation and time since entry are related only to scales that have high loadings on the CPI factor, normative regulation of behavior: socialization, self-control, achievement via conformance, and, for time of entry, sense of well-being. All correlations are negative. Thus, women who worked the most and went to work earliest tended to be the least conventional. Total participation and time since entry are also correlated negatively with Baucom unipolar femininity, $r = -.20$ and $-.22$, $p < .05$. (Not shown in Table 10.2.) These results support Zytowski's formulation of amount of participation in the labor force as constituting a departure from the norm.

In contrast to total participation and time since entry, status level of work shows no antecedent correlations with scales assessing normative regulation of impulse. However, it has abundant age-21 correlations with scales assessing confidence and assertiveness, ambition, verve, independence, and skill with people (Do, Cs, Sp, In, Em) and also with scales assessing intellectual potential and flexibility (Ai, Ie, Py, Fx). The lack of relationship to CPI socialization,

---

[1]The first two raters were Ravenna Helson and Janet Leigh. The third rater was Teresa Elliott.

TABLE 10.1
Correlations Between Several Indices of Women's Work Patterns
and Demographic Variables

	Total Participation	Time Since Entry	Status Level
	N = 107	N = 113	N = 111
Always single vs. ever married	.42***	.42***	-.07
Date of first marriage	.45***	.32**	-.02
Date of birth of first child	.27*	.13	.18
Date of birth of last child	-.04	.01	.08
Number of children	-.49***	-.45***	-.07
Years of marriage	-.57***	.54***	-.11
Years of parenting	-.51***	-.48***	-.10
Number of moves since college	.02	.01	.14
Postgraduate education	.32***	.37***	.28**
Size of present community	.12	.12	.10
Marital satisfaction	-.06	-.06	.06
Health at 43	.06	.09	.16
Total participation in work	--	.88***	.43***
Time since entry		--	.53***

*$p < .05$
**$p < .01$
***$p < .001$

TABLE 10.2
Antecedents of Work Patterns on the College CPI

CPI Scales	Total Participation	Time Since Entry	Status Level	Years of Children
	N = 105	N = 111	N = 109	N = 105
Dominance (Do)			.29**	
Capacity for status (Cs)			.36***	.20*
Sociability (Sy)				.20*
Social presence (Sp)			.23*	
Self-acceptance (Sa)				
Independence (In)			.41***	
Empathy (Em)			.32***	
Responsibility (Re)				
Socialization (So)	-.22*	-.27**		.27**
Self-control (Sc)	-.20*	-.26**		
Good impression (Gi)				
Communality (Cm)				
Well-being (Wb)		-.22*		.24**
Tolerance (To)				
Achievement via conformance	-.24*	-.22*		.21*
Achievement via independence			.34***	
Intellectual efficiency (Ie)			.23*	.27**
Psychological mindedness (Py)			.27**	
Flexibility (Fx)			.28**	
Femininity-masculinity (Fe)				-.23*

Note. Correlations significant at the .05 level on the 20 standard scales of the CPI are shown. *$p < .05$; **$p < .01$; ***$p < .001$.

self-control, and achievement via conformance suggests that women high and low in work status at age 43 were equally likely to have been norm-questioning or norm-defying when they were college seniors. Because work rated low on our status-level scale tends to be traditional women's work, this result casts doubt on Zytowski's idea that nontraditional work is more of a departure from the norm than traditional work. On the other hand, traits such as assertiveness and independence are generally considered to be masculine. In this positive sense, high status level involves departure from what is normative for women. Status level is correlated positively with unipolar masculinity, $r = .28$, $p < .01$.

Although amount and span of work show higher correlations with demographic (role) variables than with college-age personality, the last column of Table 10.2 illustrates that these role variables have personality antecedents. A young women's ability to have a family and to start it soon after graduation from college ("on time" by the norms of her cohort) involved an effective pursuit of conventional goals that did not characterize women who had children late or not at all (Helson, Mitchell, & Moane, 1984).

Regression Analyses of Work Variables

Two hierarchical regression analyses were undertaken to compare the relationships between demographic and personality factors in total participation and status level of work.

Using total participation in the work force as a dependent variable, we tested the hypothesis that years of marriage and responsibility for children were primary (negative) contributors, but that after their influence had been taken into account, the role of college-age personality characteristics could also be demonstrated. The upper portion of Table 10.3 shows confirmation of this hypothesis. After the demographic variables produced a multiple correlation of .60, CPI capacity for status was entered, which brought R to .63 and added significantly to R^2. The women's late adolescent capacity for status (ambition, discretion, sense of entitlement) thus contributed positively to participation in work, after the influence of wife and mother roles was taken into account.

Using status level as a dependent variable, we tested the hypotheses that verbal aptitude and CPI independence (self-reliance, sense of competence) would be contributors; that capacity for status (Cs) and achievement via independence (Ai) assessed other college-age personality characteristics of logical relevance to the achievement of status in work; and that after these were taken into account the effect of responsibility for children should show a demonstrable negative influence.

The middle section of Table 10.3 shows the results of this analysis. The SAT verbal score and especially the independence scale exert strong influences, and together they reduce to insignificance the contribution of Cs and Ai. Note that the

TABLE 10.3

Regression Analyses of Three Work Variables

Dependent Variable	Step	Variables Entered	R	R² Increment	Beta[a]	Simple r
Total participation at age 43 (N = 99)	1	Years of marriage	[.60]	[.33***]	-.42	-.56
		Years with children			-.26	-.51
	2	Capacity for status	.63	.04**	-.22	.11
Status level at age 43 (N = 96)	1	SAT Verbal	.27	.07**	.24	.27
	2	CPI Independence	.50	.18***	.28	.41
	3	CPI Capacity for status			.17	.37
	4	Achievement via independence	[.53]	[.03]	.11	.34
		Years with children	.55	.03	-.17	-.14
Time since entry (N = 56)	1	Years with children	.30	.09*	-.19	-.30
		Years of marriage	.40	.07*	-.21	-.30
	2	Plans for graduate school	.50	.09*	.36	.38
	3	Husband's economic value	.63	.14***	-.41	-.36
		Husband's autonomy	.67	.05*	.23	.19

[a]Beta weight in the final equation, all other predictors having been entered.

Note. CPI scores and plans for graduate school were obtained when women were in college. Measures of husbands' personality were obtained when the women were age 27.

*p < .05; **p < .01; ***p < .001.

incremental effect of years with children does not reach the .05 level of significance.

These analyses could be extended and improved, but they make the point that for this sample, *amount* of participation in work was highly predictable in terms of marriage and family, though college personality characteristics contributed additionally; but that *status level* of work was predictable largely in terms of personality variables, with motherhood failing to show a significant negative influence.

A third regression analysis included only 56 women whose husbands had participated in the first follow-up study. It tested the hypothesis that after the influence of the roles of wife and mother were taken into account, both college-age career ambitions of the women and personality characteristics of their partners would affect time of entry into the labor force.

Because all of the women in this analysis were married by age 27, years of marriage approximates a measure of years before divorce. Years with children and years of marriage show a multiple correlation (R) of .40 with time of entry (Table 10.3).

Degree of interest in going to graduate school was selected as an indicator of career ambition. This variable increases the R to .50 and makes an increment to R^2 significant at the .02 level.

Two variables were chosen to test the effect of husband's personality. One was the partner's economic value as assessed by the Allport-Vernon-Lindzey Study of Values. The assumption was that men who valued their role as provider would tend to choose and be chosen by traditionally minded women; that they would tend to be good providers, offering no economic need for their wives to work; and might even resist their wives' entry into the labor force. This variable brings the multiple R to .63 and makes the largest single contribution to R^2. The second measure of husband's personality was his need for autonomy, as assessed by his self-description on the ACL. High-scorers on the autonomy scale value independence and pursue their own goals without consideration of the needs of others. We thought that such partners would want neither to feel dependent on a wife to manage their home nor to be encumbered by a dependent woman. They might even make her feel unneeded and insecure unless she also found a sphere in which to pursue her own goals. This variable brings R to .67 and makes an additional significant contribution to R^2.

The results thus support the hypothesis that women's college-age career ambition was not submerged in the roles of wife and mother but influenced early entry into the labor force. It shows also that time since entry was related to the personality of the partner. Because of the small size of the sample and our focus on late adolescence, we did not undertake a path analysis to explore the causal structure among these variables. However, the following section provides some perspective.

Late Adolescent Personality, Divorce, and Work

Women's increasing participation in work in the 1960s was related in important and complex ways to the rising divorce rate (Cherlin, 1981). In this sample, the proportion of women who divorced by age 35 is higher among heavy participants in the labor force than among ever-married women who participated at levels below the mean for the sample, chi square $(1)(87) = 6.33$, $p < .02$. There were large college-age differences in personality between women with children who divorced by age 35 and those who did not (Mitchell, 1983). The divorcees scored lower as seniors on CPI socialization, self-control, achievement via conformance, and responsibility, ts (67) ranging from 2.93, p .005, to 2.25, $p < .03$. They also expressed more interest in attending graduate school, t $(56) = 3.13$, $p < .003$.

Thus, career ambition and inclination to behave in nontraditional ways were college-age antecedents of both divorce and work.

Late Adolescent Identity and Participation in Work

We move now to analyses based on an Eriksonian conceptualization of late adolescence. In the introduction we suggested that participation in work should be related to the identity status of the women as college seniors. Our first hypothesis was that late entrants would tend to have been college seniors who foreclosed on a traditional identity as homemaker, and early entrants would tend to have been those who were undecided or were working towards an identity defined through their own work.

It should be pointed out that questions to the seniors about the expected timing of marriage, children, and work do not show many relationships. Almost all of the women expected to marry and have large families, but except for those who were engaged, it was difficult for them to say just when. As Fig. 10.1 indicates, women of this era were unclear about the place of work in their lives. Many chose noncommittal alternatives to our questions. In the sketches that they wrote of the future life they would like, they sometimes entertained contradictory goals or reversed positions within the space of a paragraph:

> If I marry, I must be allowed to continue my creative life. I honestly do not know at this time how far I would be willing to give in should my husband's interests directly oppose this creative existence. His interests would probably come first, however, as creativity can be a flexible thing.

Nevertheless, the first set of items in Table 10.4 indicates that women who entered the labor force early were more likely to plan to go to graduate school and less likely to say that they would not work after they had children than women who entered late or never.

TABLE 10.4
Correlations Between Time Since Entry and Evidence of Foreclosed Vs.
Moratorium or Achieved Adolescent Identity Status

	Time of Entry N = 105
Traditional homemaker identity vs. self-definition in work	
Plans for graduate school	.35***
Why family and career will not conflict:	
Will not work after I have children	-.22*
Openness to change during the college years	
Amount of change	.23*
Number of areas of change	.29**
Vassar development status	.23*
Conventional vs. artistic/intellectual interests	
Interest in dating	-.26**
Interest in student organizations	-.20*
Artistic intersts	.20*
Impulse-control vs. volatility	
Self-control (CPI)	-.26**
Impulse-expression (Vassar)	.32***
Socialized behavior vs. rebelliousness and unconventional behavior	
Socialization (CPI)	-.27**
Social integration (Vassar)	-.23*
Avoidance of anxiety throuth repression	
Repression and suppression (Vassar)	-.17
Anxiety (Leventhal)(CPI)	.35***
Anxiety (Welsh)(MMPI)	.13

*p <.05; **p <.01; ***p <.001

Subsequent sets of items in Table 10.4 describe characteristics that have been found to distinguish adolescents with foreclosed identity from those in a moratorium state or those with an achieved identity (Marcia, 1980). Thus, women who entered the work force late or never, whom we hypothesize to have had a foreclosed identity, said as seniors that they had changed less and in fewer ways over the college years than those who entered the labor force early—those hypothesized to have suffered conflicts in their attempt to build their own identity and were presumably searching for ideas and clarification in college. The developmental level of the late entrants was more like that of Vassar first-year students than of seniors, where for early entrants, of course, the case was reversed. (Seniors in the Vassar studies were flexible, tolerant toward individuals but critical of institutional authority, intraceptive, nonconforming, realistic, and socially mature in comparison with first-year students. See Webster, Freedman, & Heist, 1962.)

Late as opposed to early entry is associated with conventional interests such as dating and school organizations and negatively with artistic interests. It is associated with impulse-control rather than emotional volatility, and with socialized behavior rather than with rebelliousness and unconventionality.

Finally, there is some relation between time of entry and the control of anxiety, but it is spotty: The correlation with Leventhal's scale is significant, but not those with the Vassar and Welsh measures.

In sum, the evidence is fairly convincing that early entry into the labor force had adolescent antecedents of openness to change, artistic and intellectual interests, volatility, and resistance to normative regulation of behavior, whereas late entrance was related to resistance to change and acceptance of a traditional life style. We turn now to closer examination of the extremes of the continuum.

Evaluation of Subgroups

This section compares the late adolescent personality of two groups of women who were more and less successful in achieving a career or homemaking identity by age 43. Among early entrants to the labor force, those who achieved a status level about average are compared with those whose status level is average or below. Among women who entered the labor force late, or who have never entered, women who were above average on marital satisfaction and had no major problems with children are compared with those less successful in the homemaker role.

According to Erikson's theory, successful resolution of previous stages of development engender trust (or confidence), autonomy, initiative, and industry that help the adolescent in the task of building an identity. In addition, mature cognitive functioning has been thought to contribute to the formation of identity (Marcia, 1980; Waterman, 1982). And, as previously reported, research has demonstrated that women with an achieved or foreclosed identity tend to have more ego-strength and stability than those with moratorium or diffuse identity.

Our available measures do not align perfectly with these constructs, but Table 10.5 shows scales classified as assessing trust, autonomy, and initiative; industry and intellectual efficiency; mature cognitive functioning (interpersonal perceptiveness and potential for independent intellectual achievement); and ego-strength and stability. Table 10.5 also includes a scale from each theme pertinent to the foreclosed- vs. achievement or moratorium comparisons (Table 10.4). We expect the two groups of early entrants to differ little on these last scales, since they were both considered to be of achieved or moratorium status. Among the late entrants, however, we expect the successful homemakers to have appeared in college as foreclosed and the less successful homemakers to have scored in the direction of moratorium status.

Early Entrants. Table 10.5 shows that college-age differences between more and less successful early entrants (labeled MS and LS) were particularly large on measures of autonomy and initiative, but also significant on indices of ego-strength. In addition, MS careerists were more intellectually efficient and showed more potential for independent intellectual achievement. On the fore-

TABLE 10.5

College-Age Personality Resources of Women with More and Less Successful Identities at Age 43

| | Early Entrants | | | | Late Entrants | | | |
	MS N = 24	LS N = 18	t	df	MS N = 12	LS N = 13	t	df
Trust, autonomy, and initiative								
Well-being (CPI)	32.9	30.0	2.43*	40	34.2	33.0	.80	23
Independence (CPI)	21.1	16.3	4.67***	40	19.3	17.5	1.42	18
Dominance (CPI)	25.1	20.6	3.42***	40	24.2	20.8	1.65a	23
Masculinity (Baucom)	37.0	28.4	5.24***	40	37.8	31.5	1.91a	17
Industry and intellectual efficiency								
Work orientation (Gough)	30.4	28.2	1.60	28	33.0	29.9	2.42*	23
Intellectual efficiency (CPI)	34.8	31.1	2.60**	40	35.6	33.6	1.72a	16
Achievement via conformance (CPI)	29.2	27.3	1.76a	28	31.6	29.5	1.50	16
Mature cognitive functioning								
Psychological mindedness (CPI)	18.1	16.8	1.13	40	19.3	15.8	3.01**	23
Achievement via independence (CPI)	28.6	24.5	3.05**	25	28.2	25.9	1.46	23
Ego-strength and stability								
Ego-strength (Barron)	48.4	42.8	2.91**	38	49.6	47.2	1.28	23
K (MMPI)	16.8	13.6	2.49*	38	18.9	15.3	2.64*	23
Level of effective functioning (CPI)	42.9	37.3	2.47*	28	46.2	40.5	2.38*	23
Soundness (Barron)	28.3	26.3	1.40	38	30.2	25.0	3.23*	19
Foreclosed vs. moratorium								
Amount of change in college	4.1	4.1	.36	37	3.2	4.0	3.23**	15
Interest in dating	5.4	5.1	.49	37	7.1	6.3	1.17	17
Self-control (CPI)	19.8	19.4	.30	40	24.8	21.7	1.70a	23
Socialization (CPI)	33.1	31.0	1.27	40	36.8	33.6	2.47*	23
Anxiety (Welsh)	9.4	14.2	2.28*	38	6.8	12.7	2.21*	18

Note. For early entrants, MS and LS mean more successful and less successful status in work; for late entrants, MS and LS mean more and less successful family relationships.

a p <.10, two tails
*p <.05; **p <.01; ***p <.001.

closed-moratorium comparisons, only the difference on anxiety is significant. The MS group was less anxious.

The most obvious way in which the college personality characteristics of MS and LS women influenced their work lives was in the choice of the first job after graduation. Two thirds of the LSs took traditional women's jobs, as compared to one sixth of the MSs. Later, the few MSs in these jobs switched fields or moved up into more responsible positions. Most of the LSs have moved up a little, but not very far.

The different personality resources of MSs and LSs women seem to have affected their relationships as well as their work. Of the 24 MSs, two thirds married and 14 have children. Of the 18 LSs, half married and 3 have children. Fewer LSs have become mothers, chi square $(1)(42) = 7.41, p < .01$. Because it was considered important for women of this cohort to have a family, the evidence suggests that many LSs had a long-term problem in both relational and work identity and probably in intimacy as well.

One should not picture the MS group as unambivalent or easily overcoming all obstacles. Several became careerists only after disappointments in marriage. Several have used work to maintain an identity despite fairly serious personality problems. All have had setbacks. Few MSs had achieved an identity when they were seniors, but on the whole they had a distinctive pattern of characteristics that included both a need for independent identity and the confidence, autonomy, initiative, industry, intellectual potential, and ego-strength to achieve the identity they wanted.

The LSs, on the other hand, needed an identity but lacked the resources to take hold. Thus, Meg drifted from job to job, never wanting to be tied down. When Fern was appointed to a position of responsibility over others, she became so tense that she moved to a humbler job in another city. Dorothy's real interest in life remained her parents and siblings and their health problems.

Late Entrants.   Late entrants had spent more than 15 of the 22 years since college as homemakers. Two women with severe health disabilities were omitted from analyses, because they were restricted in choice of lifestyle. Homemakers we shall label more successful (MS) scored above the mean on marital satisfaction and had no major problems with children. Those we shall label less successful (LS) scored below the mean on marital satisfaction, had divorced, and/or had major problems with children.

The last section of Table 10.5 shows that, as predicted (and despite the small size of the groups), the MS group scored higher on most of the scales used as indicators that they had been more foreclosed in college than the LS women. As seniors, they felt they had changed less in college. They scored higher on socialization, somewhat higher on self-control, and lower on anxiety. Also as predicted, they scored significantly higher on three of four measures of ego-strength and stability. In other areas, they consistently scored higher than the

LSs, but differences reached the .05 level only on work orientation (a measure of industry) and psychological mindedness (a measure of mature cognitive functioning). The difference on psychological mindedness is particularly interesting, because sensitivity and shrewdness in appraisal of others would seem to be helpful to homemakers in choosing an appropriate partner and coping with problems in family relationships.

At age 43, few of the MS homemakers expressed concern about their participation in the work world. Sue had 5 children, two still preadolescent. She was active in community activities and had several ideas for work she would like to do when her children left home. Joan was happy with a class she taught once a week at a community center. Fran was a serious amateur painter.

In contrast, a majority of the LS homemakers expressed dissatisfaction, worry, or frustration at difficulties in making a place for themselves in the labor force. Sarah's husband would not allow her to take a good job that would require a long commute. Ellen was investing her energies in art activities, but they were not likely to make her financially independent of her abusive partner. Mary did not know how to find work appropriate to her status in the community, but her marriage was foundering, and a counselor thought a job might help.

Summary and Additional Remarks.   The conspicuous finding across groups is that, as predicted, women who achieved a successful identity by age 43, whether as careerist or homemaker, scored higher on measures of ego-strength and stability in late adolescence. The more successful groups showed other of the predicted personality strengths, though each had a distinctive profile of resources. Finally, as predicted, the more successful homemakers gave evidence of having been the most foreclosed in college—least open to change and most inclined to normative regulation of behavior.

It is pertinent to ask what findings may have been ignored by analysis in terms of Eriksonian concepts. For late entrants, virtually nothing. LS women made higher grades in college. For early entrants, MS women scored higher on a variety of measures of social energy and resourcefulness. They also scored higher on measures of creativity, had higher mathematical aptitude, and made better grades in college.

DISCUSSION

The social scientist must often produce conceptualizations of problems that are important but not clearly delineated. There is often a lag between the formulation of a pattern and the living out of lives that were to be elucidated. In this chapter we have examined personality antecedents of the involvement in the labor force of a sample of socially advantaged women who entered the adult world a few years before the beginning of the women's movement. Our analyses were structured in terms of questions posed and concepts developed by social scientists as the changes of the 1960s were in progress. Retrospective evaluation of concepts in longitudinal data may be a useful way of evaluating the adequacy of theories for specific cohorts and the cohort-generality of different theoretical relationships.

We began with the succinct model of Zytowski (1969). The homemaking role, he began, was normative for women; the greater the involvement in work, the greater the departure from the norm. Our results shows that working little and entering the labor force late were indeed correlated not only with demographic indicators of emphasis on the homemaking role, such as years of marriage and children, but also with conventionality of behavior and positive aspects of femininity, as assessed by personality inventories taken by the women at age 21. So the first part of Zytowski's model received support.

Zytowski postulated also that sex-traditional work was less of a departure from the norm than work that was nontraditional for women. Here there are several points to discuss. The gender-traditionality of work remains a popular objective variable in vocational psychology (Hayes, 1986), but its meaning is complex. Work may be sex-traditional or non-traditional for a variety of reasons. Physical strength may be involved, the distinction between instrumental and expressive preference may contribute, but certainly an important consideration is status (Schrank & Riley, 1976). In the interests of clarity, we measured the status level of work rather than sex-traditionality. Our scale accords value to jobs that involve power over or responsibility for other adults, freedom from supervision by others, skill, recognition, and opportunity for self-expression and advancement. Men filled most such jobs in the 1960s, but given the opportunity, women have flocked to them. The status level scale was anchored in terms of the kinds of work that our sample actually engaged in. For use with other samples or cohorts, the points on the scale may need redefinition, but it has worked well in this study.

In our sample, traditional women's work was rated as low in status. Women in these jobs at age 43 had been neither more nor less conventional in college than women who achieved careers that by virtue of their high status were less sex-traditional. As college seniors, the women who went on to achieve a high status level were more independent and assertive—in this sense, more "masculine"—than women who were to work at a low status level. But they were not less likely to be wives and mothers.

Zytowski knew that women's roles were changing even as he formulated his model, which was admittedly a heuristic one. His outlook was open, but it was a functionalist viewpoint that made insufficient allowance for barriers due to inequalities. Thus, he did not seem to realize that many women who were not homemakers would fill traditional jobs because at that time they were the ones available to women (Barron & Norris, 1976). Not being very sensitive to issues of status in the sexual division of labor, he did not realize that the incompatibility of home and work was in part a matter of sex-role definitions and social structuring; nor that women with the capacity for status to overcome barriers and achieve high-status (and thus nontraditional) careers would often, in view of the values at that time, want the desirable status of wife and mother as well.

Because a number of other studies have shown that career women tend to be single, without children, or to have children late, one may ask whether it was an idiosyncratic feature of this study that status level in work was unrelated to family roles. The nature of the sample, the definition of career woman, and the cohort would seem to account for discrepant findings. For example, Perrucci (1970) studied engineers, for whom leaves of absence, part-time work, and other concessions to facilitate child-rearing were rare or costly. Our high-level careerists included artists, psychotherapists, lawyers, and others who could study or work part-time when their children were young. Some studies have excluded from the careerist category women who did not have histories of continuous full-time work. In the present research, amount of work was negatively correlated with wife and mother roles, though status level was not. Some studies have included as career women individuals who in this study would not be considered to work at a high status level. We believe that our finding of lack of relationship between status level and family roles is consistent with the spirit of the androgyny literature of the mid-1970s: The ideal or superior woman has personality resources for both homemaking and challenging work. Ideals were different among women of preceding cohorts, and the pattern for younger cohorts may be different again (Tangri & Jenkins, 1986).

The second question addressed in this chapter was that of the unpredictability of women's work patterns in terms of their own late adolescent personalities. We found that participation in work was indeed highly related to the roles of wife and mother and to personality characteristics of husbands. As hypothesized, however, college-age personality characteristics (capacity for status) made a significant contribution to amount of participation in the labor force after years as wife and mother had been taken into account. The relation of emotional independence at age 21 to status level of work at age 43 was particularly impressive. We showed in various ways that personality variables contributed to the predictive power of social roles. For example, years of marriage was highly correlated (negatively) with participation in work, but this high correlation was attributable in part to early divorce and the fact that most divorced women worked: Early divorce was related to both career ambition and nonconforming attitudes in college.

These various findings suggest that the attribution of dependence or pliability to the female adolescent was somewhat exaggerated. For better or for worse, a significant number of women in this sample did not fit the mold. The findings to be reviewed next add further evidence that adolescent personality characteristics did make a difference in women's work patterns.

The third topic we considered was the relation of adolescent identity, as conceptualized by Erikson and Marcia, to work patterns. On the basis of concepts from both Zytowski and Marcia, we hypothesized that late entrants to the labor force would tend to have had foreclosed characteristics as college seniors and that early entrants would have had the contrasting characteristics of those with achieved or moratorium status (openness to change, intellectual and artistic interests, nonconforming attitudes, and, for the moratorium group volatility and anxiety). This hypothesis received considerable support.

The question of the adolescent antecedents of successful identity at midlife led to additional information. As hypothesized, successful identity at age 43, whether as careerist among the early entrants or as homemaker among the late entrants, was associated with ego-strength and other personality resources at age 21. For early entrants, independence, assertiveness, and intellectual potential in college were particularly conspicuous in differentiating the more and less successful careerists; among late entrants, sensitive and shrewd perception of others differentiated the more and less successful homemakers.

We confess to being somewhat surprised at the extent to which findings from the cross-sectional research on adolescent identity in the late 1960s and early 1970s were borne out in these longitudinal findings. We believe our approach is a crude but useful one that can be further developed. It conceives of the formation of identity as a long-term process, as is particularly appropriate for women, and avoids the rigidity and awkwardness of labels that have been criticized in the original Marcia scheme (Matteson, 1977). Because there is no evidence that the various personality strengths that we assessed had been developed at particular times before late adolescence, the findings offer no differentiated support for the epigenetic postulates of Eriksonian theory. However, they support the importance for women's work patterns of the kinds of individual differences among late adolescents that have received attention in this body of research.

Conditions of life were different for women of the transitional era we have studied from what they were for women who came before or after. In the years before, there were fewer opportunities in the labor force, especially at a high status level, and divorce did not exert such a strong push toward work. Today most college women expect to work "always." For increasing numbers marriage and motherhood come later or not at all.

Zytowski's model is dated: Although home-centeredness may still be normative, the woman exclusively a homemaker has become deviant. Conceptualizations of adolescent identity status are also in need of revision. Recent research finds many fewer students classified into the moratorium group (only 2%) than was the case during the tumultuous 1960s (Whitbourne & Tesch, 1985). New "identity strategies" used by college women have been described (Côté, 1986).

The transitional character of the 1960s may have enhanced the importance of norm-upholding vs. norm-questioning, both in theory and findings. The new opportunities for women at that time may have made the influence of capacity for status and independence more conspicuous in our findings than they would be in a less open era. Though all of these characteristics will surely continue to be important influences in women's work lives, the cultural context and significance of being open or status-seeking undoubtedly change from one period to another. Social scientists must keep restudying problems under new conditions, and must take the social and historical context of adolescence into account (Elder, 1980).

Nevertheless, our findings have many points of applicability to current research in vocational psychology, and we would like to illustrate several respects in which this is so. First, some of our findings are supported in literature about more recent cohorts. For example, Betz (1984), whose work variables are similar to ours, followed up a large sample of women 10 years after their graduation from the University of Minnesota in 1968. She found that women in traditional occupations were likely to experience horizontal or downward mobility, where women in pioneer occupations experienced upward mobility. A parallel finding in our study was that the less successful careerists (among early entrants to the labor force) started out and remained in traditional occupations, where the more successful careerists did not. The personality differences presented in this article may help in the interpretation of Betz' results.

Our evidence for the long-range importance of personality characteristics in women's career development corroborates recent research and is compatible with contemporary conceptualizations. The strong relationship in this study between personality characteristics at age 21 and achievement of high status careers at age 43 corroborates Farmer's (1985) demonstration of the relationship between personality characteristics and measures of long-range career-orientation among high school women. Though we have no evidence that the independence and initiative that the successful careerists showed as college students had antecedents in childhood, it was Erikson's theory that they did. The long-range influence of early self-construals on women's career options is a part of the recent conceptualization of Gottfredson (1981). See also the review by Huston-Stein and Higgins-Trenk (1978).

The problems that our research points to remain current problems. The picture laid out by the application of the identity paradigm in this research highlights two types of client familiar to the counselor: the working woman who has trouble taking hold or moving up in the occupational world and the home-oriented woman who has trouble making the transition from her home to the work place. Our findings indicate that these women as college students had personality characteristics with enduring consequences. Such patterns are unlikely to disappear in the women of tomorrow, though that may take a different form. For some women, clinical and social interventions will continue to be needed.

Of course, it is hard to evaluate the effect of cohort on the problems of such women (Mellinger & Erdwins, 1985). The bright young woman who became a librarian in 1958 and suffered the stigma of being single might have become a lawyer in 1985 and felt much less of an oddity. It is important to keep in mind the continuing effects of the environment and of economic and social forces. We have tried to do this by providing an explicit historical context. This context attests to the particular "structures of opportunity" (Astin, 1984) within which late adolescent differences in personality shaped the work lives of our sample.

SUMMARY

This study demonstrates relationships between personality characteristics of some 100 students at a private women's college in 1958 and 1960 and the amount, span, and status level of their participation in the labor force by age 43. Questions are considered in historical context, using as guides the formulations of adolescent identity research and vocational psychology in the 1960s.

In comparison with women who came before and after them, college women of the late 1950s and early 1960s lacked consensus about the place of work in their lives. Theorists, also lacking consensus about this, tended to formulate the problem by defining as normal a pattern that was traditional but already changing. They portrayed the female adolescent as husband-oriented and without goals of her own, her participation in the labor force as a deviation from the modal role of homemaker, and the nature of any work she did as unpredictable from her characteristics as an individual. However, some theorists showed considerable interest in the description of her nontraditionality, both in personality and in work.

Although wife and mother roles and characteristics of husbands were powerfully related to the amount or span of women's work in this study, we presented evidence that our subjects' late adolescent personality was also influential. Nonnormative regulation of behavior, ego-strength (or competence), and ambition, independence, and intellectual potential were three sets of characteristics related to the women's work patterns. Thus, the passivity of the female adolescent was exaggerated in the literature.

Consistent with the theorists' emphasis on the deviant nature of women's participation in the labor force, amount and timing of work were related to personality measures of rebelliousness, unconventional interests and attitudes, and other nonnormative regulation of behavior in college. These personality measures were negatively related to years of marriage and years of children.

In our view, however, theorists and researchers of the 1960s tried to accomplish too much with the idea of nontraditionality or nonconformity. Many studies have compared the personality characteristics of women oriented to traditional vs. nontraditional or pioneering work, sometimes with discrepant results. Our study underlines the importance of using more variables to describe these groups. A woman's success in her identity is one such variable. Among both early and late entrants to the labor force, women who achieved a successful identity by age

43, whether as careerists (early entrants) or as homemakers (late entrants) showed higher ego-strength and stability in college than relevant comparison groups.

For traditionality vs. nontraditionality of work, we substituted a measure of status level that emphasizes responsibility, autonomy, and opportunity for expression. Status level in work at age 43 was strongly correlated with measures of independence, capacity for status, and intellectual potential at age 21. It was not correlated with normative regulation of impulse nor with wife and mother roles. Although independence and capacity for status may have been particularly influential in this transitional era when work opportunities for women were expanding, similar personological roots of career ambition are reported in current research on younger women.

We emphasize both the particular historical context of the study and the relevance of the findings for ongoing research on the career development of women.

ACKNOWLEDGMENT

This research was supported by a PHS Biomedical Research Support Grant to the senior author.

We thank Sharon Jenkins and W. M. Runyan for helpful criticism.

REFERENCES

Allport, G. W., Vernon, P. E., & Lindsey, G. (1960). *Study of values: Manual of directions.* Boston: Houghton Mifflin.

Angrist, S. S., & Almquist, E. (1975). *Careers and contingencies: How college women juggle with gender.* New York: Dunellen.

Astin, H. S. (1984). The meaning of work in women's lives: A sociopsychological model of career choice and work behavior. *The Counseling Psychologist, 12,* 117–126.

Bachtold, L. M., & Werner, E. E. (1970). Personality profiles of gifted women: Psychologists. *American Psychologist, 25,* 234–243.

Barron, F. X. (1953). An ego-strength scale which predicts response to psycho-therapy. *Journal of Consulting Psychology, 17,* 327–333.

Barron, F. (1954). Personal soundness in university graduate students: An experimental study of young men in the sciences and professions. *University of California Publications in Personality Assessment and Research,* No. 1.

Barron, R. D., & Norris, G. M. (1976). Sexual divisions and the dual labour market. In D. Barker & S. Allen (Eds.), *Dependence and exploitation in work and marriage* (pp. 47–69). London: Longman.

Baucom, D. H. (1980). Independent CPI masculinity and femininity scales: Psychological correlates and a sex-role typology. *Journal of Personality Assessment, 44,* 262–276.

Betz, E. L. (1984). A study of career patterns of college graduates. *Journal of Vocational Behavior, 24,* 249–264.

Betz, N. L., & Fitzgerald, L. F. (1987). *The career psychology of women.* New York: Academic Press.

Bird, C. (1968). *Born female.* New York: McKay.

Bourne, E. (1978). The state of research on ego identity: A review and appraisal, Part II. *Journal of Youth and Adolescence, 7,* 371–392.

Brown, D. R. (1956). Some educational patterns. *Journal of Social Issues, 12*(4), 44–60.

Campbell, A. (1980). *Sense of well-being in America: Recent Patterns and trends.* New York: McGraw-Hill.

Cherlin, A. J. (1981). *Marriage, divorce, remarriage.* Cambridge, MA: Harvard University Press.

Clausen, J. A. (1986). Early adult choices and the life course. *Zeitsohrift fur Sozialisationsforschung, 6,* 313–320.

Côté, J. E. (1986). Traditionalism and feminism: A typology of strategies used by university women to manage career-family conflicts. *Social Behavior & Personality, 14,* 133–143.

Donovan, J. M. (1975). Identity status and interpersonal style. *Journal of Youth and Adolescence, 4,* 37–55.

Douvan, E., & Adelson, J. (1966). *The adolescent experience.* New York: Wiley.

Elder, G. H. Jr. (1980). Adolescence in historical perspective. In J. Adelson (Ed.), *Handbook of adolescent psychology* (pp. 3–46). New York: Wiley.

Erikson, E. (1959). Identity and the life cycle. *Psychological Issues,* Monogr, 1.

Erikson, E. (1963). *Childhood and society.* New York: Norton.

Erikson, E. (1964). Inner and outer space: Reflections on womanhood. *Daedalus, 93,* 582–606.

Farmer, H. S. (1985). Model of career and achievement motivation for women and men. *Journal of Counseling Psychology, 32,* 363–390.

Fitzgerald, L., & Betz, N. (1983). Issues in the vocational psychology of women. In W. B. Walsh & S. H. Osipow (Eds.), *Handbook of vocational psychology: Vol. 1* (pp. 83–159). Hillsdale, NJ: Lawrence Erlbaum Associates.

Franz, C. E., & White, K. M. (1985). Individuation and attachment in personality development: Extending Erikson's theory. *Journal of Personality, 53,* 136–168.

Friedan, B. (1963). *The feminine mystique.* New York: Norton.

Gottfredson, L. S. (1981). Circumscription and compromise: A developmental theory of occupational aspirations. *Journal of Counseling Psychology, 28,* 545–579.

Gough, H. G. (1957/1987). *Manual for the California Psychological Inventory.* Palo Alto, Calif.: Consulting Psychologists Press.

Gough H. G. (1985). A work orientation scale for the California Psychological Inventory. *Journal of Applied Psychology, 70,* 505–513.

Gough, H. G., & Heilbrun, A. B., Jr. (1980). *Manual for the Adjective Check List.* Palto Alto, CA: Consulting Psychologists Press.

Harmon, L. W. (1970). Anatomy of career commitment in women. *Journal of Counseling. Psychology, 17,* 77–80.

Hathaway, S. R., & McKinley, J. C. (1943). *Manual for the Minnesota Multi-phasic Personality Inventory.* New York: The Psychological Corporation.

Hauser, R., & Featherman, D. (1977). *The process of stratification.* New York: Academic Press.

Hayes, R. (1986). Gender nontraditional or sex atypical or gender dominant or . . . research: Are we measuring the same thing? *Journal of Vocational Behavior, 29,* 79–88.

Helson, R. (1967). Personality characteristics and developmental history of creative college women. *Genetic Psychology Monographs, 76,* 205–256.

Helson, R., Mitchell, V., & Moane, G. (1984). Personality and patterns of adherence and nonadherence to the social clock. *Journal of Personality and Social Psychology, 46,* 1079–1096.

Hoyt, D. P., & Kennedy, C.E. (1958). Interest and personality correlates of career-motivated and homemaking-motivated college women. *Journal of Counseling Psychology, 5,* 44–49.

Huston-Stein, A., & Higgins-Trenk, A. (1978). Development of females from childhood through adulthood: Career and feminine role orientations. In P. B. Baltes & O. G. Brim, Jr. (Eds.), *Life-span development and behavior*. New York: Academic Press.

Josselson, R. (1987). *Finding herself: Pathways to identity development in women*. San Francisco: Jossey-Bass.

Josselson, R. L., Greenberger, E., & McConochie, D. (1977). Phenomonological aspects of psychosocial maturity in adolescence. Part II. Girls. *Journal of Youth and Adolescence*. 6(2), 145–167.

Kacerguis, M. A., & Adams, G. R. (1980). Erikson stage resolution: The relationship between identity and intimacy. *Journal of Youth and Adolescence, 9*, 117–126.

Leventhal, A. M. (1966). An anxiety scale for the CPI. *Journal of Clinical Psychology, 22*, 459–461.

Marcia, J. E. (1966). Development and validation of ego identity status. *Journal of Personality and Social Psychology, 3*, 551–558.

Marcia, J. E. (1980). Identity in adolescence. In J. Adelson (Ed.), *Handbook of adolescent psychology* (pp. 159–187). New York: Wiley.

Matteson, D. R. (1977). Exploration and commitment: Sex differences and methodological problems in the use of identity status categories. *Journal of Youth and Adolescence, 6*, 353–374.

Matthews, E. (1960). *The marriage-career conflict in the career development of girls and women*. Unpublished doctoral dissertation, Harvard University, Graduate School of Education.

Mellinger, J. D., & Erdwins, C. J. (1985). Personality correlates of age and life role in adult women. *Psychology of Women Quarterly, 9*, 503–514.

Mitchell, V. (1983). *Syndromes of marital inadequacy and women's identity after divorce: An object relations approach to adults*. Unpublished doctoral dissertation, University of California, Berkeley.

O'Connell, A. N. (1976). The relationship between life style and identity synthesis and resynthesis in traditional, neotraditional, and nontraditional women. *Journal of Personality, 44*, 675–688.

Osipow, S. H. (1973). *Theories of career development* (2nd ed.). Englewood Cliffs, NJ: Prentice-Hall.

Perrucci, C. C. (1970). Minority status and the pursuit of professional careers: Women in science and engineering. *Social Forces, 49*, 245–258.

Rand, L. (1968). Masculinity or femininity: Differentiating career-oriented and homemaking-oriented college freshman women. *Journal of Counseling Psychology, 15*, 444–449.

Rossi, A. S. (1965). Barriers to the career choice of engineering, medicine, or science among American women. In J. A. Mattfeld & C. G. Van Aken (Eds.), *Women and the scientific professions*. Cambridge, MA: MIT Press.

Schenkel, S., & Marcia, J. E. (1972). Attitudes toward premarital intercourse in determining ego identity status in college women. *Journal of Personality, 3*, 472–482.

Schrank, T. H., & Riley, J. W. (1976). Women in work organizations. In J. M. Kreps (Eds.), *Women and the American economy* (pp. 82–101). Englewood Cliffs, NJ: Prentice-Hall.

Stewart, A. (1980). Personality and situation in the prediction of women's life patterns. *Psychology of Women Quarterly, 5*, 195–206.

Super, D. E. (1957). *The psychology of careers*. New York: Harper & Row.

Tangri, S. S., & Jenkins, S. (1986). Stability and change in role-innovation and life plans. *Sex Roles, 14*, 647–662.

Terman, L. M. (1970). Psychological approaches to the biography of genius. In P. E. Vernon (Ed.), *Creativity*. Baltimore: Penguin. (orig. 1947).

Tiedeman, D. V. (1959). Career development of women: Some propositions. In O. David (Ed.), *The education of women*. Washington, D.C.: American Council on Education.

Vetter, L., & Lewis, E. C. (1964). Some correlates of homemaking vs. career preferences among college home economics students. *Personnel Guidance Journal, 42*, 593–598.

Waterman, A. S. (1982). Identity development from adolescence to adulthood: An extension of theory and a review of research. *Developmental Psychology, 18*, 341–358.

Webster, H., Freedman, M. B., & Heist, P. (1962). Personality changes in college students. In N. Sanford (Ed.), *The American College* (pp. 811–846). New York: Wiley.

Webster, H., Sanford, N., & Freedman, M. (1957). *Research Manual for VC Attitude Inventory and VC Figure Preference Test.* Vassar College, May Conover Mellon Foundation.

Welsh, G. S. (1956). Factor dimensions A and R. In G. S. Welsh & W. G. Dahlstrom (Eds.), *Basic readings on the MMP in psychology and medicine.* Minneapolis: University of Minnesota Press.

Williams, J. H. (1977). *Psychology of women: Behavior in a biosocial context* (pp. 56–61). New York: Norton.

Whitbourne, S. K., & Tesch, S. A. (1985). A comparison of identity and intimacy statuses in college students and alumni. *Developmental Psychology, 21*, 1039–1044.

Zytowski, D. G. (1969). Toward a theory of career development of women. *Personnel and Guidance Journal, 47*, 660–664.

11

Cultural Influences on Achievement Motivation and Orientation Toward Work in Japanese and American Youth

John W. Connor
California State University, Sacramento

George A. De Vos
University of California, Berkeley

INTRODUCTION

Impressed by the ubiquitous television ads for well-made Japanese products, most Americans believe the slogan of the Japanese is identical to that used in the past by Nissan: "We are driven." In the popular mind, the average Japanese is a hyper-workaholic who puts in a 50-hour week and whose daily form of recreation is singing the company song. Similarly, Japanese youngsters are depicted as hyperachievers with the highest mathematics and science scores in the world (Coomber & Keeves, 1973; Glaser, 1976) and mean IQs some 10 points above those of their American and European counterparts (Lynn, 1982). Americans, on the other hand, have long been beset with stories of illiterate high school graduates, decreasing achievement scores, a declining work ethic, and an education system where many students show lack of motivation (Boyer, 1983).

In both cases, the reality is somewhat different. Moreover, with respect to achievement motivation, both countries appear to be changing. In America, our recent data indicate that achievement levels are beginning to return to the levels of the 1950s. In Japan, our recent data on college students depict many emergent themes of rebellion or reluctant achievement that were almost nonexistent when De Vos did his fieldwork in Japan during the 1950s and '60s (De Vos, 1973). Moreover, in junior high schools in Japan, there are periodic reports of the appearance of forms of violence that were characteristic of American schools in the late '60s and early '70s. Recent reports by Shigenobu (1983) and Yoshiya (1983), for example, disclose that over 70% of junior high school students had witnessed such violence. In the following pages we present some of these data and our interpretation of our findings to date.

SOME RESULTS OF RECENT THEMATIC ANALYSIS

The Thematic Apperception Test (TAT)

Introduced by Murray in 1938, the Thematic Apperception Test (TAT) has remained one of the most widely used psychological projective devices for obtaining subjective data on a variety of interpersonal concerns. In our ongoing studies of the Japanese and Japanese Americans, we have found the TAT to be a very effective means of eliciting emotionally laden themes that were often only hinted at in the course of daily fieldwork.

The TAT consists of 31 cards depicting various scenes and includes one blank card. Because of time limitations and other considerations, the entire set is rarely administered at one time. Rather, certain cards are chosen to elicit certain themes. Murray TAT card No. 1, depicting a boy contemplating a violin, has been used by Caudill (1952) in his study of achievement motivation among Japanese Americans, in one version adapted to Japanese use by De Vos (1973) and by Connor (1976) in his research on the Japanese and Japanese Americans.

The administration of the TAT is quite simple. The individual is told that he or she will be shown a card depicting a certain scene and must then make up a story describing the scene. Moreover, the story must have some development over time, that is, what is going on now, what led up to it, and how it is going to turn out. When the TAT is administered to a group, as is common in a classroom, 5 minutes are allowed for each story. Given the exigencies of the average high school or college 50-minute class period, it is rare that more than seven or eight cards can be administered after roll is taken, announcements read, and the procedure explained. Nonetheless, we feel that the data so obtained are often much more productive in eliciting the deeper, mor emotionally laden value responses than are such paper-and-pencil psychological tests as the Edwards Personal Preference Schedule (EPPS), which we have also administered.

Table 11. 1 summarizes responses to TAT Card 1 by 127 American college students, 75 American high school students, 45 Japanese American college students, and 83 Japanese college students. The recent data on American college students were collected in the fall of 1983 and in the spring and fall of 1984, on the American high school students in the fall of 1984, on the Japanese Americans over a 5-year period from the late '70s to 1984, and on the Japanese students at Seinan Gakuin University and Kyushu University in 1981.

In analyzing the many hundreds of stories told, Connor found that they could be classified into two major categories: achievement–nonachievement and authority (in the form of parental pressure)–rebellion. The principle themes are: positive self-initiated achievement, achievement to please others, reluctant achievement, escape into fantasy, authority and rebellion, and "other." Positive achievement refers to stories that describe the boy practicing the violin largely because of his own volition and dreaming of becoming a great violinist some

292

TABLE 11.1
Responses to TAT Card I

	American College Students			American High School Students			Japanese American College Students			Japanese College Students		
	M	F	Total	M	F	Total	M	F	Total	M	F	Total
Total Responses	64	63	127	31	44	74	15	30	45	37	46	83
Principal themes:												
1. Positive achievement	11	2	33	17	17	34	2	5	7	10	8	18
2. Achievement to please others	8	6	14	5	6	11	3	9	12	4	13	17
3. Reluctant achievement	21	17	38	0	7	7	5	8	13	6	9	15
4. Rebellion	17	22	39	5	9	14	4	5	9	9	8	17
5. Escape into fantasy	7	9	16	2	0		1	3	4	1	2	3
6. Other	1	6	7	2	5	7	0	0	0	6	7	13

day. Achievement to please others, which is highly apparent in the Japanese and Japanese American protocols, refers to stories in which the typical response is that the primary motivation to practice comes from parental pressure.

Reluctant achievement is a category between practicing to please oneself (or another) and outright rebellion. Here the child is depicted as being forced to learn the skill. As one 21-year-old American female stated:

A young boy who is forced to take violin lessons would rather be outside playing, but his mother told him he has to practice. Violin wasn't his choice but his parents want him to be "cultured." He knows he should practice but he wants to be out with his friends. Right now he resents the practice but some day he'll look back and be thankful he learned such a skill.

Themes of outright rebellion are easy to determine; they invariably end with the boy refusing to practice. The final two categories, escape into fantasy and "other," refer to themes in which there is neither achieving nor rebelling, but simply daydreaming, or to themes where the boy is doing something else, such as waiting for his turn to practice.

Interpretation Of TAT Card 1

Table 11.1 discloses that the American style of achievement is clustered into two major areas: positive achievement (25%) and reluctant achievement (29.9%). Achievement to please others accounted for 11%, whereas rebellion themes were reported by 30%. Of the remaining two categories, escape into fantasy accounted for 12.5%, and "other" accounted for 5%.

If we total the achievement themes in all three categories, we arrive at an impressive achievement score of 66%. This is in marked contrast to only 24% achievement themes Connor recorded among college students at California State University at Sacramento in the early 1970s.

In analyzing the two sets of responses, those of today and those of the early '70s, one is impressed by the degree of change. A not atypical response by a male, age 20, in 1974 was as follows:

> The boy has never liked playing the violin, and his parents have always insisted that he learn how. His father was an excellent violin player and was determined to pass on the tradition. Tired of being told what he should do, the boy stares at the violin lying on the table. "I hate this violin," the boy cried. "Why do I have to play it?" With that the boy crushed the violin violently against the ground.

Among today's students, stories openly expressive of revolt are more tempered. There is still some resentment against being forced to practice, but more than a few students see the pressure and frustration as being for their own good. For example, a female, age 24, responded:

> The boy's parents bought the child a violin. He is being forced to practice. At this moment, he is contemplating all of his friends outside playing without him. He would rather be with them. He does not wish to practice. He is not motivated. He is bored. Eventually he will practice since his mother will insist that he do so before he can play with his friends. Years later, when he is a famous violinist, he will thank his parents a millionfold for forcing him to practice.

Another persistent theme today that was seldom seen in the early 1970s is failure followed by ultimate triumph, as in the following response from a male student:

> Eighteen months of practice and for nothing. The recital went badly, my string broke, my bow creaked, I scratched when I should have sung. Eighteen months ago I was given this violin. I practiced hard. I knew my pieces but when it came time to go through with it—it all went wrong. Maybe I should quit! This was Isaac Stern, 7-years-of-age.

Still, as Hsu (Hsu & Watrous, 1972, pp. 317-19) has pointed out, rebellion from parental authority is a recurrent theme in American culture, one that has remained strong over the years.

When Hsu administered the TAT to his students at Northwestern University in 1961—a time in the post-Sputnik period when achievement was still high—he found overall achievement themes of 53% compared with 40% obtained from

Hong Kong students. TAT Card 17BM, depicting a young man in circus tights hanging onto a rope, has often been used to measure achievement motivation; the important theme is whether the young man is ascending or descending the rope. In the early 1970s, Connor found the characteristic theme of C.S.U.S students was descent. The young man was seen as using the rope as a means of escape. More recently, the response is to see the young man climbing the rope as a personal challenge. One student, for example, gave the following interpretation.

> This is a young man in extremely good physical condition. He is showing his friends how easy it is to go up the rope. He has a good attitude about his body and life, he will make the most out of everything he does. He many even enter the Olympics.

Another reported:

> This is John F. Kennedy's high school gym class. The class has been instructed to climb ropes while being timed. John is a natural athlete and easily climbs the rope. He has one of the best times in the class. He is not surprised. Most things come easily to people as motivated as he is. Later in his life, this philosophy of "motivation brings results" helps win the hearts of Americans and John dies a great hero.

American High School Students

A series of TATs was administered to 75 high school juniors in a suburban middle-class high school in the Sacramento area in the fall of 1984. Table 11. 1 discloses that 45% gave straightforward achievement themes, 14% stated they would practice to please others, 9% reported reluctant achievement themes, 18% reported they would rebel against playing, 2.5% would escape into fantasy, and 9% gave other responses.

When totaled, the three categories of achievement yield a supprising 69% reporting achievement themes. This figure is in stark contrast to the 22% achievement themes collected in the early '70s. Equally surprising in many of the themes is that the boy wants to play the violin and cannot find a teacher. a 17-year-old Mexican American female stated:

> The boy is looking at the violin. The boy is trying to learn how to play the violin, but there is no one to teach him.

A 16-year-old Caucasian female responded:

> His mom bought him a violin because he wanted to learn how to play it, but it is more difficult than what he thought it would be because he has no one to teach him. So now it will sit in his room until someone teaches him.

Another surprising finding was the number of self-motivated themes of achievement, such as the following by an 18-year-old Mexican American male:

> The boy is looking at the violin wishing he knew how to play it, and trying to figure out how to play it before the owner comes to take it away.

A story by a Caucasian American, age 16 is:

> John is severely depressed about his upcoming violin recital. The last time he played his dad told him to play outside or give him the hatchet. John has a choice between playing and being abused by his dad, or not playing the violin and making a fool out of himself at the recital. John thinks he will pick it up and start playing it so as not to be embarrassed at the recital in front of all the adults.

Although this story might be interpreted as rebellion against the parent, a more logical explanation is that in high schools today the word is out that standards of excellence are rising and mediocre performances will no longer be tolerated. This conclusion is apparent in the totality of the responses and is made dramatically apparent in the following story by a 16-year-old Caucasian male:

> Here is a young boy sitting down feeling really depressed while he is looking at his violin. He is sitting there staring at it because he was just dropped from the orchestra and is wondering why. The boy goes back to ask his teacher why and finds out that he was dropped because there were too many people already.

Even among those youngsters who would rather be playing outside, there is an awareness that they must keep at it, as a 16-year-old Caucasian female indicates:

> He is thinking how he dislikes the violin and how he hates to practice it while all the other kids are playing outside. What led up to his depression is that his mother scolded him because he was not practicing enough and paying much attention to study. In the end he practiced as he was told and became a great violinist in later years.

The attitude of the youngsters toward education in general and higher education in particular is to be seen in the responses to a specially developed TAT card we administered along with TAT Card 1. This card depicts a young man holding a rake and staring into the distance; a building in the background prominently displays a sign reading "State College." Responses to this card included a large number of achievement themes. For example, 31% had themes such as the man was a janitor who dropped out of school and not regrets it; 32% said he was a janitor but planned to return to school; 9% saw him as a student working; 28% gave other replies, such as that he had to get married and support a wife and child, or that he is watching new students come in for orientation. Even here, however, one-half of the "other" responses indicate that the man really wants to go to college but is too poor. All in all, the theme of the importance of obtaining a good education was included in 85% of the responses.

In reading the TAT responses one is immediately impressed by how much the high school students of today differ from their counterparts in the early 1970s. Today's youngsters are definitely achievement-oriented. They see themselves as competitive and realize that what they achieve will largely be as a result of their efforts.

Yet, while the major theme emerging from the TAT responses is that of achievement, there remain some disquieting notes in the high school protocols. First, as mentioned earlier, is an awareness that the present educational system is inadequate. Many students note the lack of a suitable mentor or teacher, a theme apparent in almost one-fourth of the achievement responses, as illustrated by the not atypical reply of a 16-year-old Caucasian male:

A boy who is trying to play the violin has become discouraged. He had saved his money for close to a year and is having trouble learning to play it. After a week he walks to the park and attempts to play it. Angry and cold he throws it in a nearby bin. There is a man nearby who understands his trouble and teaches him how to play it.

An additional note is the lack of realistic, clearly thought out goals and the means of attaining them. The high school students have obviously absorbed and continue to reflect the rather deep-seated anti-intellectualism that Hofstadter (1966) so eloquently described as being a major characteristic of American life.

Achievement or success for American high school students consists largely of athletic achievement, popularity, and the cult of personality. Little in the American responses reflects the need for either suffering or the postponement of gratification, so characteristic of the Japanese responses. For example, in the card depicting a young man in circus tights hanging onto a rope, the most characteristic American response was that the young man was climbing the rope in an athletic competition to the cheers of his classmates, as the following story by a 16-year-old male makes clear:

It's rope climbing time in P.E. and all of the kids have had experience climbing ropes except the new kid, Harvey. Harvey has been dreading this day for weeks, but his time has come. The coach bellows, "Harvey, it's your turn!" All the kids gather around prepared to laugh. Harvey tries once. He fails and there is laughter. He tries again with the same result. But Harvey keeps trying and eventually gets to the top. He slides down and, as the coach calls the next name, one boy says, "Hey, kid, why don't you join us?" Harvey smiles and joins them.

This story and the overall responses are in accord with a recent survey of some 600 high school students in six states (Thirer & Wright, 1985), which revealed that the leading criterion for male popularity was success on the playing field. The second most important factor was being popular or accepted in the leading crowd. Moreover, when asked what they wished most to be remembered for in high school, 78% of the senior males responded:

They would like to remembered either as an athletic star or the most popular. Only 22% of the senior males, but some 50% of the senior females, reported that they wanted to be remembered as the most brilliant student (Thirer & Wright, 1985, p. 169).

All in all, although the American high school students are positively oriented towards achievement and work, they are somewhat unrealistic both in their goals and the means of attaining them. In a subsequent section we explore how American attitudes toward achievement have changed over time.

Japanese Americans

The Japanese American sample includes 15 male and 30 female third-generation Sansei who were administered the TAT over the past 5 years. Table 11. 1 discloses that 15% reported positive achievement themes, 27% stated they would practice to please someone else, 29% gave reluctant achievement themes, 20% gave themes of rebellion, and 9% escaped into fantasy themes. All in all, achievement themes were apparent in 71% of the Japanese American responses.

Achievement to please others remains a dominant theme in Japanese American responses as it does in the Japanese responses. First reported by Caudill and DeVos (1956) in their study of the first- and second-generation Japanese Americans in the Chicago area after World War II, the typical mode of achievement remains much the same as when first discovered over 3 decades ago. In these responses, as in those of the Japanese, the mother often plays a decisive part in getting the child to practice. A Japanese American female, age 20, responds:

The boy's mother had just told the little boy that he has to practice the violin before he goes out to play. In this picture he is sulking because he doesn't want to practice. Ultimately he practices because he wants to go outside to play.

And a 21-year-old Sansei male states:

The boy is frustrated that he cannot play his instrument properly. He probably would rather not play it at all. His mom probably is making him play it, but he would rather be doing something else.

A 17-year-old Sansei female recalls the theme of achievement through expiation that De Vos (1973, p.71) found so typical of many of the Japanese responses:

TABLE 11.2
Percentage of California Youth in School

Age Range	White American	Japanese American
18 - 19	51.0%	81.0%
20 - 21	33.9%	66.0%
22 - 24	21.8%	44.9%

Source: 1980 Census of the Population. General Social and Economic
Characteristics: California, Section 1 of 2, U.S. Department of
Commerce, Bureau of the Census, July, 1983. Tables 75 and 93.

It looks as though the boy wants to play it. He wishes he had the skill to play it. I guess that he will learn to play it because his father has died and left him this violin. And loving his father deeply he decides to play it.

A response by a 22-year-old Sansei female discloses that perhaps some of the pressure to practice is to carry on the reputation for achievement that was so typical of their parents and grandparents (Caudill & De Vos, 1956):

The boy is looking at the violin that he doesn't want to play, but is forced to by his mother. He doesn't like playing the violin specifically, but his mom makes him because her dad played it so well and she wants to keep up the tradition.

The Japanese Americans do indeed continue to play the violin well.

Japanese Americans also continue to place a higher value on academic achievement than Caucasians, as indicated in a recent report released by the Bureau of the Census. These differences, shown in Table 11. 2, continue a trend first noted in the parental and grandparental generations over 50 years ago (Strong, 1934).

Japanese College Students

The Japanese college students gave responses indicating 22% positive achievement, 20% achievement to please others, 18% reluctant achievement, 20% rebellion, 5% escape into fantasy, and 15% "other" responses. Overall, the percentage of achievement themes is very close to that of the Japanese Americans.

Although only 20% reported themes that directly stated that the child practiced to please others, it must be stressed that there are many, many references to outside pressure and others' expectations in a majority of the other themes as well. For example, a 21-year-old college male responded:

The boy practicing the violin is suffering very much because he doesn't like to play it. His mother forces him to practice. The practicing is very hard on him. What should he do later?

Another by a Japanese college female, age 20, is as follows:

> The boy is suffering in front of the violin because he doesn't want to play it. His parents force him to practice but he doesn't improve, and his teacher scolds him as well. There is no way to quit without trouble.

An additional example by a 21-year-old college male contains a powerful rebellion theme:

> All he can think of is playing outside, but his mother, who is eager for him to study, doesn't allow him to play and forces him to practice. He is suffering and thinks ill of her. He is thinking that he might stick the violin bow in his mother's throat.

It must be stressed that such themes of rebellion, reported by 20% of the students, are totally at variance with the responses recorded by DeVos in the 1950s and 1960s (De Vos, 1973). In the earlier protocols, very few themes of rebellion were associated with TAT Card 1. Where rebellion themes did occur, they were, more often than not, elicited by other cards, and in only one-fifth of the responses was the child successful in his opposition to parental wishes (DeVos, 1973, p. 98). Indeed, the majority of the earlier rebellion themes ended in punishment or misfortune.

One theme of continuity linking De Vos's earlier TAT responses with those Connor gathered more recently is moral masochism or abasement, that is, the belief that suffering is somehow ennobling. It is a belief that one must accept blame or feel guilty when things go wrong, or that personal pain and misery suffered does more good than harm.

Moral masochism is a persistent theme in a majority of those TAT responses where the boy is encountering difficulty:

> A boy who has been practicing the violin has just received the music which he is to play at the next performance. It is a little difficult and he is suffering. But he practices and practices and will do well at the concert.

The capacity to accept blame may be seen also in the responses of Japanese and American college students to a sentence completion test. In Table 11. 3, in answer to the incomplete sentence, "I could not do it because . . . . ," the largest clustering of answers by the Japanese students lies in two areas: "lack of effort" (40%) and "It's my fault" (30%). The characteristic American responses, on the other hand, were: "I didn't know how" (22%), "I didn't want to" (15%), or "It was immoral or unethical" (15%). The Americans showed little propensity to accept guilt or blame. Connor (1977, pp. 271-294) earlier reported that on the Edwards Personal Preference Schedule both Japanese and Japanese American students score much higher in the need for abasement than do the Caucasian American students.

One final note in the Japanese students' achievement themes is reluctant

TABLE 11.3
Responses to Sentence Completion "I Could Not do it Because..."

	Japanese College Students			American College Students		
	M	F	Total	M	F	Total
Total responses	29	52	83	28	41	79
Principal themes:						
1. Lack of effort	12	22	34	1	6	7
2. It's my fault	10	15	25	1	0	1
3. I didn't want to	0	0	0	4	9	13
4. It was immoral or unethical	0	0	0	4	7	12
5. I didn't know how	2	1	3	5	13	18
6. Lack of cooperation	0	4	4	0	0	0
7. Too difficult	0	0	0	5	2	7
8. Other (not time/ bad luck, etc.)	5	10	15	8	4	12

achievement, a mode used by 18%. Here we find an early indication of a possible future change in the nature of Japanese achievement. This entering wedge of lower achievement motivation is apparent in the response of a college female, age 21:

Every member of his family is a musician and he is practicing since he was a small child. He likes to play baseball much more than the violin, but he will continue to play the violin reluctantly.

Another response by a college female, also age 21, is:

I don't like to play the violin. My mother said to me, "You must continue to practice the violin today, too." But I do not like to play the violin. I put the violin on my desk and pray: Let me play it well and let me enjoy it. But it has no effect at all. Let us resign ourselves to playing the violin. When I am a father some day, I'll never insist on my son playing the violin.

In subsequent sections we examine the implications of our findings and attempt to explain them in terms of the emphasis that the Japanese place on *joge kankei,* or superior/inferior relationships, and the alternating emphasis that Americans place on the values of equality and achievement.

THE JAPANESE AND ACHIEVEMENT

For more than 4 decades the Japanese have been the subject of an extensive series of articles, monographs, and books ranging from attempts to delineate the national character (Benedict, 1946) to detailed descriptions of kinship (Brown,

1968) and the Japanese mind (Christopher, 1984). Following the amazing economic expansion of the 1960s, however, an increasing number of publications, scholarly and otherwise, have been devoted to an explanation of the political, economic, social, and psychological forces underlying the rapid economic growth. George De Vos (1973), for example, provides a detailed discussion of the psychodynamics of Japanese achievement motivation.

Based on his own fieldwork, as well as the findings of other scholars, DeVos notes that Japanese achievement is characterized by role dedication and the internalization of very high standards of performance. Indeed, the worry and fear that one will not realize one's own high standards (De Vos, 1973, p. 30) often lead to feelings of guilt and a great capacity for self-blame and moral masochism (DeVos, 1973, p. 149).

Japanese achievement motivation is a result of a socialization process that emphasizes the group or collectivity over the individual. All available evidence indicates that the Japanese household, or *ie,* was conceived as a patrilineal corporate structure extending through time. Within such a corporate entity there was little place for the rugged individualist. Indeed, the emphasis on the collectivity over the individual is so strong that it all but submerges individual identity. Matsumoto (1960, p.61), for example, states that the collectivity orientation of the Japanese emphasizes membership in the group and subordinates individual interests to the interests of the group. Membership in a group is vitally important, and the individual has little or no identification or existence outside of his group.

Subordination of the individual to the group is enhanced by creating in the child strong dependency needs. This is accomplished by providing the child with an enormous amount of gratification, which serves to establish strong emotional bonds with the mother, who can later manipulate the emotional bond to get the child to achieve or do what the mother feels is necessary. These strong emotional attachments, both to the mother and later to the group, are heightened by teasing (or shaming) (Benedict, 1946, p. 262) or inducing guilt (De Vos, 1973, p. 49) in the child—that is, by telling him that others outside the family will laugh at him for his behavior. The teasing and shaming serve to create in the child an enormous sensitivity to the opinions of others. Moreover, since the individual is a representative of a group, his behavior reflects upon the group favorably or unfavorably. Therefore, unlike other groups or extended families that rally around and support a member accused of wrongdoing, the Japanese family, in the words of Benedict (1946, p. 273), will turn against the offending member, and becomes "a solid phalanx of accusation."

The ideal child, according to De Vos (1973, p. 47) is *sunao,* or docile and obedient. He is possessed of a heightened sensitivity to what others will think and has little concept of a self independent of the attitudes of others. There is, therefore, an enormous sensitivity to being slighted, degraded, or ignored. This leads, in turn, to a vulnerability to any depreciatory attitude in others, and to a need to seek the approval of others (De Vos, 1973, p. 49).

The comments of De Vos on the enormous sensitivity of the Japanese to the opinions of others and their capacity for feeling slighted, degraded, and ignored are similar to those by William Caudill (1952) in his study of Japanese Americans in Chicago. Caudill observed: "In psychoanalytic terminology this means that the Japanese Americans have an ego structure that is very sensitive and vulnerable to stimuli coming from the outer world, and a superego structure that depends greatly upon external sanction"(1952, p. 68). De Vos (1973), however, stresses that guilt is very important in understanding Japanese achievement. It arises out of highly internalized standards and a fear that one may never achieve those standards. Moreover, DeVos emphasizes the Japanese need to repay parents for their sacrifices. Personal accomplishments in Japan are often a reflection of a need to repay others.

It seems reasonable to assume that both DeVos and Caudill have accurately described the psychodynamics of Japanese and Japanese American achievement motivation. There is, however, an additional dimension that needs amplification, namely, the enormous and overriding emphasis on hierarchy. To understand fully the nature of Japanese achievement motivation—and, indeed, much of their interpersonal behavior as well—it is incomplete to state that they are socialized to have an ego structure that is highly sensitive to the opinions of others. It is vitally important to add that they have an ego structure that is highly sensitive to the opinions of *significant* others—that is, to the opinions of those individuals or groups who are perceived to be superior to them in the highly ordered and hierarchically structured Japanese society.

JOGE KANKEI

As we have indicated, *joge kankei* (superior-inferior relationships) refers to the frequently observed Japanese tendency to think of all social relationships in hierarchical terms. This all-pervasive preoccuption with *joge kankei* is a direct legacy of the Tokugawa period (1600–1868), when social relationships were prescribed by law in great detail, and it was all but impossible to move from one social class to another. The extraordinary impact of the system is noted by Sansom (1973, p. 239), who records the experiences of Fukuzawa, Yukichi. Fukuzawa was one of the strongest advocates of Western learning in the early Meiji period (1868–1912) and had strong egalitarian views, yet he often found himself addressing the peasants in the authoritarian tones of the samurai, and unless he deliberately softened his voice, he was treated by them in a deferential and cringing fashion.

This legacy of the Tokugawa was preserved during the Meiji period, when after a time of experimenting with the liberal ideas of the West, the Japanese government decided to incorporate the authoritarian ideas of the neo-Confucian doctrine into the educational system and particularly emphasized the importance of the *shushin* or "morals" course, which became a required part of the curriculum (Hall, 1965, p. 400). This neo-Confucianism placed a great emphasis both on self-development and on superior-inferior relationships and imbued the populace with a heightened sense of duty and obligation within the family. Moreover, the samurai type of family system, with its authoritarian and hierarchical structure, was formally declared the key legal institution in the 1898 civil code (Yoshino, 1968, p. 25). With such a family system as a base, the entire nation was conceived of as being one large family with the emperor as the head.

All loyalties led up to the emperor, and the principle responsibility of the family was to develop obedient and loyal subjects. At this time great emphasis was placed on duties and obligations; there was little place for the concept of individual rights and privileges. Indeed, as Sansom states, "There was nothing in the Japanese language that stood for 'popular rights' and a term had to be invented" (1973, p. 311). Further, the Japanese spoken language reflected the all-abiding concern with superior-inferior relationships. Lafcadio Hearn, (1955) who lived in Japan during the late Meiji period, observed the following:

> This hierarchial organization of society was faithfully reflected in the conventional organization of language. . . . Early training enforced caution in this regard: everybody had to learn that only certain verbs and nouns and pronouns were lawful when addressing superiors, and other words permissible only when speaking to equals or inferiors. . . . Of terms corresponding to "you" or "thou" there are sixteen in use; but formerly there were many more. There are yet eight different forms of the second person singular used only in addressing children, pupils, or servants. (pp. 170–171).

Hearn's comments are supported by Nakane (1970), who notes that "The Japanese have failed to develop any social manner properly applicable to strangers, to people from 'outside.' In the store of Japanese etiquette there are only two patterns available: one which applies to a 'superior' and another which applies to an 'inferior'; or to put it another way, there are expressions of familiarity and expressions of hostility, but none which apply on the peer level or which indicate indifference" (p. 130). Furthermore, in the first quarter of this century, guests were still required to indicate their social class when registering at Japanese inns. Haring (1967) mentions that misrepresentation could bring police attention. Finding a category in which to place foreigners was a problem. An indication of the high regard or "superior" status accorded Occidentals is to be seen in the solution to the problem. According to Haring, (1967) "The problem was solved by according 'Gentry' status to all Euro-Americans" (p. 136).

Indeed, in reviewing the literature it seems that the one Japanese characteristic that appears to have been noticed by all observers has been the persistent emphasis on hierarchy. Ruth Benedict, (1946) devotes an entire chapter to the subject and makes repeated reference to it throughout her book. As she states in the chapter entitled, "Taking One's Proper Station:"

Any attempt to understand the Japanese must begin with their version of what it means to "take one's proper station." Their reliance upon order and hierarchy and our faith in freedom and equality are poles apart and it is hard for us to give hierarchy its just due as a possible social mechanism. Japan's confidence in hierarchy is basic in her whole notion of man's relation to his fellow man and man's relation to the State, and it is only by describing some of their national institutions like the family, the State, religious and economic life that it is possible for us to understand their view of life. (p. 43)

It can be seen, then, that in order to clarify the nature of Japanese achievement, not only is it necessary to stress the socialization practices that give rise to an internalized ego structure emphasizing self-motivated achievement, it is also necessary to emphasize that the overriding Japanese concern with hierarchy adds to that ego structure a heightened sensitivity to the opinions of *significant* others. We believe that it is the Japanese preoccupation with hierarchy that creates a status anxiety and is primarily responsible for an oft-noted paradoxical characteristic of the Japanese—their ability to appear both arrogant and submissive at different times. Others have commented on this contrast. Beardsley, (1965) for example, states that the "Japanese might well oscillate between seeing themselves as the heirs of age-long civilization and viewing themselves as ignorant simpletons. Ambivalence and hypersensitivity feed on each other, and it has been extreme and contradictory expressions of these sentiments that have caught attention: deep humility and self-denigration at one point and exceptional arrogance at another" (p. 360).

Reischauer (1965) reached similar conclusions. He notes that the Japanese have alternated between "abject humility toward outside civilizations and arrogant cultural independence and self-assertiveness" (p. 109).

JOGE KANKEI AND JAPANESE INTERNATIONAL AND DOMESTIC ACHIEVEMENT

In saying that the Japanese have a marked tendency to think in hierarchical terms and are acutely aware of the opinions of significant others, we are open to the accusation that we are perpetuating stereotypes, or, worse yet, engaging in a simplistic description of the Japanese national character. Nevertheless, we believe that considerable evidence bolsters our inferences.

Both history and geography contribute to the Japanese having a far greater sense of national identity than almost any other modern nation. As Beardsley (1965) notes:

Few areas of comparable population anywhere in the world have had such a culturally homogeneous people who were so long isolated from other peoples. As far back as history goes, these islands were the home of an essentially single people who spoke one language and had a common body of customs, institutional traditions and values. (p.360)

That such a feeling of national identity is not confined to the past is confirmed in a study by Goodman (1968, p. 47). When asked to describe themselves, French, English, Canadian, German, Brazilian, and American children replied first of all that they were boys or girls. The Japanese children, on the other hand, first replied that they were Japanese.

The keen sense of a Japanese national identity, coupled with the ubiquitous concern with hierarchy and the heightened sensitivity to the opinions of significant others, goes far to explain the periodic cycles of borrowing from abroad. Writing of the Japanese willingness to borrow from others and their concern with their standing vis-a-vis other nations, Reischauer (1965) characterizes the Japanese as having a "national self-consciousness and a sense of inferiority" (p. 109). Passin (1968) supports Reischauer's comments, writing:

> . . . the Japanese appear to have an inordinate preoccupation with their relative standing on some implicit scale of values. This results in sharply alternating periods of excessive humility and willingness to borrow, on the one hand, and arrogance and total rejection of "foreign" influence, on the other. (p. 240)

It was the Japanese concern for status and their "proper station" in the world, among other things, that was a motivating force for the ultranationalism of the period before World War II. Indeed, according to Benedict, (1946) the preoccupation with status was seen as a prime reason (or principal rationalization) for Japan's action at Pearl Harbor, as reflected in the statement handed to Secretary of State Cordell Hull on the day of the attack:

> It is the immutable policy of the Japanese Government . . . to enable each nation to find its proper place in the world . . . The Japanese Government cannot tolerate the perpetuation of the present situation since it runs directly counter to Japan's fundamental policy to enable each nation to enjoy its proper station in the world. (p. 44)

In examining the Japanese concern with hierarchy, it is essential to know that a high social position does not necessarily entitle one to deferential treatment in all social interactions. A Japanese executive, for example, will have his position clearly stated on his greeting cards and expects to be treated deferentially by his subordinates and those social inferiors to whom he is introduced. If, however, he decides to take English lessons from a much younger and otherwise socially inferior college student, he, in turn, will behave differentially toward the student because the student is enacting the highly regarded role of *sensei,* teacher.

We believe that the concept of *joge kankei* is also invaluable in understanding the seemingly paradoxical behavior of the Japanese when they travel abroad. In much of Southeast Asia the Japanese are rapidly gaining a reputation for being the "ugly" Japanese. And while it is true that a part of this image is due to their aggressive economic penetration of foreign markets, more than a little is due to their feelings of superiority and often downright arrogance toward other Asians. Ironically, we are now witnessing the postwar resurgence of the "Greater East Asia Co-Prosperity Sphere," without the sword, with Japan, as the first industrialized Asian nation, taking its "rightful place" as the leader. In conversations with Japanese it is easy to detect at least a patronizing attitude, if not always an arrogant one, toward other Asians. It is readily apparent that they regard them in hierarchical terms as being *meshita,* or in an inferior position.

Nor may we assume that the arrogance and associated behaviors of the Japanese are simply due to the Japanese habit of forgetting about social responsibilities while traveling, as the Japanese psychiatrist Doi maintains. In his book *The Anatomy of Dependence* (1973), Doi makes reference to a common Japanese saying, *tabi no haji wa kakizute* (you can lose your shame while traveling), as an explanation for the ill-mannered behavior of some Japanese when traveling abroad (pp. 40-41). Yet Doi does not mention that when Japanese tourists and businessmen traveled to Hawaii, the United States, or Europe in the 1970s more often than not they were regarded as model visitors. Not only did they behave in a very unassuming and often diffident manner, they also acquired reputations for being very neat and tidy, often to the extent of making their hotel beds in the morning before the maid arrived. Undoubtedly these behaviors are related to the high prestige accorded Euro-Americans.

Such practices are a far cry from the behavior exhibited by Japanese tourists on their own trains and within Japanese national parks and recreation sites, which are frequently more littered than our own. Such littering is in great contrast to the behavior of a group of Japanese Boy Scouts at the International Boy Scout Jamboree held in Butler County, Pennsylvania, in the summer of 1973. It was a common observation that far from littering the landscape, the Japanese kept their campsites the cleanest and neatest in the entire camping area. Indeed, one highly impressed visitor remarked to Connor at the time that when the Japanese contingent departed, there wasn't a single scrap of paper or bit of refuse to be found anywhere within their allotted camping area.

The Japanese sense of national identity and their consciousness of their standing vis-a-vis other nations was also given dramatic expression during the 1964 Olympic games in Tokyo. Not only did the Japanese spend enormous sums of money in the creation of first-rate facilities for both the participants and visitors, they also went to considerable effort to make certain that the visitors would receive the right impression. Households near the Olympic facilities, for example, were urged to install flush toilets so that the visitors would not be offended by the sight and smell of the "honey carts" draining off the night soil. Moreover, the word went out in the underworld from the Tokyo police force that foreigners were to be left alone during the games, and even the notorious Tokyo taxi drivers were advised to drive carefully and not to frighten their foreign passengers.

Although it is true that such a heightened sense of national pride and the accompanying attempt to present the best possible image are not at all unusual in newly emerging nations or those with a marked sense of nationalism, we believe that the behavior of the Japanese during the Olympic games was more in keeping with their keen sense of ranking and their sensitivity to the opinions of significant others. This is a sensitivity that earlier prompted the Japanese government to advise farmers to remove the phallic statues in their fields so that foreign tourists would not be offended. Further, Japanese workers are acutely aware of the standing of their company in relation to all other similar companies, and it is not at all unusual to stress the competition in company songs. Indeed, as Nakane (1970) states, it is the all-pervasive concern with ranking that is most responsible for the hypercompetition that is so characteristic of Japanese industry and among Japanese in general:

> Because competition takes place between parallel groups of the same kind, the enemy is always to be found among those in the same category. . . To illustrate this, competition arises among the various steel companies, or among import-export firms. Among schools it is just the same, university against university, high school against high school. In rural areas competition develops among neighboring villages and also among households with a village. . . If this competition is expressed very pragmatically, the prize is the rating. A common Japanese reaction may well take the form, "Their rating is higher than ours, so. . . ." (pp. 87-88)

Undoubtedly this tremendous competitive drive had a direct influence in the rapid economic recovery of Japan after World War II.

Nakane's conclusion that Japanese competition is related to ranking, and that competition takes place among those in the same category, provides additional support for our findings on the relationship of hierarchy to achievement. Moreover, we believe that the sociological concept of a reference group gives an added dimension to her discussion and enables us to understand the acculturation of the Japanese Americans and their remarkably rapid rise to middle-class status (Caudill & De Vos, 1956); it also provides us with some valuable insight into their achievement drive and oft-observed hypercompetition.

The concept of *joge kankai*, together with an understanding of the sense of a national identity, also provides us with some insight into the means whereby the Japanese were able to raise themselves from the humility of defeat to the second greatest economic power in the world today.

Beginning in the mid 1950s, with a great sense of national purpose, and guided by such government agencies as the Ministry of Finance, the Ministry of Education, and the Economic Planning Agency, Japan set upon the task of recovering its rightful place in the family of nations. It was not an easy task for a crowded country so poor in natural resources that it must import 99.9% of its oil and 85% of its iron ore and coking coal. Indeed, as we have already seen, the only real resource is a well-educated, highly-skilled, and well-disciplined work force.

This transition from a national feeling of inferiority to one of near superiority is documented by Fukutake (1982, pp. 218–219) in his analysis of data collected by the Japanese Institute of Statistical Mathematics. In 1953 only 20% of the Japanese thought they were superior to Western peoples. By 1968, however, that percentage had increased to 47%, and a 1978 NHK survey reported that while 70% still thought Japan had a lot to learn, nearly one-half saw Japan as a first-rate nation.

In a speech delivered at Hiroshima in 1980, the late Prime Minister Masayoshi Ohira declared: "The United States has changed from a superpower to just another power" (Christopher, 1984, p. 298). Apropos of the above, the Japanese government has predicted that by the year 2000, the per capita Gross National Product of Japan will be 20% higher than that of the United States (Christopher, 1984, p. 298).

SIGNS OF REBELLION IN CONTEMPORARY JAPANESE YOUTH

On a typical Sunday afternoon in a park or a blocked-off street in many of the large cities of Japan, one can observe groups of young Japanese males clad in the black leather jackets and sporting the duck-tailed haircuts of the 1950s, listening and dancing to the music of Bill Haley and the Comets, Sha Na Na, Chuck Berry, and, of course, Elvis. Their female companions will be dressed in very bright blouses and skirts. Most will form small groups where they will dance with members of the same sex—there is little male-female dancing. In dancing, the great emphasis is on getting the steps right. There is little evidence of the loose spontaneity one finds when American youth dance together. These are the *Bosozoku* or "wild driving tribe" who first appeared in Tokyo about 1980 and whose style has rapidly spread to the rest of Japan. They are also known as *Amegurazoku* from the film "American Graffiti."

The Bosozoku are mostly of high school age. They express a keen interest in the youth culture of America in the 1950s. Black leather jackets and American army uniforms are highly prized, and in most of the larger cities there are shops that specialize in these and other items of the 1950s. These costumes, including the American army uniforms, are not parodies such as the Hippies once wore; rather the great emphasis is on authenticity, and *Life* magazines of the period are highly prized and sought after. James Dean's "Rebel without a Cause" and Marlon Brando's "The Wild One" are cult films that are shown repeatedly and attract large audiences.

Despite the search for authenticity, these groups differ significantly from their

American counterparts of the 1950s. There is, for example, little or no cruising. These are mostly high school students, and it would be extremely unusual for someone of that age to own or even be licensed to drive a car. Another difference is that there is little violence, individually or collectively, in or between groups. Although expressive of rebellion, by American standards these groups are very quiet, even gentle. Why then do they exist, and what are they trying to express? These are not easy questions to answer. Even when Connor interviewed them, they found it difficult to express just why they found the music and the symbols of the '50s so appealing. What are some of the various reasons for the appearance of such groups in Japan and their relationship to changing trends in achievement motivation among the young?

DISCUSSION

We believe some insight into the signs of rebellion and changing attitudes towards achievement motivation in Japanese youth can be had if we examine four main areas: (1) the present generation is the second adult generation after the war; (2) Japan's educational system; (3) Japan's prosperity; and (4) Japanese culture and Japan's relationship with the United States. Although each of these topics could be examined in great detail, and some are more influential than others, we will confine ourselves to those aspects that appear to be the most relevant.

First, the fact that those of high school age are the children of those who completed their education after World War II means that they were not subjected to the severe discipline imposed by the traditional Japanese family system, with its rigid, authoritarian, and hierarchical structure. Nor were they exposed to the neo-Confucian, highly moralistic, and often frankly chauvinist *shushin* or morals course that was the principal means of indoctrinating children in the prewar educational system. Both the traditional family system and the educational code were among the early targets of reform by the American occupation. As a result, parents are often at a loss as to what standards to impose, and most mourn the loss of the *shushin* course, even though a modified morals course was re-introduced in 1958. Most adults believe that the decline of the traditional family system and the loss of the old *shushin* or morals course are directly responsible for the growing incidence of teenage crime and violence. In 1985, for example, Prime Minister Nakasone stated that he wanted to reintroduce ''moral education'' in the classroom (Waldman, 1985, p. A22).

The second feature is the appearance of some underlying resistance to the stringencies of the educational system. Japan's educational code was completely revised after the war and remodeled after the American system of 6 years of elementary school, 3 of junior high school, and 3 of high school. The first 9 years are mandatory and free. Attendance is almost 100%. The last 3 years of high school are not mandatory, and fees are required. Attendance is 94%. Moreover, Japanese youngsters go to school 5½ days a week. In elementary and junior high school, 40% attend the *juku* or cram schools. In Tokyo, some 75% of 4th, 5th, and 6th graders are in cram schools (*Time*, March 15, 1982, p. 80). The Japanese school year is about 70 days longer than the American school year. There is a 6-week summer vacation during which all students must work on a project that will be submitted in the fall. Although children are more or less automatically promoted in the elementary grades, by junior high school there are competitive examinations to enter the higher grades.

Furthermore, by junior high school most of the curriculum involves much rote memorization and frequent drills to prepare the students for the college entrance examinations, which are quite severe. When they enter the 10th grade, the students are told how many days remain before *shiken jigoku,* or "examination hell." Additionally, only one-third of the Japanese work force enjoys life-time employment security. These are generally the top corporations, and it has been the practice of the top corporations to recruit their prospective employees from a handful of elite universities. One survey disclosed that of 3,000 top corporation executives, nearly half come from five major universities. As late as 1970, 32% of the business elite came from Tokyo University alone (Woronoff, 1981, p. 133). Since most of the top corporations employ for life, the implication is that to secure your future, you must graduate from one of the best universities. And to get into one of the major universities, you must graduate from one of the best high schools, and so on down the line. For many students, a crunch comes at 16 or 17. By junior high school, must of the students already know who will be going on to college—about 35% overall—yet 65% are enrolled in college prep courses (*Time*, March 15, 1982, p. 80).

Moreover, since Japan is still largely an age-graded society, there is little opportunity for a second chance once you have missed the career escalator. By early adulthood, most Japanese youth have a fairly clear idea of where they will be 20 or 30 years later. Hence, in late adolescence, there is a growing awareness that only a very few will have really important jobs and high incomes. For many, the pressure that results from rote memorization and school discipline becomes intolerable. As a result, there are frequent suicides. In 1978, the number reached a record 335 (Woronoff, 1981, p. 118).

In recent years the trend has been toward venting one's anger at the teacher. In Miyazaki, a 13-year-old junior high student retaliated against a teacher who had scolded him by blowing up his car with dynamite (*Japan Times,* October 6, 1981). In Osaka, a 15-year-old boy stabbed his teacher (*Japan Times,* October 3, 1981), and in Hokkaido, a junior high school was closed for 4 days because of violence (*Japan Times,* July 4, 1981). In January, 1982, a gang of 20 students in a school near Tokyo surrounded a group of teachers and began to beat them up. It took 20 policemen to subdue the boys (*Time*, March 15, 1982, p. 81). In 1981 there was a particularly rapid increase in school violence; the number of cases of students assaulting teachers was more than three times that of 1978 (*Japan Times,* October 20, 1981, p. 14). A government white paper disclosed that the delinquents wanted to lead an easy life, and were self-centered, with a strong desire to draw attention to themselves; and over 80% of them were below average academically while apparently aspiring for advanced education (*Japan Times,* December 12, 1981, p. 2). In 1983 Japan experienced 2125 incidents of school violence including 929 assaults on teachers (*Newsweek,* November 19, 1984).

More recently, violence has given way to *ijime,* bullying or hazing. Most often this takes the form of "in group" against "out group" bullying. About 75% of the cases involve stronger students bullying weaker, passive, handicapped, or nonconformist students (Wysoki, 1985, p. 1). Bullying sometimes results in suicides or even murders. One recent survey disclosed that 85% of the junior high schools polled had an *ijime* problem (Wysoki, 1985, p. 24). Susume Abe, a prominent critic of the education system, states that bullying is the result of 40 years of postwar education methods in Japan (Wysoki, 1985, p. 1).

A third factor in rebelliousness is the effect on youth of Japan's increasing prosperity. For centuries many of the essential Japanese values derived both from Zen Buddhism, with its emphasis on simplicity and austerity, and from practical experience. Japan is about the size of California, with 114 million people, but only 15% of the land is arable. Throughout Japan's history there were periodic famines, and for the impoverished samurai, poverty became a virtue. There is a famous saying: "*Bushi wa kuwanedo takayoji*" (even if a samurai hasn't eaten, he holds his toothpick at a high angle). With Japan's rapid modernization during the last century, particularly with the rise of the militarists in the 1930s, any display of luxury was considered frivolous and unpatriotic. During World War II, Japanese women wore *mompei* or baggy trousers, and even the use of cosmetics, such as lipstick or rouge, was frowned upon. A few years after the war, a common expression was *hitotsubu okome demo muda ni suro to me ga tsubareru* (if you waste even a grain or rice you will go blind). This emphasis on austerity and the postponement of gratification were enforced and maintained after the war when Japan has to rebuild its shattered economy. Even today, the Japanese save 17% of their income—the highest in the world. The point is, can one have an affluent society and still maintain a set of values more appropriate to an age of austerity? Can a society create a vast cornucopia of consumer goods, efficient highways, and some of the world's finest automobiles and expect a generation born in the late 1960s at the crest of the Japanese economic miracle simple to keep their noses to the grindstone and forever postpone gratification? A change in values is reflected in the fact that thefts account for 75% of all criminal offenses by minors. Of these, 80% involve shoplifting or stealing bicycles and motorcycles (*Japan Times,* December 27, 1981).

Today many Japanese are worried that the young may be contracting the "British disease"—a decline in the work ethic. In 1980 a government poll

revealed that only 28% of the youth between 15 and 19 were consciously working toward future goals. More than 50% said that they were simply doing what
they wanted to do now, without concern for the future. Compared with a similar
poll conducted 20 years earlier, the 1980 figures were an almost exact reverse.
Additionally, the 1980 poll revealed that more than 71% of the youngsters said
they craved an individual life style; only a little over 9% expressed a desire to
lead lives useful to society. A poll taken a year later showed that, in contrast to
the youths, the number of Japanese between 40 and 60 who wished to be of
service to society substantially exceeded those who did not (Christopher, 1984,
p. 136). A more recent "White Paper on Youth," released by the government in
December, 1984, reported that only 3.7% of Japanese aged 18 to 24 intend to
devote themselves to the cause of society; 38% stated they wanted to be rich; and
43.3% said they wanted to live a life matching their interest (Waldman, 1985, p.
A82).

A final factor in rebelliousness is an increasingly discussed awareness of the
emphasis placed on *joge kankei,* superior-inferior relationships, and the Tokugawa heritage stressing hierarchy, order, and "everything in its place." A continuing emphasis on superior-inferior relationships means that the Japanese are
acutely conscious of where they are in relationship to others at all times. These
cultural values are important when we juxtapose them to the direct influence on
youth of Japan's relationship with the United States. The influence of the United
States on Japan has been considerable. Japan's defeat was extremely traumatic.
The militarists were totally discredited. In the eyes of the Japanese just after
World War II, the Americans becam Japan's elder brother who could do no
wrong. America came to stand for all that was good, great and powerful. American manufactured goods were thought to exceed by far anything the Japanese
could produce. During the Occupation, Japanese police uncovered a company
that was counterfeiting American labels and affixing them to Japanese canned
goods and other products. During the early 1950s, a Japanese friend thought that
Connor's photographs were far superior to his because Connor was using an old
Argus C3 and American film. America had become the model to emulate, and
success for the Japanese was in terms of American models. Even today the
amount of information about America on Japanese TV and other mass media is
about eight to ten times as much as we dovote to news of Japan.

With Japan's economic recovery and rapid advancement in the world's eyes,
and America's shaken position in world leadership after Vietnam, it is little
wonder that many Japanese now think of themselves and Japan the way Americans thought of themselves in the 1950s. In newspaper articles it is apparent that,
while conceding American excellence in R & D and in outer space, the Japanese
are already considering themselves to be morally and spiritually superior to the
U.S. On Japanese TV, many commercials feature individuals who are contemplating the good life and exclaiming, "*Ah, nihonjin ni umareta yokatta*! (Ah,
how good it is to be born Japanese). The symbols of rebellion taken by some

restless, out-of-touch Japanese youth are American, but there are many differences in the style of revolt. The Japanese youngsters, for all of their aping of American costumes and other symbols of rebellion, are not yet completely alienated. They are behaving rebelliously, with tensions expressed against Japanese values—not American. When Brando is asked in "The Wild One" what he is rebelling against, he answers, "What have you got?" The Japanese youths, on the other hand, put on their leather jackets, comb their ducktails, grab their tape players and head for the park for a few hours of fantasy and escape on a Sunday afternoon; by Sunday evening most of them are back at their books. Even the older motorcycle gangs are only weekend "Hell's Angels"; early Monday morning they are back on their jobs singing the company song along with everyone else. This is a far cry from such alienated American groups as the Hell's Angels, who, because of their contempt for work and middle-class values, rely on drugs and crime to support themselves. Sonny Barger, president of the Oakland chapter of the Hell's Angels, once told Connor that he loved his freedom and lack of responsibility. If he suddenly got an impulse to go to Los Angeles, he would simply jump on his motorcycle and take off.

A final observation is that we think that the rebellious themes reported in the TAT material and dramatically expressed by the youth groups are indicative of some potentially major social changes in Japan that are as yet not fully apparent. We see them as a sign that the youngsters sense there is a growing discrepancy between the future the Ministry of Education is preparing them for and the future they see before themselves. In other words, many believe their educations— especially the endless preparation for entrance exams and the blunting of one's youth—to be totally irrelevant. According to one study, by 1990 only 30% to 40% of university graduates will be placed in managerial positions, as opposed to nearly 70% today (Woronoff, 1981, p. 139). The remainder will have to be employed in professional, clerical, or lesser posts. Additionally, how can one maintain the ethics of frugality and the endless postponement of gratification in an age of affluence? For the young of Japan, World War II and its aftermath are already ancient history. The great sense of national purpose that prompted Japan to catch up with the West no longer motivates the young. They see the older generation "hung up" on problems that are already solved. What is the value of spending one's life working 5½ days a week and saving money for a future that has already arrived? If, as Ezra Vogel (1979) says, Japan *is* number one, why not sit back and enjoy it?

ACHIEVEMENT VERSUS EQUALITY IN AMERICA

In America, for those of us who survived the campus turmoil of the '60s and early '70s, it seems axiomatic that the students of the '80s are in many ways different from their Hippie counterparts of 2 decades before. Indeed, a few of us with longer memories can easily find echoes of the '50s in today's youth. Rebellion and drug use are down; schools have reintroduced dress codes; S.A.T. and other scores are rising, and the society itself seems to be moving more and more in the direction of the tranquillized '50s. Is this a form of cultural regression or what? We believe an answer can be found in the manner in which public institutions mirror changes in a society. We also believe that when seen against the broad panorama of American history and values, the transition from Hippie to Yuppie (Young Urban Professional) is not only understandable, but also predictable. We further believe that an understanding of the transition from Hippie to Yuppie can best be understood as an expression of periodic oscillations between the emphasis that Americans place on the major—and often contradictory—values of equality and achievement or success.

American institutions developed in response to the central values of American society. In every society, certain values predominate, and most members of the society absorb them through socialization. Values can effect a change in social institutions in various ways. For one thing, values predispose people to react to one set of proposals more favorably than others. Values, moreover, affect the behavior of people, causing them, for example, to insist that certain rights be provided or that certain laws be enacted. Values, then, are premade decisions. They are held with deep convictions; they have strong, emotional overtones, and can directly move a people to action.

American Values.   The values that Americans prize are a direct outgrowth of the unique American experience. From their beginning as a nation, Americans have placed high value on individualism, self-reliance, equality, achievement through active mastery, self-assertion, and a pronounced emphasis on one's rights and privileges (Connor, 1977, pp. 45-65). Accompanying these values are their negative concomitants: a fear of dependency, a grudging acceptance of authority, a resentment or dislike of rules and controls, and a tendency to mask or play down the superiority of others. For brevity, we focus our attention on what many feel to be a major source of tension in American society—the conflict between the value of equality and that of achievement or success.

In 1927, V. L. Parrington advanced the thesis that the two major influences in American thought were democratic egalitarianism stemming from the French enlightenment and laissez faire individualism stemming from the English liberal tradition articulated by Adam Smith and others. In time, egalitarianism became associated with Jeffersonian agrarianism, while individual achievement became associated with industrial capitalism (Parrington, 1927, pp. vvi–xiv).

Indeed, among the most persistent observations in the voluminous commentaries made by European and other travelers in the 19th and 20th centuries (Joseph, 1959; Hartshorne, 1968; Rapson, 1971; Reid, 1977) has been the repeated emphasis on the value that Americans place on both equality and individual achievement or self-fulfillment. On another level, these values are given political expression in the form of liberalism or conservatism. Although obviously an oversimplification, by and large, liberalism has been associated with egalitarianism and conservatism with individual achievement.

Equality.   No observation was more widely reported than that of equality. From De Toqueville during the 1830s to Lord Bryce near the end of the 19th century, visitors were amazed and often appalled by the value that the Americans placed on equality. Europeans were impressed that children were allowed to speak out during meals and that often their wishes were deferred to. Others noted that Americans consistently deemphasized any superior status and insisted that they call each other by their first names (McGiffert, 1965, pp. 32-82). When the first Japanese diplomatic mission reached America during the administration of President Buchanan (1857–1861), the leader of the Japanese delegation wrote in his diary that he was offended by the plain clothes and speech of the American president and could not understand why the common people were allowed in the White House (Iriye, 1975, p. 56). To this day, foreign visitors are often amazed and puzzled by the friendliness and easy informality of the Americans. To many it is much like wandering into a neighbor's backyard barbeque wearing a full-dress suit. Lipset (1967, pp. 115–158) notes that when European professionals migrated to the United States before and after World War II, they felt declassed, even though they often made far more money than in Europe.

Achievement Or Success.   Because America was known as the land of opportunity, it was thought only natural that any person can rise as far as his or her ambition or talent permitted. If an individual remained poor or at the bottom of society, that individual was considered unlucky, stupid, or lazy. The great emphasis placed on achievement is still found in all levels of society, although it is often expressed in a different fashion. There is one theme that is found throughout America today; that is, no one loves a loser. No matter what you might be, you must be the best. If you can't succeed intellectually, then at least you can succeed financially. Moreover, success is open ended. What does it mean to be at the top? If one is still young and vigorous, one is still expected to excel in other areas later. One can never rest on one's laurels. Because success is open ended, one never really knows when one has arrived at the top. Once there, it quickly vanishes, only to be replaced by a new and distant vista of success. One of the saddest of American sights is the "has been." As Americans are fond of saying, "I know, but what have you done recently?" This great American value of success can also be seen when one compares America with a closed, stratified society, such as existed in Europe. Such a society values not so much one who "succeeds," but one who is as good as possible in the role or social status into which he was born. In the open, egalitarian society of America, everyone is expected to rise and is assumed to have the means to do so. This is one of the major reasons so many Americans feel guilty and believe they are failures when they reach age 40 and are working at the same job they were doing 10 or 20 years earlier; it is also one of the major reasons why Americans seem to be restless and often change jobs.

In 1964, when a national sample was asked to account for the outcome of two people described as having the same skills, one of whom has succeeded and one of whom has not, only 1% of the American sample suggested that it was due to God's will or fate. In six developing countries the average was 30%, and in Bangladesh, 60% (Inkeles, 1977, p. 277).

Similarly, Michael Harrington reports the surprising experiences of a friend who had campaigned for George McGovern in 1972 among predominately female Puerto Rican, low-paid garment workers in New York. Whenever his friend explained McGovern's proposal to place a substantial tax on estates of more than a half million dollars, he was met with angry protests: "You mean that if I have a half million dollars, I can't leave it all to my kids?" (Harrington, 1984).

Dilemmas Created By The Tension Between Equality And Success.   If one believes that America is the land of opportunity and attempts to rise to a position through self-sacrifice, postponement of gratification, hard work, and extraordinary ability, how can one remain the equal of those who have not subjected themselves to the same efforts? For most of their history Americans have seen this as a dilemma. One solution thought of in the 19th century by such men as Rockefeller, Morgan, Ford, and especially Andrew Carnegie, was to return at least part of the money to the public in the form of bequests to libraries, hospitals, and the like. Carnegie went so far as to create a trust fund for his wife and daughters—he had no sons—that would provide handsomely for their welfare while they were alive, but could not be passed on to the next generation.

With the advent of the 20th century, the emphasis has been more of being discreet in the use of wealth rather than in ostentatious display. Moreover, with the rise of modern corporations, it became much wiser to hire competent, trained professionals rather than to trust the family fortune to one's offspring. Of the middle class, at least, this meant that education became the great highway to upward mobility. In turn, a college degree became a prerequisite for many jobs formerly held by high school graduates. A dilemma was created for those who could not go to college—or even finish high school. They shared the great American dream of success—a dream continually fostered by the mass media—but felt they had no legitimate access to it. Many felt resentment and searched for other means to show their success.

Because America is still an open society where one's success or status is measured in terms of how much money one makes, one obvious way to indicate that you are a success is to make a great deal of money. In America one of the easiest ways to make money is through crime. As the sociologist Daniel Bell (1960) pointed out more than 2 decades ago, crime is very often the means for upward mobility for deprived and some newly arrived immigrant groups. These groups, like all Americans, accept the great emphasis on success and feel that they are denied access to success by legitimate means. It is not at all surprising that many decide to prove their success by illegitimate means. Connor once administered a series of psychological tests to the inmates of Folsom State Prison in California and found that the inmates scored higher on achievement than his own college students. The great emphasis that Americans place on equality and success can be seen, then, in the fact that both the high crime rate and the educational level are interrelated. The United States has both the highest crime rate of any developed nation and one of the highest rates of college attendance; both are responses to the value that Americans place on success.

Reducing the Tension Between Equality and Success. One of the major means of reducing the tension between the two is by downplaying one's success. It is no accident that the title of Bing Crosby's autobiography was *Call Me Lucky* (1963). Similarly, no candidate for public office must act in any way that indicates that he is superior; Nelson Rockefeller was successful because he adopted what some have called the "common touch." In the same manner, Americans have institutionalized ways in which they can remind the successful that no matter how high they have risen, they are no better than the rest of us. One such means is the "celebrity roast" in which those who are successful are subjected to a great deal of often biting and sarcastic humor about their personal foibles and idiosyncracies. It has become commonplace during the presidential inaugural ball to have the newly elected president subjected to some rather pointed humor by the nation's comedians. Should he exceed the limits of his office, as did former President Nixon, the humor becomes extremely sarcastic. This ability to downplay success and remain egalitarian is also the reason why foreigners, especially Japanese, are first struck by the friendliness of Americans and are then dismayed by the shallowness of the friendship. This is a direct result of the tension between upward mobility and equality. If you are upwardly mobile, you cannot afford to make a strong emotional commitment to someone you may shortly have to leave.

In addition to having ways of reducing tension between the two major values of equality and achievement, American culture also periodically emphasizes one or the other (Lipset, 1960, 1967). When the ethic of equality is dominant, achievement with its emphasis on elitism, competitiveness, and self-assertiveness is played down. When achievement is emphasized, there is a downplaying of equality and less of a tendency to blame society for inequality; individuals are held more accountable for their behavior; and there is a deprecation of some of the consequences of equality, such as lowered standards of education and excellence and influence of popular taste on culture. Yet, because of the great value Americans place on equality, there remains an innate fear that unbridled achievement will result in the creation of an elite who will ultimately destroy equality. From the beginning, Americans have been very suspicious of any attempt to create a closed class system based on any form of inherited aristocracy.

These swings have long been recognized by many scholars. For example, in a perceptive article published in the *Yale Review*, Arthur M. Schlesinger, Sr. (1939) stated that with the exception of the 32-year period of unbridled achievement following the Civil War, conservatism had, on the average, alternated with liberalism approximately every 16 years since the beginning of the Republic. He made the following, rather surprising, prediction:

> On the assumption that no such catastrophe such as totalitarianism lies ahead, it is evident that the revolt against conservatism which began in 1931 will last until 1947 or 1948, with the possible error of a year or so one way or the other. The next run of the tide will be due in the neighborhood of 1963. (p. 223)

Schlesinger was not far off the mark. Although Harry Truman was reelected in 1948, the country was definitely in a conservative, success-oriented mood in those heady postwar years. By 1948 the Cold War had begun; in Congress the conservatives were returned to power, so much so that Truman despaired of having any social legislation passed by that "damn 81st Congress." Only a few years later Senator McCarthy accused the Democrats of 20 years of treason. By 1963, however, the pendulum had swung in the other direction. The decade of the '60s was marked by civil rights and antiwar demonstrations, the war on pverty, grade inflation, and a general lowering of standards of excellence and achievement.

It can be seen, then, that the periodic oscillations between the emphasis we place on equality and success are directly related to a need to redress in imbalance caused by the excesses created by an overemphasis on one or the other values. Thus the growing inequality created by rampant capitalism and rugged individualism around the turn of the century led to Populism and the Progressive Movement. The liberalism and social advances occasioned by unlimited immigration, the liberal reforms of the Progressives and the social upheaval of World War I led to the reactionism and hyperachievement of the "Roaring Twenties," with Jay Gatsby in Fitzgerald's "The Great Gatsby" (1925) as its crowning symbol. Similarly, the excesses of the 1920s led to the stock market crash of 1929, which ushered in The New Deal and the age of the common man. The egalitarianism of the 1930s was reflected in the films of Frank Capra, the music of Aaron Copland, the works of Steinbeck, and the New Deal itself. It is significant that in this period Mayor LaGuardia of New York City abolished the Townsend Harris High School for the gifted on the grounds that it was undemocratic and elitist (Lipset, 1967, p. 145). World War II was also a period when the ethic of equality prevailed. An obligatory scene in every war movie was an "all-American" platoon consisting of Americans of every ethnic group (except blacks), from every region of the country and every walk of life. It was also a time when the most characteristic gripe of the enlisted men was against the elitism of the officer caste (Spindler, 1948). Additionally, it was during the war that the Swedish sociologist, Gunnar Myrdal, published *An American Dilemma* (1944), which anticipated the black civil rights movement 2 decades later by clearly pointing out that segregation was directly counter to the great value that Americans place on equality.

By the late 1940s and early 1950s, with the advent of the cold war and McCarthyism, egalitarianism and liberalism were in decline. In New York City, by 1958, 25 new high schools for the gifted were proposed (Lipset, 1967, p. 146); Russell Lynes wrote his book *Snobs* (1950); Louis Kronenberger wrote *Company Manners* (1958), his scathing book deprecating popular taste; Vance Packard was writing *The Status Seekers* (1959); William Whyte published *The Organization Man* in 1956; and the characteristic novel and film of the decade was Sloan Wilson's *The Man in the Gray Flannel Suit* (1955), which, along with Herman Wouk's *The Caine Mutiny* (1953) completed the message, "Don't rock the boat." In 1963, Jules Henry published *Culture Against Man* based on his research in the late 1950s. Rereading this book in the 1970s, one was immediately struck by how much had changed. Henry's major criticism was that the hyper-competition of the school system created alienated, aggressive youth. In the 1970s, competition and achievement were down, and the book seemed quaint.

With the advent of the Kennedy and Johnson years, and the emphasis on civil rights, the pendulum swung back again toward equality. In 1962 Harrington published *The Other America* in which he called attention to the neglected urban poor. The elitism and button-down Ivy League look of the late '50s and early '60s gave way to the war on poverty, folk music, mass protests, and the wearing of blue jeans and work shirts to symbolize one's identification with the working class. This was a time of Hippie communes, the Woodstock experience, anti-elitism, and a Jeffersonian return to the soil, at least according to *The Greening of America* (1970) by Charles Reich. It was also a time of student protest, grade inflation, ethnicity, lowered graduation requirements, lowering SAT scores, and scandalous stories about illiterate high school graduates.

By the late 1970s, all that began to change. Blue jeans gave way to designer jeans, and in state after state more rigorous graduation requirements were introduced. By 1977, the California Department of Corrections changed its policy from rehabilitation to punishment, and the Supreme Court upheld the death penalty. In 1978 came the Bakke decision, union membership was declining, and the country was caught up in a wave of running and physical conditioning.

These trends are documented in a poll that the Yankelovich organization conducted for *Time* magazine in 1974 and again in 1981. Between 1974 and 1981 there was a 10-point increase (from 38% to 48%) in agreement with the statement, "There is too much concern with equality and too little concern with law and order." Similarly, when asked whether "there is more concern today for the welfare recipient who doesn't want to work than for the hard-working person who is struggling to make a living,'' there was an increase in agreement from 53% in 1974 to 64% in 1981 (*Time,* June 1, 1981, pp. 18-19).

Additional evidence for the transition from equality to achievement is to be seen in that great microcosm of American society, the public high schools. In the high schools the dilemma created by our opposing values of equality and achievement become painfully obvious. In its attempt to be all things to all people, the American high school does not lead; it only follows and reflects public opinion. As Cohen and Neufeld (1981) report:

> With the launch of Sputnick, federal funds for improved curriculum and teaching followed in short order, especially in science and language *and exclusively for college-bound students.* . . . In the mid-1960s concern about the quality of secondary education shifted briefly from excellence for the talented to equality for the disadvantaged. . . . In practice, the definition of equality that has developed in American secondary education has left less and less room for schools to control student exit on grounds of achievement. (pp. 77-84); italics added

By 1982, however, after more than a decade of slump, SAT scores began to rise (*Time,* October 4, 1982, p. 87).

By the early 1980s the concern for academic excellence had so increased that many school districts were creating special schools for high achievers. One such school is Walter Reed Junior High School in North Hollywood, California, which has an honors program that has attracted national attention. In answer to charges of elitism from local egalitarians, one teacher commented:

> To put these highly gifted students in a regular classroom would be to punish them and hold them back. Some people think democracy means being absolutely equal and having the same curriculum for each student. But in a *real democracy,* we owe to each individual the opportunity to develop his talents to the utmost. (*Time,* March 18, 1985, p. 66); italics added.

Additional evidence for the transition from equality to achievement can be seen in the fact that the proportion of citizens favoring unions dropped from 66% in 1967 to 55% in 1981 (*Time,* November 16, 1981, p. 28). When Caplow and his associates restudied Muncie, Indiana (Middle Town) in the late 1970s, some 47% of Muncie high school students agreed to the statement, ''It is entirely the fault of a man if he does not succeed.'' The figure of 47% was identical to that obtained by Lynds in 1924 (*Time,* October 16, 1978, p. 106).

In keeping with transition from Hippie to Yuppie there has been a spate of recent articles on proper etiquette and snob appeal. It is fitting that over 30 years after Russel Lynes' book *Snobs* (1950) and 22 years after Vance Packard's *The Status Seekers* (1959), a minor best seller was John Brooks' *Showing Off in America* (1981), in which he re-examined and re-applied Thorstein Veblen's

(1899) early caustic comments on conspicuous consumption in America. It is also fitting that the cover story of the November 5, 1984, issue of *Time* was entitled "Mind Your Manners: The New Concern with Civility." By the end of 1984 the transition was so complete that *Newsweek's* final cover story of the year was entitled "The Year of the Yuppie" (*Newsweek*, December 31, 1984).

In Connor's research, and that of others, the swing from equality to achievement or success is clearly evident. For example, scores on the Edwards Personal Preference Schedule administered by Connor in the early 1970s disclosed student values that contrasted starkly with those of college students in the early 1950s. Students of the 1970s had a greater need for change, were less dominant, had far less sense of order and endurance, and were less aggressive than their 1950 counterparts (Connor, 1977, pp. 271–284). Similarly, in the TAT protocols achievement themes were low, but there were many themes of rebellion. More recently, as we have already reported, achievement scores are up and rebellion is down.

Our data are comparable to those collected by George Spindler of Stanford over a 30-year period. In the early 1950s fully 59% of his subjects agreed with the statement, "Everyone should want to achieve." By 1974, at a time of equality and anti-achievement, agreement had declined to 2% (Spindler, 1977, p. 25). More recently, Spindler has reported a return to an emphasis on achievement. "Work, success, achievement, and individualism are stated in the 1979-82 sample in ways very similar to the 1952 sample" (Spindler & Spindler, 1983, p. 58).

SUMMARY AND CONCLUSIONS

We believe our data from Japanese and American TATs provide clear evidence of a rather substantial shift in achievement motivation in both Japan and the United States over the past several decades. We attempt to understand these changes in terms of certain broad cultural themes or values that influence achievement motivation in the two countries.

Succinctly stated, a major theme in Japanese culture is the great emphasis on *joge kankei*, or inferior relationships. This overriding sense of hierarchy or ranking is a prime consideration in understanding Japanese domestic and international competition. As De Vos (1973) noted, however, this does not negate the deep-rooted need for personal achievement that arises out of both a need to repay others and a fear that one never quite achieves one's own internalized high standards of role performance. But our recent data indicate that the younger generation is no longer as highly motivated to postpone gratification or work a 50- or 60-hour week as were their parents and grandparents. For example, many reluctant and antiachievement theses are given expression in the TATs of youth groups and are reflected in the periodic polls conducted by various Japanese agencies. These theses of reluctance and antiachievement were almost nonexistent when DeVos did his research in Japan during the 1950s and 1960s.

While it must be emphasized that achievement motivation remains high in Japan, we are now witnessing in the young a perception of the world very different from that of their elders. Today's youth are the product of an affluent Japan. Born during the height of the Japanese economic miracle in the late 1960s, they experienced neither the humiliation of defeat nor the austerity of the postwar period that motivated their parents and grandparents to catch up with the West. Surrounded since birth by the visible evidence of Japan's growing prosperity and enhanced international reputation, they feel they have much more of an opportunity to enjoy the good life and less of a need to prove themselves in the eyes of the world.

Americans, on the other hand, have moved from the youth turmoil and antiachievement emphasis of the late '60s and early '70s to a renewed sense of national purpose and dedication. Patriotism and nationalism are once more in vogue, and the country itself is in a conservative, achievement-oriented, entrepreneurial mood. We believe that these trends are, among other things, reflections of periodic changes in the alternating emphasis that Americans place on the values of equality and achievement or success.

American youngsters today differ considerably from their Hippie counterparts of nearly two decades earlier. Our TAT data clearly indicate some major shifts in achievement orientation. Today's youth are far more achievement-oriented than were the students of the late 1960s and early 1970s. Yet there are some disturbing themes in the TAT responses.

First, it appears that youngsters are aware of some serious inadequacies in the education system. The surprisingly large number of students who were searching for a suitable mentor or teacher is a reflection on the inability of the high schools to provide the quality instruction that many students are seeking.

Secondly, despite the present emphasis on achievement, many of our youth seem naive with respect to occupational goals and the means of attaining them. American youth are also the product of an affluent society. Many have little awareness, or perhaps are even unwilling, to sacrifice and postpone gratification for long-term goals. Until recently, it appears, there was little need for either sacrifice or effort in obtaining a high school diploma. We may be unrealistic, therefore, to expect them easily to develop adequate work habits and qualities of persistence and endurance when they first enter the work force.

Finally, it must be stressed that although our test protocols indicate achievement themes quite different from the late 1960s and early 1970s, when expressed academically that achievement remains rather pale if the Caucasian American youth are compared with their Asian American counterparts. As reported by the United States Department of Commerce (1983), of those in school in the 18-19, 20-21, and 22-24 age ranges, Asian Americans outnumbered their California white contemporaries by two to one in nearly every category. More recent surveys (*Time*, August 31, 1987, pp. 42-51) show that although Asian Americans are utilizing the same educational facilities, they are academically outscoring their peers of other races throughout the United States. Clearly much more needs to be done to direct the energy and achievement motivation of the majority of American youngsters toward academic goals. It will not be easy. As Hofstadter (1966) indicated more than two decades ago, anti-intellectualism remains a potent force in American life.

REFERENCES

Beardsley, R. K. (1965). Personality psychology. In J. W. Hall & R. K. Beardsley (Eds.), *Twelve doors to Japan*. New York: McGraw Hill.

Bell, D. (1960). Crime as an American way of life. In D. Bell (Ed.), *The end of ideology*. Glencoe, IL: The Free Press.

Benedict, R. (1946). *The chrysanthemum and the sword*. New York: Houghton-Mifflin.

Boyer, E. (1983). *High school: A report on secondary education in America*. New York: Harper & Row.

Brooks, J. (1981). *Showing off in America*. New York: Atlantic-Little Brown.

Brown, K. (1968). The content of dozoku relationships in Japan. *Ethnology, 7*, 113-138.

Caudill, W. (1952). Japanese-American personality and acculturation. *Genetic Psychology Monographs, 45*, 3-102.

Caudill, W., & De Vos, G. (1956). Achievement, culture, and personality: The case of the Japanese Americans. *American Anthropologist, 58*, 1102-1126.

Cohen, D., & Neufeld, B. (1981, summer). The failure of high schools and the progress of education. *Daedalus*, pp. 69-89.

Christopher, R. C. (1984). *The Japanese mind*. New York: Ballantine Books.

Connor, J. (1976). Family bonds, maternal closeness and the suppression of sexuality in three generations of Japanese Americans. *Ethos, 4*(2), 199-222.

Connor, J. (1977). *Tradition and change in three generations of Japanese Americans*. Chicago: Nelson-Hall.

Coomber, L. C., & Keeves, J. P. (1973). *Science education in nineteen countries*. New York: Wiley.

Crosby, B. (1963). *Call me lucky*. New York: Pocket Books.

De Vos, G. (1973). *Socialization for achievement*. Berkeley: University of California Press.

Doi, T. (1973). *The Anatomy of Dependence*, trans. J. Bester: New York and San Francisco: Kodansha international.

Fitzgerald, F. S. (1925). *The great Gatsby*. New York: Scribners.

Fukutake, T. (1982). *The Japanese social structure*. Tokyo: University of Tokyo Press.

Glaser, N. (1976). Social and cultural factors in economic growth. In H. Patrick & H. Rosovsky (Eds.), *Asia's new giant*. Washington, D.C.: The Brookings Institution.

Goodman, M. E. (1968). Influences of childhood and adolescence. In E. Norbeck et al. (Eds.), *The study of personality: An interdisciplinary appraisal*. New York: Holt, Rinehart and Winston.

Goodman, M. E. (1970). *The culture of childhood*. New York: Teachers College Press.

Hall, J. W. (1965). The historical dimension. In J. W. Hall & R. K. Beardsley (Eds.), *Twelve doors to Japan*. New York: McGraw Hill.

Haring, D. G. (1967). Japanese character in the twentieth century. *Annals of the American Academy of Political and Social Sciences, 370*, 122-142.

Harrington, M. (1962). *The other America*. Baltimore: Penguin Books.

Harrington, M. (1984, March). Does America still exist? *Harpers,* p. 48.

Hartshorne, T. L. (1968). *The distorted image: Changing conceptions of the American character since Turner.* Cleveland: Case Western Reserve Press.

Hearn, L. (1955). *Japan: An interpretation.* Rutland, VT: Charles E. Tuttle. (original 1904).

Henry, J. (1963). *Culture against man.* New York: Random House.

Hofstadter, R. (1966). *Anti-intellectualism in American life.* New York: Vintage Books.

Hsu, F. L. K., & Watrous, B. (1972). An experiment with TAT. In F. L. K. Hsu (Ed.), *Psychological anthropology.* Cambridge, MA: Schenkman.

Inkeles, A. (1977, August). A continuing national character. *Change,* p. 277.

Iriye, A. (1975). *Mutual images: Essays in American-Japanese relations.* Cambridge, MA: Harvard University Press.

Japan Times. (July 4, 1981). Hokkaido school reopens after 4-day closure.

Japan Times. (October 3, 1981). 15-year-old boy stabs ex-teacher.

Japan Times. (October 6, 1981). Blasting of teacher's car shocks local residents.

Japan Times. (October 20, 1981). Crime trends in Japan.

Japan Times. (December 12, 1981). Student delinquency hitting 3rd postwar peak, govt. report reveals.

Japan Times. (December 27, 1981). Juvenile crime may set postwar record.

Joseph, F. M. (ed.). (1959). *As others see others: The United States through foreign eyes.* Princeteon, NJ: Princeton University Press.

Kronenberger, L. (1958). *Company manners.* New York: Signet Books.

Lipset, S. M. (1960). Trends in American society. In L. Bryson (Ed.), *An outline of man's knowledge of the modern world.* New York: Nelson-Doubleday.

Lipset, S. M. (1967). *The first new nation.* New York: Anchor books.

Lynes, Russell. (1950). *Snobs.* New York: Pocket Books.

Lynn, R. (1982). I.Q. in Japan and the United States shows a growing discrepancy. *Nature, 197,* 222-223.

Matsumoto, Y. S. (1960). Contemporary Japan: The individual and the group. *Transactions of the American Philosophical Society, 50,* Part 1.

McGiffert, J. (Ed.) (1965). *The character of Americans.* Homewood, IL: Dorsey Press.

Myrdal, G. (1944). *An American dilemma.* New York: Houghton-Mifflin.

Nakane, C. (1970). *Japan society.* Berkeley: University of California Press.

Newsweek. (November 19, 1984). The aimless generation (p. 71).

Newsweek. (December 31, 1984). The year of the Yuppie (pp. 14-31).

Packard, V. (1959). *The status seekers.* New York: Pocket Books.

Parrington, V. L. (1927). *Main currents in American thought* (Vol. II). *The romantic revolution in America, 1800-1860.* New York: Harcourt Brace.

Passin, H. (1968). Japanese society. *International Encyclopedia of the Social Sciences, 8.*

Rapson, R. L. (1971). *Britons view America: Travel Commentary 1860-1935.* Seattle: University of Washington Press.

Reich, Charles (1970). *The Greening of America.* New York: Pocket Books, Inc.

Reid, J. T. (1977). *Spanish American images of the United States 1790-1960.* Gainsville: University of Florida Press.

Reischauer, E. O. (1965). *The United States and Japan* (3rd ed.). New York: Viking Press.

Sansom, G. (1973). *The Western World and Japan.* New York: Random House.

Schlesinger, A. M. (1939). Tides of American politics. *Yale Review, XXIX*(2), 217-230.

Shigenobu, S. (1983, June). Nihon no. Kyoiku no. Saiken no tame ni. *Bunka Kaigi,* pp. 24-35.

Spindler, G. (1948). American character as revealed by the military. *Psychiatry, XI,* 275-281.

Spindler, G. (1977). Change and continuity in American core values: An anthropological perspective. In G. J. DiRenzo (Ed.), *We the people: American character and social change* (pp. 49-78). Westbrook, CN: Westbrook Press.

Spindler, G., Spindler L. (1983). Anthropologist View American Culture. In B. J. Siegel (Ed.), *Annual Review of Anthropology*. Palo Alto: Annual Reviews, Inc.

Strong, E. K. (1934). *The second generation Japanese problem*. Stanford: CA Stanford University Press.

Thirer, J., & Wright, S. D. (1985). Sport and social status for males and females. *Sociology of Sport Journal, II*(2), 164-171.

Time Magazine. (October 16, 1978). Middle Town revisited (pp. 106-109).

Time Magazine. (June 1, 1981). It's rightward on (pp. 18-19).

Time Magazine. (November 16, 1981). Labor's unhappy birthday (pp. 28-29).

Time Magazine. (March 15, 1982). The test must go (pp. 80-81).

Time Magazine. (October 4, 1982). The seniors' slump may be over (pp. 26-27).

Time Magazine. (November 5, 1984). The new concern with civility (pp. 42-50).

Time Magazine. (March 18, 1985). Launch pad for superachievers (p. 66).

Time Magazine. (August 31, 1987). The new whiz kids (pp. 42-51).

United States Department of Commerce. 1980 Census of the Population. (1983, July). *General social and economic characteristics in California*. Section 1 of 2. Washington, DC: U.S. Government Printing Office.

Veblen, Thorstein (1899). *The theory of the leisure class*. New York: MacMillan.

Vogel, E. (1979). *Japan as No. I: Lessons for North America*. Cambridge, MA: Harvard University Press.

Waldman, P. (1985, February 10). Coming of age in Japan. *The Sacramento Bee*, p. A22.

White, W. (1956). *The organization man*. New York: Doubleday Anchor Books.

Wilson, S. (1955). *The man in the grey flannel suit*. New York: Pocket Books.

Woronoff, J. (1981). *Japan: The coming social crisis*. Tokyo: Lotus Press.

Wouk, H. (1952). *The Caine mutiny*. New York: Pocket Books.

Wysoki, B., Jr. (1985, November 12). Asian bullies. *The Wall Street Journal*, p. 1

Yoshino, M. Y. (1968). *Japan's managerial system: Tradition and innovation*. Cambridge, MA: MIT Press.

Yoshiya, S. (1983, May). Konai boryodu o kangaeru. *Sekai*, pp. 57-69.

12 Competence in Work Settings*

Sheri Mainquist
Dorothy Eichorn
University of California, Berkeley

INTRODUCTION

In the psychometric approach to vocational psychology, differences between persons in interests, personality, and specific abilities or aptitudes are measured to match persons with jobs, with the assumption that success and greater productivity are more likely when the characteristics of the individual and the demands of the job are well matched. In this chapter, we are concerned instead with behavioral characteristics significant for adjustment and success across a variety of work settings, including attributes that may contribute to a successful transition from school to work.

We assume such a general approach is both warranted and needed. First, although differences certainly exist among the requirements of different jobs, they also entail some common tasks. For example, one must first get a job, which usually requires successful completion of an interview. Then come the tasks of adjusting to a new job and retaining it. In the same vein, Sternberg and Caruso (1985) argue that to adapt and be successful in their work new employees usually must learn much on the job.

In addition, because of practical constraints, trainers in vocational preparation programs typically must take a general approach. With at-risk populations, trainers are often more concerned with helping youth to obtain steady employment than in achieving the optimal match. They are thus interested in the essential

---

*Prepared for the Symposium on Adolescents' Orientation toward Work, Institute of Human Development, University of California, Berkeley, March 8 and 9, 1985.

knowledge and skills needed to succeed in such tasks as obtaining and retaining a job.

Unfortunately, many problems arise in attempting to address the question of which characteristics are important to success across work settings. The tripartite nature of influences (person, job and setting) and the existence of reciprocal and indirect effects complicate the task of understanding and describing the relative contribution of pertinent psychological variables. So also do differences in research design, such as considerable variation in the dependent variables selected as measures of work outcomes. Major dependent variables have included work satisfaction, occupational aspirations, and effective work performance or work success. Work success has been defined in terms of income, advancement or job level, occupational status, job performance, and success in simply obtaining and retaining a job. Job performance is sometimes described in terms of productivity and quality of work, but often it is not defined or is poorly defined. Nor is it clear that the measures utilized to assess work performance are valid ones.

Another design issue is sampling. Longitudinal and cross-sectional samples sometimes yield different results and, hence, conclusions about effective variables. Further, although we seek to identify some of the most salient independent variables influencing work success, subject variables, such as sex and socioeconomic status, may have considerable bearing on the relevance of a given independent variable or a particular theoretical framework. Different groups are confronted with different barriers in the world of work (including psychological ones). As a result, the task is not the same. We may expect that explanations of success or failure in the domain of work will at least sometimes vary by group membership. For example, need for achievement may be more useful in predicting advancement for middle-class individuals. Other motivational theories may be more useful in predicting achievement for groups more likely to encounter intense discrimination.

Disadvantaged youth have generally been regarded as at risk for employment difficulties. Despite expressed concern about preparing such adolescents, "The literature does not yet provide a good understanding of the most salient skills needed by disadvantaged youth in order to make a successful transition from school to work" (Passmore & Wircenski, 1981, p. 7).

Having noted these cautions, we turn first to longitudinal studies of career success that began with subjects at adolescence or earlier stages of development, together with a training study of hard-to-employ young adults, because of their potential for suggesting psychological characteristics central to, or at least most predictive of, later work success.

The following four sections review theory and research on the role of cognitive ability, achievement motivation, self-esteem and social competence. The first two are major, traditional topics that have been relatively heavily researched and for which there is fairly good evidence for causal relationships. The latter two represent newer approaches to understanding success in work that are becoming increasingly important as the labor market shifts toward more service-oriented work.

For these topics we discuss: concepts and methods developed to explain the relationship between the given variable and work (for example, in the past, heavy reliance has been placed on need for achievement in understanding the role of motivation), limitations of past approaches (for example, the predictive utility of need for achievement is dependent upon certain conditions), conceptual and methodological issues or problems (for example, varying conceptualizations of intelligence), representative studies and major findings, and new approaches that seem promising for understanding psychological factors in work outcomes.

PSYCHOLOGICAL ATTRIBUTES AND WORK—SOME EMPIRICAL DATA

This section "fleshes out" Table 12.1 by providing examples of some of the empirical studies from which listed attributes were drawn. Our sampling of the literature includes a long-term longitudinal study of the later vocational success of adolescents from a "typical American community," research with groups that typically have high unemployment rates (e.g., inner-city black teenagers), longitudinal studies of children from low-income and minority families, as well as samples who entered professional or managerial occupations.

After considering attributes that young workers are inferred to have brought with them into work situations, we conclude with a brief consideration of inverse or reciprocal effects. These include a few sociological studies examining the effects of working conditions on the workers' psychological attributes and data on reciprocal effects between characteristics of the individual (e.g., cognitive skills) and situational variables (e.g., cognitive demands of the job).

Adolescent Attributes Predictive Of Later Success In The Workplace.   Probably the most long-term assessment of adolescent predictors of ultimate occupational attainment is the current work of Clausen (1986). He is using longitudinal data from the Guidance, Berkeley Growth and Adolescent Growth Studies conducted at the Institute of Human Development at the University of California at Berkeley to examine the association between occupational status at age 55-62 and IQ, father's occupation, and "planful competence" at adolescence. The three personality components comprising his index of "planful competence" were derived from a component analysis of items from Block's California Q-sort. Those components and their major definers were: dependable ("dependable" and "productive" as opposed to "rebellious" and "undercontrolled"), cognitively committed ("values intellectual matters" as opposed to "uncomfortable with uncer-

TABLE 12.1
PSYCHOLOGICAL ATTRIBUTES RELATED TO WORK

TRAITS/DISPOSITIONS

    Planful
    Responsible (in acquisiiton of information)
    Dependable
    Purposeful (goal-oriented, takes initiative)
    Independent (self-reliant, self directive)
    Pragmatic/practical
    Future oriented
    Active-involved style (includes active exploration)
    Utilization of resources (personal and environmental)
    Self-confident assertiveness
    Persistence (with flexibility)*
    Optimistic realism*
    Stamina*
    Ego strength[a]
    Adaptable[b]

MOTIVES

    Achievement motivation

        Need for achievement (and hope for success)
        Assertive competence motivation
        Task competence motivation
        Specific attainment values
        Mastery vs. competitive orientation*

    Need for power*
    Need for affiliation*

ATTITUDES TOWARD ENVIRONMENT

    Attitudes toward work
    Attitudes toward hierarchy in social structures[b] (e.g., supervisors)
    Work habits[b] (e.g., time management)

SELF-CONSTRUCTS

    Self-concept
    Self-esteem
      global self-esteem
      competence self-esteem (task-specific esteem) or perceived competence

    Self-efficacy or self-confidence (sense of competence)
    Locus of ontrol

CONCEPTS/KNOWLEDGE (of the world)

    Understanding of society[a]
      concepts of work
      understanding of social conventions (appropriateness; includes notions
        of role and norms)
      concepts of hierarchical structure (in the workplace)

    Psychological understanding[a]
      understanding of people's feelings
      understanding of people's motives
      understanding of people's cognitions

    Practical knowledge (procedural knowledge useful in everyday life, can
      be social and cognitive; includes tacit and practical knowledge about
      one's job)

    Formal knowledge*

SKILLS/APTITUDES

    Basic skills
    Cognitive abilities
      Ability to learn[b]
      Logical ability*
      Conceptual ability*
      Cognitive complexity* (multidimensional thinking and strategicness)
      Intellectual flexibility*
      Planning ability*
      General cognitive abilities (measured by professional tests in
        industrial settings: verbal, quantitative, spatial, mechanical,
        inductive and deductive reasoning)

(Table 12.1 continued)

General problem-solving and decision-making skills[b] (Means-ends thinking in particular)

Social/communication skills
    Self-monitoring skills*
    Oral presentation skills*
    Oral communication skills[b]
    Social sensitivity*
    Social problem-solving skills[b]

Skill in coping with challenging soical situations
    Ability to work with others and as a team[b]
    Conflict resolution[b]
    Facilitation of resolution of others' conflicts*
    Collaboration*
    Negotiation*
    Ability to develop alliances*
    Entering and leaving a group[a]

*Limited to specific work roles
[a]Theoretically relevant; no empirical basis
[b]Practitioner's opinion; no empirical basis

tainty"), and self-confident/victimized ("satisfied with self," "calm," and "cheerful" as opposed to "feels victimized" and "fearful"). Many of the items loading on these components imply planfulness.

For the men the multiple correlation for the three personality components is more strongly predictive of later occupational attainment than are IQ, educational attainment, and father's occupation. The strongest single predictor of status at age 55-62 is dependability during the high school years, with a correlation of .63.

For women, dependability in adolescence "accounted for a higher proportion of variance in educational attainment than either IQ or father's social class but was not predictive of occupational attainment" (Clausen 1986, p. 318). These results are not surprising, given the emphasis on marriage experienced by the women in this sample, who were adolescents before and shortly after World War II. However, assertiveness and cognitive commitment in later maturity did correlate with occupational attainment.

The longitudinal work of Jordaan and Super (1974) also offers data on the characteristics of adolescents that predict success as an adult. In their Career Pattern Study, males were assessed at 14-, 15- and 18-years-of-age. Then the investigators evaluated the extent to which the participants had achieved success, satisfaction, and a "place for themselves" in the world of work at age 25.

The major findings offer some support for the developmental, vocational theory of Super, in that realistic goals (goals in keeping with person's intellectual functioning) and knowledge of the occupation the youth was interested in pursuing were both predictors of later vocational success. Predictors of vocational behavior in early adulthood included future orientation, planfulness, and responsibility in the acquisition of information.

These investigators further summarize their findings with the following psychological description of the "adolescent who becomes a successful adult":

> In short, he uses resources to good effect, both his own and those provided by the school and community. He is active and involved: He not only engages his environment but actively explores it. (p. 124)

Interestingly enough, effective utilization of resources and an active orientation to one's environment are also the major dimensions of competence identified in preschool studies of socially competent behavior (Kohn & Rossman, 1972; White, Kaben, Marmor, & Shapiro, 1972). Jordaan and Super (1974) also found that "access to resources of society through middle class home" was a predictor of successful completion of later developmental tasks.

Similarly, in follow-ups of these subjects, exploration at ages 15 and 25 is predictive of career and vocational success at age 36 (Walvoord, 1979). Both general and purposeful exploration were related to career satisfaction, occupational satisfaction, attained status, and career progress in adulthood. Increasing commitment to occupation also emerges as a predictor of career success by age 36, although such an association is not evident at age 25 (Phillips, 1979, 1982a, 1982b).

Other recent data further establish linkages between adolescent or young adult behavior and specific elements of the process of adaptation to work, in this case aspects of job search. Stumpf, Austin, and Hartman (1984) conducted a 6-month longitudinal study of graduate business students, collecting data on career exploration and interview readiness prior to job interviews. They, too, found exploration to be an important predictor of success in obtaining a job.

Exploration also predicted self-perception of interview readiness. In addition, two aspects of psychological readiness predicted interview ratings and outcomes (job offers). These aspects were "preceiving one had performed effectively in similar situations" and experiencing support regarding the interview task. Knowledge of what the interviewer believes to be effective interview performance was also felt to be important to interviewee success (an inference drawn from a more informal post-hoc analysis).

Minority Youths And Children.   Policy makers have been particularly concerned about the young hard-core unemployed (Gurin, 1968; MDC, Inc., 1983) and have funded training programs developed to address this problem. Some of the major findings from one such demonstration project (Gurin, 1968) are presented here for their potential value in providing some sense of priority in the development of training goals.

Participants were trainees in the Chicago JOBS Project (1963–1964). They are described as primarily Blacks between the ages of 18 and 22. Most had dropped out of school and had not held regular jobs for more than a few months.

Emphasis in training was on basic skills, attitudes, and behavior deemed "appropriate to the world of work." Data were collected on the trainees at several points, beginning with their entry into the program and ending 6 to 12 months after they completed the program. Unfortunately, the group was not a random sample, no control group was used, and the dropout rate was fairly high. However, the report offers some suggestions as to the trainee and training characteristics important to successful transition to work for such a group.

Gurin assessed the relationship between trainee characteristics and attitudes and success in work, measured in terms of earnings on the job. Contrary to expectation, he found that values were not an issue among these trainees, i.e., they tended to share the work ethic. However, another motivational variable, sense of personal efficacy while in the program, did predict success. Further, the trainee's job success had an even stronger effect on his or her feelings of efficacy. Muene (1983) also obtained consistent findings in her study of juvenile unemployability—lack of confidence in ability to obtain a job was associated with unemployment.

Anxiety was also an issue for trainees as they began jobs after completion of the program. Gurin (1968) emphasizes that support (e.g., emotional support from a counselor) in the transition to beginning a job is another need on which interventions should be focused. Some substantiation of this informal finding is provided in later studies of the hard-to-employ—a supportive supervisor was found to be a significant factor in successful employment (Beatty, 1974).

In a broader long-term analysis, educational and occupational outcomes of low-income minority children were assessed together with the correlates of educational and occupational success. Data from a number of longitudinal studies evaluating later effects of the early intervention programs of the 1960s and 1970s, such as Head Start, were analyzed by the Consortium for Longitudinal Studies (Royce, Lazar, & Darlington, 1983). Early intervention was associated with greater achievement motivation, which, in turn, had a positive impact on later occupational attainment. The investigators believe such beneficial long-term results may have been mediated by the programs' effects on the children's self-confidence.

Young Adults.   Self-confidence was similarly related to competence in work among teachers (Peace Corps volunteers). Using factor analysis, Smith (1968) found that competent teachers shared the characteristic of "self-confident maturity," a factor described as including a "pattern of self-confidence, high self-esteem, principled responsibility, optimistic realism, and persistence with flexibility" (p. 558). The competent teachers also appeared to be motivationally different from the less competent in their response to challenge. They exhibited both a "readiness to commit (themselves) to demanding tasks" and initiative and an active approach to attaining desired outcomes, along with the ability to see clearly the means to obtain such objectives.

In another longitudinal study (Heath, 1976), psychological maturity in young men was also found to be predictive of later vocational adaptation in professional and managerial fields. Test, interview, and questionnaire data were obtained to assess the men's personalities and competence at adolescence, when they were in college, and when they were in their early 30s. Maturity was conceptualized in terms of the following dimensions: symbolization of personal experience and aspects of the environment, the ability to take different perspectives and viewpoints and to integrate them, stability, and autonomy.

Both psychological maturity, as measured by the Self-image questionnaire, and psychological health, as appraised by the Rorschach, predicted later vocational adaption. Vocational adaptation was defined as "competence and success in meeting occupational demands" and fulfillment of needs. Stability and integration of self-concept were also relatively strong predictors of later vocational success.

Recent studies of successful managers (Boyatzis, 1982; Wagner & Sternberg, 1985) suggest the importance of another psychological variable, practical intelligence. Cognitive abilities, such as the ability to spot patterns in an array of facts (conceptual ability) and social abilities, such as skill in collaboration, negotiation and building alliances, were all found to differentiate effective managers from other managers. Self-esteem, need for power, and spontaneity in expression were identified as components of effective performance (Boyatzis, 1982).

In summary, motivation, sense of efficacy/self-confidence, self-esteem, practical intelligence, and social competence are personal attributes that may be relevant to work success *across* groups. Other traits with general relevance (as opposed to being specific to only one group or setting) are planfulness, responsibility, and an active style (e.g., taking initiative, utilizing resources and exploring one's environment). To provide a broader perspective we next consider the impact of situational variables, in this case, work conditions, on work performance and psychological attributes.

Psychological Consequences Of Work Conditions And Reciprocal Effects. The effects of work environments on an individual's self-concept, sense of competence, and intellectual functioning (particularly intellectual flexibility) and work involvement have been studied by sociologists (e.g., Kohn & Schooler, 1978; Lorence & Mortimer, 1981; Mortimer & Lorence, 1979a, 1979b). Major findings from two longitudinal studies are reported here.

Over a period of 10 years that began when the men were in college, Mortimer and Lorence (1979a) collected data on college graduates. Their group included a large proportion of highly educated workers (professionals and Ph.D.s). Job experiences that allowed for decision-making, innovative thinking, and challenge enhanced the subjects' self-concept and increased their sense of competence. In a related study, Mortimer and Lorence (1979b) found these same conditions also enhanced intrinsic and person-oriented reward values. A third study (Lorence & Mortimer, 1981) yielded evidence that these sorts of working conditions led to increased work involvement (positive orientation to work, e.g., "takes work seriously," "important values at stake in job," etc.) as well. Work involvement correspondingly affected income and work autonomy 10 years later.

Kohn and Schooler (1978) focused on the effects of complexity of work on an individual's "intellectual flexibility." They tested for reciprocal effects between these two variables. In this longitudinal study, a more representative male sample ("representative of all men employed in civilian occupations") was also followed for 10 years. Substantive complexity was defined as the "degree to which the work requires thought and independent judgment" (p. 30). Intellectual flexibility was defined in terms of "flexibility in attempting to cope with the intellectual demands of a complex situation" (p. 36) and appraised through a variety of standard techniques and interviewer's judgment of subject's intelligence. Substantive complexity had a more rapid impact on workers' intellectual flexibility than the subjects' initial intellectual flexibility had on the substantive complexity of work.

Cumulatively, these studies indicate that work experiences may have a substantial influence on important aspects of an individual's psychological functioning. Moreover, they provide evidence that important positive personal changes can continue to occur in adulthood, given the opportunity for facilitative work experiences.

ACHIEVEMENT MOTIVATION

Of all the psychological attributes posited to influence preparation for, and performance in, the workplace, none has more intuitive appeal than achievement motivation. Achievement behavior is defined as "behavior directed toward the attainment of approval or the avoidance of disapproval (from oneself or from others) for the competence of one's performance in situations where standards of excellence are applicable" (Crandall, Katkovsky, & Preston, 1960). The "standards of excellence" element in this definition is essential for discriminating between achievement behaviors and other goal-directed activities, such as "mastery" behaviors in young children. Early efforts that result in improvement in walking or talking are not categorized as achievement behaviors because very young children are not considered capable of evaluating their performance against standards of excellence. The "approval/disapproval" element may be tangible or intangible, but it distinguishes achievement behavior from behavior carried out "just for the fun of it."

Since Murray (1938) introduced the concept of need for achievement as a component of personality, achievement motivation has been the subject of literally thousands of empirical and theoretical papers and books. Within this outpouring, Dweck and Elliott (1983) identify four major theoretical approaches—need achievement, social learning, test anxiety, and attribution/learned helplessness. The later two deal with more limited aspects of achievement motivation, whereas the first two provide more comprehensive frameworks.

Many efforts have been directed toward applying the construct of achievement motivation to understanding academic achievement and, although to a lesser extent, performance in the workplace. Data on task performance, such as quality, amount, or speed are relatively sparse, for example; more data are available on level of aspiration, task persistence, and risk taking.

Our emphasis here is on the implications of achievement motivation for work adaptation. The following discussion briefly outlines efforts to differentiate both achievement orientation constructs and components of achievement orientation that seem most strongly related to work adaptation. Also included are recent representative studies illustrating issues important to understanding the nature of the association between achievement motivation and work, as well as data on the development of achievement motivation. In addition, we address Bandura's (1977, 1982) more recent self-efficacy theory of achievement motivation and discuss its possible utility in understanding individual differences in adolescents' adaptation to the world of work.

Constructs Of Need Achievement Theory. Most of the constructs used in studies of achievement motivation are represented within the expectancy-value theory developed by Atkinson, McClelland, and their collaborators. Beginning with Murray's need for achievement, conceived as a global, stable personality characteristic, and his projective method of measurement, this theory has evolved over the years. The theory postulates that the strength of the achievement motive in a given situation is the sum of the tendency to approach success (positive) and the tendency to avoid failure (negative). The strength of these contradictory tendencies is determined by: (1) the motive to approach success or to avoid failure, (2) the expectancy (probability) of success or failure, and (3) the incentive value of success or failure. Both the motive to approach success and the motive to avoid failure are acquired through experience, but become stable personality characteristics. The incentive value of success is assumed to increase with task difficulty.

Among the constructs added later are the tendency to seek extrinsic rewards (under the original formulation, persons in whom the tendency to avoid failure was greater than the tendency to approach success would avoid all achievement-related activity). Two other additions are the concepts of future orientation (to allow for the fact that success on one task often permits a person to go on to another step) and the well-publicized but still controversial fear of success.

Other kinds of extensions include the use of objective measures to avoid some of the problems inherent in projective devices (particularly low reliability), increasing stress on cognitive and attributional processes, greater attention to real life situations and groups other than white males, and work on the differentiation of achievement motivation.

Differentiation Of Achievement Orientation. Because achievement motivation was for so long regarded as a unitary disposition in expectancy-value theory (an assumption not made in social learning theory), the work on differentiation is of interest in its own right. For our purposes it has particular interest because of linkages to work.

Veroff, McClelland, and Ruhland (1975) had a cross-sectional sample of adults aged 18- to 49-years. Varimax rotation of data on work outcome and a variety of objective, projective, and behavioral measures of achievement orientation yielded six factors: (1) assertive competence motivation, (2) task competence motivation, (3) fear of failure, (4) social comparison motivation, (5) future achievement orientation, and (6) hope of success.

Of these factors, *assertive competence motivation* (defined as positive interest in competence, stemming from a desire to see oneself as successfully performing valued achievement activity in the society) and *task competence motivation* (motivation to achieve the demands of a task) were most strongly and significantly related to occupational success for both men and women. *Hope of success* (motive to approach success) was the factor that most closely corresponded to need for achievement as measured by projective tests and to what previous researchers meant by achievement motivation. It was also correlated with occupational success for both men and women, but less strongly than were the competence motivation factors. Veroff and his colleagues define this factor as measuring "how gratifying meeting standards of excellence (success) is to a person."

In short, need for achievement appears to be a less potent predictor of occupational success than is competence motivation, defined as motivation to perform competently for intrinsic reasons or for reasons of social evaluation. Moreover, the findings point to a need for more attention to task competence motivation and personal efficacy, topics on which little research has been done.

Spence and Helmreich (1983) accept much of classic need achievement theory, such as the stable, dispositional nature of achievement motivation and intrinsic achievement motivation as striving toward excellence in performance for its own sake. They seek, however, to broaden the applications of motivation from academic and vocational situations to any kind of performance that can be evaluated for its excellence and to develop an objective assessment tool. Using their objective self-report instrument, the Work and Family Orientation Questionnaire, with a variety of populations, including children and adolescents, they, too, find evidence for differentiation of achievement motivation into three relatively independent factors: work (the desire to work hard), mastery (preference for challenging tasks), and enjoyment of interpersonal competition (competitiveness). The factor structure for adolescents is like that for adults.

One finding with implications for the design of training programs and work settings is that persons high on competitive motivation perform less well than do those who score high on work and mastery. This result is tentative because the circumstances under which this differential occurs have not been well explored. Competitiveness may not be disadvantageous for all persons nor in all situations.

Development Of Achievement Motivation.   Actually, evidence for the differentiation of achievement motivation was available long before Veroff et al. (1975) and Spence and Helmreich (1983) began their work. It came from developmental studies done within a framework of social learning theory, but using the concepts of expectancy-value theory, by Virginia Crandall and her collaborators at the Fels Research Institute. Their Achievement Development Project was initiated in 1958, and publications from it began to appear in 1960 (Crandall, Katkovsky, & Preston, 1960). Participants in the Fels Longitudinal Study were followed from birth through early adulthood, and findings were verified with cross-sectional or short-term longitudinal groups. "The clarity of their concepts and the precision of their measures provided, from the beginning, findings that remain among our most reliable and important" (Dweck & Elliott, 1983).

Achievement behaviors were reliably assessed, even in preschool-age children, with a variety of observational, experimental, and self-report methods. Individual differences were detected during the first 3-years-of-life, "but it is perhaps only toward the end of that period that children can impose standards on their own efforts" (Crandall, 1972). At that point achievement motivation was undifferentiated or global. Between 3½ and 6 years the area of physical skills became differentiated; later the artistic and cognitive areas became differentiated from one another. By young adulthood, the cognitive area had differentiated into academically oriented achievement and intellectual achievement. Each of the different areas had different concurrent correlates and predictors, e.g., parental behaviors.

Representative Studies Of Achievement Motivation And Work.   Longitudinal studies provide evidence that achievement motivation or commitment to achievement (achievement aspirations) in children and adolescents predicts later occupational attainment and success (Block & Haan, 1971; Royce, Lazar, & Darlington, 1983). However, other recent studies point to additional issues in attempting to understand the specific conditions under which achievement motivation may predict successful occupational attainment.

One such study is an investigation of achievement values and women's occupational attainment. Faver (1982) correlated women's specific achievement needs with their values and participation in paid employment. Assessments included career and family values and achievement orientation measured in terms of two components of the multidimensional achievement orientation concept: personal efficacy (positive confidence in personal ability) and self-esteem about achievement. In part, the achievement orientation measures were influenced by the findings of Veroff et al. (1975). One of Faver's major findings is that "specific values attached to attainment through career and family" is a stronger predictor of labor force participation than is general achievement orientation. Attainment values are defined as "the value(s) an individual attached to performing well in a given achievement area" (Stein & Bailey, 1976). Career and family values predict employment status for all three age groups examined (22–34, 35–44, 45–64) and the relationships are stronger than for achievement orientation. Achievement orientation is also predictive but for only two of the three age groups (35–44 year-olds and 45–64 year-olds). These results indicate that the particular value placed on a specific achievement area is a better predictor of participation in the labor market than is a woman's general achievement orientation.

Another study suggests that strength of motivation may be important in determining when achievement motivation will be positively correlated with successful work adaptation. Gould (1980) examined the association between need for achievement and career mobility using the methodology of McClelland, Atkinson, Clark, and Lowell (1958) and a projective measure (TAT) of need for achievement. Subjects were Mexican-American college graduates employed in public and private organizations. An index of mobility was obtained by summing measures of salary and career achievement aspirations. Results of an analysis of covariance indicate a curvilinear association between need for achievement and career mobility. Those with a moderate need for achievement had the highest upward mobility; high or low need for achievement was predictive of lesser mobility. Although the generality of these findings is not clear, given the nature of the sample and methodological limitations, they are consistent with Atkinson's view and his research (Atkinson, 1974; Atkinson & Reitman, 1956).

A Process Model Of Achievement Motivation.   Dweck and Elliott (1983) describe previous theories of achievement motivation as including varying degrees of emphasis on expectancies and values. However, they note that "In virtually every theory of achievement motivation *expectancy of goal attainment* is a *critical determinant* of *goal-directed activity.*" They contrast cognitive theories of achievement motivation with attribution theory, emphasizing that attribution theory focuses exclusively on expectancies and explaining "why people *expect* to succeed," ignoring the question of "why they *want* to succeed" (Dweck & Elliott, 1983, p. 651; italics added).

Seeing a need for a more comprehensive model of achievement motivation, Dweck and Elliott (1983) present a process model that addresses both cognitive and affective processes. (They note that Bandura's social learning model also offers a more comprehensive approach.) The major components of the Dweck and Elliott model are expectancies, values, and goal tendencies. This model attempts to explain processes such as the impact of "cognitive sets" (e.g., beliefs about the nature of intelligence) on goal expectancies–expectancies about the probability of attaining goals and obtaining desired judgments of competence. And it delineates different types of motivational goals: *learning goals* (mastery oriented) and *performance goals* (or more normatively, competitively-oriented goals). Goal values are defined in terms of the importance of a "competence increase" (a learning goal value) or "competence judgment" (a performance goal value) for the individual (p. 664). This approach is relevant to recent findings on work orientations in adolescence and work functioning in adulthood because Dweck and Elliott maintain that different types of goals will impact differently on how a person copes when faced with obstacles. Their distinction between learning and performance goals seems related to the mastery vs. competitive dimension discussed by Spence and Helmreich (1983).

A Self-Efficacy Model Of Achievement Motivation.   In contrast to the need achievement theory of McClelland, Atkinson, Clark, and Lowell (1953) are cognitive models emphasizing the importance of one's "beliefs or cognitions about one's capacity to control one's own environment" (Zimmerman & Ringle, 1981, p. 485). One recent model that shares such an assumption is the social learning "self-efficacy approach" of Bandura (1977). Sense of efficacy is very similar to White's (1963) concept of sense of competence.

Bandura's model is emphasized here because (1) "sense of efficacy" predicts later occupational success in high unemployment groups (Gurin, 1968), and (2) personal efficacy has been found to be an important component of assertive competence motivation, an achievement orientation factor strongly associated with occupational success. Self-efficacy or sense of competence is also increasingly regarded as an important component of another attribute related to work, self-esteem.

Self-efficacy or personal efficacy is defined by Bandura (1977) in terms of efficacy expectations. "An efficacy expectation is the conviction that one can successfully execute the behavior required to produce outcomes" (p. 193). The basic propositions of this motivational theory are that one's feelings of efficacy will determine whether coping efforts are initiated, how much effort will be applied, and how much persistence will be demonstrated in the face of obstacles and "aversive experiences" in a given task situation (Bandura, 1977, pp. 193-194). Factors influencing one's beliefs regarding self-efficacy and behavior are held to include the following social experiences: other's relevant verbal statements, exposure to models, and consequences of one's own personal actions (i.e., successes and failures). Also included in this model is the concept of outcome expectancies—"a person's estimate that a given behavior will lead to certain outcomes" (p. 193).

This model deserves further investigation because it presents an efficient way of understanding a psychological attribute—positive belief in one's ability to perform given tasks—that appears to be central to successful transition to the workplace, at least in certain groups. It spans issues addressed in theories about locus of control and attribution and makes explicit the relationship and relevance of particular components of these theories to the self-efficacy model of motivation. Bandura's approach also merits further attention as a possible intervention model for enhancing adolescents' sense of efficacy and changing behavior.

COGNITIVE ABILITIES

Like achievement motivation, general intelligence is an attribute widely assumed to influence performance in many kinds and levels of occupations. Asked to identify essential qualities for success, employers and, indeed, many laymen, would probably place both the desire and ability to do well at the top of the list, and the term ability would imply general intelligence as well as skills specific to the job. If further questioned, they would probably state that specific skills could be learned on the job or in training programs if the individual had sufficient general aptitude.

Although aptitude testing is a well-established area of research that has demonstrated its usefulness in predicting occupational success, for example, during both World Wars (Super, 1985), the relevance of general intelligence to performance in the work place has been in dispute for many years (Featherman, 1980; Ghiselli, 1966; McClelland, 1973; Schmidt & Hunter, 1981; Wagner & Sternberg, 1985).

Cross-Sectional And Longitudinal Studies Of Ability And Work. Some of the findings most frequently cited in this controversy are those of Ghiselli (1966), who summarized an extensive research literature on a variety of occupations (clerks, protection providers, operators of service vehicles, all trades and crafts people, and all industrial occupations). He found the average validity coefficients between IQ and performance to be .30 for training criteria and .19 for proficiency criteria, levels too low to be of much practical significance. On the other hand, Ghiselli did note that both general intelligence and some more specialized abilities or aptitudes were substantially correlated with success in a number of occupational settings. Such equivocal results are subject to at least three interpretations, each of which is represented in subsequent research.

First, many argue that for methodological reasons most research on employment testing, perhaps especially that on general intelligence, underestimates the strength of the associations. Restriction of range on either variable attenuates observed correlations, and under the circumstances in which most aptitude correlations are obtained, both are restricted, i.e., neither the full range of ability nor the full range of occupational performance is sampled. Within types of employment this problem is difficult to avoid. Some jobs can be performed by those with relatively little ability. Increments above this level may bring some improvement in performance, but the "ceiling" is limited. Conversely, some jobs require a sufficiently high level of ability that few persons falling below this level will be found in them.

Unreliability of measures is another methodological problem. "Pencil and paper" tests are typically used for assessment of ability in occupational settings because the more reliable individual tests, such as the Wechsler Scales, require more time and expense than is feasible. Unreliability of the criteria for occupational success may be an even greater problem (Hunter & Schmidt, 1982; Schmidt & Hunter, 1981). Among the criteria that have been used are ability to secure employment, success in training programs, work satisfaction, productivity, proficiency as rated by supervisors, earnings, and occupational status. Little is known about the relative reliability and validity of these various measures.

Schmidt and Hunter (1981) are among those who believe that the correlations between cognitive abilities and work have been underestimated. Their review presents evidence that professionally developed objective tests of verbal, quantitative, and spatial ability, inductive and deductive reasoning, and mechanical comprehension can be valid predictors of job performance ("productivity" in many cases). They support their case with an analysis that provides coefficients corrected for the effects of small sample size, unreliability of performance measures, and restriction of range of ability.

However, they also report considerably smaller validity coefficients for lower level jobs, suggesting that the strength of the association may be related to the cognitive complexity of the job. In Hunter's (1980) study, jobs were assigned levels according to complexity of information-processing requirements; then cognitive ability was related to job performance. The independent measures in this study were verbal and quantitative composites. Obtained coefficients ranged from .56 for the highest-level job grouping to .23 for the lowest.

In another paper, Hunter and Schmidt (1982) present a model involving both general intelligence and a limited number of specific cognitive abilities. They assume there are, for all practical purposes, four "distinct" types of jobs and that "general ability correlates .4 with performance in all jobs" (p. 264). Most jobs are thought to require additional specific abilities for success, and spatial aptitude and perceptual ability are included in their model. The four types of jobs are professional/managerial, skilled trades, clerical, and unskilled or semi-skilled.

Another line of research leads to a more differentiated picture of the association between adolescent ability and later occupational status and earnings. This series of studies on high school students from Wisconsin includes analyses of the impact of education, socioeconomic status, and aspirations as well as ability. Some of the analyses include only men; others assess both sexes. Participants took the Henmon-Nelson Test of Mental Ability when they were in the 11th grade. This is a group-administered test with a heavy emphasis on verbal ability—the items include vocabulary, logical selection, verbal analogies, sentence completion and design analogies.

In an analysis of these data reported by Sewell, Hauser, and Wolf (1977), occupational status was assessed with Duncan's socioeconomic index when the participants were age 35. The correlations between adolescent ability and adult occupational status were .40 for men and .30 for women. With SES controlled, the standardized regression coefficients for effects of ability were still statistically significant for both sexes.

Also using this data base, Hauser and Daymont (1977) examined the "changes in influence of parental income, mental ability and post-secondary education" on earnings, with the assumption that measured mental ability depends on socioeconomic background (p. 188). The results indicated that the effect of ability increased with age, with the largest effect evident at the 12th year after graduation from high school.

A cross-sectional study by Gottfredson and Brown (1981) with a number of male age groups—18-, 20-, 22-, 24-, 26- and 28-year-olds—yielded similar results. Here the IQs were obtained with a variety of measures (unspecified). The correlations between IQ and occupational status increased from .14 for the 18-year-old sample to .45 for the 28-year-olds. The authors attribute the lower correlations at younger ages to the greater homogeneity (lesser variability) of the men in educational and occupational status during that age period. Hauser and Daymont (1977) comment that the increase in correlation with mental ability may be partly a function of education and changes in the effect of schooling.

Gottfredson and Brown also found education to be a much stronger predictor of occupational status than was IQ, as evidenced by the pattern of correlations obtained in a discriminate analysis. They view their findings as consistent with "previous status attainment work which shows via path models that education is a more important determinant of occupational status than IQ" (Sewell & Hauser, 1975, p. 284). In reviewing the work of Sewell, Hauser and Wolf (1977), Featherman (1980) concludes that IQ has an indirect effect on occupational outcomes through its effect on successful completion of education and certification.

Unfortunately, some of the assumptions on which these analyses are based are questionable. The reader is referred to Wilson's chapter in this volume for a critique of such use of path models.

Practical Intelligence And Vocational Success: Concepts And Research. Other investigators believe that standard psychometric tests of cognitive abilities are generally not well-suited for predicting job performance because they were designed primarily for predicting school performance and do not do a good job of sampling the types of behaviors required in work settings (McClelland, 1973). Sternberg and his colleagues take a similar view (Sternberg & Caruso, 1985; Wagner & Sternberg, 1985), agreeing with Neisser (1976) that traditional IQ tests measure "academic intelligence," primarily "analytical intelligence."

Sternberg's work on practical intelligence is based on a different conceptualization of intelligence and draws on assessment center methodology. He argues that his triarchic theory of intelligence contrasts with the traditional psychometric approach in that it is "intended to get at the kind of intelligence that counts in real life" (Hammer, 1985, p. 34).

In this alternative conceptualization, intelligence has three aspects: (1) componential ("mental components involved in analytic thinking"), (2) experiential (synthesis and creativity), and (3) contextual ("that aspect of intelligence which involves knowing the environment and how to manipulate it"). Practical intelligence is related to the contextual domain and includes aspects of intelligence important to coping with everyday situations, including everyday tasks at work (Trotter, 1986).

Wagner and Sternberg (1985) describe a comprehensive theory of practical intelligence in real world pursuits "as encompassing general aptitudes, formal knowledge, and tacit knowledge that is used in managing oneself, others, and one's career" (p. 436). They refer to Neisser in defining practical intelligence as "responding appropriately in terms of one's long-range goals and short-term goals, given the facts of the situation as one discovers them" (Neisser, 1976, p. 137). Practical intelligence implies a process that includes utilization of knowledge gained through experience.

Thus far, Wagner's and Sternberg's research on practical intelligence has dealt with the practical knowledge component. Their empirical work is on tacit knowledge in particular, and its role in success in the fields of business and academic psychology. They define tacit knowledge as "knowledge usually unverbalized and not explicitly taught" (Wagner & Sternberg, 1985, p. 437) and are concerned with the ability to acquire and apply tacit knowledge.

Tacit knowledge in the areas of managing self, managing others, and managing career refers to knowledge about how to manage oneself to "maximize one's productivity," how to manage subordinates and social relationships, as well as knowledge about how to establish and enhance one's reputation and others' perceptions of the worth of one's work (Wagner & Sternberg, 1985, pp. 9-11). As such, tacit knowledge may be important both to performance of the social tasks of a job and to carrying out the central responsibilities of one's work.

To evaluate the role of tacit knowledge, these investigators constructed several hypothetical work-related situations, generated on the basis of (1) interviews with experienced and successful members of the field, (2) a review of relevant literature, and (3) the authors' theoretical framework. In the test items, tacit knowledge was assessed by requiring the subjects to make judgments and decisions about management of self, others, and career. For example, "given the goal of gaining tenure and becoming a leading figure in your field, how would you prioritize a variety of job tasks (e.g., research, teaching, attending conferences, etc.)?'' The results support the hypothesis that differences in tacit knowledge are related to job performance in business students and managers, students of psychology, and academic psychologists.

Operationalization of this construct requires further evaluation. Nonetheless, Wagner and Sternberg cite evidence from independent investigations of the relevance of practical knowledge to other occupations, including computer programming and unskilled jobs (Scribner, 1983; Soloway, Erlich, Bonar, & Greenspan, 1982). From a longitudinal study of youthful characteristics and later occupational success, Vaillant (1974) also reports findings that imply the importance of practical knowledge for success in the world of work. He found that for the 19-year-old it was not so much knowing *what* one wanted to do as "knowing *how* to go about it" that was predictive of occupational success. Again, studies of exploration and success in the job search process also provide support for the importance of understanding of the environment as a significant preparatory step for work success (Stumpf, Austin, & Hartman, 1984). In sum, there is reason to believe that practical knowledge/intelligence may be an important component of a successful transition to the world of work.

Sternberg and Caruso (1985) maintain that practical knowledge can be brought to bear on the processes of adaptation, shaping of environments (i.e., changing environments to one's advantage), and selecting of environments (i.e., choosing and/or leaving). Use of practical intelligence may thus involve more than adaptation to existing conditions.

Practical knowledge may also develop in a variety of ways, e.g., through direct instruction, mediated learning, or tacit learning. Sternberg and Caruso's present conceptualization suggests that the manner of acquisition is likely to differ among age groups. In children, practical knowledge is believed to be acquired more through mediated learning (i.e., through adult structuring of the child's learning experiences). For adults, practical knowledge is thought to be acquired more through tacit learning. For example, when teachers begin their first teaching jobs, they often find that their training has not prepared them adequately to meet all the situational demands. To cope with the demands, much knowledge must be gained on the job; it is knowledge that typically is not directly taught (Sternberg & Caruso, 1985).

The nature of late adolescent and adult acquisition of practical knowledge for work needs to be further explored. Some adolescents and adults certainly gain much valuable knowledge directly from mentors in the workplace (for example, fortunate starting teachers and school psychologists receive direct suggestions for dealing with thorny problems on the job). It may be that this learning is more significant to work adjustment than has been recognized. Having a caring and helpful mentor may, in turn, depend on social skills and personality characteristics.

SELF-ESTEEM

The topic of self-esteem has been relatively heavily researched in efforts to understand the interactions of psychological variables and work experiences. Both the effects of self-esteem as a moderator of work adjustment and satisfaction and the impact of the work situation on self-esteem have been examined.

Definitions. Although often used interchangeably with self-esteem, self-concept refers more generally to one's perceptions of one's self (Tharendou, 1979), whereas self-esteem implies an evaluation of those perceptions that includes an affective component. A typical definition of self-esteem is "the evaluation which the individual makes and customarily maintains with regard to the self: It expresses an attitude of approval or disapproval, and indicates the extent to which the individual believes the self to be capable, significant, successful and worthy" (Coopersmith, 1967, pp. 4-5).

Although some researchers continue to treat self-esteem as a global unidimensional construct, the weight of opinion tends to a "more differentiated aggregate of self-evaluations" (Harter, 1983, p. 323). Drawing on her own developmental research as well as a review of the literature, Harter concurs with Rosenberg (1979) that "we should retain the notion of global self-esteem and focus on the constituent parts of the whole" (p. 20). In vocational psychology a similar distinction has evolved between global self-esteem (general self-worth) and task-specific self-esteem (evaluations of competence). This distinction is of both theoretical and practical importance because different types of self-esteem predict different aspects of work adjustment (see below).

Influences On Self-Esteem. A variety of factors are cited as influences on self-esteem. Coopersmith (1967) identifies four familial variables in his study of parenting styles and children's self-esteem: accepting and affectionate attitude toward child, clearly defined limits, noncoercive discipline, and democratic child-rearing practices. Brookover (1965) stresses experiences with challenge, freedom to make choices, respect, warmth, control, and success. Work stress and role conflict, role overload, and role ambiguity are factors that appear to have negative impact on adult self-esteem (Tharendou, 1979).

Although many researchers and practitioners seem to regard the evaluations and degree of acceptance by significant individuals in a person's life as central to the development and maintenance of self-esteem, the list of influences above contains items that are not necessarily mediated by feedback from other persons. Gecas and Schwalbe (1983) propose two fairly distinct types of self-esteem— outer self-esteem and inner, or efficacy-based, self-esteem. Outer self-esteem is "based on the opinion of others" and correlates with the approval or acceptance of others. In contrast, inner self-esteem is rooted in efficacious action and is "earned through one's own competent actions." It derives from experiences of

346

efficacy and a corresponding "perception of self-as-cause." Gecas and Schwalbe emphasize the importance of general aspects of social contexts and work conditions in "determining the possibility for efficacious action." Such conditions include degree of autonomy, degree of individual control, and the resources available for attaining intended outcome.

Inner, efficacy-based self-esteem appears to correspond fairly closely to the term "competence self-esteem" as used in the vocational literature and to "task-specific self-esteem," a term that seems to be used interchangeably with "competence self-esteem." Task-specific self-esteem is defined as self-perceived competence in the task at hand (Ellis & Taylor, 1983).

Self-Esteem And Motivation.   Although the association between self-esteem and motivation is not clearly articulated, some argue that these personal characteristics are closely intertwined and that self-esteem has a significant impact on motivation. Korman (1970), in particular, postulates that self-esteem is an important factor in work performance and satisfaction. In his "consistency theory of work motivation" he proposes that individuals strive to act in ways that are consistent with their self-images.

To the extent that one's sense of competence or self-perceived competence is considered to be one facet or type of self-esteem, self-esteem would also be expected to have an impact on motivation and performance. Again, Bandura (1977, 1982) asserts that one's perceptions of self-efficacy will affect the extent to which effort is initiated, how much effort is expended, and how long an individual persists in the face of obstacles and negative aversive conditions. Recent studies of women and nontraditional career choices (Betz & Hackett, 1981) also suggest that perceptions of one's self-efficacy may have an impact on occupational aspirations and choice.

Self-Esteem And Work: Some General Findings.   Self-esteem has been studied extensively enough to warrant a major review on the vocational correlates of self-esteem (Tharendou, 1979). After summarizing some of the general findings of Tharendou's review, we discuss a few more recent studies of self-esteem and work search and performance outcomes.

Tharendou (1979) indicates that self-esteem has aroused considerable interest because many correlates of self-esteem seem to have strong implications for an individual's creativity, performance, and interpersonal relations, such as effectiveness in handling conflicts at work. Individuals with low self-esteem "are more likely to

(a) exhibit anxiety, depression, and neurotic behaviors (Fitts, 1972a, 1972b, 1972c; Wylie, 1961),

(b) perform less effectively under stress and failure (Schalon, 1968; Shrauger & Rosenberg, 1970,

(c) exhibit poorer social skills and less sociability (Berger, 1955; Fitts, 1972b; Rosenberg, 1965),

(d) are more persuasible and conforming (Wells & Marwell, 1976),

(e) lack initiative and assertiveness (Crandall, 1973), and

(f) have lower aspirations and expectations of success (Rosenberg, 1965)."

Some associations between different types of self-esteem and work variables do emerge. Competence self-esteem (self-perceived competence) best predicts work performance. Global self-esteem seems to be a better predictor of performance under stress, a frequent finding supported again recently in a study of firefighters' global self-esteem and stress (Petrie & Rotheram, 1982).

The influence of self-esteem on another dimension of work-related behavior, success in the job search process, has also been examined. Given established associations between low self-esteem and poor social skills (Berger, 1955) and reduced initiative (Crandall, 1973), Ellis and Taylor (1983) studied the predictive efficacy of global self-esteem and task-specific esteem (self-perceived competence in job seeking, in this case) for process variables of job search (e.g., sources used to find jobs, interview evaluations) and outcomes of job search (e.g., number of job offers received). Subjects were students from business college. Global and specific self-esteem were assessed prior to their job searches. Task-specific and global self-esteem were both significant predictors of search outcomes. However, global self-esteem was more highly correlated with outcomes "dependent on participant's social skills" (p. 639), whereas task-specific self-esteem was the stronger predictor for search motivation and satisfaction.

In short, there is evidence that competence self-esteem is associated with work performance and global self-esteem with response to stress and that both types of self-esteem influence success in the job search process. As emphasized by Tharendou (1979), however, the research thus far raises more questions than it answers, particularly with respect to causal issues.

One major question is the extent to which self-esteem is a dependent variable or a moderator variable. The longitudinal study of Bachman and O'Malley (1977) on adolescent and subsequent adult self-esteem offers some helpful data. As part of the Youth in Transition Project, these investigators collected data from 1600 young men over the period from 1966, when the subjects were in 10th grade, to 1974. A 10-item scale, similar to Rosenberg's self-esteem scale, was used to assess self-esteem. It included items from the scales of Rosenberg (1965) and of Cobb, Brooks, Kasi, and Connelly (1966). Tests for causal relationships between self-esteem and educational and occupational attainment were conducted by path analysis. Contrary to expectation, no evidence was found for a direct causal impact of self-esteem on later educational and occupational attainment. Bachman and O'Malley (1977) further state, "self-esteem and attainment are correlated primarily because of shared prior causes including family background, ability and scholastic performance" (p. 365). However, occupational status did have "direct positive impact on self-esteem." The results of this study suggest that self-esteem functions more as a dependent variable in its association with work variables, but further investigation of this question is warranted.

Developmental Trends.   The controversy about global versus differentiated self-esteem extends into childhood. In a frequently cited study, Coopersmith (1967) found no differentiation at ages 10 to 12 years. Yet Harter (1983) reports that "across the age span from third to tenth grades, pupils make clear distinctions between cognitive, social and physical competence, as well as what we have labeled general self-worth" (p. 331). It is of more than passing interest that the three more specific kinds of competences identified by the factor structure of Harter's "Perceived Competence Scale for Children" essentially parallel the areas of achievement motivation differentiated by children in the work of Crandall and her collaborators (Crandall, 1972).

Although she cites studies supporting each side of the differentiation controversy, Harter believes the weight of the evidence favors the existence of differentiation. She attributes the contrasting results to methodological differences. For example, scales developed to assess self-esteem, whether in children or adults, vary considerably in the types of items included. Further, clear distinctions are not always made between self-esteem, self-efficacy, and self-confidence.

Another controversy surrounds the question of age trends in self-esteem. In her review of the literature on self-esteem, Wylie (1979) concluded that age and self-esteem are not correlated. McCarthy and Hoge (1982) challenge this conclusion on the basis of Wylie's heavy reliance on cross-sectional evidence. Their longitudinal study across the 7th, 9th, and 11th grades showed increases in self-esteem, as did the longitudinal data of Bachman and O'Malley (1977) covering a longer period (from 10th grade to 8 years later). In both studies, however, the changes were relatively small and gradual. Harter and her colleague (Connell, 1981; Harter & Connell, 1982), as well as Simmons, Rosenberg, and Rosenberg (1973) all report a decrease in self-esteem during the shift to junior high school. More recent analyses by Simmons and Blyth (1987) indicate more complex interactions between satisfaction with body-image, self-esteem, and school environment. Although satisfaction with weight may decline during early puberty, self-esteem seems to decline only when there is a simultaneous shift in school environment, i,e., from elementary to junior high school.

Such findings suggest some cautions in the design of training or intervention programs. The developmental status of the participants, the extent of the change in environment, and the coexistence of other life changes may exert considerable influence on apparent program outcomes.

Training For Self-Esteem And Motivation.   Although many have asserted that self-esteem becomes fairly firmly established during childhood, parents' responses during their children's adolescence (Brookover, 1965), school experiences of success and failure, and later work experiences may also have a significant impact on level of self-esteem. Self-efficacy theory (Bandura, 1977) suggests that opportunities to experience oneself as a competently functioning individual and a corresponding perception of "one's self-as- cause" in such experiences may also be important determinants of self-esteem and specifically, competence self-esteem. Increases in self-esteem may occur during adolescence, when opportunities for autonomy, and presumably, the experiences of effectiveness that may accompany such opportunities, are greater. This hypothesis needs empirical substantiation.

Enhancement of self-esteem and self-confidence is an important goal of collaborative school-industry programs to prepare adolescents for the world of work (MDC, Inc., 1983). Reasoner (1983) describes a school program for building self-esteem and motivation in children and adolescents. His model, developed through collaborative efforts with Coopersmith at an elementary school in Walnut Creek, California, promoted five basic "attitudes": (1) sense of security, (2) sense of identity or self-comcept, (3) sense of belonging, (4) sense of purpose, and (5) sense of personal competence. The program was successful in increasing children's short-term motivation and self-confidence. Compared to students who did not participate, subjects presented fewer disciplinary problems, and more of them held leadership roles in their later school years. However, no immediate impact on school achievement was evident.

SOCIAL COMPETENCE

The past decade has seen an increase in the study of social competence by developmental and behavioristic psychologists. Over the same period, concern about social skills in the workplace has grown. With the increasing emphasis on teamwork in occupational environments, social skills (such as the ability to resolve interpersonal conflicts) are being emphasized in programs to prepare youth for work (e.g., MDC, Inc., 1983; R. C. Smith, personal communication, 1984).

As compared to other psychological attributes reviewed here, however, social competence has been relatively little studied in terms of its association with work success and work adjustment. In part, this deficiency in the literature is attributable to a lack of specificity in understanding how social competence may influence work (Sypher & Sypher, 1983). Indeed, psychologists are still struggling to reach some agreement on a definition of social competence, so this section begins with an overview of attempts to define the construct, followed by recent theoretical frameworks and models of assessment of social competence. Then we move to empirical data on social competence and work, the development of social competence, and training strategies for enhancing social competence in adolescents and young adults.

Definitions Of Social Competence.   Various frameworks have been brought to bear in attempts to define social competence. In the earlier efforts, large numbers of specific "competencies" were listed in what has been referred to as the "bag of virtues" approach (Greenspan, 1981). In some cases the bag was very large indeed. Anderson and Messick's (1974) well-known formulation includes 29 "competencies," with motor skills among the items on the list. Zigler and Trickett (1978) subsequently developed a narrower approach, emphasizing success in meeting societal expectancies and self-actualization or personal development, but including physical health as well. Both approaches have been criticized as overly inclusive.

Other investigators adopt more focused ways of describing social competence. During the mid-1970s, O'Malley (1977) classified such approaches as falling into one of three categories: (1) personality structure (Baumrind & Black, 1967; Kohn & Rossman, 1972); (2) social interaction (Spivack & Shure, 1974; Weinstein, 1969); and (3) behavioral skills (e.g., assertiveness).

Baumrind and Black (1967) base their approach on an analysis of personality structure. Initially they defined social competence in terms of two factors, independence and social responsibility, and emphasized the centrality of purposefulness in distinguishing different groups of children. Recently (Baumrind, 1984) this approach has been refined to include definition in terms of three dimensions: *cognitive competence, social responsibility* (friendliness, cooperativeness, and maturity) and *social assertiveness*—socially confident (self-assertion in social situations), peer ascendant (agonistic, competitive self-assertion), and social agency (both social assertiveness and peer dominance).

Social interactionists place emphasis on "interpersonal goals" and identification of components of effective interactions (O'Malley, 1977; Weinstein, 1969). The psychological components delineated included (1) role-taking ability, a process by which inferences are drawn about others' thoughts, emotions, intentions, and viewpoints (Shantz, 1975), (2) repertoire of responses, and (3) "intrapersonal resources to deploy effective tactics in situations where they are appropriate." Hartup (1979) emphasizes the exchange aspect of social interactions and defines social competence in terms of the child's ability to engage in "mutually regulated relations."

In a similar vein, O'Malley (1977) proposes that social competence be defined in terms of productive and mutually satisfying interactions. "Productive" refers to attainment of goals and "mutually satisfying" to the manner in which goals are attained. The aspect of value judgment in defining social competence is addressed by including the criterion of "mutually satisfying." Such interactions are described as ones in which "actions in pursuit of the goals are received in either a benign or positive manner" by the other individual in the dyad (O'Malley, 1977, p. 29).

Behavioristic approaches typically focus on social skills, such as assertiveness. Social competence is defined in terms of quality of performances and the adequacy of the individual's behavioral repertoire (Hops, 1983). Some researchers attempt to describe interpersonal resources in terms of positive and negative interpersonal traits, as in the Social Performance Survey of Lowe and Cautela (1978). They recognize, however, the need to examine the extent to which such traits reflect social desirability.

Currently, the definition with the greatest degree of consensus is the concept of social competence as *effective functioning* (Ford, 1985; Waters & Sroufe, 1983). Ford (1985) differentiates previous approaches as variously emphasizing processes (e.g., role-taking, the drawing of social inferences in ongoing social interactions, and applying inferences in choosing an action/response) versus outcomes (e.g., the success of the individual in actually achieving some goal relevant to the situation). Although he views previous attempts as complementary, he suggests an emphasis on outcomes as the central criterion in evaluating an individual's effectiveness.

A fourth approach to the study of social competence also focuses on effectiveness and, specifically, attempts to explain social performances through a process model framework. Ford's (1982) open system model and McFall's (1982) information processing model are examples of this current approach.

Ford (1982), a developmentalist, specifically defines social competence as "the attainment of relevant social goals in specified social contexts, using appropriate means and resulting in positive developmental outcomes" (p. 324). He explains social performances through an examination of the following processes: direction (goal-directedness and interest in social goals), regulation (empathy and consideration of consequences), control (e.g., goal improvement, means-ends thinking), information collection, and transaction with the environment.

This model addresses the issue of value judgments, viewing such judgments as inevitable, and considers such dimensions as "intent" and "manner of achieving goals" in evaluating social performances. For example, manipulativeness would be judged differently depending upon the intent and tactics used.

McFall's information-processing model of social performances overlaps with Ford's somewhat, but focuses on a set of specific skills. He describes three types of skills important to the outcomes of social interactions: (1) *decoding* (e.g., discrimination/interpretation of social cues), (2) *decision* (e.g., selecting and evaluating a response alternative), and (3) *encoding* (execution and self-monitoring during execution, with attention to feedback and adjustments in selected response in light of feedback). In this approach more attention is placed on the subjective aspect of people's everyday assessments of others' competence. McFall defines competence as "a general evaluative term that reflects somebody's *judgment* on the basis of certain criteria that a person's performance on some task is adequate" (p. 13).

Ford (1985) relates his process model of social competence to the personality trait approach by recognizing that some personality traits may reflect generally effective, organized patterns of social functioning. Self-assertiveness is an example of such a trait, and in Ford's view may be seen as a particular organization of the components alluded to in his living system's model. At the same time, however, Ford emphasizes the importance of social contexts and developmental levels. He sees some limitations in the personality trait framework, stating that "In most task domains, different skills and resources will need to be tapped at different times in order to maintain effective patterns of behavior" (p. 8).

Ford and Miura (1983) have developed an additional approach to conceptualizing social competence by examining laypersons' conceptions of a socially competent person. Subjects were asked to identify the most socially competent person they knew and reasons for their choice. Students then clustered the reasons, yielding a prototype of the socially competent adult. The clusters, in order of importance, were:

Cluster 1. Prosocial skills (e.g., responds to the needs of others, sensitive to the needs of others, socially responsible, can be counted on).

Cluster 2. Social-instrumental skills (e.g., knows how to get things done, likes to set goals, has leadership abilities).

Cluster 3. Social ease (e.g., enjoys social activities and involvement, appears at ease with people, easy to be around).

Cluster 4. Self-efficacy (e.g., has a good self-concept, likes challenges).

Ford (1985) notes consistent empirical and theoretical support for the centrality of self-assertion (e.g., effective at acquiring resources for self) and integration (e.g., responsible—dependable, trustworthy, has integrity and concern for equity) as "fundamental criteria for evaluating human competence" (p. 34) if, again, one adopts a personality trait approach. Androgyny with regard to these dimensions is the attribute adaptive for most situations. Interestingly, the most important aspects of laypersons' conceptions of social competence, prosocial skills, and social-instrumental skills correspond fairly well to these concepts of self-assertion and integration. Ford (1985) also indicates that these two dimensions appear to reflect shared cultural meanings of social competence.

In summary, a variety of approaches to definition have been taken, and several facets of social competence have been identified. Currently, there seems to be some consensus in defining social competence in terms of effective functioning. Two *generally* effective, organized patterns of such functioning involve self-assertiveness (including accomplishment of personal goals) and prosocial skills or integration (skills that have to do with helping others and understanding others' feelings). At the same time, because social contexts vary individuals must often "fine tune" their responses to the specific demands of the situation in order to remain effective in their social interactions. They must be able to discern when a pattern of behavior, such as assertiveness, is appropriate and when it is not.

Social Competence In Adolescence.   Social competence is manifested differently at different developmental stages (Waters & Sroufe, 1983), but as yet most of the work has been with preschoolers and adults. Fortunately, interest in exploring the meaning of social competence during adolescence is increasing.

Ford (1982) applies his process model to the relationship between social cognition and social competence in adolescence. Social cognition generally refers to the "child's understanding of his social world" (Shantz, 1975, p. 1). In the present case, Ford defined social competence in terms of goals "relevant to the social interactions of most adolescents." Such relevant tasks were viewed as including the judged ability of the subject to "behave effectively in challenging social situations." To assess this ability, descriptions of situations, including tasks demanding negotiation, collaboration, and interpersonal sensitivity were developed. Students in the 9th and 12th grades read these descriptions and judged which of their peers would be most effective at dealing with each situation. Three additional measures of social competence were obtained: interview ratings (based on how subject handled self in interview), and teacher ratings and self-ratings of how effectively the individual could handle these situations. Seven measures of social cognition were also obtained.

A multivariate analysis showed that social cognition was associated with social competence and that *means-end thinking* (a social-cognitive variable measuring cognitive resourcefulness in developing "coherent" plans/strategies and ways to deal with social problems) and *empathy* were the best predictors of social competence. A *goal-directed* disposition—persists towards goal, tries to choose own goal—similar to Baumrind and Black's (1967) concept and consideration of consequences also were related to the composite measure of social competence. These findings are consistent with previous studies of means-end thinking and empathy in adolescence; both have been found to be significant variables in other contexts. These dimensions are also very similar to those identified in Smith's (1968) study of competence in Peace Corps teachers.

Among the adolescents in Ford's study, those judged to be more effective in challenging situations also gave high priority to interpersonal goals, such as helping others. They also seemed to have feelings of efficacy around such goals, i.e., they were "likely to describe themselves as possessing the intrapersonal resources required to accomplish these goals" (p. 335). Ford's (1982) measure of social competence was correlated with intelligence, but had some variance independent of intelligence.

In another study, social knowledge predicted peer popularity. Adams (1983) obtained three measures of social competence (social knowledge, empathy, locus of control) from four groups of adolescents—14-, 15-, 16-, and 18-year-olds. Rothenberg's (1970) role-taking task was used to assess social knowledge. This task required the subject to describe the feelings of characters in pictured social situations; it is believed to require understanding of feelings and motives in different social contexts. Locus of control was measured with Rotter's (1966) scale and refers to "belief in self-initiative and self-effort in problem-solution" (Adams, 1983). A Likert scale was used to measure empathy.

Social knowledge about emotional states correlated with peer popularity among both males (.57) and females (.64), but locus of control was correlated only for males and empathy only for females. Thus some of the qualities important to receiving positive views from others during adolescence appear to vary with gender. Adams also observed some increase in social knowledge, empathy, and locus of control with age. His results provide further support for the importance of social knowledge (including accurate perceptions of feelings and understanding of motives) and interpretation (aspects of McFall's decoding skills) in interpersonal relations.

In summary, the evidence suggests that means-ends thinking, empathy, goal-directedness, and social knowledge (understanding others' feelings and motives) are all important dimensions of social competence and peer relations in adolescence. Further, there is some correspondence between important facets of social competence in adolescence (Ford, 1982) and conceptions of social competence in adulthood (Ford, 1985).

Social Competence And Work.   Two of the few empirical studies examining the role of aspects of social competence in the domain of work are those of Sypher and Sypher (1983) and of Boyatzis (1982). The former focuses on self-monitoring, a component skill of social performances, and communicative effectiveness, a major aspect of social interaction. Boyatzis' study attempts to delineate clearly the general competencies that comprise effective managerial performance, including skill in social "tasks," such as negotiation and the building of alliances.

Sypher and Sypher (1983) obtained measures of self-monitoring behavior (Snyder's 1974 Self-monitoring Scale), self-perceptions of communicative effectiveness, and job level for male and female employees in the corporate headquarters of an insurance company. The authors view self-monitoring as an important aspect of interpersonal success, noting that "self-monitors" are believed to be more sensitive and "responsive to situationally appropriate interpersonal cues" and to "monitor situational demands" and engage in perspective taking (Snyder, 1979). Such characteristics are considered to be significant because they are expected to be instrumental in achieving interpersonal goals. Self-monitoring skills may also be important for "fitting in," and understanding and meeting implicit expectations on the job. Although the findings are somewhat lacking in consistency and clarity (the study provides general correlations only), evidence was found for an association between job level and both self-monitoring and perceived communicative effectiveness. Why the investigators chose to study perceived communicative effectiveness rather than studying communicative skills directly is not clear.

Boyatzis' (1982) aim was to develop a "model of effective performance" in management. The managers were employed at different levels and working in various functions. A wide range of psychological characteristics were found to be correlated with effective performance, such as motivation, intellectual skills, social skills, self-image, self-confidence, and self-esteem. Social competencies that distinguished effective managers from less effective ones included skills in such tasks as negotiation, developing alliances and coalitions, building teams, and in "managing group process" (getting people to cooperate and facilitating the resolution of conflicts). Effective managers were described as collaborators and integrators.

Boyatzis delineated social tasks relevant to success only in business management. The significance of effectiveness in handling such tasks for other types of occupations and levels within occupations has not been established. However, several kinds of social competencies have been proposed as important to one or more aspects of occupational adjustment and success. For example, Sypher and Sypher (1983) cite "interactional competence" as influential in job satisfaction, ability to work with others, productivity, and commitment to organization (Farace, Stewart, & Taylor, 1978) and career success (Argyris, 1962).

Practitioners typically view social skills, such as skill in conflict resolution, as important in *retaining* a job (MDC, 1983). Recently, researchers have focused on the role of social skills in the process of searching for a job.

There is evidence that social assertiveness, one of the three major dimensions of social competence identified by Baumrind (1984), is important for both obtaining and holding a job. Some empirical support exists for the hypothesis that social assertiveness and general social performance strongly influence the outcomes of interviews (Greenwald, 1978; Sands, 1978). As Crites comments in his chapter in this volume, nonassertive persons may be more likely to be released during layoffs and passed over for promotion because their supervisors are insufficiently aware of their competence.

In short, these few studies provide support for the general importance of one trait or organized pattern of social functioning, assertiveness. However, they also suggest that flexible adaptation and at least one processing skill for making such adaptations, self-monitoring, may also be important for job success. Specific social skills for getting along with others (e.g., conflict resolution) are also commonly recognized as significant to successful work adjustment.

Inadequate social skills are posited as particularly relevant to the difficulties of hard-to-employ groups in obtaining and retaining jobs (Foss & Peterson, 1981). Speaking of educable mentally retarded adolescents, Niziol and De-Blassie (1972) comment, "most work maladjustments of this group are, in general, attributed to poor interpersonal skills." Gable (1982) reports that many behavior-disordered adolescents are also handicapped in their vocational adjustment by deficits in social skills (Adams et al., 1979; Kaufman, 1977). He indicates that although behavior-disordered adolescents may possess a wide repertoire of skills, they frequently fail to discriminate accurately when particular social responses are appropriate. In the work experiences of juvenile delinquents, both poor presentation in interviews (Spence, 1981) and poor skills in conflict resolution (Price, 1978) have been identified as potential problems.

Recently others have suggested that learning-disabled youth may experience vocational problems because of deficits in social skills (Kroll, 1984). Studies on the social-vocational adjustment of learning-disabled students are sparse and somewhat inconsistent. However, the research of Mathews, Whang, and Fawcett (1980) indicates that learning disabled youths are more likely than others to have poorer skills in job interviewing, accepting and giving constructive criticism to co-workers, and explaining a problem to a supervisor—all skills important to obtaining and retaining a job. What proportion of learning-disabled adults are also handicapped in their vocational adjustment by lack of social skills is not clear.

Development And Training Of Social Competence.   How does social competence develop? Answers to this question seem to vary with age, as well as with the particular facet of social competence under consideration. The work of Sroufe and his colleagues suggests that quality of mother-infant attachment predicts ego resiliency and social competence in the preschool years when social competence is defined in terms of peer relations/popularity (Arend, Gove, & Sroufe, 1979; Sroufe, 1982). Ego resiliency refers to an individual's adaptive flexibility and engagement with the world. It is defined as "the ability to modify one's behavior in accordance with contextual demands" (Block & Block, 1980, p. 50) and "to be engaged with the world but not subservient to it" (Block & Block, 1980, p. 48).

Research by Baumrind and Black (1967) and Baumrind (1984; in press) suggests that parenting style is an important determinant of social competence, where social competence is defined in terms of such personality traits as independence, social responsibility (friendliness, cooperativeness, and maturity), and social assertiveness. However, just as there may be more than one way to be competent (McFall, 1982; Smith, 1968), there may also be more than one way to socialize competence. Parenting styles that are either authoritative (demanding and responsive) or harmonious (characterized by cooperation, equanimity, rationality, and parental control, but infrequent exercise of such control) may engender the personality traits identified as aspects of social competence in early and middle childhood (Baumrind, 1984) and adolescence (Baumrind, in press). Intrusive and officious or disengaged (undemanding and unresponsive) parenting practices interfere with the development of competence in adolescence.

Until quite recently, little research had been done on the development and correlates of the type of responsibility important to employers (see Hansen & Johnson in this volume), other than what is suggested by general socialization theory on the internalization of norms and values. Ford, Wentzel, Siesfeld, Wood and Feldman (1986) began to explore such processes by examining correlates of choices to behave in responsible or irresponsible ways in hypothetical conflictual situations. They defined social responsibility in terms of (1) conformity to legal and moral rules, (2) meeting social role expectations (complete homework, household chores, and work obligations), and (3) living up to interpersonal commitments made to parents, friends and other individuals.

None of the adolescents was uniformly responsible or irresponsible. Irresponsibility was most likely to occur in a context with peers (e.g., at a friend's house or with several peers). More irresponsible choices were made by adolescents who were (1) more concerned with personal goals, (2) more susceptible to social-evaluative process, (3) better at generating excuses, and (4) "more likely to indicate that their irresponsible choices were typical of their usual behavior." The clearest predictor of responsible behavior was a "more autonomous, task-oriented approach to decision-making" (e.g., "if I oughta do it, I gotta do it," Ford et al., 1986, p. 5).

Although irresponsibility appears more likely to occur in peer contexts, other developmentalists maintain that peers play an important, positive role in some aspects of social development. According to Piaget's theory of moral (social-cognitive) development, the child's cooperative experiences with peers promote the development of social knowledge. Hartup (1979) also hypothesizes that peer interactions, rather than parent-child interactions, facilitate the development of an appropriate repertoire for interacting with peers on an egalitarian basis because important differences in learning experiences arise with different roles.

Dodge, Murphy, and Buchsbaum (1984) report that growth in decoding and interpretation skills (the processing skills from McFall's model) continues during adolescence. Opportunity for such development is important because socially incompetent children are deficient in interpreting cues about social situations.

Finally, recent evidence indicates that opportunities for decision-making, whether in the family or in the classroom, may foster the development of social-problem-solving skills (Fry & Addington, 1984; Herman & Shantz, 1983). A stronger sense of efficacy in social interactions may also develop as a result of strengthening social-problem-solving and assertive skills.

Efforts to enhance social competence in educational and research settings have stemmed mainly from social learning and more cognitive, social-problem-solving approaches. Social learning theorists attempt to remediate inadequate behavioral repertoires through teaching methods (modeling, role playing). Social-cognitive-problem-solving skills have been taught through classroom curricula (Spivack, Platt, & Shure, 1976; Spivack & Shure, 1974) and through small group work with adolescents. Such skills could be taught in adolescent vocational training programs as well.

Only limited evidence exists that efforts to enhance social competence lead to better outcomes in the workplace. However, the consistent finding of an association between social assertiveness and success in job search and job retention provides support for the inclusion of training for social assertiveness job preparation programs.

Training in the social tasks of conflict resolution, communication, and self-confident assertion has been included in some job preparation programs for adolescents and youth (MDC, Inc., 1983; Kurtz, 1981). Social-vocational programs have also been developed to address the specific social handicaps of educable mentally retarded (LaGreca, Stone, & Bell, 1983) and behavior-disordered adolescents (Gable, 1982).

LaGreca et al.'s (1983) program for educable mentally retarded was developed to remediate difficulties in getting along with coworkers and supervisors and focused on improving appropriateness of social responses in problem situations. This intervention had positive effects on length of employment of retarded young adults (LaGreca et al., 1983). Gable's (1982) program on prevocational instruction for severely behavior-disordered adolescents includes both academic-remedial and social skills components, with an emphasis on appropriate language, appropriate interactions with peers and adults, and self-control. The impact of this program has not yet been clearly assessed.

In summary, the development and evaluation of social skills interventions to prepare adolescents for work is thus far quite limited. Such intervention may be strengthened with a fuller understanding of the social tasks important for work success. A processing model may be helpful in pinpointing the source of difficulty once deficits in performing relevant social tasks are identified.

SUMMARY

Our purpose was to review research on psychological attributes influencing preparation for, and performance of, work. Rather than specific abilities, such as mechanical aptitude, the focus was on characteristics important for success at many levels and in many settings.

Several conclusions are warranted. First, achievement motivation is important to vocational success, but the common sense notion of achievement motivation as desire to succeed is overly simplistic. Some types of achievement orientation, such as mastery and competence motivation, seem more predictive of success than do others, e.g., need for achievement. Distinctions between the value and expectancy aspects of achievement motivation are also essential, as illustrated here by studies of training programs for youths at high risk for unemployment. This conclusion is further supported by results reported in several other chapters in this volume, e.g., Hansen and Johnson's large-scale study in public schools, Ogbu's work with minority youngsters and their families, and Werner's cross-cultural longitudinal research. Among all of these groups, vocational success was predicted, not by valuation of the work ethic, to which they *did* subscribe, but by perceptions of personal efficacy, outcome expectancies, or internal locus of control.

Cognitive ability, as measured by standard psychometric tests of intelligence, does have some direct effect on occupational attainment independent of such associated and mediating factors as educational level. Prediction is poorer during the earlier phases of careers and for jobs requiring less cognitive complexity, two related observations obviously linked to the extent of sampling variability with respect to both intelligence and occupational level.

A recent line of research suggests that practical intelligence may also explain differences in work outcomes. Some evidence indicates that tacit knowledge, one aspect of practical intelligence, is associated with successful adaptation on the job. For example, knowledge about the relative importance of various tasks and about how to set priorities is predictive of success in business. Practical knowledge may also be important in the process of obtaining employment. Many may fail to get a job because they lack knowledge about how to lay the proper groundwork and how to present themselves in application forms and interviews.

Although the influence of social competence has been less thoroughly studied, empirical evidence supports practitioners' opinions that social skills are important both in obtaining and retaining a job. Here too, better definition of component skills seems to improve prediction. A more differentiated approach both to the assessment of self-esteem and to aspects of employment may also prove helpful. For example, self-esteem may be more important to some aspects of work, such as getting a job, than to others. As yet the effects of self-esteem are not well understood, nor is it clear whether self-esteem is a causal or dependent variable.

Long-term longitudinal research indicates that an active, engaged style of interacting with the environment during adolescence is predictive of later occupational success, at least for males. Those who actively explore their environment and utilize their personal and environmental resources are more likely to perform well in the workplace from early through late adulthood. Terms such as "purposeful exploration" (Super, 1985) and "planful competence" (Clausen, 1986), used to summarize attributes found predictive in long-term studies also fit well with Waters and Sroufe's (1983) developmental view of social competence "as an integrative concept which refers broadly to an ability to generate and coordinate flexible, adaptive responses to demands and to generate and capitalize on opportunities in the environment" (p. 80).

In sum, the literature reviewed argues for two kinds of methodological strategies both for basic research and for construction and evaluation of intervention programs: (1) a more differentiated approach to the assessment of personal attributes and of performance in the workplace, and (2) developmental longitudinal designs. The latter are needed for at least three reasons. First, sociological research indicates that experience on the job may influence personality characteristics, so findings for experienced adults may not be valid for drawing inferences about adolescent predictors. Second, short-term prediction is sometimes misleading, as illustrated by studies contrasting prediction to earlier and later phases of careers. Third, any given attribute is likely to be manifested differently at different developmental phases. Knowledge about linkages among these manifestations would be helpful in determining how to foster characteristics important in the adult world of work.

Promising theoretical frameworks include the social-cognitive approach and self-efficacy theory. The former may prove fruitful in understanding the development of components of social competence. For example, individual differences in responsibility may be a function not only of socialization experiences but also of understanding the role of responsibility in social systems, including the social organizations of the workplace. Bandura's (1977, 1982) self-efficacy theory suggests guidelines for effectively structuring adolescents' experiences in school and part-time employment so they are psychologically better prepared to make the transition to adult employment.

REFERENCES

Adams, T., Strain, P., Salzberg, C., & Levy, S. (1979). A model program for prevocational/vocational education with moderately and severely handicapped adolescents. *Behavior Disorders, 3,* 36-42.

Adams, G. R. (1983). Social competence during adolescence: Social sensitivity, locus of control, empathy, and peer popularity. *Journal of Youth and Adolescence, 12,* 203-211.

Anderson, S., & Messick, S. (1974). Social competency in young children. *Developmental Psychology, 10,* 282-293.

Arend, R., Gove, F. L., & Sroufe, L. A. (1979). Continuity of individual adaptation from infancy to kindergarten: A predictive study of ego-resiliency and curiosity in preschoolers. *Child Development, 50,* 950-959.

Argyris, C. (1962). *Interpersonal competence and organizational effectiveness.* Homewood, IL: Irwin-Dorsey.

Atkinson, J. W. (1974). Strength of motivation and efficiency of performance. In J. W. Atkinson & J. O. Raynor (eds.), *Motivation and achievement.* New York: Winston & Sons.

Atkinson, J., & Reitman, W. (1956). Performance as a function of motive strength and expectancy of goal attainment. *Journal of Abnormal and Social Psychology, 53,* 361-366.

Bachman, J. G., & O'Malley, P. M. (1977). Self-esteem in young men: A longitudinal analysis of the impact of educational and occupational attainment. *Journal of Personality and Social Psychology, 35,* 365-380.

Bandura, A. (1977). Self-efficacy: Toward a unifying theory of behavioral change. *Psychological Review, 84,* 191-215.

Bandura, A. (1982). Self-efficacy mechanism in human agency. *American Psychologist, 37,* 122-147.

Baumrind, D. (1984, March). *Familial antecedents of social competence in young children.* For Program in Social Ecology, University of California, Irvine.

Baumrind, D. (in press). Parenting styles and adolescent development. In J. Brooks-Gunn, R. Lerner, & A. C. Petersen (eds.), *The encyclopedia on adolescence.* New York: Garland.

Baumrind, D., & Black, A. E. (1967). Socialization practices associated with dimensions of competence in preschool boys and girls. *Child Development, 38,* 291-327.

Beatty, R. W. (1974). Supervisory behavior related to job success of hardcore unemployed over a two-year period. *Journal of Applied Psychology, 59,* 38-42.

Berger, E. M. (1955). Relationships among acceptance of self, acceptance of others and MMPI scores. *Journal of Counseling Psychology, 3,* 279-283.

Betz, N. E., & Hackett, G. (1981). The relationships of career-related self-efficacy expectations to perceived career options in college women and men. *Journal of Counseling Psychology, 28,* 399-410.

Block, J., & Block, J. (1980). The role of ego-control and ego-resiliency in the organization of behavior. In W. A. Collins (Ed.), *The Minnesota Symposia on Child Psychology* (Vol. 13). Hillsdale, NJ: Lawrence Erlbaum Associates.

Block, J., & Haan, N. (1971). *Lives through time.* Berkeley: Bancroft Books.

Boyatzis, R. (1982). *The competent manager.* New York: Wiley.

Brookover, W. B. (1965). *Self-concept of ability and school achievement,* U.S. Office of Education Cooperative Research Project No. 1636, Michigan State University. Cited by Reasoner, R. W. (1983). Enhancement and self-esteem in children and adolescents. *Family and Community Health, 6,* 51-64.

Clausen, J. A. (1986). Early adult choices and the life course. *Zeitschrift für Sozialisationsforschung und Erzichungssociologie, 6,* 313-320.

Cobb, S., Brooks, G. H., Kasi, S. V., & Connelly, W. E. (1966). The health of people changing jobs: A description of a longitudinal study. *American Journal of Public Health, 56,* 1476-1481.

Connell, J. P. (1981). A model of the relationships among children's self-related cognitions, affects, and academic achievement. Unpublished doctoral dissertation, University of Denver. Cited by Harter, S. (1983). Developmental perspectives on the self-esteem. In P. Mussen (Ed.), *Handbook of child psychology* (Vol. 4). New York: Wiley.

Coopersmith, S. (1967). *The antecedents of self-system.* Palo Alto, CA: Consulting Psychologists Press.

Crandall, R. (1973). The measurement of self-esteem and related constructs. In J. P. Robinson & P. R. Shaver (Eds.), *Measures of social psychological attitudes.* Ann Arbor: University of Michigan.

Crandall, V. (1972). The Fels Study: Some contributions to personality development and achievement in childhood and adulthood. *Seminars in Psychiatry, IV,* 383-397.

Crandall, V. C., Katkovsky, W., & Preston, A. (1960). A conceptual formulation for some research on children's achievement development. *Child Development, 31,* 787-797.

Dodge, K., & Murphy, R. (1984). The assessment of social competence in adolescence. *Advances in Child Behavioral Analysis and Therapy, 3,* 61-96.

Dodge, K., Murphy, R., & Buchsbaum, K. (1984). The assessment of intention cue discrimination skills in children: Implications for developmental psychopathology. *Child Development, 55,* 163-173.

Dweck, C. S., & Elliott, E. S. (1983). Achievement motivation. In P. Mussen (Ed.), *Handbook of child psychology* (Vol. 4). New York: Wiley.

Ellis, R. A., & Taylor, M. S. (1983). Role of self-esteem within the job search process. *Journal of Applied Psychology, 68,* 632-640.

Farace, R. V., Stewart, J. P., & Taylor, J. A. (1978). Criteria for evaluation of organizational communication effectiveness: Review and synthesis. In B. D. Ruben (ed.), *Communication yearbook II.* New Brunswick, NJ: Transaction Books.

Faver, C. (1982). Achievement orientation, attainment values, and women's employment. *Journal of Vocational Behavior, 20,*67-80.

Featherman, D. L. (1980). Schooling and occupational careers: Constancy and change in worldly success. In J. Kagan & O. G. Brim (Eds.), *Constancy and change.* Cambridge: Harvard University Press.

Fitts, W. H. (1972a). *The self concept and psychopathology.* Nashville: Counselor Recordings and Tests.

Fitts, W. H. (1972b). *The self concept and performance.* Nashville: Counselor Recordings and Tests.

Fitts, W. H. (1972c). *The self concept and behavior: Overview and supplement.* Nashville: Counselor Recordings and Tests.

Ford, D. H. (1987). *Humans as self-constructing living systems: A developmental perspective on behavior and personality* Hillsdale, NJ: Erlbaum.

Ford, M. E. (1982). Social cognition and social competence in adolescence. *Developmental Psychology, 18,* 323-340.

Ford, M. E. (1985). The concept of competence. In H. A. Marlowe & R. B. Weinberg (Eds.), *Competence development.* Springfield, IL: Charles C. Thomas.

Ford, M. E., & Miura, I. (1983, August). *Children's and adults' conceptions of social competence.* Paper presented at the 91st Annual Convention of the American Psychological Association, Anaheim, CA.

Ford, M. E., Wentzel, K. R., Siesfeld, G. A., Wood, D., & Feldman, L. (1986, April). Adolescent decision-making in real-life situations involving socially responsible and irresponsible choices. Paper presented at the annual meeting of the American Educational Research Association, San Francisco.

Foss, F., & Peterson, S. L. (1981). Skills relevant to job tenure for mentally retarded adults. *Mental Retardation, 19,* 103-106.

Fry, P. S., & Addington, J. (1984). Comparison of social problem-solving of children from open and traditional classrooms. *Journal of Educational Psychology, 76,* 318-329.

Gable, R. A. (1982). *A program for prevocational instruction for adolescents with severe behavioral disorders.* Paper presented at the Minnesota Conference on Programming for the Developmental Needs of Adolescents with Behavioral Disorders, Minneapolis.

Gecas, V., & Schwalbe, M. (1983). Beyond the looking-glass self: Social structure and efficacy-based self-esteem. *Social Psychology Quarterly, 46,* 77-88.

Ghiselli, E. E. (1966). *The validity of occupational aptitude tests.* New York: James Wiley & Sons.

Gottfredson, L., & Brown, V. (1981). Occupational differentiation among white men in the first decade after high school. *Journal of Vocational Behavior, 19,* 251-289.

Gould, S. (1980). Need for achievement, career mobility, and the Mexican-American college graduate. *Journal of Vocational Behavior, 16,* 73-82.

Greenspan, S. (1981). Defining childhood social competence: A proposed working model. In *Advances in special education* (Vol. 3), 1-39.

Greenwald, M. A. (1978). The effects of physical attractiveness, experience, and social performance on employer decision-making in job interviews. *Dissertation Abstracts, 39,* 4-B, 1956.

Gurin, G. (1968, December). *Inner-city Negro youth in a job training project: A study of factors related to attrition and job success.* Final Report to the Manpower Administration. U.S. Department of Labor and the Office of Education. USDHEW. Institute for Social Research, University of Michigan, Project No. 2798, Contract No. OE 5-10-243.

Hammer, S. H. (1985). Stalking intelligence: IQ isn't tne end of the line; you can be smarter. *Science Digest, 93,* 31-37.

Harter, S. (1983). Developmental perspectives on the self-system. In P. Mussen (Ed.), *Handbook of child psychology* (Vol. 4). New York: John Wiley & Sons.

Harter, S., & Connell, J. D. (1982). A comparison of alternative models of the relationships between academic achievement and children's perceptions of competence, control, and motivational orientation. In J. Nicholls (Ed.), *The development of achievement-related cognitions and behaviors.* Greenwich, CT: J.A.I. Press.

Hartup, W. (1979). Peer relations in the growth of social competence. In M. Kent & J. Wolfe (Eds.), *The primary prevention of psychopathology* (Vol. 3) *Promoting social competence and coping in children.* Hanover, NH: University Press of New England.

Hauser, R. M., & Daymont, T. N. (1977). Schooling, ability, and earnings: Cross-sectional findings 8 to 14 years after high school graduation. *Sociology of Education, 50,* 182-206.

Heath, D. H. (1976). Adolescent and adult predictors of vocational adaptation. *Journal of Vocational Behavior, 9*, 1-19.

Herman, M. S., & Shantz, C. U. (1983). Social problem-solving and mother-child interactions of educable mentally retarded children. *Journal of Applied Developmental Psychology, 4*, 217-226.

Hops, H. (1983). Children's social competence and skill: Current research practices and future directions. *Behavior Therapy, 14*, 3-18.

Hunter, J. E. (1980). *Validity generalization for 12,000 jobs: An application of synthetic validity and validity generalization to the General Aptitude Test Battery (GATE).* Washington, D.C.: U.S. Employment Service, U.S. Department of Labor.

Hunter, J. E., & Schmidt, F. L. (1982). Fitting people to jobs: The impact of personnel selection on national productivity. In M. D. Dunnette & E. A. Fleishman (Eds.), *Human performance and productivity: Human capability assessment* (pp. 233-284). Hillsdale, NJ: Erlbaum.

Jencks, C., Smith, M., Acland, H., Bane, M. J., Cohen, D., Gintis, H., Heyns, B., & Michelson, S. (1982). *Inequality.* New York: Basic Books.

Jordaan, J. P., & Super, D. E. (1974). The prediction of early adult vocational behavior. In D. F. Ricks, A. Thomas, & M. Roff (Eds.), *Life history research in psychopathology* (Vol. 3). Minneapolis: University of Minnesota Press.

Kaufmann, J. (1977). *Characteristics of children's behavior disorders.* Columbus, OH: Charles E. Merrill.

Kohn, M., & Rossman, B. D. (1972). A social competence scale symptom checklist for the preschool child. *Developmental Psychology, 6*, 430-444.

Kohn, M., & Schooler, C. (1978). The reciprocal effects of the substantive complexity of work and intellectual flexibility: A longitudinal assessment. *American Journal of Sociology, 84*, 24-52.

Korman, A. K. (1970). Toward a hypothesis of work behavior. *Journal of Applied Psychology, 54*, 31-41.

Kroll, L. G. (1984). LD'S - What happens when they are no longer children? *Academic Therapy, 20*, 133-148.

Kurtz, P. (1981). *Preparation for the world of work training sessions.* CETA Staff Development Project. San Mateo County Office of Education, Redwood City, CA.

LaGreca, A. M., Stone, W. L., & Bell, C. R., III. (1983). Facilitating the vocational-interpersonal skills of mentally retarded individuals. *American Journal of Mental Deficiency, 88*, 270-278.

Lorence, J., & Mortimer, J. (1981). Work experience and work involvement. *Sociology of Work and Occupations, 8*, 297-326.

Lowe, M., & Cautela, J. S. (1978). A self-report measure of social skill. *Behavior Therapy, 9*, 535-544.

MDC, Inc. (1983). *Job readiness training for high school aged youth.* Division of Employment and Training. North Carolina Department of Natural Resources and Community Development. MDC, Inc. Chapel Hill, NC.

Mathews, R. M., Whang, P., & Fawcett, S. B. (1980). *Behavioral assessment of job-related skills: Implications for learning disabled adults* Research Report No. 6). Lawrence, KS: University of Kansas Institute for Research in Learning Disabilities. Cited by Alley, G. R., Deshler, D. D., Clark, F. L., Schumaker, J. B., & Warner, M. M. (1983). Learning disabilities in adolescent and adult populations: Research implications (Part II). *Focus on Exceptional Children, 15*, 1-14.

McCarthy, J. D., & Hoge, D. R. (1982). Analysis of age effects in longitudinal studies of adolescent self-esteem. *Developmental Psychology, 18*, 372-379.

McClelland, D. C. (1973). Testing for competence rather than for "intelligence." *American Psychologist, 28*, 1-14.

McClelland, D., Atkinson, J. W., Clark, R., & Lowell, E. L. (1953). *The achievement motive.* New York: Appleton-Century.

McClelland, D., Atkinson, J. W., Clark, R. A., & Lowell, E. L. (1958). A scoring manual for the achievement motive. In J. W. Atkinson (Ed.), *Motives in fantasy, action and society.* Princeton: Van Nostrand.

McFall, R. M. (1982). A review and reformulation of the concept of social skills. *Behavioral Assessment, 4,* 1-33.

Messick, S., & Anderson, S. (1974). Social competency in young children. *Developmental Psychology, 10,* 282-293.

Muene, J. C. (1983). Understanding juvenile unemployability: An exploratory study. *Journal of Adolescence, 6,* 247-261.

Mortimer, J., & Lorence, J. (1979a.). Work experience and occupational value socialization: A longitudinal study. *American Journal of Sociology, 84,* 1361-1385.

Mortimer, J., & Lorence, J. (1979b). Occupational experience and the self-concept: A longitudinal study. *Social Psychology Quarterly, 42,* 307-323.

Murray, H. A. (1938). *Explorations in personality: A clinical and experimental study of fifty men of college age by the workers at the Harvard psychological clinic.* New York: Oxford University Press.

Neisser, U. (1976). General, academic, and artificial intelligence. In L. Resnick (Ed.), *The nature of intelligence.* Hillsdale, NJ: Lawrence Erlbaum Associates.

Niziol, O. M., & De Blassie, R. R. (1972). Work adjustment and the educable mentally retarded adolescent. *Journal of Employment Counseling, 9,* 158-166.

O'Malley, J. M. (1977). Research perspective on social competence. *Merrill-Palmer Quarterly, 23*(1), 29-44.

Passmore, D. L., & Wircenski, J. L. (1981), *School-to-work transition skills for disadvantaged youth. Final report. Vocational-technical education research report.* (Vol. 19, No. 3). Pennsylvania State University Department of Vocational Education, University Park, PA. Bureau of Vocational Education (Project No. 94-1004).

Petrie, K., & Rotheram, M. J. (1982). Insulators against stress: Self-esteem and assertiveness. *Psychological Reports, 50,* 963-966.

Phillips, S. D. (1979). *The post-high-school development of vocational choice.* Unpublished doctoral dissertation, Teacher's College, Columbia University, New York, NY. Cited by Super, D. E. (1985). Coming of age in Middletown: Careers in the making. *American Psychologist, 40,* 405-414.

Phillips, S. D. (1982a). Career exploration in adulthood. *Journal of Vocational Behavior, 20,* 129-140.

Phillips, S. D. (1982b). The development of career choices: The relationship between patterns of commitment and career outcomes in adulthood. *Journal of Vocational Behavior, 20,* 141-152.

Price, T. F. (1978). Conflict resolution among juvenile delinquents. *Dissertation Abstracts, 39,* 5A, 3161.

Reasoner, R. W. (1983). Enhancement of self-esteem in children and adolescents. *Family and Community Health, 6,* 51-64.

Rosenberg, M. (1965). *Society and the adolescent self-image.* Princeton: Princeton University Press.

Rosenberg, M. (1979). *Conceiving the self.* New York: Basic Books.

Rothenberg, B. (1970). Children's social sensitivity and the relationship to interpersonal competence, intrapersonal comfort, and intellectual level. *Developmental Psychology, 2,* 335-350.

Rotter, J. B. (1966). Generalized expectancies for internal versus external control of reinforcement. *Psychological Monographs, 80,* (Whole No. 609).

Royce, J., Lazar, I., & Darlington, R. (1983). Minority families, early education, and later life chances. *American Journal of Orthopsychiatry, 53*(4), 706-720.

Sands, L. (1978). The influence of sex, competency and style of self-presentation on interviewer decisions. *Dissertation Abstracts, 39,* 7-B, 3568-69.

Schalon, C. (1968). Effect of self-esteem upon performance following failure stress. *Journal of Consulting and Clinical Psychology, 32,* 497.

Schmidt, F. L., & Hunter, J. E. (1977). Development of general solution to the problem of validity generalization. *Journal of Applied Psychology, 62,* 529-540.

Schmidt, F. L., & Hunter, J. E. (1981). Employment testing: Old theories and new research findings. *American Psychologist, 36,* 1128-1137.

Scribner, S. (1983). *Mind in action: A functional approach to thinking.* Paper presented at the meeting of the Society for Research in Child Development, Detroit.

Sewell, W. H., & Hauser, R. M. (1975). *Education, occupation and earnings: Achievement in the early years.* New York: Academic Press.

Sewell, W. H., Hauser, R. M., & Wolf, W. (1977). *Sex, schooling and occupational careers.* Center for Demography and Ecology Working Paper No. 77-31. University of Wisconsin, Madison.

Shantz, C. U. (1975). *The development of social cognition.* Chicago: The University of Chicago Press.

Shrauger, J., & Rosenberg, S. (1970). Self-esteem and the effects of success and failure feedback on performance. *Journal of Personality, 33,* 404-414.

Simmons, R. G., & Blyth, D. A. (1987). *Moving into adolescence.* New York: Aldinede Gruyter.

Simmons, R. G., Rosenberg, F., & Rosenberg, M. (1973). Disturbance in self-image in adolescence. *American Sociological Review, 38,* 553-568.

Smith, M. B. (1968). Competence and socialization. In J. A. Clausen (Ed.), *Socialization and society.* Boston: Little, Brown.

Snyder, M. (1974). The self-monitoring of expressive behavior. *Journal of Personality and Social Psychology, 30,* 526-537.

Snyder, M. (1979). Self-monitoring processes. In L. Berkowitz (Ed.), *Advances in experimental social psychology* (Vol. 12). New York: Academic Press.

Soloway, E., Erlich, K., Bonar, J., & Greenspan, J. (1982). What do novices know about programming? In B. Schneiderman & A. Badre (Eds.), *Directions in human-computer interactions.* Norwood, NJ: Ablex.

Spence, J. T., & Helmreich, R. L. (1983). Achievement-related motives and behaviors. In J. T. Spence (Ed.), *Achievement and achievement motives: Psychological and sociological approaches.* San Francisco: W. H. Freeman.

Spence, S. H. (1981). Differences in social skills performance between institutionalized juvenile male offenders and a comparable group of boys without offence records. *British Journal of Clinical Psychology, 20,* 163-171.

Spivack, G., Platt, J. J., & Shure, M. B. (1976). *The problem-solving approach to adjustment.* San Francisco: Jossey-Bass.

Spivack, G., & Shure, M. B. (1974). *Social adjustment of young children.* San Francisco: Jossey-Bass.

Sroufe, A. (1982). Infant-caregiver attachment and patterns of adaptation in preschool: The roots of maladaptation and competence. In M. Perlmutter (Ed.), *Minnesota Symposium in Child Psychology* (Vol. 16). Hillsdale, NJ: Lawrence Erlbaum Associates. ·

Stein, A. H., & Bailey, M. M. (1976). The socialization of achievement orientation in females. In A. G. Kaplan & J. P. Bean (Eds.), *Beyond sex-role stereotypes: Readings toward a psychology of androgyny* (pp. 240-261). Boston: Little, Brown.

Sternberg, R. J., & Caruso, D. R. (1985). Practical modes of knowing. In E. Eisner (Ed.), *Learning the ways of knowing* (pp. 133-158). Chicago: University of Chicago Press.

Stumpf, S. A., Austin, E. J., & Hartman, K. (1984). The impact of career exploration and interview readiness on interview performance and outcomes. *Journal of Vocational Behavior, 24,* 221-235.

Super, D. E. (1985). Coming of age in Middletown: Careers in the making. *American Psychologist, 40,* 405-414.

Sypher, B. D., & Sypher, H. S. (1983). Perceptions of communication ability: Self-monitoring in an organizational setting. *Personality and Social Psychology Bulletin, 9,* 297-304.

Tharendou, P. (1979). Employee self-esteem: A review of the literature. *Journal of Vocational Behavior, 15,* 316-346.

Trotter, R. J. (1986). Three heads are better than one. *Psychology Today, 20,* 56-62.

Vaillant, G. E. (1974). Commentary in reaction to Jordaan, J. P., & Super, D. E. (1974). The prediction of early adult vocational behavior. In D. F. Ricks, A. Thomas, & M. Roff (Eds.), *Life history research in psychopathology* (Vol. 3). Minneapolis: The University of Minnesota Press.

Veroff, J., McClelland, L., & Ruhland, D. (1975). Varieties of achievement motivation. In M. Mednick. S. Tangri, & L. Hoffman (Eds.), *Women and achievement.* New York: Wiley.

Wagner, R. K., & Sternberg, R. J. (1985). Practical intelligence in real-world pursuits: The role of tacit knowledge. *Journal of Personality and Social Psychology, 49,* 436-458.

Walvoord, J. E. (1979). *Correlates and outcomes of exploratory behavior in adolescence and early adulthood.* Unpublished doctoral dissertation, Teacher's College, Columbia University, New York.

Waters, E., & Sroufe, L. A. (1983). Social competence as a developmental construct. *Developmental Review, 3,* 79-97.

Weinstein, E. A. (1969). The development of interpersonal competence. In D. Goslin (Ed.), *Handbook of socialization theory and research.* Chicago: Rand McNally.

Wells, L. E., & Marwell, G. (1976). *Self-esteem.* London: Sage.

White, B. L., Kaban, B., Marmor, J., & Shapiro, B. (1972). *Child rearing practices and the development of competence.* Cambridge: Laboratory of Human Development, Harvard University.

White, R. S. (1963). *Ego and reality in psychoanalytic theory.* New York: International Universities Press.

Wylie, R. C. (1961). *The self-concept: A critical review of pertinent research literature.* Lincoln: University of Nebraska Press.

Wylie, R. C. (1979). *The self concept* (Vol. 1, rev. ed.). Lincoln: University of Nebraska Press.

Zigler, E., & Trickett, P. (1978). IQ, social competence, and evaluation of early childhood intervention programs. *American Psychologist, 33,* 789-798.

Zimmerman, B. J., & Ringle, J. (1981). Effects of model persistence and statements of confidence on children's self-efficacy and problem-solving. *Journal of Educational Psychology, 73,* 485-493.

Author Index

Subject Index

For Product Safety Concerns and Information please contact our EU representative GPSR@taylorandfrancis.com Taylor & Francis Verlag GmbH, Kaufingerstraße 24, 80331 München, Germany

Printed and bound by CPI Group (UK) Ltd, Croydon, CR0 4YY

01/05/2025

01858380-0001